GUIDE TO ENGLAND'S INDUSTRIAL HERITAGE

GUIDE TO
ENGLAND'S INDUSTRIAL HERITAGE

KEITH FALCONER

Introduction by
Neil Cossons

B. T. BATSFORD LTD

London

© Keith Falconer 1980
First published 1980
ISBN 0 7134 13433

Filmset by Photobooks (Bristol) Ltd
28/30 Midland Road, St Philips, Bristol
Printed and bound in Great Britain by
Redwood Burn Limited
Trowbridge & Esher
for the publishers
B. T. Batsford Ltd
4 Fitzhardinge Street, London W1H 0AH

CONTENTS

ACKNOWLEDGEMENTS

The preparation of a guide such as this involves a great deal of assistance from a great many individuals and organisations. First and foremost I would wish to thank all the past and present members of the Industrial Archaeology Research Committee of the Council for British Archaeology. The committee was for many years a most solicitous parent to the National Survey of Industrial Monuments and I would wish to thank its successive chairman, Professor Grimes, the late L T C Rolt and Dr Neil Cossons for their support and advice. I would especially like to thank the secretary of the committee, Dr Angus Buchanan of the University of Bath, for being such a kind host to the Survey over the last nine years, and to record my debt to my predecessor as Survey Officer, Rex Wailes. The regional representatives on the committee formed the core of the battalion of willing guides without whom my fieldwork would not have been possible. I would wish to thank these guides and all my friends who gave so freely of their time and advice, notably Simon Adamson; David Alderton; Owen Ashmore; Maurice Barbey; Mike Bishop; Frank Booker; John Booker; Fred Brooks; Sandy Buchanan; Michael Bussell; Chris Charlton; Mike Corfield; John Cornwell; Elwin Course; Martin Doughty; Stuart Feather; Ron Fitzgerald; John Goodchild; John Hazelfoot; Bob Hawkins; John Horne; John Hume; David Humphries; Francis Kelly; Michael Lewis; Stafford Linsley; Ken Major; John Marshall; Martin Meade; Walter Minchinton; David & Marlyn Palmer; Keith Reedman; Philip Riden; Michael Rix; Martin Robertson; Ken Rogers; Chris Schmitz; Mike Davies Sheil; John Stengelhofen; David Tomlins; John Townsend; Barry Trinder; Owen Ward; George Watkins; Peter White; Lyn Willies; Paul Wilson; Neil Wright; Don Young.

I should also like to thank the members of industrial archaeological societies throughout the country and especially those in Avon; Cornwall; Gloucestershire; Greater London; Hampshire; Leicestershire; Somerset; Sussex; Teeside.

Thanks are also due to Judith Burchell, Nicky King, Anne Pearson, Clare Slater, and Joanna Valentine for their typing of a virtually indecipherable manuscript.

For help with photographs I am most grateful to: J Cornwell (pp. 36, 41, 43, 51, 61, 64, 68, 70, 75, 78, 82, 85, 112, 139, 151, 164, 169, 184, 185, 188, 189, 196, 199, 230, 231, 232, 235, 241, 243, 244); N Cossons (pp. 104, 134, 137, 155, 157, 159, 161, 250, 251); E Delony (pp. 77, 87, 225); S Linsley (pp. 95, 96, 171, 217, 219); J K Major (p. 204); J Sawtell (p. 203); B Bracegirdle (p. 119); G Payne (p. 205); N Wright (p. 141) and to the University photographers, James Phillips and Colin Wilson.

Lastly, I would like to thank my wife and family for putting up with all the inconveniences the preparation of a guide like this causes both to the home and family holidays.

LIST OF ILLUSTRATIONS

INTRODUCTION

The Industrial Revolution in Britain, which gained momentum during the middle years of the eighteenth century and dominated the nineteenth, was more than a revolution in the techniques of making things. It was a revolution in cultural, in social, in economic and in environmental terms which radically altered the way in which people thought and lived, not only in Britain but ultimately throughout the world. It has left us a unique physical legacy in the form of a landscape which, both urban and rural, is predominantly the product of industrialisation and its side effects. It has also left us a legacy of attitude, the overwhelming emotional ambivalence which dominates so strongly our view of this important period of our past.

Our understanding of the Industrial Revolution has been greatly enhanced by the study of the evidence still surviving on the ground, of blast furnaces, mills, factories and warehouses, of canals and railways, and of whole industrial landscapes combining all these things and many more with the houses in which the new industrial population lived, their pubs, chapels, churches and shops. Today we recognize the importance of these industrial monuments and landscapes as part of the national estate and attempt to record and preserve them. We may not yet accord the Iron Bridge in Shropshire, Albert Dock in Liverpool, or Brunel's great railway terminus at Temple Meads, Bristol the same reverence as Hadrian's Wall or York Minster but we are right to see them in the same sort of context, as the supreme symbols of their age and all it represented. Unlike the Wall however, or even York, these great industrial monuments derive little from cultures overseas. They represent the achievements of a completely new epoch in the evolution of man when Britain, for a brief period of perhaps five generations, held the centre of the world stage as the first industrial nation, birthplace of the Industrial Revolution.

In several respects Britain's own Industrial Revolution was unique and this must colour the way in which we view its remains. Firstly, it took a long time to gain momentum, to reach the so-called point of take-off into self-sustained growth, and even after this the relatively rapid transformation of the national economy into one based primarily on industrialization was spread over several generations. Secondly, this pace of change, although it put strains upon the political and social institutions of the country did not destroy them in the process. The effects were in many respects evolutionary rather than revolutionary. After a century and a half of industrialization Britain was certainly a very different place from what it had been before but it had avoided the cataclysmic upheavals which had characterized other European states in the same period. Thirdly, the fact that industrialization evolved in parallel with the largely home-grown step-by-step processes of innovation meant that each stage was characterized by its own technology making its peculiar mark on the economy and the landscape before being rendered obsolete.

In examining today the growth of industrialization in Britain it is still frequently possible to trace the individual stages of growth of a particular technology. The blast furnace, the textile factory and the railway, for example, all passed through tentative developmental stages to mature in concept and design before they had any significant impact on the outside world. These 'firsts' abound in Britain and it is only by recording and preserving them that we can gain any real insight into why and how the Industrial Revolution took place.

The events of the last century too have put us in a unique position to examine our industrial origins. The roots of decline are clearly visible as early as the 1870s, in a complacency, and a reluctance to innovate and change. The protected markets of empire, an over-abundance of craft skills and an unwillingness to re-capitalize coincided with the emergence of Germany, the United States and Japan as industrial powers. At the same time Britain felt the leap-frog effects suffered by all pioneers; her out-of-date technologies had provided the foundation for others to forge ahead based on the experience she had contributed. Two world wars, with little of the destruction that affected much of continental Europe, perpetuated still further these nineteenth- and even eighteenth-century industrial practices, machines and buildings so that the 1950s and 60s found the Britain of the Industrial Revolution still surprisingly intact. But by the time industrial and urban renewal did begin to gather strength, and indeed largely because of it, society as a whole was becoming increasingly concerned about its surroundings and what was happening to them.

These anxieties stemmed in part from the revival of industrial activity itself with its attendant problems of air and water pollution and unrestrained encroachment on rural and coastal areas, but in addition the more deep-seated economic and technological changes of the post-war years which led to the destruction of town centres for road and office building all combined to fuel the fires in the bellies of the new environmentalists. Conservation trusts, preservation and civic societies sprang up all over the country determined not only to resist these new intrusions on the landscape but to sweep away the worst effects of the Industrial Revolution as well. But tastes were changing too; 'Victorian' ceased to be a derogatory term and assumed a connotation initially of delight in newly discovered eccentricities but soon a firm respectability born of imperial wealth and traditions. For the first time it was possible to view with some degree of objectivity not only the legacy of the nineteenth century in general but of the Industrial Revolution, the aftermath of which is associated in the minds of many people with appalling living and working conditions, unemployment and landscapes of destruction and decay. For the first time the monuments of those who had so spectacularly generated growth in the Industrial Revolution became widely appreciated in a way which would previously have been impossible.

Out of this period of environmental awareness and rapidly changing attitudes grew industrial archaeology, concerning itself with the examination and analysis of the remains of industrial activity before they disappeared under the tidal wave of modernization and our new-found desire for tidiness. This paradox has caused the industrial archaeologist some difficulty in establishing his credibility, particularly when it comes to the preservation of sites and areas which are historically significant but are outside the currently accepted and relatively narrow areas of contemporary aesthetic appreciation.

This is not the only paradox however as the other reaction of the new environmental conservation movement has been a widespread disenchantment with contemporary planning philosophies which of course also had their origins in a previous generation's reaction to the problems of industrialization and urbanization. Town planning arose in response to social distress, a condition that could be alleviated, *inter alia*, by improvement of the physical environment. But over the years environmental improvement appears increasingly to have become an end in itself and the original social objectives have been forgotten. The concept of amenity promoted by advocates of pleasantness, civic beauty and visual order like Octavia Hill, William Morris, and T.C. Horsfall had as its goal the development of sylvan and genteel suburbs which were soon to evolve into white towers in green parks. The postwar period has seen a rejection of many of these basic planning tenets coupled with a loss of direction made all the worse by a widespread lack of confidence in our ability to create new urban environments in which people can live.

It is possible to detect, however, the emergence of a conservation ethic which may perhaps provide a more satisfactory reconciliation of society's demands for 'amenity' with the economic realities of a so-called post-industrial society largely devoid of ritual expectations of growth. Thus society is showing an increasing interest in the physical infra-structure of the existing landscape and is beginning to see in it assets with intrinsic social and economic values. The nature of the British landscape, dominated as it is by eighteenth- and nineteenth-century developments, means that it will inevitably be the physical remains of industrialization that provide the building bricks, so to speak, for the future and this places special responsibilities upon us in terms of how we view their conservation.

Origins of the Industrial Revolution

England at the end of the seventeenth century was still a fairly thinly populated country and the large proportion of that population derived a living from agriculture. The traditional village craftsman was still the most important industrial producer and every locality had its baker, tailor, carpenter, blacksmith and bricklayer who was both worker and capitalist. In the towns these crafts were organized in guilds many of which were to strongly influence and in some cases control the way in which their craft-based activities evolved into full-scale industrial enterprises during the eighteenth and nineteenth centuries. It would be wrong however to imagine that the Industrial Revolution was simply a product of the eighteenth century, growing out of a series of ingenious inventions like the steam engine or the spinning jenny. Its origins lie in a whole complex of inter-related movements, some with their origins as far back as the Middle Ages, which reacted one with another to produce a situation in the second half of the eighteenth century when the economy could be said to have reached a point of take-off. Nor should the extent of industrial activity in the seventeenth, or even sixteenth, century be underestimated for despite the preponderance of locally based self-employed craftsmen there were many areas of the economy including wool textile manufacture and coal mining for example which had reached a substantial scale of operation.

Our understanding of why the Industrial Revolution took place is a subject of much controversy but what is certain is that at some point, probably in the second half of the eighteenth century – although some would put it slightly earlier – Britain reached the point of 'take-off into self sustained growth' based on radical changes in methods of production. These changes, occurring over a relatively short time, had widespread repercussions throughout society, the national economy and the landscape. The beginning of the Industrial Revolution, therefore, is marked by the start of a rapid rate of change in the economy from one of a backward or underdeveloped country to that of a modern industrial nation. In quantitative terms it might be possible to pinpoint the start of the Industrial Revolution as the date when the gross national product, representing the national income or the total value of goods and services produced in the economy, first began to increase by about 2 per cent per year. In any pre-industrial economy the rate of growth would be less than 1 per cent per annum. This take-off point occured in Britian somewhere between 1740 and 1780. Britain was the first country in the world to undergo this industrial transformation of its national economy. The change occurred spontaneously, without any outside direction, without any conscious policy of stimulating industrial growth, without any momentum being directly imparted through taxation or through capital being made available. Indeed the state showed no interest whatsoever in promoting industrial activity or encouraging new skills.

What were the factors which lead to the occurrence of this Industrial Revolution? There were the direct economic forces of population growth, of agricultural improvement, of increasing trade and the growth of markets, of capital accumulation and the development of a flexible banking system, of the breakdown of medieval conditions of control and regulation and their supersession by those of competition, of business enterprise, of improvements in communication and of technological innovation. There must also have been many subtler influences resulting from deep-seated stirrings within society – changes in religion and conditions of religious tolerance, for example, scientific advances and the political situation in which government, if not giving active support to industrial enterprise, was at least acquiescent. Conditions of relative stability in Britain must also have been important and the country became a haven for political and religious refugees many of whom brought with them manufacturing techniques and the enterprise necessary to put them into practice. There are also natural advantages in the availability of raw materials such as good quality sheep pasture, consistently flowing streams for power, iron ore and coking coal. Also of some unknown importance must have been those entirely fortuitous occurrences such as the succession of good harvests in the 1730s which contributed to a general prosperity and the creation of surplusses and thus helped to generate a climate within which the other forces of change could interact more satisfactorily.

The population of England in 1700 was probably slightly more than 6,000,000; it had increased to 6,500,000 by 1750 and then started climbing rapidly to reach over 9,000,000 by 1801, the date of the first census. The increase of real incomes provided a market incentive, a stimulus to producers of goods and importers of commodities. The increase in foreign trade, in addition to the new home demand, was opening up colonial markets to home manufacturers. But was population growth a cause or a consequence of the economic changes? The dramatic rate of growth after 1770 may have been a result of the rise in birthrate, itself resulting from the demand for labour leading to earlier marriage and therefore earlier parenthood. On the other hand social and economic factors such as improved food supply and better clothing and housing substantially reduced the death rate, a trend accentuated by the beginnings of smallpox inoculation and improved medical knowledge applied to the feeding of children. In the middle of the eighteenth century the initial growth took place before the period of rapid economic expansion and must therefore be regarded as one of its causes. What is also certain is that once the balance had been tipped in favour of self-sustained growth, an increased number of consumers and workers became a necessary condition of further industrially-based economic advance.

Population growth was by no means evenly distributed and once industrial-ization had got underway the effects of the reorientation of the population axis were, in terms of landscape changes, of very great importance. In 1700 the population was thickest along a line running south-west to north-east through the rich agricultural lands of lowland England. By 1800 that axis had been turned through 90 degrees and there it lies today. The areas in which industry was centred saw a more rapid population growth than the predominantly rural counties which, although in a few small areas suffering an actual decline, continued to grow but at a less rapid rate. But the growth in the new industrial areas was not only generated entirely from within; there were massive migrations from the countryside. By 1831 about one third of England's population was engaged in industry, a proportion, but not of course a total number, which remained more or less stable throughout the rest of the century. New industrial towns developed although London which had always been much larger than all other towns continued to dominate. In 1800 London had nearly 900,000 inhabitants but there were only 14 other towns with populations of more than 20,000. By 1851 when London had a population of over 2,250,000 there were 54 towns and cities with a population between 20,000 and 100,000 and seven (Birmingham, Bradford, Bristol, Leeds, Liverpool, Manchester and Sheffield) with over 100,000 inhabitants.

Feeding the new industrial and urban population was made possible by changes and improvements in agriculture. The first was enclosure, the second the superior methods of husbandry and of farming technology introduced by the great improvers. Both were closely interlocked, enclosure being the essential prerequisite for the introduction of the new techniques. Much of the new equipment introduced after 1750 would have been useless on the old strips of the open field system. Similarly, introduction of new crops or rotations and methods of animal breeding was out of the question in an essentially feudal agricultural system where custom, tradition and the standards of the poorest quality cultivator were dominant. Enclosure then was the largest single movement affecting land use, and therefore output, because it made possible all other innovations. In 1750 perhaps half of England was enclosed as in some areas open fields have never existed and in others they had been long outmoded. For the remainder of England the major period of the enclosure movement was 1760 to 1815 when most enclosures, in contrast to the earlier period, were made as the result of Parliamentary awards. In this period over 1,800 acts, covering some 10,000,000 acres, were passed. With the almost total enclosure of agricultural England by the early years of the nineteenth century it became possible for the first time for the theories on new crops and mechanization which had been actively promoted in the seventeenth century to be applied on a wide scale.

Although capital availability was significant to this 'agricultural revolution', it was much more important to the new industrial entrepreneurs. Most of the capital that financed the early phase of the Industrial Revolution came from two main sources. Firstly there was accumulated capital, the result of the more or less continuous expansion in the economy in the middle years of the eighteenth century before industrialization really got underway. Accumulation of capital in the hands of landowners and merchants, for example, was considerable, and much of this found its way into industry, often industry within the family network. The other main source was investment and this came from many sectors of the community including the landed aristocracy, traditional holders of wealth who were frequently energetic investors. In addition however the savings of the professional classes, craftsmen and working men, often through their friendly societies found its way into industry also. One of the great strengths of industry in Britain, and conversely one of the greatest heartaches when a company failed, was the broad base of industrial investment, seen at its extreme in the capitalization of the railways.

The early growth of banks, not only in London but in country areas too, made short term credit available for agriculture, industry and transport. By 1780, when there were 100 banks outside London, a network of credit extended throughout the country, facilitating the transfer of funds, the settling of debts and the obtaining of cash. By the late 1820s there were 554 country banks, a situation unique in Europe. The banks did not, however, provide the key to the much larger quantities of capital required by industrialists to launch their enterprises. Most manufacturing industry was in the hands of family businesses or partnerships in the middle of the eighteenth century. This to some extent was inevitable as without the protection of the Limited Liabilities Acts, which did not come in until 1855–62, each partner in an unincorporated business was totally liable for his debts. Partners tended therefore to be found within the framework of a family or a church where the ties of trust were strongest. With some sections of the community, such as the Quakers, family and faith were often closely interwoven.

Another important factor, which applied to many industrial enterprises, was the relatively low cost of the initial fixed assets. It was possible to start on a small scale and expand almost entirely on the reinvestment of profits. Technology was relatively simple and the cost of buildings and equipment not inordinately large. Given technical expertise in the process, perhaps the most valuable single asset in the setting up of a new manufacturing concern, it was not too difficult to make a start. The number of skilled craftsmen who left established organizations to set up on their own with no more than the traditional 'life's savings' was considerable and in some sections of industry was the most typical method of expansion.

Although at home population increase provided both a new source of labour and also a new market for manufactured goods, of increasing significance throughout the eighteenth century was the development of Britain's overseas trading connections. In the 1570s England had one major export commodity, woollen cloth, which accounted for some 80 per cent of the value of her trade, nearly all of which was with the North Sea ports or the Atlantic seaboard of Europe. Two hundred years later she had a diverse range of manufactured exports of which wool still constituted the largest and her trade extended not only throughout Europe but to America, Africa, India and China. Indeed the century after about 1660 has been titled the period of the 'Commercial Revolution', so important was it to the development of merchant organization, to capital accumulation and investment and to the market opportunities which were provided to the new industries. The collapse of Antwerp in the late sixteenth century as the *entrepôt* for Europe led eventually to English merchants having to seek their own connections by sea with European markets and as the eighteenth century progressed London became the mercantile centre of the world and the base for merchants, financiers, bankers, insurance companies and shipping underwriters. By the end of the eighteenth century Britain had trading connections throughout the world and much of the capital which was being accumulated in London was redistributed into mining and manufacturing industry. Bristol and London merchants helped finance coal mining and iron making in South Wales, and Glasgow and Liverpool merchants put capital into the cotton industries of Scotland and Lancashire respectively.

These economic and demographic origins of the Industrial Revolution have been mentioned first if only to put the heroic age of invention into the right sort of perspective. Successful invention and innovation demand a number of prerequisites: a climate of acceptability, an obvious need, and development of genius, perseverance or opportunism, or possibly all three. The climate of acceptability certainly existed in England in the early years of the eighteenth century as witnessed by the immigrants fleeing persecution elsewhere in Europe who as Dutch brassfounders settled in the valley of the River Avon between Bath and Bristol or as French silk-weavers occupied the Spitalfields area of London. Throughout the seventeenth century too a new class of bourgeoisie was developing in Britain who, although they were not often the people who created the new ideas themselves were prepared to listen, were capable of understanding, and were prepared to offer backing. Some inventions relied on intellectual genius, others on the systematic investigation of possible alternatives until the right answer came up, while still others required some almost fortuitous outside factor to intervene. Abraham Darby was undoubtedly aware of the social and economic need for an alternative fuel to charcoal for iron smelting, although how far that need was being directly felt in Coalbrookdale in 1709 is difficult to assess. The geological accident of the eminent suitability of the Coalbrookdale 'Clod' coal for making coke for smelting purposes must be borne in mind when measuring the significance of the coke smelting technique which he perfected. Over a century and a half later another attempt to find an alternative fuel, in this case the substitution of coal for coke in locomotive fireboxes, was systematically pursued for years with innumerable patents and experimental designs before the perfection of the brick arch in 1859 allowed coal to be burned successfully.

Undoubtedly the cumulative effect of innovation in technology was beginning to be felt on a large scale by the end of the eighteenth century. Using the simple indicator of patents, of the 2,600 for the whole of the century, more than half were registered after 1780. But often the new machine would prove disappointing to its patentee or promoter perhaps because it did not do what it was supposed to, or for want of precision or because the raw material was of inconsistent quality. Patent could follow patent without anything like profitability being achieved and the employers' dream of a self-acting machine which would equal the best hand labour but would be driven by itself remained elusive. In other words mechanization was a process spread over a long period rather than, as is commonly supposed, an event to which the label 'Industrial Revolution' could be applied. The process was not smooth but discontinuous and subject to a whole complex of competing pressures. For the most part it advanced by small increments and in some areas, such as the textile industry for example, where the effects of mechanization were felt strongly in terms of redundancy the small forward movements were often followed by retreats as groups of workers reasserted their claims. There was resistance to machinery, some of it ill-informed, but it was nevertheless an endemic feature of eighteenth- and nineteenth-century industrial life.

We must, however, allow innovation in technology no more than its proper importance, for although the products of many of the great inventive engineers provide much of the inspiration for the study of industrial archaeology, they have relevance only when combined with entrepreneurial ability and the effective organization of capital, the market and the methods of production. Thomas Telford was arguably an organizer of men first and foremost and an engineer second. The canal network owed little or nothing to advanced technology but much more to the organization of large numbers of men and the mobilization of capital. In the textile industry a whole range of closely interlinked inventions provided the base line from which the industry could free itself from its medieval shackles, though it was in the factory, which was primarily a symbol of organization rather than technology, that the potential of these inventions was realized. The factory system was being exploited for its organizational advantages by people like Benjamin Gott in Leeds, for example, before the advantages of power applied to a multiplicity of machines were fully realized.

Impact of the Industrial Revolution

Let us examine the magnitude of the effects of industrialization on Britain. The economic consequences are measurable and staggering in their scale. National income in England and Wales was £130,000,000 in 1770; in Great Britain as a whole in 1800 it was £230,000,000, in 1830 £350,000,000 and in 1850 £525,000,000. This shows a doubling of average income per head. By the end of the nineteenth century the national income had increased by a factor of about 14 and real income per head had roughly quadrupled. Despite the traditionally pessimistic view of the horrors of industrialization seen in terms of poverty, of appalling living conditions and of periodic heavy unemployment, the real wages of the majority of workers in British industry were rising and their living and working conditions, *on average* were improving.

The statistics of growth for individual industries provide some of the more startling indicators of the effects of industrial activity. There were less than 20 blast furnaces in 1760. By 1790 this figure had increased to over 80 and in 1797 England became for the first time an exporter of iron and iron goods. There were 177 blast furnaces in 1805, 372 in 1830 and 655 in 1852. The majority were coke-fired after 1800. Pig-iron output increased from 30,000 tons in 1700 to 250,000 tons by 1805, 650,000 by 1830 and 2,000,000 tons by mid-century. In the cotton industry growth was still more spectacular, largely as the result of the improvements made in machine spinning by James Hargreaves, Richard Arkwright and Samuel Crompton with the introduction of the jenny, the waterframe and the mule respectively. Import of raw cotton, which was less than 8,000,000 lb per year in 1780 had risen to over 25,000,000 lb by 1790, 37,500,000 lb by 1800 and nearly 60,000,000 lb in 1805. The 100,000,000 lb point was reached in 1815, 250,000,000 lb in 1830 and 620,000,000 lb in 1850. The number of cotton spindles increased similarly from less than 2,000,000 in 1780 to 21,000,000 by the middle of the nineteenth century. Mechanization in weaving of cloth developed slightly later but, once underway, the results in terms of production were no less remarkable. With hardly any power looms in 1820 the industry grew to have 50,000 in 1830 and 250,000 in 1850. The cotton industry as a whole employed more than 500,000 people in 1830, of whom about half were working in factories. Over 50 per cent of total production was exported, representing in value about 40 per cent of all British exports.

Good communications provided the basis for the factory growth of the iron, the cotton and many other industries. In 1750 there were about 1000 miles of navigable river in England. In the following century over 4,000 miles of canal had been built, linking the main industrial areas with the rivers, ports and coalfields. What is more significant, however, is that nearly three-quarters of that canal mileage had been completed by 1800, thus providing at the beginning of the Industrial Revolution period the consolidation and unification of the English market that was so essential for growth. The significance of railways was still greater and between 1840 and 1850 5,000 route miles were built, more than the whole of the country's total canal mileage. The effects of railways were felt in many fields beyond those connected directly with the transport of goods. Besides reducing the time and cost of travel and extending the communication system over a wider area than that covered by the canal network, the railway increased the mobility of labour and further encouraged concentrations of population, gave an enormous boost to the iron and engineering industries with its demand for rails and locomotives and was largely responsible for the new and widespread habit of investment in industry. By 1850, for the first time ever, a nation was devoting at least 10 per cent of its total income to capital accumulation in one form or another.

In addition to communications, coal was essential to the development of industry, and the discovery of ways of using coal where once wood had been essential was a decisive technological factor in allowing many industries to develop. The use of coal to generate steam removed industry still further from its reliance on nature by reducing dependence on water power. As early as the beginning of the eighteenth century England had been unique in Europe for its large consumption of coal, probably then about 3,000,000 tons per year. By 1800 this had grown to 10,000,000 tons, almost entirely as the result of increased industrial activity. Coal in the form of coke began to replace charcoal for iron smelting and later for puddling of wrought iron, it was the primary fuel of the rapidly expanding brick industry and, of ever increasing importance, it powered the new steam engines. By 1800 there were perhaps 1,000 steam engines in use in England, the large majority pumping water. About 250, however, were driving machines in the cotton industry and, as the nineteenth century progressed, steam engines increasingly replaced human, animal, wind and water power. Thus by 1838 the cotton industry was using 46,000 steam horsepower and the woollen industry 17,000. By 1850 the textile industry as a whole was using nearly 100,000 steam-generated horsepower. All of this was provided by coal, the first raw material in history to be measured in millions of tons. From 10,000,000 tons produced in 1800 output grew to 25,000,000 tons in 1830 and 50,000,000 tons in 1850. These statistical indices of growth tell only part of the story of industrial development in Britain during the eighteenth and nineteenth centuries, covering up at a single sweep the subtleties of social change and enormities of social cost which can never be fully documented. The remains of the landscape changes brought by industry are still there to be seen and studied by the industrial archaeologist but the effects on ordinary people of those changes, the most radical changes of environment which any society has ever experienced, can only be pieced together from fragmentary evidence. In examining therefore the remains of industrial activity it is essential to have some understanding of the technological, social, and economic background in order to fully appreciate the relevance of a waterwheel to the machinery it drives, to the stream valley in which it is situated, to the community of which it might form a focal point, to the men who made it and used it, to the families whose livelihood depended upon it, and to the processes of technological innovation of which it might form a part. Similarly we must learn to look at industrial monuments, not in isolation but as part of the total landscape.

THE INDUSTRIAL HERITAGE

Britain's industrial heritage is unique in its richness and variety and it is appropriate that industrial archaeology – the study and, where appropriate, the preservation of that heritage – had its origins here. Archaeological analysis of the remains of industry is making an increasing contribution to our understanding of them. Not only is the industrial archaeologist, as a field-worker and interpreter of the landscape, able to provide an extra dimension to the findings of historians who have used only documentary sources but there are numerous areas where field evidence is itself the primary source material. The development of early iron railways from the mid-eighteenth century onwards, the evolution of iron-framed buildings out of their timber- and composite-framed predecessors, virtually the whole of our knowledge of early blast furnace design, has been revealed by archaeological study. A completely different approach to site evidence is the area surveying and mapping of types of industrial installation, workers' housing, water mills or mineshafts as a means of establishing distributional patterns. Here the techniques of the geographer and statistician are required. An understanding of the evolution of industrial technology has similarly been enhanced by study of the artefacts. Many technical innovations of the early Industrial Revolution period were brought about by craftsmen whose contribution was rarely, if ever, documented. The machine he made may well be our only clue to its design and method of operation. It can provide an insight into the life and intellect of the man who made it far more potent than any written evidence could do, even supposing it existed. James Nasmyth, himself a notable inventor, wrote of that great craftsman and innovator Henry Maudslay, with whom he worked for a time as an assistant: 'To be permitted to stand by and watch the systematic way in which Mr Maudslay would first mark or line out his work, and the masterly manner in which he would deal with his materials and cause them to assume the desired forms, was a treat beyond all expression. Every stroke of the hammer, chisel or file, told as an effective step towards the intended result. It was a never-to-be-forgotten lesson in workmanship in the most exalted sense of the term.' Here is the key to what much of industrial archaeology is all about – the appreciation and understanding of the genius of innovation and the skill in making things combined with a recognition of the practical and aesthetic qualities of workmanship, for which the original object is essential.

For the remains of industry to continue to provide us with an insight into the past it is essential that we record or preserve at least the most important and the most typical of them. The industrial archaeologist is concerned with both these activities. As yet there is no systematic approach to the recording of industrial remains and numerous sites disappear each week without even the simplest photographic record being made of their existence. There have, however, been regional and national surveys of the most important sites and it has thus become possible, in the last few years, to build up a broad-brush picture of priorities for legislative protection. The most important of these surveys – the Industrial Monuments Survey – begun by Rex Wailes and now being undertaken by Keith Falconer – has resulted in many hundreds of industrial structures being listed and scheduled. This *Guide* is one of the useful by-products of this work although it can contain only a minute proportion of the sites which have been examined.

Preservation of the industrial heritage has been energetically pursued in the last ten years with wind- and watermill preservation groups, railway and canal societies and open air museums all making their contribution. The problems, however, have been quite different from those facing the preservation of more traditional sites in that industrial buildings are not only more numerous, but they tend to be bigger, occupy valuable urban sites and can present formidable technical difficulties. In the case, for example, of a medieval building its importance is heightened by its very survival whereas when a country railway station, row of workers' cottages or tollhouse is considered for preservation there may well be a choice to be made between several dozen. This makes preservation more difficult for whilst we still on occasion have a chance to select the best or most typical example of a type of site, the fact that it is not the sole survivor weakens the case for its retention. Purely archaeological considerations can only be applied in the case of a relatively small proportion of sites, however. Increasingly it is recognized that the only chance for retention of a building is to make it work for its living – by finding a new use for it. Although there are undoubtedly adequate historical and archaeological justifications for the preservation of the great Albert Dock warehouse complex in Liverpool purely as a monument, it is inconceivable that this would be allowed to happen. If we want to keep Albert Dock we must pay for it and then ensure that the new users provide sufficient economic justification for its continued existence. The voices of the past must be reconciled with the pragmatic necessities of today and tomorrow. Industrial archaeological preservation will, therefore, increasingly be a collaboration between historians, planners, designers and architects and the measure of their success will be the extent to which the archaeological and design integrity of the site has survived the processes of adaptation.

The physical remains of the first industrial nation, with which this book is wholly concerned, thus far transcend in importance their role as pure historical evidence. To an increasing number of people the engines, machines, factories and mills, railways and canals, pit mounds and rows of terrace houses, which came to dominate the landscape in the last two centuries have become significant as part of a wider cultural heritage. They are implanted in the subconscious of innumerable ordinary people who with no background of scholarship or training in artistic or architectural appreciation recognize their significance as a part of the national estate. It would be all too easy to see the sites featured in this book through the eyes of an antiquarian or collector – like butterflies on pins – but what they represent and what their study so often reveals with startling vividness and clarity, is the skill, inventiveness, panache, adventurousness and suffering of the world's first Industrial Revolution.

Neil Cossons
Ironbridge
February 1980

MAPS

Union Suspension Brid[ge]

Keilder Viaduct

Ridsdale Ironworks

Co[a]

Brampton Station

Lambley Viaduct

Port Carlisle

Shaddon Mill Carlisle

Smelthill Allenh[e]

Alston Station

Nenthead

Kilhope

Saltpans Allonby

Jane Pit Workington

Cumbria

Wether riggs Pottery Clifton

Duke Pit Whitehaven

Cleator Moor

Elterwater Gunpowder Mill

Stoney Hazel Forge

Snuff Mill Kendal

Duddon Furnace

Stott Park Bobbin Mill

Backbarrow Furnace

Holme Mill

Hodbarrow Mine

Ulverston Station

Barrow in Furness

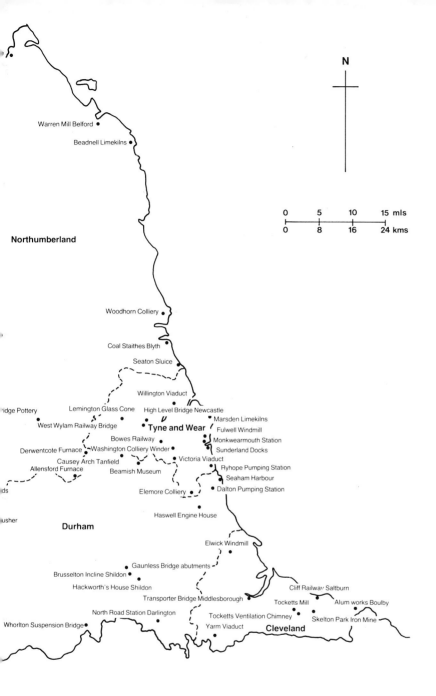

N

Northumberland

Warren Mill Belford ●

Beadnell Limekilns ●

Woodhorn Colliery ●

Coal Staithes Blyth ●

Seaton Sluice ●

Willington Viaduct

Lemington Glass Cone   High Level Bridge Newcastle
●idge Pottery   ●
West Wylam Railway Bridge   **Tyne and Wear**   ● Marsden Limekilns
                                                              Fulwell Windmill
                        Bowes Railway ●   ● Monkwearmouth Station
Derwentcote Furnace ●   ● Washington Colliery Winder ●
Causey Arch Tanfield   ● Victoria Viaduct   ● Sunderland Docks
Allensford Furnace ●   ● Ryhope Pumping Station
                      Beamish Museum   ● Seaham Harbour
ds   Elemore Colliery ●   ● Dalton Pumping Station

usher   Haswell Engine House

        Durham

                      Elwick Windmill ●

                      ● Gaunless Bridge abutments
Brusselton Incline Shildon ●
Hackworth's House Shildon ●   Cliff Railway Saltburn ●
        Transporter Bridge Middlesborough ●   Tocketts Mill ●   Alum works Boulby ●
North Road Station Darlington ●   Tocketts Ventilation Chimney ●   Skelton Park Iron Mine ●
Whorlton Suspension Bridge ●   Yarm Viaduct   **Cleveland**

| 0 | 5 | 10 | 15 mls |
| 0 | 8 | 16 | 24 kms |

Grinton Smelt Mill •

Yorks N

Smeltmills Greenhow •
Grassington Flues •
• Toftgate Limekiln

• Lune Aqueduct

Corn Mill Skipton •
Glasson Dock • • Galgate Silk Mills
Cononley Engine House •
Lighthouses Fleetwood
Dale End Mill Lotherdale •
Lancashire
• Bramhope Tunnel me
• Wyre Aqueduct
Bingley Locks •
Saltaire Mill •
• Pollard Bridge H
Marsh Hill Thornton Cleveleys
• Whalley Viaduct
Armley Mills Leeds •
Woollen Mills Bradford •
• Th
Leeds & Liverpool Canal Burnley •
Windmill Lytham St Annes • Cotton Mill Preston •
Yorks W
Coke Ovens Oswaldthwistle •
Piece Hall Halifax •
Higher Mill Helmshore •
Dewbury Canal Basin •
• C
Southport Pier •
Huddersfield Station •
• Caphouse Collier
Burrow Bridge village •
Weavers Cottages Colne Valley •
March Barn Bridge Castleton •
• Dee Mill Shaw
Low Mill Furnace Silkstone •
Manchester
• Cotton mills Oldham
Hartleys Jam Factory •
Canal Basin Worsley •
Liverpool Road Station •
• Wortley Forge
Glassworks St Helens •
St Helens Canal
Castlefield Basin •
Yo
Oriel Chambers •
Rainhill Station •
Barton Aqueduct •
Albert Dock •
Merseyside
Viaduct Stockport •
• Marple Aqueduct
Edgehill Cutting •
Cementation Furnaces Sheffield •
Port Sunlight •

N

Warren Moor Chimney •

Railway Tunnel Grosmont •

Moorgate Railway Bridge •

Kilns Rosedale •

Spa Bridge Scarborough •

0   5   10   15 mls
0   8   16   24
                    kms

Flamborough Light •

• Maltings Boroughbridge

Railway Museum York
                    •
• Stamford Bridge Mill

Naburn Lock
        •   Pocklington Station
                              •
• Breweries Tadcaster
                              Humberside
rth

Putty Mill   Skidby Windmill •

                    Springhead Pumping Station •
                                          • Hull Docks
ley Ferry Aqueduct   • Goole Docks
Quays Wakefield   • Ferriby Sluice
                    Horkstow Bridge •

                                          • Grimsby Docks

                    Wrawby Windmill •
sborough Mill
secar Engine House
    Crags Tramway Conisborough •

• Catcliffe glass cone
ydale Industrial Hamlet

Alvington Mill

Tealby Thorpe Watermill

Warehouses Gainsborough

Louth Station

North Levington Windmill

Canal Warehouse Worksop

Alford Windmill

Notts

Central Station Lincoln

Canal Basins Horncastle

Maltings Mansfield

Lincolnshire

Maltings Newark

Dog Dyke Pumping Station

Papplewick Pumping Station

Colliery Winder Bestwood

Sleaford Maltings

Hospital Bridge Boston

Bennerley Viaduct

Boston Quay

Lace Market Nottingham

Anglo Scotia Mills Beeston

Londonthorpe Mill

Ruddington Workshops

Spalding Marsh Pumping Station

Ashby Station

Moira Furnace

Leics

Warehouses Measham

Bagworth Incline

Oakham Station

Abbey Lane Pumping Station

Glenfield Tunnel

Railway Bridges Peterborough

Workshops Wigston

Brickworks Old Fletton

Workshops Hinkley

Cambridgeshire

Foxton Incline

Market Harborough Station

Northants

Kilsby Tunnel

Braunston Canal Basin

Billing Watermill

Shoe Factories Northampton

Magdalene Bridge

Bourn Post Mill

Blisworth Tunnel

Canal Museum Stoke Bruerne

Cosgrove Bridge

N

0   5   10   15 mls

0   8   16   24 kms

• Burnham Overy Mills

• Fakenham Gasworks

• Kings Lynn Docks

Norfolk

Jarrolds Works Norwich •

Stracey Arms Windmill •

Yarmouth smokehouses •

Berney Arms Mill •

• Eagle Mills Downham Market

Herringfleet Windmill •

St Olave's Bridge •   • Lound Waterworks

• Maltings Oulton Broad

• Hoxne Mill

• Stretham Engine

• Wicken Fen Mill

• Pakenham Windmill

• Newmarket Station

• Saxtead Green Windmill

• Cheddars Lane Pumping Station

• Drinkstone Windmill

• Fleam Dyke Pumping Station

• West Wratting Mill

Suffolk

• Woodbridge Tidemill

Maltings Ipswich •

Flatford Mill •

Cannon Foundry Chesterfield

Cat & Fiddle Windmill Dale

Lace Factories Long Eaton

Tramway Bridge Ticknall

Bottle Ovens Swadlincote

Colliery Engine house Eckington

Caudwells Mill Rowsley

Morley Park Furnaces

Calver Mill

Stone Edge Smelt Mill

Leawood Pumping Station Cromford

Belper Mills

Eden Mine Crushing Circle

Cressbrook Mill

Crich Quarry

Darley Abbey Mill

Buxworth Canal Basin

Newhaven Tunnel
Cromford Mills

Silk Mill Derby

Derby Station

Derbys

Cotton mills Glossop

Clarence Mill Bollington

Magpie Mine Sheldon

Middleton Top Winding Engine

Silk Workshops Macclesfield

Brindley Mill Leek

Breweries Burton

Quarry Bank Mill Styal

Alderley Old Mill

Chatterley Whitfield Colliery

Cheddleton Flint Mill

Gladstone Pottery

Stone Station

Staffs

Shugborough Railway Tunnel

Aqueduct Congleton

Avenue Bridge Brewood

Canal Locks Wolverhampton

Transporter Bridge Warrington

Lion Salt Works Marston

Harecastle Tunnel

Etruscan Bone Mill

Stoke on Trent Station

Cheshire

Dutton Viaduct

Railway works Crewe

Runcorn Railway Bridge

Anderton Lift

Longdon Aqueduct

Hadley Locks

Ironbridge Gorge

Sankey Viaduct

Shot Tower Chester

Beeston Lock

Lift Bridge Wem

Shrops

Bage's Mill Shrewsbury

Howard Street Warehouse

Snailbeach Mine

Ellesmere Port

Chirk Aqueduct

Pant Incline

N

15 mls
24 kms
0   5   10   15 mls
0   8   16   24 kms

Anker Mill Nuneaton
Hawkesbury Canal Junction
Goods depot Rugby
Cash's Topshops
Rock Mill Leamington
Chesterton Windmill
Berkswell Windmill
Jewellery Quarter Birmingham
Gasholder Buildings Warwick
Wooten Wawen Aqueduct
Edstone Aqueduct
Stratford Tramway Bridge

Warwickshire

West Midlands

Chances Glassworks
Langley Maltings
Galton Bridge
Sarehole Mill
Engine House Tardebigge
Needle Mills Redditch
Canal Basin Worcester

Donnington Brewery

Gloucs

Bottenham Locks
Cobbs Engine House Dudley
Stourbridge glass cones
Churchill Forge
Brintons Mills Kidderminster
Arlington Mill Bibury
Sapperton Tunnel
Gloucester Docks
Mythe Bridge
Over Bridge
Frogmarsh Woolstove
Dunkirk Mill

Bridgnorth Station
Eardington Forges
Victoria Bridge Arley
Bewdley Station
Canal Basins Stourport
Holt Fleet Bridge
Powick H E P

Hereford & Worcs

Stanley Mill

Charlecote Furnace
Quarries Clee Hills
Watermill Mortimer's Cross
Sharpness Docks
New Mill Kingswood

Fairplay Engine House
Whitecliffe Furnace
Redbrook bridge
Clearwell Caves
Scowles Bream
Lydney Harbour

Broomy Hill Pumping Station

Stevington Wi

Tickford Bridge

Wolverton Aqueduct

Stewart?

Beds

Hook Norton Brewery

Bucks

Bliss Tweed Mill

Linsdale Tunnel

Oxon

Ford End Watermill

Pitstone Windmill

Brill Mill

Blanket Mills Witney

Gad

Canal Bridges Oxford

G

Lacey Green Windmill

Didcot Engine Shed

Marlow Bridge

Railway Estate Swindon

Medmenham Winch

Brakspear's Brewery

Wharncliffe

Railway Bridge Maidenhead

Old Forge Eastbury

Kew Bridge P

Berkshire

Royal Waiting Room Windsor

Box Tunnel

Sheffield Lock

Kempton Park P

Crofton Pump

Caen Hill Locks

Cobham Telegra

Dundas Aqueduct

Wey Nav

Abbey Mill

Wadworths Brewery

Wilton Windmill

Woollen Mills Trowbridge

Silk Mill Whitchurch

Crane Guildfo

Mills Farnham

Wilts

Hop Kilns Binstead

Hants

Headley Mill

City Mill Winchester

Twyford Pumping Station

Shipley Wi

Downton Tannery

Sussex W

We

Eling Tidemill

Funtley Ironworks

Southwick Brewhouse

Arundel Pumping Station

G

Bucklers Hard

Dockyards Portsmouth

Eastney Pumping Station

Salterns Lymington

Ryde Pier

Yarmouth Tidemill

Warehouses Newport

Upper Mill Calbourne

Donkey Wheel Carisbrooke

Bembridge Windmill

I of W

mill

Cardington Hangers

Herts

Cromer Windmill

Maltings Bishops Stortford

Welwyn Viaduct

Maltings Ware

New River Hertford

idge Park Bridge

Brick kiln Broxbourne

e Park Bridge

Arms Factory Enfield

London

Walthamstow Copper Mill

Camden Round House

Regents Canal

Three Mills

Abbey Mills Pumping Station

aduct

St Katharines Docks

ping Station

Fulham Gasworks

Crossness Pumping Station

Deptford Incline

Ram Brewery

Brixton Windmill

bing Station

Crystal Palace Station

Morden Mills

Keston Windmill

Tower

tion

Hayle Paper Mill Maidstone

Surrey

Reigate Windmills

Outwood Windmills

Kent

Horsewheel Otterden Place

Ouse Viaduct

Nutley Windmill

Oast House Sissinghurst

Union Windmill

mill

Cobbs Mill

Sussex E

Warehouses Rye

ls Mill Henfield

Clayton Tunnel

Brede Pumping Station

Jack & Jill Windmills

Animal Wheels Stanmer

Harveys Brewery

Cliff Lifts Hastings

Net Shops Hastings

stone Pumping Station

Piers Brighton

Polegate Windmill

Thaxted Windmill

Maltings Mistley

Harwich Crane

Bourne Mill

Sauls Bridge

Saltworks Maldon

Essex

Stock Windmill

Upminster Windmill

Southend Pier

Pier Gravesend

Boatstore Sheerness

Chatham Dockyard

Mierscourt Horsewheel

Chart Gunpowder Mills

Chillenden Windmill

Crane Dover Harbour

N

0   5   10   15 mls
0   8   16   24 kms

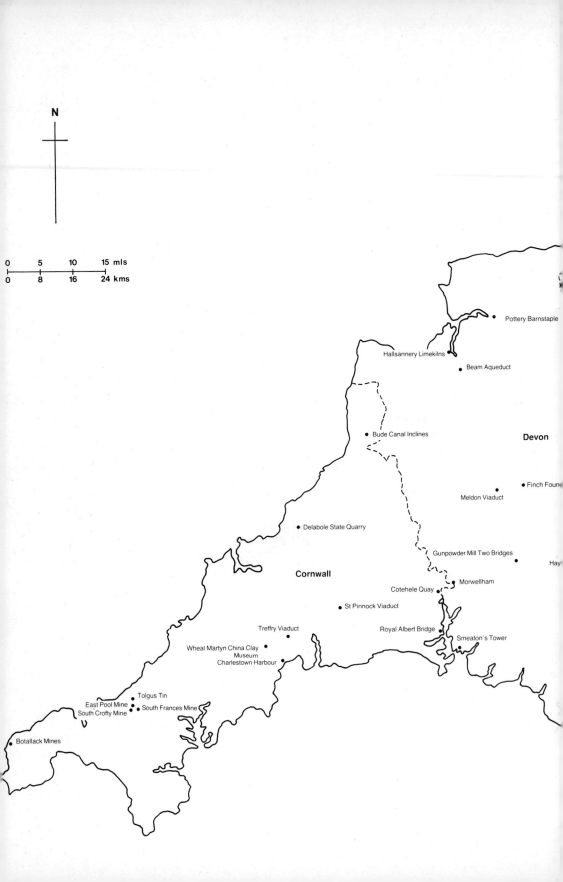

N

| 0 | 5 | 10 | 15 mls |
| 0 | 8 | 16 | 24 kms |

Pottery Barnstaple

Hallsannery Limekilns

Beam Aqueduct

Devon

Bude Canal Inclines

Finch Foun

Meldon Viaduct

Delabole State Quarry

Gunpowder Mill Two Bridges

Cornwall

Hay

Morwellham

Cotehele Quay

St Pinnock Viaduct

Treffry Viaduct

Royal Albert Bridge

Smeaton's Tower

Wheal Martyn China Clay
Museum
Charlestown Harbour

Tolgus Tin

East Pool Mine
South Frances Mine
South Crofty Mine

Botallack Mines

Tormarton Tollhouse

Avon

Clifton Bridge
Temple Meads
Clevedon Pier
Bristol Docks
Kelston Brassmill
Albert Mill
Kennet & Avon Canal Bath
Victoria Bridge Bath
Claverton Pump
Birnbeck Pier
Blagdon Pumping Station
Priston Mill
Charterhouse Leadworks
Smitham Chimney
Fussells Ironworks
Ashton Windmill
Paper Mill Wookey
Train shed Frome
Kilve Retort
Somerset

Brendon Incline
Bridgewater Docks
Traversing Bridge
Shoe Factory Street
Burrow Farm Engine House
Westonzoyland Pumping Station
Stembridge Windmill
Burrow Bridge Pumping Station

Holywood Mill Chard
Sherborne Water pump
Tiverton Housing
Fox Bros Mill Uffculme
Leatherworks Yeovil

Honiton Tollhouse
Dorset

cklepath
Canal Basin Exeter
Seaton Bridge
Palmers Brewery Bridport

Turbine Pump Sutton Poyntz
Tramway Tunnel Corfe
Starcross Engine House
Water Tower Swanage
Bovey Potteries
arries
Windmill stumps Portland

PREFACE TO GAZETTEER

The gazetteer is arranged by county in alphabetical order. For reasons of geographical cohesiveness the two Sussex counties and three Yorkshire counties are listed under S and Y respectively. Greater Manchester and Greater London are to be found under M and L respectively. Sites within a county are listed alphabetically under the place name by which they can most readily be found: all place names are on the Ordnance Survey 1:250,000 ($\frac{1}{4}$″) sheets or in the 3 miles to 1 inch AA Great Britain Road Atlas. In London sites are listed under common neighbourhood names.

In compiling such a gazetteer problems of selection and compression must be faced. Thus an attempt has been made to provide a representative selection of the industrial monuments in each county. This has resulted in the omission of many significant monuments especially in those counties with a particularly rich legacy of industrial monuments. Thus Cornwall, Derbyshire, London, Shropshire, Staffordshire and Yorkshire have suffered the most but only, it is hoped, proportionately. Throughout the emphasis has been on sites where there are complete or substantial remains: many interesting locations have thus been omitted. In the case of relatively common monuments, such as milestones, tollhouses and bridges, only a small representative sample is included. In most cases the buildings are described with reference to their original use but where conversion has altered the character of the site this may be mentioned.

Most of the sites have been visited in the last six years but many of the historical details have been gathered from a wide variety of secondary sources, some of these sources have been of suspect accuracy. The author begs the reader's forgiveness for those inaccuracies that have occurred. Similarly, though every effort has been made to remove references to buildings known to have been demolished since they were visited, inevitably by the time the book is published some material will have disappeared.

One final point: many of the sites listed are not normally open to the public, some are still in active use, others have been converted to other purposes and some are on private land. Permission to view should always be sought.

Avon

A creation of the 1974 local government reorganization, Avon gains its name and its unity from the river on which it is focussed. Bristol, at the limit of tidal water, was for long the second city and port of England and dominates the region. It has a wealth of industrial sites in its environs relating to both its function as a port and a major manufacturing centre. Bath, in addition to its Georgian splendour has also a rich industrial heritage including, on the Kennet & Avon Canal, several of the finest canal monuments in the country. The Avon and its tributaries drain the heartland area of the West of England woollen industry and there are numerous water power sites which have undergone many changes of use ranging from fulling mills and dye grinding mills to brass mills and gunpowder works. The northern Mendips also lie within the county with a history of lead mining dating from Roman times. More recently calamine, coal and stone have been mined in the county but all such activity has now ceased. Many relics of coal mining survive in the valleys around Radstock, in the Kingswood area and around Nailsea.

Museums: Bristol City Museum has an industrial annex situated in a transit shed on Princes Wharf in the City Docks. There are railway preservation centres at Bitton and Weston-super-Mare.

BATH
Bairds Maltings, Sydney Buildings (ST758647)
¹/₂ mile E town centre
Situated at the top of the Widcombe flight of locks (*qv*) this former maltings dates from *c* 1850 and was in production using traditional hand-powered techniques until 1972. The main building has been converted into offices with a dwelling in the square-plan pyramidal-roofed roasting kiln. The canal façade of dressed stone has paired circular headed windows and a central loading door opening on the first floor.

BATH
Green Park Station, Green Park (ST745647)
¹/₄ mile W town centre
Built in 1870 by the Midland Railway, this station was formerly known as Queens Square and operated as the terminus of the Somerset & Dorset Railway until 1966. It has an impressive Georgian-looking entrance block leading to a magnificent iron train shed with a large central span over the track bed flanked by smaller aisles over the platforms. After many years of disuse and neglect, its future is being hotly debated at present (1978).

BATH
Canal and Railway Cuttings, Sydney Gardens (ST758654)
¹/₄ mile E of A36
The lines of both the Kennet & Avon Canal and the Great Western Railway traverse fashionable Sydney Gardens. They both achieve this by cuttings which, with their dressed masonry retaining walls and ornamental overbridges, contribute greatly to the attractions of the gardens. The 2 cast-iron canal bridges bear the inscription 'Erected Anno 1800' and are thus 2 of the oldest cast-iron bridges in the country. The larger of the 2 with 7 cast-iron ribs on the skew is the earliest such metal bridge. The railway of 1840 is spanned by both masonry and cast-iron ornamental bridges. The portals of the 2 short

canal tunnels at either end of the gardens are exceptionally fine.

BATH
Victoria Bridge, Victoria Bridge Road
(ST741650)
³/₄ mile W town centre off A4
A 120-ft-span suspension bridge built in 1836 to the designs of James Dredge, a local engineer. Reputedly, this bridge was built as a demonstration of Dredge's novel principles of bridge design which had been unsuccessful in the competition for the Clifton Bridge, Bristol (*qv*). The catenary chains are made up of flat section iron rods whose number decrease towards the centre with suspension rods arranged at increasingly acute angles. The northern Bath stone pylon bears a plaque with Royal Arms and 'Dredge, Patentee, Bath'.

BATH
Widcombe Locks (ST755643–ST758646)
¹/₂ mile E town centre
One of the major engineering problems of the Kennet & Avon Canal was to effect a junction with the River Avon in Bath. This was eventually achieved by a flight of 7 locks down the hillside at Widcombe with a basin and pumphouse at Dolemeads wharf. The locks were completed in 1810 some 10 years after most of the western section of canal was open. After years of neglect the locks have been restored and the lowest 2 amalgamated into one very deep new lock. The flight is spanned by 2 masonry road bridges and 2 cast-iron footbridges.

BLAGDON
Blagdon Pumping Station (ST503600)
¹/₂ mile N Blagdon off A368
A fine Edwardian water pumping station constructed in 1905 in red brick with stone quoins and dressings. Two elegant engine houses flank a central (truncated) campanile chimney and each contained 2 1902 compound beam engines by Glenfield & Kennedy of Kilmarnock. The engines in the southern engine house are preserved and illustrate the final development in beam engine technology.

BRISTOL
City Docks (ST566724–ST590729)
These docks owe their present configuration to a scheme implemented by William Jessop in the first decade of the 19th century with some modifications in detail by Brunel in the 1840s

BRISTOL: *Steam crane in City Docks – the ships have gone but the crane has been restored.*

and Howard in the 1870s. Most commercial activity has shifted downstream to Avonmouth and Portishead. The numerous sites of industrial interest are briefly described from west to east.
Gridiron (ST567723). Built in 1884 on part of the site of Jessop's original northern entrance lock. Used for doing minor repairs to vessels at low tide.
Northern Entrance Lock (ST567724). Built by Howard in 1873. 350 ft by 62 ft – the only lock now in use giving access to City Docks. The tubular girder swing-bridge may be Brunel's original.
Brunel Lock (ST568723). Jessop's 33-ft-wide southern lock was enlarged by Brunel to 54 ft in 1848 and given a distinctive U-cross-section. The tubular girder swing-bridge may be a replica of Brunel's but built by Howard. **Cumberland Basin** (ST570723). An outer basin to the Docks now virtually disused. Massive stone quay walls with cast-iron bollards.
Junction Lock (ST572723). Part of Howard's improvements of the 1870s with to the north an Italianate shell of a hydraulic engine house of 1871.
Old Junction Lock (ST572721). The only original Jessop lock of 1809 to survive though now blocked. The attractive 2-storey cottages to the north are somewhat later, the block nearest being dated 1831.
Underfall Yard (ST572722). Named after the surplus water culverts on whose embankment it is built. Underfall Yard is the Port of Bristol Authority's workshops. Housed in red brick buildings of 1884 and powered by a 2-cylinder horizontal Tangye steam engine the workshops contain a great variety of interesting engineering machinery. The pumps of the hydraulic system for the City Docks are also in the Yard though the system has greatly contracted. (BIAS 10)
Wapping Dock (ST574724). Also known as Great Western dock, this stepped masonry dry dock was started in 1839 for the construction of Brunel's second steamship the *Great Britain*. The SS *Great Britain*, launched in 1843 as the first screw-driven metal-hulled vessel, once again occupies the dock after a career which saw her abandoned as a hulk in the Falkland Islands. She is being restored to her former glory and is the centrepiece of a museum open to the public.
Fairbairn Crane, Wapping Wharf (ST584722). This large curved jib steam crane capable of lifting 35 tons was constructed by Stothert & Pitt (Bath) in 1875 and has recently been restored as a working exhibit of the nearby industrial museum. It is now the only steam

driven Fairbairn-type crane in the country. (BIAS 8)

Bush's Warehouse, Prince Street (ST585724). A massive 4-storey warehouse built in 2 parts in 1830 and 1847. Probably designed by R S Pope. It has tall narrow semi-circular headed recesses between the vermiculated ground floor and the moulded cornice at attic level. It now houses the Arnolfini Gallery and offices in sympathetic conversion utilizing a tinted-glass roof-storey.

Seed Warehouse, The Grove (ST586725). Early 19th-century squared rubble 5-storey warehouse with small elliptically headed barred windows with central loading doors on each floor. Most of the right-hand windows have been altered to large rectangular openings. A parapet obscures the roof.

Swing-Bridge, Prince Street (ST586724). A riveted plate girder dual roadway swing-bridge of 1879. The masonry engine house contains original hydraulic machinery with applewood toothed gearing. The weather-boarded accumulator tower is given an Italianate appearance by its shallow pyramidal roof with bracketed eaves.

Bathurst Basin (ST587722). Part of Jessop's scheme of 1809 originally giving alternative access for small craft to the New Cut of the River Avon. Stone wharves enclose a triangle of 2 acres of dock. Both junction and entrance lock are now disused. The large arched openings below the General Hospital were reputedly for warehousing.

WCA Warehouse, Redcliff Backs (ST590724). The Western Counties Agricultural Co-operative Association warehouse completed *c* 1910 by W H Brown is a striking example of early reinforced-concrete construction. The red brick infill between concrete floor bands contrasts strongly with the cantilevered concrete goods hoists.

The Granary, Welsh Back (ST589726). The most extravagant example of the so-called Bristol Byzantine style of architecture. Dated 1869 and built by Ponton & Gough, all 7 storeys differ in architectural detail which is picked out in blue and yellow brickwork against a red brick background. The building is topped by a battlemented parapet over a stepped cornice with tall tapering chimney stacks. Now used as a jazz club.

BRISTOL
Clifton Suspension Bridge (ST564731)
2 miles W city centre above A4
The project for a bridge over the Avon gorge originated in a bequest of £1,000 in 1753. When the fund had accumulated to £8,000 by 1829 an Act of Parliament for a toll bridge was obtained and a design competition held which attracted 22 entries. The young I K Brunel's modified design was accepted and work commenced in 1836 but funds ran out by 1840 by which time the Pennant rubble pylons had been built. Work was recommenced in 1861 by Hawkshaw & Harlow as a tribute to the memory of Brunel using chains from the latter's Hungerford Bridge. It was opened in 1864 with a centre span of 702 ft 3 in.

BRISTOL
Goldney Tower, Goldney House, Clifton (ST576727)
1 mile W city centre
In the unlikely setting of an 18th-century landscaped garden stands what is probably the earliest extant pumping engine house in the country. It was built in 1764 to house a tiny Coalbrookdale engine with cylinder dimensions 8 ft long by 11 in diameter though this proved of insufficient power to pump water for the cascade in the adjacent grotto and was replaced by a cylinder 9 ft x 15 in in 1766. The 4-storey masonry engine house is built to resemble a Gothic tower with pointed arched windows and doorway and battlemented parapet. The large opening on the second floor most probably accommodated the beam pivot of the wooden beam as the well is situated immediately below.

BRISTOL
Harveys' Cellars and Wine Museum, Denmark Street (ST584728)
City centre
The extensive cellars under this old street in the centre of the city possibly date back to the 12th century when they were used as storerooms for the monastery of St Augustine. They eventually passed into the hands of William Perry and the company he founded in 1796 is now Harveys of Bristol. When Harveys moved the processing side of the business to Whitchurch they converted the cellars into a museum of sherry and wine. In addition to a magnificent collection of antique wine glasses and silver wine labels it contains many wine workers' tools and a display of the development of wine containers through the centuries. Opposite the showroom entrance is an early 19th-century 5-storey rubble-built bonded warehouse.

BRISTOL
Redcliff Glass Cone, Prewett Street (ST593723)
½ mile S city centre
The most prominent relic of Bristol's illustrious history of glass making is the truncated

glasscone in Redcliff built *c* 1780. The surviving 25 ft high brick structure with its many arched openings has been converted into the dining suite of the adjacent Dragonara Hotel. The upper portion of the original brickwork has been obscured by a storey of hung slates.

BRISTOL

Sea Mills Dock, The Portway (ST549759)
3 miles NW city centre off A4
Only ruinous sections of rock-faced rubble walls survive of this, the first wet dock on the River Avon. Built by John Padmore *c* 1715 it was the third earliest floating dock in the country but its rather isolated situation militated against its success. It was mainly used as a whaling station and as a base for privateers until its closure in 1776.

BRISTOL

Temple Meads Station (ST595724)
½ mile E city centre
Temple Meads Station is the regional focus of the present day rail system and as such is vastly larger than the original terminus of Brunel's Great Western Railway. However, some original features remain, most notably the 1840 train shed one of the outstanding national railway monuments, though now relegated to a car park. The 72 ft clear span simulates hammer beam construction but is in fact cantilever with the load being on the columns of the aisles with the tail ends tied in to the side walls. Beyond the train shed is the 4-aisled engine shed carried on rows of slender cast-iron columns. The neo-Jacobean offices flanking the station approach date from the 1850s and are a relic of the Bristol & Exeter terminus which was swept away in the major rebuilding of the complex in the 1870s. The final enlargement providing 5 further platforms was completed in 1935. (BIAS 4)

CHARFIELD

Huntingford Mill, (ST716935)
2 Miles SW Wotton-under-Edge off B4058
A large former grist mill on the Little Avon now converted into an hotel but retaining its large overshot waterwheels.

CLAVERTON

Claverton Pumphouse, Ferry Lane (ST792644)
2 miles SE Bath off A36
Designed by John Rennie to supply water to the 9-mile pound of the Kennet & Avon Canal prior to its descent down Widcombe Locks in Bath (*qv*), this waterwheel pump is the largest such installation in the country. Contained in a custom-built pumphouse on a former mill site in the Avon valley, the cast-iron beam pump driven by a massive 25 ft broad x 17½ ft diameter breast shot waterwheel can raise some 100,000 gallons an hour from the river to the canal 53 ft above. Construction started in 1809 with Fox of Bristol as one of the contractors and the pump began operation in 1813. The machinery was modified in 1843 by Harveys of Hayle and again in 1902–3 when a central pedestal bearing was inserted in the middle of the waterwheel. The waterwheel was damaged in 1952 and was disused until 1979 when it was restarted after some 8 years of restoration by volunteers. It is open, under the aegis of the Kennet & Avon Canal Trust, on Sundays in the summer.

CHELVEY

Chelvey Pumping Station (ST474678)
3½ miles NE Congresbury off A370
Though steam pumping on this Bristol Waterworks Company site goes back to 1866 the only relic is the last of a series of engines – a 1923 Lilleshall triple expansion vertical engine designed to pump 4,000,000 gallons per day to a head of 420 ft. Now disused.

CLEVEDON

Clevedon Pier, Marine Parade (ST402719)
Town foreshore
Designed by R J Ward and J W Grover and built in 1867–8 by Hamiltons Windsor Ironworks Co of Liverpool, this is surely the most graceful of all piers in the country. It is also one of the most unusual in its construction. It comprises a masonry approach 180 ft long and 20 ft wide with 8 100-ft-spans of wrought-iron girders carried on wrought-iron screw piles. The upper parts of these columns consist of pairs of Barlow rails riveted back to back. The 2 outermost spans of the neck collapsed under test loading in 1970. Stone toll house, gates and dwelling of the pier master were designed by a local architect, Hans Price.

COMBE HAY

Canal Locks and Incline (ST744605)
3 miles S Bath off A367
The Somerset Coal Canal was promoted in 1794 to link the mines of the Somerset coalfield with the Kennet & Avon Canal at Dundas basin at Limpley Stoke (*qv*). It comprised a mainline to Paulton and a branch to Radstock (see Midford Aqueduct *qv*). The mainline had to overcome a difference of height of 130 ft and originally this was to be achieved by a series of caisson locks at Combe Hay. Although one lock to the design of Robert Weldon was built and trials conducted successfully, this idea was abandoned and an incline substituted. The incline was replaced in

1805 by a flight of 22 narrow locks which survive in a state of dereliction.

FRAMPTON COTTERELL
Haematite Mine, The Close (ST669819)
6 miles NE Bristol off A432
The mines were worked in the period 1862–74 producing some 68,000 tons of ore most of which was sent to Seend and Westbury in Wiltshire for smelting. Water seepage was a great problem and after abandonment this plentiful supply was tapped by a water pumping station built over the Roden Acre shaft in 1884. This has preserved access to some of the underground galleries. Nearby (ST673814) is the tapering shell of one of the few windmills in the county.

FRESHFORD
Dunkirk Mill (ST785595)
4 miles SE Bath off A36
This impressive ruin, situated on a hillside near the confluence of the Rivers Frome and Avon was in fact powered by a small stream which issued only 200 yds further up the hillside. The 5-storey rubble built main block with free stone quoins and window openings probably dates from 1795 and measures 72 ft by 32 ft. The engine house extension with its square stack is likely to date from the introduction of steam power in 1810. The southwest elevation has a large wheel arch for the leat to the 32 ft internal waterwheel (gone). The mill was never very successful and had several owners until its final closure in 1912. The mill house is still occupied.

HINTON CHARTERHOUSE
Embankment and Underpass (ST780592)
5 miles SE Bath under A36
The prosperous Black Dog Turnpike Trust obtained an Act of Parliament in 1833 to construct a new road from Woolverton in Somerset to Sydney Gardens in Bath thus bypassing the road via Midford which was in 'parts very steep, hilly and dangerous'. This new road, now the A36, was a major engineering achievement involving considerable earthworks and an embankment at Limpley Stoke, Wiltshire (*qv*). One of the embankments crossed the head of a small valley leading down to Freshford (*qv*) and necessitated accommodating an existing path. This path was led under the embankment in a short tunnel whose western portal was embellished with a Gothic arch in keeping with the nearby Hinton priory.

KELSTON
Brass Annealing Furnaces (ST694679)
4 miles W Bath off A431
This site was developed by William Champion in the late 1760s and was used until the 1840s. The 2 tall stacks of the annealing furnaces may date from the 18th century and although their linings have gone, the long vertical slots above the furnace door openings are evidence of the pivot beams used to facilitate opening of the heavy fireproof furnace doors. Several watercourses can be traced though recent landscaping has obliterated the original layout.

KEYNSHAM
Albert Mill, St Clement's Road (ST656679)
¼ mile E town centre
When production ceased in 1964 the logwood mill at Keynsham was the last dyewood grinding mill in the country. Though the production of dye from exotic woods has been practised in England since the 16th century this site was only used for this purpose from 1874. Previous uses having been as a grist mill, a fulling mill, a cotton mill, a flax mill and a lime and paint works. The layout of the present main building dates from 1875, after the last of a series of disastrous fires. Parts of the fabric of the 3-storey rubble built mill may be earlier. There are 2 breast shot waterwheels probably predating the fire, both *c* 18 ft in diameter by 10 ft wide. The internal waterwheel drives edge runner crushing equipment, the external wheel operated a wool chipper machine. (BIAS 7)

LIMPLEY STOKE
Canal Wharf and Crane, Dundas Basin (ST785626)
3 miles SE Bath off A36
The Kennet & Avon Canal and the Somerset Coal Canal connected at the western end of the Dundas Aqueduct (*qv* Wiltshire). The junction lock itself has been incorporated into a rose bed in a private garden but the small turning basin with its wharf, warehouse and iron hand-crane by Acraman of Bristol still survive. An unusual wood and masonry footbridge carries the towpath across the canal.

MIDFORD
Canal Aqueduct (ST758605)
3 miles S Bath off B3110
A ruinous 2-arched masonry aqueduct which carried the Radstock branch of the Somerset Coal Canal over the Midford Brook. Opened in 1805, the Radstock Arun never provided a completed waterway link and it was replaced throughout its length in 1812 by a railroad. Its early demise as a canal was probably due to water supply problems.

NAILSEA
Engine House, Old Church Road (ST477698)
8 miles W Bristol off B3128
The rather poor reserves of coal at Nailsea were worked throughout the period when transport costs favoured local production. The advent of rail transport made them less competitive and all the collieries had been closed by the end of the 19th century. The shells of 2 engine houses bear witness to late attempts to revive the trade in this district.

OLDLAND
Willsbridge Tunnel (ST666706)
1 mile N Keynsham off A431
The 5½-mile long Avon & Gloucestershire Railway was opened in 1832 by a consortium of local coal merchants and the proprietors of the Kennet & Avon Canal. It ran from Short-wood to the River Avon opposite Keynsham where there are remains of a wharf (ST666693). The line was always operated as a horse-drawn tramway but nevertheless involved quite extensive engineering works including a deep rock cutting leading to the 156-yd-long Wills-bridge Tunnel. Though the line closed shortly after 1865, the tunnel is still open as it is used for water pipes. Remains of a second wharf can be seen below Londonderry Farm at ST662698.

PRISTON
Priston Mill (ST695615)
5 miles SW Bath off A367
The 3-storey rubble built twin-gabled mill building dates from the early 18th century and occupies a pre-Domesday milling site. The 21 ft diameter pitchback wheel was installed in 1850 parallel to the high dam under a large wheel arch opening integral with the building. It drives 2 pairs of stones, one modern composition, the other Derbyshire Peak. The mill is locally famous for its stone-ground wholemeal flour and is open to the public in the summer on weekday afternoons and weekends. (BIAS 7)

KELSTON: *Brass annealing furnaces incorporated in a marina on the River Avon.*

PUCKLECHURCH
Shortwood Brickworks (ST679769)
2 miles E Pucklechurch off B4465
Though closed in 1969, these brickworks are remarkably intact and contain within a large 19th-century main building a fine selection of brick making machinery including pugmills, grinding pans and presses. The works has also possibly the earliest surviving modified Hoffman kiln in the country. Dating from the end of the 19th century, it has 16 chambers. There is also a 20-chamber Guthrie kiln of 1946. (BIAS 8) Being dismantled in 1980.

RADSTOCK
Kilmersdon Colliery Incline (ST693542)
½ mile S Radstock, unclass road
The Kilmersdon and Writhlington collieries were, until their closure in 1974, jointly worked as the last coal mine in the Somerset coalfield. Coal was wound at Kilmersdon and taken by a shunting engine to the head of a gravity worked incline connecting the main line. Though the colliery site has been cleared, the mineral line and its incline are easly traced.

SALTFORD
Old Brass Mill, The Shallows (ST687670)
4½ miles W Bath off A4
The 18th-century complex on an island between the Avon and a leat was the last site to process brass in an area with some 200 years tradition of brass production. The battery mill ceased operation in 1908 and the rolling mill in 1925. There are 3 parallel rubble built ranges running east–west with ashlar dressings and steeply pitched pantile roofs and a further range at right angles. Parts of 2 internal waterwheels which drove the rolling mill survive and there are traces of a further 3 wheel pits as well as a substantially intact connecting furnace and remains of a pair of others. (BIAS 9)

STANTON DREW
Toll House (ST595635)
1 mile E Chew Magna on B3130
A most unusual hexagonal 2-storey toll house at the junction of the B3130 and the road to Stanton Drew. It has a conical thatched roof, thatched awning to the porch, pointed windows and white rendered walls.

TORMARTON
Toll House, (ST757784)
An attractive 8 sided 2-storey rough limestone cottage with dressed quoins and slate roof. Just north of the A46 and M4 interchange.

WARMLEY
Warley Tower, (ST669728)
5 miles E Bristol off A420
Though most of the buildings of William Champion's pioneer integrated brass works at Warmley have now gone, there is still a windmill tower of *c* 1761 and a large late 18th-century clock tower building which may have been a pin factory. Copper slag blocks are used extensively for quoins and opening dressings. Champion's house is now the local authorities offices.

WESTON SUPER MARE
Birnbeck Pier, (ST308624)
N of town centre
This pier is most unusual in that Eugenius Birch incorporated an island in its design. It was built by the Isca Iron Co of Newport in 1867 and consists of a 1,000 ft section on cast-iron columns from the mainland to Birnbeck Island and a further 200 ft metal girder landing section on iron piles. The island itself which carries amusement facilities, bars, a restaurant, a museum and a lifeboat station had to be levelled, stepped and bricked to form a suitable base. The pier with its small projecting bays and 5 iron ornamental lamp standards and decorative seating has an unrivalled Victorian charm.

Bedfordshire

A predominantly rural county with relatively few industrial monuments, the southern portion of the county is becoming a dormitory settlement for Greater London. The industrial monuments that do exist are mainly associated with agriculture, eg watermills and windmills, with the provision of pumped water supply or with brick making and quarrying. Three national historic lines of communications touch this county – Watling Street, the Grand Union Canal and the London & Birmingham Railway.

Museums Luton: The museum at Wardown Park has collections featuring lace making and the hat industry and has a 15 ft donkey wheel from a local farm. Shuttleworth Collection: historic aeroplanes and other transport items housed at Old Warden Aerodrome near Biggleswade.

AMPTHILL
Pump in Market Place (TL034382)
9 miles S Bedford on A418
A stone obelisk with pump handle and spout and the distance to an important town in each direction is engraved on the appropriate faces, also this inscription: Erected by the Earl of Upper Ossory AD MDCCLXXXV.

BEDFORD
Great Ouse Lock (TL082468)
E city centre
Although the River Ouse had been made navigable as far as Bedford by 1690, the upper reaches become impassable as trade declined at the end of the 19th century. The lock in Bedford is the furthest upstream and was restored in 1955–6 as part of the Great Ouse Restoration Society's efforts to reopen the navigation. It has a guillotine type gate at the river entrance.

CARDINGTON
Airship Hangars (TL082468)
3 miles SE Bedford off A600
These 2 enormous hangars are the major relic of the ill-fated airship industry. The earlier

CARDINGTON: *Airship hangar, home, once again, of the British airship industry.*

hangar was constructed in 1916–17 with a steel frame and measured 700 ft by 254 ft with a clear height of 110 ft. It was enlarged 1924–26 to enclose a floor area of 4½ acres, with a clear height of 145 ft and a length of 812 ft.

DUNSTABLE
The Windmill, West Street (TL015218)
W of town centre
A grey brick 5-storey tower with green copper sheathed cap. It was gutted in 1942 and the sails have also gone.

HEATH
Village Pumphouse and Clock Tower (SP925277)
2 miles N Leighton Buzzard
This prominent feature of the village green still contains some iron pumping machinery inside the single-storey brick building. A 2-stage square brick tower surmounted by a louvred belfry holds the clock dial.

KENSWORTH
Donkey Wheel, Church End Farm (TL029190)
2 miles S Dunstable off A5
A 15 ft diameter by 4 ft 2 in wide donkey wheel dating from 1688 but now removed from its well house. A similar wheel from the nearby Nash Farm is in Luton museum.

LEIGHTON BUZZARD
Narrow-Gauge Railway (SP928241)
¼ mile SE town centre
A 3½ mile long 19th-century narrow-gauge mineral railway connecting sand quarries in an area to the east of Leighton Buzzard. The 2-ft-gauge line is operated by a preservation society with several steam and diesel loco-motives including the 100-year-old 'Chaloner' built by De Winton.

LINSLADE
Linslade Tunnel Portals, (northern SP911261) (southern SP912259)
¼ mile N town centre off B488
The original London & Birmingham Railway tunnel of 1834 is still in use flanked by 2 later single-track tunnels. All 3 have 2 similar horseshoe arches with moulded surrounds on both portals of the 272-yd-long tunnel and are embellished with 3 semi-octagonal battle-mented turrets. Stone sleeper blocks line the cutting from the original track.

STEVINGTON
Windmill (SP992527)
4 miles NW Bedford off A428
A fine restored timber post mill with brick and tile roundhouse and a red corrugated iron roof. Dating from *c* 1770, it has 4 common sails and one pair of stones *in situ*. It is owned by the county council and is open daily.

STEWARTBY
Company Town and Brickworks (TL0242)
6 miles S Bedford off A418
Stewartby, named after its founder Sir P Malcolm Stewart, is a company town in the most literal sense. Planned in 1926 as a model village complete with schools, shops etc, there are now 378 living units, all of which are owned by the London Brick Company or its associated charitable trust. The brickworks themselves are the largest in the world with a weekly capacity of *c* 17,000,000 bricks. There are 20 transverse arch Hoffman-type kilns, one of which has no less than 80 chambers. The works originated in the small Pillinge brickworks started by B J H Forder in 1897.

Berkshire

A rich agricultural county crossed by the main historical routes from London to the West. Industrial monuments are typically associated with these transport systems viz, the Thames, the Kennet & Avon Canal, the Bath Road (A4) and the Great Western Railway. Agricultural processing industries and the raising of water by animal or wind power also typify the county.

BEEDON
Parish Pump (SU488777)
7 miles N Newbury off A34
This most attractive pump, cast by Baker of Compton, stands over a well at the entrance to Beedon near the Newbury to East Ilsey road.

BEENHAM
Water Pump (SU623696)
6½ miles W Reading on A4
The old Bath Road was liberally provided with pumps for watering horses and many survive in various degrees of delapidation. This example in the forecourt of a public house is in good condition, the 4 in shaft standing 3 ft above ground.

BISHAM
Suspension Bridge (SU851860)
See Marlow, Bucks

BISHAM
Toll House (SU850853)
4 miles NW Maidenhead on A404
A single-storey brick building dating from *c* 1800 on the east side of the Reading to Marlow road. It originally had 2 windows and a door onto the street but this latter has been blocked and a further bay added.

BRADFIELD
Brewery (SU602728)
2 miles W Theale
A small brewery dating from *c* 1880 and built of brick, flint and timber. The central portion is 2-storeyed with single 'lean-tos' on either side. The upper part of the main block is louvred to provide cooling air to the tanks but neither these nor any other machinery has survived.

BUCKLEBURY
Foundry (SU552710)
3 miles NE Thatcham, unclass road
This complex of buildings in the centre of Bucklebury has had a tradition of iron working dating from the 18th century. The early stave cupola which dated from *c* 1820 has recently been removed for preservation at Ironbridge Gorge Museum.

BUCKLEBURY
Wind Generator, Highlands (SU537686)
2½ miles NE Thatcham
Built *c* 1945 this small triangular section tower supported a 3-bladed windmill driving a generator through gears. The blades which are 7 ft long are adjusted to wind direction by fan tail. Nearby is a working wind pump which supplies water to a series of cattle troughs and

a garden swimming pool. Built *c* 1900 it combines a 'Hercules' 8 ft-wheel on a 'Climax' tower over 32 ft high.

CHADDLEWORTH
Horse operated corn mill, Woolley Manor (SU410802)
5 miles S Wantage off A338
Housed in the west bay of a large 16th-century timber barn is a mid-18th-century 2-horse wheel with an 18 ft diameter main gear which drove via other wooden gears 2 pairs of millstones on floor above. A second upright shaft drove a wire brushing machine.

CROWTHORNE
Windmill Stump (SU868638)
2 miles NE Crowthorne off A3095
In the Crown Forest behind Broadmoor Asylum the parish boundary crosses an artificial mound 40 ft diameter and some 4 ft high. This was the base mound of a post mill, sections having been cut through the mound to establish its identity.

EASTBURY
Old Forge (SU347773)
1 mile SE Lambourn
This working forge is housed in a 19th-century 1½-storey brick building with a red tile roof. It contains 2 hearths and 2 anvils, its main trade being shoeing race horses.

FRILSHAM
Brickyard (SU552732)
4 miles N Thatcham
Behind the public house on the Bucklebury to Frilsham road these are a group of buildings associated with a small brickyard which worked *c* 1900–45. There are remains of a 10 ft by 10 ft chamber Scotch Kiln used to fire wire-cut bricks and agricultural drains and tiles.

HUNGERFORD
Horse Threshing Engine House (SU338717)
1 mile S Hungerford
This engine, at Old Hayward Farm, was housed in a semi-circular extension to an 18th-century thatched and weatherboarded barn. The top bearing is in position but all other gear removed.

HUNGERFORD
Old Hayward Farm Donkey Wheel, (SU339718)
1 mile S Hungerford
A rather dilapidated donkey wheel of small proportions – diameter 12 ft width 3 ft. Reconstruction of the building in which it is

housed has disorientated the wheel and the well has been sealed.

MAIDENHEAD
Railway Bridge (SU902812)
½ mile E town centre
Built in 1838 by I K Brunel on this Great Western Railway out of London, this bridge has 2 of the largest and flattest arches that have ever been built in brickwork. Each had a span of 128 ft with a rise of only 24 ft 3 in to the crown and critics confidently predicted its collapse under any traffic, yet the bridge still carries the West Country expresses as a vindication of Brunel's design. The main arches are flanked by flood relief arches and these with the piers are arranged in the form of classical triumphal arches.

NEWBURY
Old Brewery (SU469667)
The Phoenix brewery was established 1841 behind the inn and brewers house on Bartholomew Street. Long since converted to a furniture store, it is still an impressive

WINDSOR: *The royal waiting room now relegated to office use.*

building with Gothic brick arches over cast-iron windows.

READING
Railway Bridge, Kennet Mouth (SU730738)
½ mile E town centre
The south side of this bridge is the original 1839 Brunel Great Western Railway bridge while the north side has 2 further tracks added. The main elliptical river arch has a span of 70 ft and a rise of only 20 ft. It is flanked by round headed flood relief arches and there is also a supplementary iron and wood towing path bridge.

READING
Rosehill Water Tower (SU722745)
1 mile N town centre
Built *c* 1935 at the highest point in Emmer Green, this is a good example of a concrete water tower. 70 ft to the tank, the tower is faceted with corner butresses and is still in use.

RUSCOMBE
Milestone (SU797771)
½ mile E Twyford
The 'transit' nature of Berkshire is well illustrated by the milestones throughout the county. This example erected in 1824 shows

distances to London and Bath as well as Maidenhead, Colnbrook and Reading.

THEALE
Sheffield Lock, Kennet Navigation (SU649706)
1 mile S Theale
The Kennet Navigation comprises 7 miles of river and 11½ miles of canal. Opened to traffic in 1723, it was bought by the Kennet & Avon Canal in 1812 for £100,000. Its 21 locks overcome a height of 134 ft and can take boats up to 109 ft by 17 ft. Sheffield lock is a good example of early lock construction with timber and turf sides instead of the usual masonry or brick.

WELFORD
Ice House, Welford House (SU408732)
4 miles NW Newbury off B4000
In a clump of yews some distance from the house a mound covers an ice house. The entrance arrangement has been changed at some time but the chamber itself would appear to date from the mid-18th century. 10 ft in diameter, this is built of brick without batter with a cemented dome and 8 drain holes at the base of the wall.

WINDSOR
Railway Bridge, The River Thames (SU961773)
¼ mile W town centre
This bow and string girder bridge was designed by Brunel in 1847–8 and opened in 1849. It has a river span of 202 ft and carries the Slough to Windsor branch over the flat meadows. Originally the approaches were of timber and the girder bridge itself was supported by cast-iron cylindrical piers but all has been replaced by arcaded brick abutments. The 3 main girders are 213 ft long built up of riveted wrought-iron plates.

WINDSOR
Royal Waiting Room, Windsor Riverside Station (SU968772)
Designed by Sir William Tite for Queen Victoria in 1851, this small building is linked to the station proper by an arched wall. It has a main room with a ribbed ceiling and pendant finial and an ante room. It has a Tudor arched bay window and is crowned by a turret with spirelet.

WINDSOR
Windsor Bridge, Thames Street (SU967773)
A cast-iron bridge of 3 spans dating from 1823 on rusticated ashlar pointed cutwaters and ashlar abutments. Good ornamental ironwork including original lamposts.

WOOLHAMPTON
Swing-Bridge, (SU573666)
3½ miles E Thatcham off A4
A wooden swing-bridge over the Kennet & Avon Navigation built *c* 1810 and consisting of a wooden deck on wooden framing. The under side is weighted with 'Vignoles' top hat section rails while rotation is achieved with a standard Rennie ball race. Cantilever suspension of wrought-iron chains and hooks.

Buckinghamshire

A rural county crossed by major lines of communication and bounded by the River Thames to the S. Its stock of industrial monuments are thus associated with agriculture, e.g. Pitstone and Lacey Green windmills, or with transport. Amongst the latter are the fine road bridges at Marlow, Newport Pagnell and Tyringham displaying quite different solutions to similar problems, the cast-iron aqueduct on the Grand Union Canal at Old Wolverton and Denbigh Hall Railway Bridge on the London & Birmingham Railway. The county has also several fine series of milestones e.g. on the A5, the A413, and A422.

BLETCHLEY
Denbigh Hall Railway Bridge (SP853353)
2 miles N of Bletchley on A5
A single-arch, ashlar and cast-iron bridge carrying Stephenson's London & Birmingham Railway across Watling Street (A5) at a point where a temporary terminus was established in 1837. Massive masonry abutments support cast-iron ribs with masonry dentilated cornice and low parapet above. The latter have delicate geometric patterned cast-iron railings.

BRILL
Post Mill (SP653142)
7 miles NW of Thame off B4011
A fine post mill dating from *c* 1668. The open trestle which originally supported it was protected by a brick roundhouse this century. Owned by the County Council, it is open to the public on Sunday afternoons in the summer.

CADMORE END
Brick Kiln, Cadmore End Common (SU793930)
4 miles W of High Wycombe off A40
Amongst the scanty remains of an early 19th-century brickworks on the common is an updraught kiln with a central cylindrical chimney in its low vaulted brick roof. The kiln which has internal dimensions 9 ft by 12 ft with 4 ft thick brick walls may originally date from *c* 1800 though the present structure has been much rebuilt. The brickworks ceased production *c* 1839 and the kiln is now incorporated into a private garden.

FENNY STRATFORD
Milestone (SP885339)
1 mile E of Bletchley on A5
Situated on Telford's Holyhead road (A5) between bridges over the Grand Union Canal and the River Ouzel, this milestone is one of a series dating from *c* 1815. These are typically pentagonal cast-iron plates 20 in by 13 in fastened to stone blocks and bearing simple distances and a maker's name – in this case Tarver Foundry, Daventry.

IVINGHOE
Ford End Watermill, Station Road (SP941165)
5 miles SW of Dunstable off B489
A 2-storey brick and weatherboarded, mansard-roofed mill dating from 1773. An overshot waterwheel 11 ft 6 in in diameter by 5 ft wide drives one pair of French stones and one pair of Peak stones. Open to the public on Sundays and Bank Holidays in the summer.

LOOSELY ROW
Lacey Green Windmill (SP819008)
3 miles S of Princes Risborough off A4010
Timber smock mill originally erected at Chesham (Bucks) *c* 1650 and moved to present site in 1821. Unique early wooden machinery possibly 17th-century. Ceased milling in 1921 and slowly deteriorated until the Chiltern Society started restoration in 1971. Open to the public on Sunday afternoons in the summer.

MARLOW
Suspension Bridge (SU851860)
S of town centre
Built from 1829 to 1831 by a local contractor, W Bond, to the designs of Tierney Clark, this 235 ft iron suspension bridge over the River Thames was widened in 1861 to include 2 footways. A further recent reconstruction has preserved the general appearance of Clark's design.

MARSWORTH
Canal Locks and Reservoirs (SP920142–SP928138)
7 miles E of Aylesbury A41/B489
A flight of 7 locks allows Jessop's Grand Junction Canal to descend 42ft from Tring summit pound. Water supply to this summit level was always a problem and a series of reservoirs were built from 1802 onwards to store surplus water and to return it to the summit by pumping.

MEDMENHAM
Flashlock Winch (SU820843)
4 miles W of Marlow off A4155
On the N bank of the Thames upstream from Hurley weir is a winch used to pull barges through Hurley Flash before the pound lock was built in 1773. The 6-arm post and capstan winch, though partly buried, is of great significance as the only such structure on the Thames.

NEW BRADWELL
Bradwell Windmill (SP831411)
3 miles E of Stony Stratford on A422
Owned by the local authority, this fine 3-storey limestone tower mill built in 1876 for Samuel Holman stands on the low mound of a former post mill. The 4 common sails originally drove 2 pairs of stones but the machinery is incomplete.

NEWPORT PAGNELL
Tickford Bridge (SP878438)
E of town centre on A5130
A narrow single-span cast-iron bridge with

stone abutments carrying a trunk road over the River Ouzel. It was begun in June 1810 to the plans of Henry Provis, architect of Paddington, reputedly after an original design of Thomas Paine modified by Wilson and Burdon of Sunderland. It was opened in September 1810 with 6 cast-iron ribs with circles in spandrels. The date 1810 is cast at the top of the arch.

NEWPORT PAGNELL
Tyringham Bridge (SP858465)
2 miles NW of Newport Pagnell off B526
A graceful single-span masonry bridge designed and built by Sir John Soames from 1793–7.

OLD WOLVERTON
Wolverton Aqueduct (SP801418)
1 mile E of Stony Stratford off A422
Built 1809–11 to replace Jessop's masonry aqueduct which had been destroyed by floods in 1808, this double-span iron trough aqueduct carries the Grand Union Canal over the River Ouse. Popularly known as the Iron Trunk it is over 100 ft long and its weight is supported by the iron arched ribs let into its sides – a pioneer example of the arch suspension bridge. The high embankment on either

MEDMENHAM: *Danesfield barge winch, a relic of river navigation before pound locks.*

side is pierced by cattle creeps – small accommodation tunnels.

PITSTONE
Pitstone Windmill (SP945157)
7 miles SW of Dunstable off B489
A very early post mill with a black weatherboarded buck above a painted brick roundhouse. Owned by the National Trust it has been restored to working order. The 4 common sails, which are adjusted from ground level, drive 2 pairs of stones, one Peak, and one French. Nearby is a 2-storey watermill (SP942160) with a granary and malting attached. Now converted into a studio.

WENDOVER
Windmill (SP867082)
N of town centre
This large hexagonal brick-built tower mill was built 1796–1804. The 66 ft high tower is 25 ft diameter at the base and 18 ft at the curb. The huge aluminium sheathed cap was rebuilt in 1969 but no machinery survives and the tower has been a dwelling for many years.

WOBURN SANDS
Railway Station (SP815422)
6 miles SE of Newport Pagnel on A5130
A small Gothic-style timber framed 2-storey station of *c* 1846 on the Bedford branch of the London & North Western Railway. The dia-

gonal pattern of the timber framing is similar to that of the nearby Fenny Stratford Station (SP882343) on the same line.

WOLVERTON
Railway Viaduct and Settlement, (SP815422)

2 miles E of Stony Stratford on A422
A 6-arch viaduct of 1838 carrying **Stephenson's London & Birmingham Railway** over the River Ouse just N of the railway town of grid iron terraces established by the railway company in association with their engineering works.

Cambridgeshire

The industrial monuments of this low-lying agricultural county are very much a product of its geography. They are mostly associated with the control of water for navigation, drainage or consumption and with agricultural processing.

BOURN
Post Mill (TL312580)
8½ miles W of Cambridge A45/A14, 1½ miles W of A45 A14 crossroads
This very early post mill possibly dating from before 1636 was partially rebuilt *c* 1741 after extensive gale damage. The buck is black and rests on an open trestle while the sails, stairs and tailpole are white. The 4 sails, 2 common, 2 patent, drive a single pair of stones in the breast of the mill. Restored in 1931, the mill is open to the public.

CAMBRIDGE
Cambridge Station (TL463573)
1 mile SW of town centre
Cambridge Station, with its prominent colonnade of 15 round arches taking up most of the façade, was, in 1845, one of the last commissions of Sancton Wood for the Great Eastern Railway before his dismissal the following year. It has retained the once common early arrangement of a single platform for both directions with a scissor crossing half way along.

CAMBRIDGE
Cheddars Lane Pumping Station (TL465593)
1 mile E of town centre off A45
The station was completed in 1895 to pump Cambridge's sewage through a 24 in main to a new sewage farm at Milton just outside the city. The 2 original Hathorn Davy horizontal tandem compound non-rotative steam engines

are substantially intact and there is a collection of other steam engines preserved by the Cambridge Museum of Technology Trust. Fine 170 ft decorated chimney stack.

CAMBRIDGE
Hobson's Conduit – Aqueduct (TL452577)
½ mile S of town centre on A10
Hobson's conduit was built in 1614 to carry water from the Nine Wells spring S of Cambridge to Conduit Head, a distance of some 3½ miles. This pretty stone cistern with its lead tank was moved to the site in 1856. The northern section of the conduit is channelled into a raised aqueduct puddled with clay. At the entrance to the Botanic Gardens it is crossed by a cast-iron bridge (TL453570) with the name Hurrell and the date 1850 cast on it.

CAMBRIDGE
Magdalene Bridge (TL447589)
town centre
This early cast-iron bridge was built in 1823 over the River Cam to replace the Great Bridge – a masonry structure of 1754. The main cast-iron girders were supplied by Balfour Browne of Derby while the railings were made locally by Finch's Foundry.

FOWLMERE
Milestone (TL408430)
3½ miles NE of Royston on A505

BOURN: *One of the earliest post mills in the country.*

Some distance to the S of Fowlmere at the junction of the B1368 with the A505 is one of the milestones in the 'Trinity Hall' series. These stones were erected by the Master of Trinity Hall between 1729 and 1733 with money from a fund established 1586. Most of the original stones display a variation of the Trinity Hall crest and the distance to Cambridge and indicate the direction of London. In this example, however, there is a second face with hands pointing to Royston and Wittlesford.

FULBOURN
Fleam Dyke Pumping Station (TL539548)
5 miles SE of Cambridge
This brick pumphouse contains a pair of 1920 Hawthorn Dovey horizontal tandem compound engines which were in use until 1976. Fulbourn pumping station itself (TL512565) has an impressive masonry engine house built 1886 for 2 Lilleshall rotative beam engines but now housing electric pumps.

GREAT CHISHILL
Post Mill (TL414389)
5 miles SE of Royston on B1039
Dating from 1819 this post mill has an open trestle and 4 common sails which were formerly patent. The fantail is mounted on the stairs and the buck has an extension to the rear. Altogether there are 3 pairs of stones – 2 in breast and one in tail.

HILDERSHAM
Watermill (TL548485)
9 miles SE Cambridge off A604
This corn milling complex comprising mill, mill house, grain store and bakery dates partly from 1868, though the mill itself is probably 18th-century. The overshot waterwheel is 12 ft in diameter and 10 ft wide and was used to produce power when grinding ceased in 1906. Most of the milling machinery has disappeared and the granary has been converted into flats and its chimney truncated.

HOUGHTON
Houghton Watermill (TL282719)
3 miles E Huntingdon off A1123
The fabric of this large 4-storey rectangular mill dates variously from the mid-17th century to the 19th century. Constructed of brick and timber with tarred weatherboarding, it has prominent lucans on side and end elevations. The mill ceased working in 1930 and is now owned by the National Trust who use it as a youth hostel. The 3 waterwheels have been removed though some of the other machinery survives.

HUNTINGDON
Huntingdon Station (TL233716)
SW of town
Typical GNR station with 2-storey station house and single-storey offices and fine platform canopy with cast-iron pillars.

OLD FLETTON
Brickworks (TL194968)
1 mile S of Peterborough
Original home of the Fletton brick industry developed since 1880 and now extensive area of brickworks in varying degrees of use. All remaining works under control of London Brick Company, including
LBC Yard 1 (TL194968) 2 Hoffman kilns
LBC Yard 3 (TL186966) 1 early double Hoffman
LBC Yard 4 (TL187963) 1 Hoffman, 1 Belgian kiln
Hicks Yard 1 (TL191956) 5 early Hoffman kilns
New Peterborough Yard 2 (TL196956) 4 Hoffman kilns

OVER
Tower Mill (TL381689)
8 miles NW of Cambridge off A604
This small 3-storey, brick built tower mill is being renovated although only 2 of its original 4 patent sails remain. The body of the mill is tarred while conical dome cap is white.

PETERBOROUGH
Railway Bridge (TL191982)
S of town centre
By the mid-19th century Peterborough had become an important railway centre served by 4 of the main companies and with extensive workshops. Little survives of the original stations but this fine 1850 3-span iron bridge is a significant survival. The river piers are clusters of cast-iron fluted columns while the spans are of cast-iron ribs now strengthened. To the E (TL201978) is one of the last timber trestle railway bridges to survive in use.

ST IVES
Corn Mill (TL314710)
$\frac{1}{4}$ mile S of village off A1096
This large, 6-storey, brick-built steam mill was erected in the early 19th century to take advantage of the water borne grain trade on the River Ouse. This trade was seriously affected by the opening of the St Ives–Huntingdon line of the Ely & Bedford Railway Co in 1847 and the mill has been used for a variety of occupations including a jam factory and an electronic component factory.

SHEPRETH
Railway Station (TL392482)
8 miles SW Cambridge off A10
This rather austere, yellow brick station on the Great Northern Railway branch from Hitchin to Cambridge was built in 1850 and is typical of the intermediate stations of this company. The 2-storey station house is flanked by single-storey offices.

STOW-CUM-QUY
Coprolite Workings (TL515627)
5 miles E Cambridge off A45
Coprolite, which is rich in phosphate, was mined *c* 1888 in the Stow-cum-Quy fen and used to make fertiliser. The workings yielded some 300 tons per acre and have 10 ft long, water-filled pits and extensive spoil heaps. The remains of a chemical works at Burwell (TL573683) built to process coprolite can still be seen.

STRETHAM
Stretham Old Engine (TL517730)
5 miles S of Ely off A10
This single cylinder, rotative beam engine was built in 1831 by the Butterley Company for the Waterbeach Level Commissioners. The engine drives a huge scoop wheel 37 ft 2 in in diameter by 2 ft 3 in wide built in 1896 to replace the original smaller wheel which had been enlarged in 1848 as the peat had shrunk. The wheel is capable of lifting 120 tons of water per minute. Stretham Engine is now preserved by a voluntary trust.

SWAFFAM BULBECK
Wharf (TL555630)
6 miles E Cambridge on B1102
In the latter half of the 18th century a considerable commercial enclave developed at the head of Swaffam Bulbeck lode. By 1858 it comprised 3 granaries, a coal yard and shed, a smith's shop, coke shed and oven, lime sheds, deal shed, a salt house and tile yard as well as 2 barns, stables, 5 maltings, numerous dwellings and a public house. The lode is now silted up and only some of the commercial buildings survive though now converted to dwellings, garages etc.

WATERBEACH
Bottisham Lode Staunch, (TL516651)
5 miles N of Cambridge off A10
The brick foundations are all that now remain of one of the last staunches to survive in the region. The wooden superstructure which was built in 1875 by the Swaffam & Bottisham Drainage Commissioners was finally demolished in 1969, fortunately the staunch survived long enough to be adequately recorded.

WEST WRATTING
Smock Mill, (TL605510)
3 miles NE Linton off B1052
This 3-storey smock mill dates from *c* 1726 and has 2 spring sails and 2 common sails. The upper 2 storeys are octagonal and timber-built and rest on a single-storey round brick base. The body is black while the dome cap is white and a tailpole is fitted.

WICKEN
Wicken Fen Drainage Mill, (TL562706)
8 miles NE of Ely off A1123
This small smock mill of *c* 1910 was rebuilt on its present site in 1956. The timber body rests on a concrete base and the 4 common sails drive a scoop-wheel. It stands in Wicken Fen in a noted National Trust Reserve.

Cheshire

Cheshire is a county with a long and varied industrial history reflected by a wealth of industrial monuments. Many of these are associated with canals, notably the Trent & Mersey with its spectacular connection with the Weaver Navigation via Anderton Lift, the cast-iron aqueducts of the Shropshire Union and Macclesfield canals and the canal basins of Ellesmere and Runcorn. The major salt workings of the Northwich area have left few monuments but of these the Lion Salts works, Marston, is most impressive.

The north of the county contains many significant monuments to the textile industry especially Quarry Bank Mill at Styal, the silk workshops of Macclesfield, and Clarence Mill, Billington. Several agricultural mills also survive, including the early restored mill at Alderley Edge.

ANDERTON
Anderton Canal Lift (SJ647753)
1 mile NW Northwich off A533
This, the only canal lift still in use in the country, allows boats to pass between the Trent & Mersey Canal and the River Weaver some 50ft below. Completed in 1875 to the designs of Edwin Clark following the proposals of E Leader Williams the lift was originally worked hydraulically, the 75 ft wrought-iron caissons counterbalancing each other by transfer of water. In 1908 the lift was modified to electric operation with each caisson separately counterbalanced by weights and so it remains now used mainly by pleasure craft.

BEESTON
Cast-Iron Canal Lock (SJ554599)
8 miles NW Nantwich off A49
A unique cast-iron lock on the Chester Section of the Shropshire Union. Built by Telford in 1828 to overcome problems of acute loss of water due to unstable foundations. The lock chamber itself and its immediate approaches are lined with cast-iron plates. The lock gates, however, are conventional.

BICKERTON
Chimney, Gallantry Bank (SJ516540)
9 miles W Nantwich off A534
A hammer-dressed sandstone chimney in 2 stages, both square in plan. The upper one tapering is all that remains of a pumping engine installation which drained the copper mine of the Egertons of Oulton. Though the mine itself dated from the 17th century, the chimney is probably early 19th-century.

BOLLINGTON
Clarence Mill (SJ934782)
3 miles NE of Macclesfield
A 5-storey masonry cotton mill of varying date built alongside the Macclesfield Canal. The earliest section *c* 1824 has tall narrow segmental headed windows. A massive staircase tower with square pilasters at each corner and surmounted by a water tower projects out over the wharf at the junction of the earlier and later parts of the mill. Single-storey engine house with tall cylindrical red brick chimney.

BURTONWOOD
Sankey Viaduct (SJ569947)
5 miles NW Warrington off A49
A fine 9-arch stone-faced viaduct carrying Stephenson's Liverpool & Manchester Railway of 1830 some 70 ft above the Sankey Brook and the St Helen's Canal.

CHESTER
General Station (SJ413669)
½ mile NE city centre
The 2-storey red brick façade with stone window dressings and cornice was designed in a vaguely Venetian symmetry by Wild & Thompson in 1847–48. Its immense length of some 1000 ft is punctuated by projecting towers of slightly higher elevation with colonnaded ground floors. The canopy is a later addition.

CHESTER
Canal Cutting and Bridges Canal Street (SJ404666)
¼ mile N city centre
The Shropshire Union Canal occupies a cutting below the city walls. Indeed, Northgate locks themselves are partly cut in solid rock. Along this section of canal there is an attractive early 19th-century iron roving bridge, a lock-keeper's house of 1772 and the Bridge of Sighs – a graceful sandstone arch built in 1793 for taking felons from prison to chapel.

CHESTER
Shot Tower, Broughton (SJ415667)
½ mile E city centre
In the works of Associated Lead stands one of the few remaining shot towers in the country. The process of making lead shot involves pouring molten lead through a perforated tray and allowing the droplets to solidify by falling from a great height into water, hence the need for such a tall structure. The Chester tower is brick built with small round headed stair windows.

CONGLETON
The Old Mill, Mill Green (SJ854635)
W of town centre
Built *c* 1752 by John Clayton of Stockport, this red brick building was the first silk mill in

Congleton. Now truncated to only 2 storeys with a flat roof, it was originally powered by a waterwheel constructed by James Brindley.

CONGLETON
Iron Aqueduct (SJ866622)
1 mile SE town centre
An attractively painted cast-iron trough aqueduct of *c* 1835 carrying the Macclesfield Canal over a minor road on the outskirts of Congleton. This aqueduct with its sweeping curved masonry abutments with low relief pilasters and cast-iron railings between masonry pillars bears a striking resemblance to Telford's aqueducts on the Shropshire Union at Nantwich and Stretton.

CREWE
Railway Settlement and Workshops (SJ605555)
Almost synonomous with the works railway, Crewe is truly a child of the great railway expansion in the middle decades of the 19th century. Francis Trevithick established railway works here in 1843 for the Grand Junction Railway and these now cover a huge area. Much of the associated terraced housing has recently been cleared, but good examples such as Duke Street (SJ603554) still survive close to the massive range of the Deviation Works which included carpentry, joinery, electrical and machine workshops.

DUTTON
Viaduct (SJ583764)
5 miles NW Northwich off A533
An early 20-arch masonry viaduct across the Weaver Valley on the Grand Junction Railway built by George Stephenson and Joseph Locke to link Birmingham and Manchester and Liverpool. Dating from 1837, Dutton viaduct has unusually large spans of 60 ft.

ELLESMERE PORT
Canal Basins, Locks and Toll House (SJ405773)
7 miles N Chester
The canal complex at Ellesmere Port is one of the most extensive on the canal system. At this point the Shropshire Union Canal drops down the hillside to join the Manchester Ship Canal. There are basins at the top of the flight and at the bottom, the latter formerly dominated by Telford's magnificent 'island' warehouses which recently burnt down leaving only the island foundations. The upper warehouses, pump house and toll house are still intact and form the nucleus of the new Boat Museum. The nearby Porters Row is the only surviving

workers' housing from Telford's Dock Estate of 1833.

HANKELOW
Hankelow Mill (SJ659451)
6 miles S Nantwich off A529
A large 19th-century 3-storey and attic fireproof brick and slate watermill with 7 bays of iron-framed windows on ground floor. The interior floors are carried on brick or tile jack arches on inverted Y-shaped cast-iron beams supported by cast-iron columns. Most of the machinery is of iron and the 16 ft by 6½ ft waterwheel has been modified to make its original undershot operation more efficient and to partly utilize the weight of the water as well.

MACCLESFIELD
Chester Road Mills (SJ909737)
W of town centre
Formerly the card factory of Henry & Leigh Slater and before that a silk mill, this late 18th-century building is typically Georgian in style. Built of red brick, it has 4 storeys and 17 bays on the road façade with a pediment and clock cupola and wind vane projecting over the central 5 bays. The right hand return elevation also has a pediment.

MACCLESFIELD
Frosts Mill, Park Green (SJ918737)
town centre
A 5-storey red brick silk mill of 13 bays dated on the rainwater heads 1785. The central projecting 3-bay section has a pedimented gable with clock and a vane on the roof.

MACCLESFIELD
Messrs Arighi Bianchi's Showrooms (SJ920737)
E town centre
This most attractive store dates from *c* 1883. The side and rear walls are of load bearing brick but the cast-iron and glass front is curtain walling. The interior is supported on cast-iron columns.

MACCLESFIELD
Silk Weavers' Workshops, Paradise Street (SJ914733)
town centre
Early 19th-century 3-storey brick terrace with 'weavers' garretts' comprising the uppermost floor. This range which rises in steps from east to west is the best example of tenement workshops in the area. Other examples can be seen in Bridge Street, Mill Lane and Buxton Road.

NETHER ALDERLEY: *Alderley Old Mill, restored by the National Trust.*

MARSTON
Lion Salt Works (SJ671755)
1½ miles NE Northwich
Situated beside the Trent & Mersey Canal this firm is the only survivor of the once common type of salt works – pumping brine from extensive Cheshire salt beds and reducing it to crystals by open pan boiling. The resulting product is sufficiently different from the salt produced in vacuum chambers to command a prestige market. The works themselves are an untidy group of wood and brick buildings with remains of early steam driven pumps. They are set in a landscape devastated by subsidence with large 'flashes' – water filled depressions – disrupting communications. The canal itself is now significantly higher than the surrounding land surface as only it has preserved the original level.

NANTWICH
Iron Canal Aqueduct (SJ643526)
1 mile W of town centre on A534
Carrying the Birmingham & Liverpool Junction Canal over the Wrexham road this aqueduct was completed in 1835 some 6 months after Telford's death. It has a span of *c* 30 ft with 5 rectangular plates visible.

NETHER ALDERLEY
Alderley Old Mill (SJ843763)
1½ miles S of Alderley Edge on A34
A very interesting and early watermill belonging to the National Trust and open to the public. The low stone building is set into the mill dam and has a stone flagged roof which almost reaches the ground. The tandem arrangement of the 2 overshot waterwheels 13 ft by 4 ft and 12 ft by 3 ft is also most unusual as they occupy the same water channel on different levels. The mill worked commercially until 1939 and after a period of disuse has now been restored to working order.

PRESTON BROOK
Canal Tunnel (SJ570799)
4 miles SE of Runcorn on A533
This 1,239-yard tunnel was the longest of the 3 tunnels on this section of Bradley's Trent & Mersey. Completed in 1775, 3 years after his death, it vies with the Norwood Tunnel on the Chesterfield Canal in Nottinghamshire as being the earliest canal tunnel of any length in the country. The nearby tunnels at Saltersford (SJ624725) and Barton (SJ630749) was com-

pleted within a further 2 years and are 424 yards and 572 yards respectively.

RED BULL (KIDSGROVE)
Canal Junction (SJ830549)
1 mile NW Kidsgrove off A50
The Macclesfield Canal makes an unusual and complicated junction with the much earlier Trent & Mersey Canal to the W of Kidsgrove. The former is at a higher level where their lines first intersect and it crosses the latter by an aqueduct and parallels it for 600 yards until the Trent & Mersey gains sufficient height by means of 2 locks to allow a level junction.

RUNCORN
Railway Bridge (SJ509835)
N of town centre
A fine example of a large wrought-iron girder bridge built in 1863 to take the London & North Western Railway to Liverpool across the Mersey. It has 3 305-ft spans and the landward masonry arches are embellished with masonry turrets and battlements.

RUNCORN
Waterloo Bridge (SJ508828)
NW of town centre
A 3-span masonry and cast-iron road bridge across the basin at the top of the flight of locks by which the Bridgewater Canal descended to the Mersey (and latterly the Manchester Ship Canal). The locks have since been infilled leaving the bridge sited rather incongruously.

STYAL
Quarry Bank Mill and Village (SJ834830)
2 miles N Wilmslow off B5166
Built, witness an inscription over the door, by Samuel Greg of Belfast in 1784, the mill at Styal is one of the finest Georgian industrial buildings in the country. Though it underwent some enlargement and alteration in the early 19th century, the red brick mill with its central pediment and clock surmounted by a bellcote was essentially the same when given to the National Trust as at Greg's death in 1834. It is now proposed to develop the mill as a major textile museum. Styal is also most notable for the survival of the associated self-contained community founded by Greg. Besides Greg's own house, there is an apprentice house, a shop, a chapel (1822), a school (1823), an institution (1823) and rows of attractive workers' cottages, e.g. Oak Cottages *c* 1800. The Arcadian setting of this model industrial development contrasts strongly with its urban counterparts only a dozen miles away in Manchester and Stockport.

WARRINGTON
Bridge, River Mersey (SJ607878)
S of town centre
Opened in 1913 by King George V, this single-span road bridge was designed by John J Webster and is an early example of reinforced-concrete construction.

WARRINGTON
Transporter Bridge (SJ596876)
SW of town centre
Built 1913 – 14 by Sir William Arral & Co to provide communication for vehicles and railway trucks between parts of Joseph Crosfields works separated by a loop of the River Mersey. Two pairs of lattice steel piers 70 ft high support a clear span of 200 ft from which the transporter deck is suspended. Although no longer used for rail traffic, the bridge survives in apparently good condition.

WARRINGTON
Winwick Locks & Dry Dock, St Helens Canal (SJ595917)
2 miles N Warrington off A49
The St Helens Canal is generally accepted as being the first typical English Canal. Much of the line has now been dismembered but a stretch immediately S of the M62 contains several features of interest including Hulme Lock and attendant's house and a dry dock and swing-bridge on Winwick Quay. The lock, although in poor condition, retains both pairs of gates and must be one of the earliest surviving broad locks, possibly *c* 1758. The dry dock which is of stepped construction is at right angles to the canal. The swing-bridge at a narrowing in the canal is now fixed.

WILLASTON
Windmill, Mill Lane (SJ328785)
9 miles NW Chester off A540
One of 3 disused windmills in this part of the Wirral, this example dates from *c* 1800, the others being earlier and located at Burton and Neston. It is a tall circular 5-stage red brick tower with a weatherboarded cowl-shaped cap but only the cross arms of the sails. Now converted to a dwelling.

Cleveland

A creation of the 1974 local government reorganization, Cleveland boundaries reflect its industrial past. At its heartland are the ports of the Tees estuary and it embraces the foothills of Cleveland Hills whose wealth of iron ore led to a remarkable expansion of the iron and steel industry in Teeside in the late 19th century. The continuous modernization of plant on the same sites has virtually obliterated any significant remains of the iron smelting industry but the abandoned extractive industries have left several relics and the transport systems, which were vital to the development of the area, contribute further monuments.

BOULBY
Alum Works (NZ761191)
6 miles E Saltburn off A174
The shale cliffs at Boulby have been quarried since the 17th century to obtain alum. The last works closed *c* 1873 and there are remains of the alum house where the liquid extract, obtained by calcining and steeping the shale, was boiled and concentrated to crystallization. At the quarries themselves there are remains of a calcining clamp, steeping pits, storage cisterns, culverts and flues. Both the quarries and the alum house had access to the sea via inlets cut in the wave platform. The southern inlet, the New Cut as it was called, was connected by a vertical shaft to the alum house.

ELWICK
Windmill (NZ449316)
4 miles W Hartlepool beside A19
This brick-built tower mill, despite its semi-derelict state is the second most complete example in NE England.

GREATHAM
Railway Viaduct (NZ490260)
4 miles S Hartlepool off A689
Built in 1840 by John Fowler as part of the Stockton & Hartlepool Railway, the brickwork of this structure rests on timber piling to stabilize its foundations in the marshy ground. Only 34 of the original 92 arches are now visible, the remainder now being embanked.

GUISBOROUGH
Tocketts Ventilation Chimney (NZ621183)
1½ miles NE of Guisborough off A173
Built in 1875 by Walker, Maynard & Co, this chimney has a hole for the fire grate at the base. The fire in the grate would have drawn air up the shaft from the seam below causing a current of air in the mine itself.

GUISBOROUGH
Tocketts Mill (NZ627182)
1½ miles NE of Guisborough off A173
Tocketts Mill is a stone-built corn mill of 4 storeys with an adjoining mill house and steading. The internal waterwheel is high breast and measures 18 ft diameter by 4 ft broad. There are 3 pairs of stones, 2 elevators, a grain dresser, a set of silk screens and a sack hoist *in situ*. Although there has been a mill on this site since the 17th century, the present buildings probably date from the 19th century.

HART
Windmill (NZ473346)
2½ miles NW Hartlepool off A179
Early 19th-century stone-built 4-storey tower mill in ruinous condition though with remains of some machinery.

LINGDALE
Ironstone Mine (NZ676165)
4½ miles E of Guisborough off A171
A major ironstone mine dating from *c* 1878 with its own rail link from the Kilton Branch.

Formerly supplied Skinningrove Ironworks but ceased production in the 1960s and mine-head buildings used for a variety of purposes. Recent demolition has cleared much of the site.

MIDDLESBOROUGH
Dock Sheer Legs (NZ494215)
½ mile N of town centre off A178
At Dents Wharf on the S bank of the Tees, an enormous sheer legs is in use. This tripod of hollow metal legs was built in 1897 by Day Summers & Co of Southampton for West-garth Forster and was used for lifting ships' engines. Capable of lifting up to 85 tons, it was originally operated by a steam engine but in 1966 it was electrified.

MIDDLESBOROUGH
Transporter Bridge (NZ500213)
½ mile N of town centre on A178
This, the largest transporter bridge in the world, was built in 1911 by Sir Wm Arrol & Partners to replace a ferry service between Middlesborough and Port Clarence. The total length of the bridge and approach spans is 850 ft, and 225 ft high. This allows a clear span across the channel 570 ft broad and 160 ft high. The platform which is suspended by cables from a high level trolley can carry 9 cars and 600 passengers and is worked by an electric motor on the S side.

MIDDLESBOROUGH
Vulcan Ironworks (NZ501211)
½ mile N of town centre off A178
Started by Bolckow & Vaughan in 1841 as a rolling mill, eventually this site acquired blast furnaces and large workshops. Now only the office building remains and what is possibly one of the furnace bears.

REDCAR
Old Lifeboat Station (NZ607252)
Promenade
This custom built station of 1877 has been superceded and now houses a small maritime museum containing one of the famous Redcar lifeboats. When the station was in use these boats had to be hauled across the promenade and down a ramp onto the beach.

SALTBURN
Cliff Railway (NZ666217)
¼ mile N of town centre

MIDDLESBOROUGH: *Transporter Bridge built 1911.*

Yorkshire was a pioneer area for cliff railways, that at Saltburn being one of the earliest. Although the present line dates from 1884 it replaced an earlier vertical lift of 1869 which rose 100 ft from the pier. 270 ft long, the railway rises 114 ft at a gradient of 1 in 1.33. The method of operation is by water ballast which, after discharge from the lower car, is pumped back to the upper tank, originally by gas engine, now electrically.

SALTBURN
Station Complex (NZ665215)
town centre
This station complex was an ambitious development rather out of scale with the town it served. Built *c* 1868, the railway ran behind the classical façade of the station itself, through a goods yard with its associated warehouses to the rear of the Zetland Hotel on the cliff top. Passengers for the hotel could thus alight directly into the hotel in a similar manner to railway hotels at major termini. The warehousing and goods yard are screened by a highly ornamental, windowless wall and the warehouse itself has a rear elevation conforming with this wall. The side facing the goods yard has a much more traditional appearance.

SKELTON
Skelton Park Iron Mine (NZ644180)
2½ miles E of Guisborough off A173
This mine was sunk in 1872 by Bell Brothers to work the ore of the Main Seam. The shaft was 380 ft deep and also gave access to the 2-Foot Seam. The mine was taken over in 1923 by Dorman Long & Co and finally ceased production in 1938. The surviving buildings represent the most complete mine head complex in the Cleveland iron field. Besides the very large, stone-built, 2-storey winding house

there is a ventilation fan chamber, stabling workshops, a smithy and offices.

STOCKTON-ON-TEES
Ticket Office (NZ447184)
½ mile S of town centre on A174
This tiny structure at the road crossing leading to the river quays was the original ticket office for the Stockton end of the Stockton and Darlington Railway.

THORNABY-ON-TEES
Navigation Cuts (NZ463190)
2½ miles W of Middlesborough off A66
In former times the Tees between Middlesborough and Stockton made 2 large loops in the vicinity of Thornaby. To improve navigation the Mandale Loop was cut out in 1810 and the Portract Loop in 1831.

YARM
Warehouses (NZ421125)
Town centre
Until 1771 Yarm with its medieval bridge built *c* 1400 by Bishop Skirlaw was the lowest bridging point on the River Tees. The warehouses to the E of the bridge are a reminder of its former role as the most important port on the river handling lead from the Pennines as well as agricultural produce.

YARM
Yarm Viaduct (NZ418132)
W of town centre
This railway viaduct which was completed in 1849 has 43 arches and runs from one end of the small town to the other. All but 2 of the arches are brick, the exceptions are of stone and span the river itself. The masonry section bears a lengthy inscription commemorating the engineers, superintendent and the contractors.

Cornwall

The history of Cornish industry is indeed long – most of it is associated with metal mining which has been conducted for over 2,000 years. There has been, however, a drastic contraction of most of the staple industries in the last century leaving an extremely rich legacy of industrial monuments. Most numerous are the engine houses of the former tin and copper mines, over 300 such structures survive some even retaining their distinctive steam engines. The ore processing plant and the attendant industries such as foundries and shipping facilities add to the stock of monuments. One extractive industry which shows no signs of contraction is the china clay industry centred on St Austell though it too has left numerous abandoned workings, one of which has been restored as the Wheal Martyn museum. The Cornish landscape has long posed problems for transport engineers and some of their solutions such as high tramroad and railway viaducts and canal inclined planes have survived.

BOTALLACK
Botallack Mine (sw362337)
1 mile N St Just on B3306
Spectacularly perched on the cliff edge stand 2 of the engine houses of Botallack Mine. The earlier house was probably built before 1816 and latterly contained a 30 in Harvey of Hayle engine of 1823 which did pumping duty. The smaller engine house higher up the cliff was built in 1858–9 and was used for winding. Whereas the earlier engine house has a chimney incorporated within its shell, the latter engine house had a flue running up the cliff to a chimney some distance away.

BOTALLACK
Levant Mine (sw370340)
1½ miles N St Just on B3306
This celebrated mine produced more tin and copper than any other in the Land's End peninsula. First worked in the 1790s it worked

BOTALLACK: *Mining landscape on cliffs at Bottallack.*

well into the 20th century. In 1919 the rod of a main engine broke killing 31 men and from then on production from the deep workings below the sea bed virtually ceased. Inland working finally ceased in 1930 but the setts have now been acquired by the neighbouring Geevor mine which is still in operation. The National Trust own the 1840, Harvey of Hayle, beam whim engine which is still *in situ* with its original machinery. The engine, which was partially rebuilt in 1862, is double acting with a 24 in cylinder and a 4 ft stroke.

BUDE
Sea Lock and Basin (sw203065)
$\frac{1}{4}$ mile W of town centre
This sea lock, constructed *c* 1820 and enlarged in 1836 and 1856, gives access to the basin of the Bude Canal. Some of the 19th-century dock offices and stores survive and an early life boat station. For features on the abandoned section of the Bude Canal, see Launcells and Marhamchurch (*qv*).

CALLINGTON
Kit Hill Stack (sx375713)
1 mile E Callington. Minor road off B3257
This 85 ft high square chimney stack marks the site of the Kit Hill Great Cansols mine and is a conspicuous landmark for many miles.

CALSTOCK
Calstock Viaduct (sx434687)
2 miles S Gunnislake. Minor road off A390
This graceful railway viaduct over the Tamar was completed in 1907 as part of the Plymouth, Devonport & South Western Junction Railway plan to service the soft-fruit trade of the Tamar Valley. Built of over 11,000 concrete blocks manufactured on site, it is over 1,000 ft long with 12, 60 ft-span arches and stands $117\frac{1}{2}$ ft above the river.

CAMBORNE
Dolcoath Mine (sw661405)
E outskirts of Camborne, $\frac{1}{4}$ mile S A3047
This was the deepest and perhaps most celebrated mine in Cornwall employing in 1864 over 1,200 persons. Worked from the 1720s it eventually descended to a level of 550 fathoms and had 10 engines, 7 waterwheels and a man engine. Little remains of this famous mine but the nearby housing was associated with it.

CAMBORNE
East Pool & Agar Mine (sw679419)
2 miles E of Camborne, $\frac{1}{4}$ mile N A3047
The beam pumping engine over Taylors Shaft at this mine is an example of the largest size of pumping engine normally used in Cornwall. It

has a 90 in diameter cylinder and was made in 1893 by Harveys of Hayle for the neighbouring Carn Brea Mine. It was moved to Taylor's Shaft *c* 1924. The beam alone weighs 52 tons and working at 5 strokes per minute the engine could deliver 450 gallons per minute from a working depth of 1700 ft. It is now owned by the National Trust.

CAMBORNE
East Pool Whim (sw675416)
2 miles E of Camborne, beside A3047
This small double-acting, rotative beam winding engine or 'whim' was built in 1887 to the designs of F W Mitchell of Redruth by Holman Bros of Camborne. Its cylinder diameter is only 30 in and it is claimed to be the last such engine to have been built in Cornwall. Originally preserved by the Cornish Engine Preservation Society it is now owned by the National Trust.

CAMBORNE
South Crofty Mine (sw669409)
1 mile E of Camborne, $\frac{1}{2}$ mile S A3047
The 80 in (2.03m) Cornish pumping engine over Robinson's Shaft at this mine was working up to the 1950s although it is one of the oldest engines in the county. Built in 1854 to the design of the celebrated Cornish engineer Samuel Grose, a pupil of Trevithick, by Sandys, Vivian & Co of Copperhouse Foundry Hayle it was first erected at Wheal Alfred Mine near Hayle. After use at 2 other mines it was finally re-erected at South Crofty in 1903 where it worked continuously night and day for over 50 years. It is now owned by the National Trust.

CAMBORNE
Trevithick's Cottage (sw636389)
$\frac{1}{2}$ mile W of town centre off B3303
This cottage at Penponds to the SW of Camborne was given to the National Trust in 1967. It is the birth place of Richard Trevithick the famous engineer (1771–1833) and may be seen on application to the tenant.

CAMBORNE
Wheal Seton Engine House (sw655416)
1 mile NE town centre
Built *c* 1860 this engine house is unusual in its decorative use of brick and in its parapet wall which originally concealed a hipped roof.

CARTHEW
Wheal Martyn China Clay Works (sx004557)
3 miles N St Austell on A391
China clay has been mined at this site since *c* 1820 though the present works are typically

late 19th century in design. There is a traditional coal fired pan-kiln and a small mica kiln forming an L-shaped building and a series of mica drags, settling pits and settling tanks. There is also an 18 ft-diameter waterwheel which operated a pump some 100 yds away by means of a cable held in tension by a large balance box. Nearby there is a larger wheel, 35 ft diameter, which worked the main pumps in the pit itself some 400 yds away. The works ceased operation in 1968 but are now being preserved as the focus to a museum of the china clay industry.

CHACEWATER
Great Wheal Busy Mine (SW739448)
4½ miles NE Redruth, minor road S A30
This is one of the most important mining sites in West Cornwall. Worked from the beginning of the 18th century, it was reputably the site where, in the 1770s, James Watt introduced some of his early improvements to the steam engine. In 1909 an 85-in cylinder Cornish-type steam pumping engine was erected with the large granite engine house which, however, dates from *c* 1856. The engine itself was scrapped in 1945 but the engine house, stack and substantial 3-bay boiler house still remain. Nearby there are also remains of the associated arsenic calciner and stack.

CHACEWATER
Great Wheal Busy Mine Workshops
(SW738448)
4½ miles NE Redruth, minor road S of A30
When a mine closed most of the surface structures were dismantled and re-used at another site and hence few Cornish mines have significant remains other than engine houses. Wheal Busy is an exception, not only does the boiler house survive (see above), but also a fine workshop building. The latter accommodated the mines carpenter and smith and has a large span timber roof and 2 cast-iron lintels made by the Perran Foundry bearing the inscription 'Great Wheal Busy Mines' and dated 1872.

CHARLESTOWN
Charlestown Foundry (SX038519)
1 mile SE at Austell
Started in 1827, this foundry still has a 30 ft waterwheel, which, served by a syphon, drove the forge hammers and workshop. Much of the building is original with cast-iron fluted columns and massive timber beams.

CHARLESTOWN
Charlestown Harbour (SX039518)
1 mile SE St Austell
This artificial harbour was excavated 1792–8

to enable Charles Rashleigh to ship china clay and copper ore from the nearby mines he owned. Designed by John Smeaton the harbour was relatively unaltered until 1971 when the mitre dock gates were replaced. The underground railway and clay loading bays were built in 1908 by John Lovering to handle clay from the Carclaze Mine.

COTEHELE
Quay and Warehouse (SX423681)
2½ miles S of Gunnislake, unclass roads
A typical Tamar quay which has been restored by the National Trust. There are 2 sets of limekilns and an impressive warehouse which now houses a museum display arranged by the National Maritime Museum. A traditional Tamar barge is being restored on the slipway.

COTEHELE
Mill, Wheelwright's Shop (SX417681)
2½ miles S of Gunnislake, unclass roads
A complex of exceptional interest comprising a watermill, cider house, wheelwright's shop and blacksmith's forge, all of which have been restored by the National Trust and are open to the public. An external overshot waterwheel powers 2 pairs of stones in the corn mill while in the cider house which was originally the bakery, there is a donkey wheel.

CHILSWORTHY
Greenhills Arsenic Stack (SX418718)
1 mile W of Gunnislake off A390
This immense stack is the only surviving stack of the once important east Cornwall arsenic industry. Some 30 ft across the base it is at the end of a long flue built *c* 1894.

DELABOLE
Old Delabole Slate Quarry (SX075840)
1½ miles W of Camelford. Minor road off B3314
This, the most famous of all Cornish slate quarries, has been worked since at least 1396. Originally there were several quarries but these coalesced in the mid-19th century to form one huge pit which by 1882 was 1,300 ft long and 400 ft deep employing 500 hands. Throughout the 19th century steam and water power were employed side by side but by 1924 all the historic machinery had been scrapped. The quarry is still in production though at a much reduced scale.

EAST TAPHOUSE
St Pinnock Viaduct (SX178638)
S A38, 4 miles E Liskeard
With the obvious exception of the Royal

Albert Bridge Saltash (*q.v.*) this is perhaps the finest of Brunel's viaducts in Cornwall. The 150 ft high brown slate piers carried timber spans when the viaduct was built in 1854–5 but these spans were replaced by iron girders in 1882.

GERMOE
Great Work Mine (sw596306)
4 miles E Marazion 1 mile N A394
The only remaining engine house on an important old mine between Tregonning and Godolphin Hills. It has a very fine and unusual stack.

GOLDSITHNEY
Tregurtha Downs Mine (sw539311)
1 mile E Marazion A394 off B3280
This tin mine has an outstanding engine house that once accommodated the 80-in pumping engine that is now preserved at South Crofty mine (*q.v.*). The engine house has unusual slit windows and brick arches.

GRAMPOUND
Manor Tanyard (sw936438)
5 miles E of Truro A390
Owned by J. Craggan & Son this is the last tannery in Cornwall producing heavy leather. It makes extensive use of the tannin from oak bark – a rare practice nowadays. The original lime pits and some of the old machinery survive.

GWENNAP HEAD
Landmarks (sw368217)
2 miles SE Lands End. Minor road off B3315
These two landmarks were erected *c* 1830 by Trinity House on the extreme SW corner of the mainland.

HALTON QUAY
Limekilns (sx413656)
5 miles SE Callington off A388
The use of lime as a soil conditioner became widespread in the Tamar Valley in the late 18th century. Both banks of the Tamar were lined with limekilns and those at Halton Quay are perhaps the most impressive on the Cornish side. They were capable of producing up to 1,000 tons of burnt lime a year and continued in operation until 1916. Faced with alternating courses of slate and limestone they are built against a ledge in the river bank, the wells, 20 ft deep and 10 ft across, being hewn out of the rock.

CHARLESTOWN: *A harbour purpose built for the export of china clay.*

HAYLE
Ellis Brewery (sw565378)
A small range of good brewery buildings dating from 1873 and now used as a distribution depot.

HAYLE
Harveys Foundry (sw558372)
This famous foundry was started in 1779 by John Harvey a local blacksmith and by the mid-19th century it had grown to be the most illustrious of all Cornish engine manufacturers. Richard Trevithick was Harvey's son-in-law and when Watts' patents lapsed Harveys took full advantage of Trevithick's improved designs. This foundry in 1849 cast the largest steam engine cylinder in Europe – the 144-in Cruquius engine which is preserved *in situ* at Vijfhuizen in Holland. The foundry finally closed in 1903.

LANIVET
Tin Stamps (sx035643)
2 miles SW Bodmin off A30
These stamps for crushing ore were last used in 1953. The 16 metal shod heads were powered by a 15 ft waterwheel.

LAUNCELLS
Hobbacott Incline (ss244049)
2½ miles E Bude A 3072
With the exception of the first 2 miles the Bude canal was built to tub-boat specifications. Its total length of 35½ miles was the greatest of any tub-boat canal in Britain and it used incline planes, 6 in all, to surmount the problems of relief. The incline at Hobbacott was the largest of these with a total rise of 230 ft. It was worked by the bucket-in-the-well system and indeed there is reputedly a bucket still at the bottom of the well which is situated alongside the incline-keeper's house. The tub boats which used the incline were 20 ft by 5 ft 6 ins. There is an example preserved in the maritime museum at Exeter.

LIZARD
Lighthouse (sw705115)
11 miles S Helston A 3083
Fonnereau's brick tower of 1752 is the most southerly lighthouse on mainland Britain.

LOOE
Fish Cellar (Cornish Museum) (sx255532)
This museum in Lower Street, East Looe, is housed in an old fish cellar and besides items concerned with fishing such as a fish press, pilchard-oil pit and smoking hearth, there is an interesting collection of mining exhibits.

LOOE
Harbour Warehouse (sx255533)
Quays on both banks of the River Looe have been in use since the Middle Ages but the opening of the canal from Liskeard in 1827 gave impetus to the port development. This particular warehouse dates from this period (*c* 1850) and predates the arrival of the railway in 1860.

LUXULYAN
Treffry Viaduct (sx055572)
1½ miles NNW of St Blazey, unclass road
This immense granite viaduct was the first major railway engineering feat in Cornwall. It was built 1839–42, to the designs of James Palmer, as part of the line of Treffry's private mineral railway across Cornwall. It is 660 ft long with 10 arches of 40 ft span and at its highest is some 100 ft above the river valley. Below the track itself was a stone covered water channel carrying water to power the china stone crushing plant at Ponts Mill, hence the structure is sometimes referred to as the Treffry Aqueduct.

MADRON
Ding Dong Mine (sw435344)
3 miles NW of Penzance, unclass road, 1½ miles NW of Madron
Reputedly worked in Roman times the famous mine restarted in 1814 and closed in 1878, although attempts were made to re-open in 1912 and 1928. The massive engine house now marks the site.

MARHAMCHURCH
Incline Plane (ss220037)
1½ miles S of Bude A39 E of road
This was the first of the inclines on the Bude Canal (*q.v.*) with a rise of 120 ft overcome by a 836 ft long incline. This incline was reputedly worked by a 50 ft waterwheel as distinct from bucket-in-the-well system of the Hobbacott example.

MINIONS
Phoenix Mine (sx260715)
4 miles N of Liskeard B3254 1 mile W of B3254
This fine engine house contained the last large pumping engine built in Cornwall. This area around Caradon Hill abounds in copper mines with significant engine houses at South Phoenix (sx268720) Wheal Jenkin (sx264712) and South Caradon (sx268698).

NANCLEDRA
Tin Stamps (sw500356)
4 miles NE of Penzance B3311 ¼ mile SE of Blancedra unclass road

This eight-headed set of tin stamps was powered by an 18 ft waterwheel made *c* 1890 by E T Sara Foundry, Camborne.

NEWLYN EAST
East Wheal Rose Mine (sw838555)
4 miles S of Newquay unclass road
This was Cornwall's most celebrated lead mine – it was also the most infamous. Some 40 men were drowned underground in 1846 when a cloudburst of exceptional intensity flooded the mine workings. The present massive engine house was built in the 1880s to contain an enormous 100 in cylinder engine.

PENPILLICK
Ponts Mill (sx072562)
1 mile N of St Blazey, ½ mile NW of A390, unclass road
This complex of china-stone grinding mills was powered by Pelton type turbines fed by a complicated system of leats high up on the valley side. One of these leats utilized the Treffry Viaduct (*q.v.*) to cross the valley. The Par canal, built in 1847, terminated at Ponts Mill while the Carmears incline of the Treffry mineral railway descended the valley nearby.

PERRANARWORTHAL
Perran Foundry (sw775384)
4 miles SW of Truro A39
Perran Wharf Foundry was established in 1791 by a consortium led by the Fox family. Within a few years it was one of the most important firms in the South West of Britian with extensive interests in South Wales including the famed Neath Abbey ironworks. The foundry is situated on a tidal inlet of the Fal Estuary and by 1860 covered some 6 acres in area and employed 400 men. However the foundry's output was heavily concentrated on pumping engines and the firm was not able to survive the mining depression of the 1870s. From its closure in 1879 until recently it was used by a milling firm and little deterioration has taken place in many of the impressive timber roofed buildings while two cast-iron arches bear the inscription 'Perran Foundry 1791'.

PERRANARWORTHAL
Perran Foundry Footbridge (sw775385)
4 miles SW of Truro A39
This small, private, iron footbridge was cast in a single piece some 30 ft long. It gives access from the foundry site to the manager's house and was one of the last products before the closure of the foundry in 1879.

POLGOOTH
Polgooth Mine Count House (SW994506)
$1\frac{1}{2}$ miles SW of St Austell A390
This is a good example of a mine count house or office very few of which now survive.

POLKERRIS
Fish Cellar (SX095521)
6 miles E of St Austell 2 miles W of Fowey A3082
Some of the extensive ruins of this pilchard curing factory may date from the 16th century. In its heyday it was claimed to be the largest such cellar in Cornwall.

REDRUTH
Ped'n-an-Drea Stack (SW702420)
This conspicuous stump in the centre of Redruth is all that remains of a 145 ft-high stack associated with a noted tin mine. The stack was disused as early as 1827.

REDRUTH
South Frances Mine (SW680395)
The buildings grouped round Marriott's shaft of the South Frances section of the Bassett Mines are some of the most impressive monuments to the late 19th-century Cornish mining industry. The engine house itself is most unusual – it is much squatter and broader than the normal Cornish engine house as it contained an inverted compound engine unique in Cornwall, though to be found elsewhere. Built by Hatham Davey & Co, Leeds, in 1897–8 it was a Cornish engine with 40 in and 80 in cylinders with the beam below the cylinders with direct access to the circular shaft. This shaft was ultimately 310 fathoms deep and provision was allowed for a second engine in the engine house. There are also remains of the boiler house which latterly contained 6 Lancashire boilers, massive ore bins and ancillary buildings to make this one of the most complete mining sites in Cornwall. Throughout the 19th century this group of mines was one of the most productive for both copper and tin.

REDRUTH
Tolgus Tin (SW690438)
1 mile N of Redruth B3300
These tin streaming works still extract tin from old mine waste and contain the last working set of Cornish stamps. The firm's main support is the income from the many thousands of visitors who pay to see round the works.

REDRUTH
Tolgus Tin, Brunton Calciner (SW691429)
$\frac{1}{2}$mile N of Redruth B3300
Built *c* 1910 and installed at Tolgus in the 1930s, this is probably the only remaining intact arsenic calciner of this kind in which the tin ore was roasted in a rotating furnace to give off arsenic.

ST AGNES
Gooninnis Mine (SW742504)
$1\frac{1}{2}$ miles E of St Agnes B3285
The St Agnes area was a very productive source of tin from the 16th century to the close of the 19th. Gooninnis, though not one of the major mines, has an engine house in a very conspicuous situation. The 50 in cylinder engine it originally contained was moved to Goovean.

ST DENNIS
Parkandillack Engine House (SW945568)
5 miles NW of St Austell B3279 1 mile S of St Dennis
At the English Clays Parkandillack Clayworks a tall masonry engine house contains a preserved Cornish beam engine still capable of being run on compressed air. It was built at Sandys Vivian & Company's Copperhouse Foundry in 1852 and has a 50-in diameter cylinder and a 10 ft stroke. It ceased working in 1953.

ST STEPHEN
China stone grinding mill
Chapel Mill ceased production in 1953 and is representative of the once numerous grinding mill around St Stephen. Originally it was driven by a 21 ft Charlestown Foundry waterwheel.

SALTASH
Royal Albert Bridge (SX435587)
2 miles W of Plymouth (A38)
The spanning of the 1,100 ft wide Tamar estuary was one of Brunel's greatest and last engineering feats. Construction started in 1853 and the second of the 2 great iron trusses was completed in 1859 and the railway opened in April of that year. The bridge is 2,200 ft long and made use of iron chain links originally intended for the Clifton Bridge.

Cumbria

Cumbria comprises the former counties of Cumberland and Westmorland and the northern part of Lancashire. The Lake District with its associated woodland, slate and metal mining industries forms the core of the county with, on its fringes, the pitheads and ports of the Cumbrian coalfield, the charcoal-based iron smelting districts and the 19th-century developments at Millom and Barrow-in-Furness. The former county towns of Carlisle and Kendal developed a range of service industries and were both termini of canals. A distinct metal mining area was centred on Alston in the NE with closer ties to Northumberland and Durham than with the rest of the county.

These comparatively early industrial developments were not followed by equivalent modern industries and therefore abandoned works have survived to provide a stock of industrial monuments much more numerous than the conventional image of the 'Lake Counties' would suggest.

ALLONBY
Crosscanonby Salt Pans (NY066402)
3 miles N Maryport on B5300
The Cumberland salt trade closed down *c* 1790 because of competition of the Cheshire salt industry and has left very few traces, apart from place-names, of a once flourishing industry. At this site however, there are the earthwork forms of 2 settling tanks, or sleech pans, the lower example now occupied by a beach hut. Sea water was pumped to these enclosures to concentrate prior to being boiled over coal fires.

ALSTON
Alston Station (NY717467)
Town centre
1852 Terminus of the Alston branch of the Newcastle and Carlisle Railway. Built in stone in a mock Tudor style it still retains some of its 19th-century equipment such as lamps though the later overall roof was subsequently removed. In the yard is a handsome, stone built goods shed which, with its corner buttresses resembles a medieval barn.

REDRUTH: *Marriott's shaft South Frances Mine – evocative ruins of a once glorious industry.*

BACKBARROW
Backbarrow Furnace (SD356846)
7 miles NE Ulverston off A590
This site has a very long tradition of iron-making. The original water-powered blast furnace was erected in 1711 the first in the area on the site of an earlier bloom smithy. The furnace itself was modified several times and the present cast-iron lintel commemorates the 1870 reconstruction. The furnace was still fired by charcoal until 1926 and in 1963 a double-skinned water-circulating steel furnace was installed. The works finally closed a few years ago though the masonry of the furnace survives as does a horizontal steam blowing engine.

BACKBARROW
Cotton Mill (SD356849)
7 miles NE Ulverston off A590
This mill, which now produces dolly blue – the whitening agent, contains in its fabric the shell of the original cotton mill of *c* 1785. The associated workers housing nearby is also very early – *c* 1800.

BARROW-IN-FURNESS
Industrial Housing (SD197695)
Town centre
Barrow-in-Furness is a mid-19th century

BACKBARROW: *Backbarrow Furnace arch illustrating several periods of use.*

creation – the tiny village of Barrow which preceded it was obliterated. The earliest development of industrial Barrow was the row of red sandstone cottages in Salthouse Road built by the Furness Railway in 1846. However some of the later houses for the shipyard workers were influenced by the Clydebank housing tradition hence the grim barrack-like tenements such as the Old Barrow Flats of the 1880s.

BLAWITH
Nibthwaite Furnace (SD295883)
7 miles E of Broughton-in-Furness
When this furnace went out of use last century a bobbin mill was erected on top of the loading ramp and furnace. The furnace has thus been preserved in very good order below the mill and it is complete with its cast-iron lintel dated 1736. The fine charcoal barn has been converted into a dwelling but the ore store remains virtually unaltered.

BOOT
Corn Mill (NY176013)
6 miles NE of Ravenglass
This inconspicuous watermill is typical of many mills in the area in both size and appearance. The machinery is largely intact and was driven by overshot waterwheels in tandem to the rear of the building.

BARROWDALE
Honister Slate Quarry (NY210143)
8 miles SW of Keswick off B5289
This quarry produced the famous green slate but exploitation was always limited by severe transport problems. Originally the slate had to be taken by pack horse to Ravenglass some 15 miles away. Latterly when the Lake District roads were improved opening local markets, a self-acting tramway was installed in 1878 to bring the slate down to the road.

BRAMPTON
Brampton, Junction Street (NY550559)
7½ miles E of Carlisle off A69
A typical example of the smaller station on the

Newcastle & Carlisle Railway. Built 1836–7 the original part is a small 2-storey mock-Tudor red sandstone building on a rectangular plan but with a small projecting windowed cross gable over the platform. This station predated the higher platforms which were universally introduced and the later platform was built at window sill level hence so reducing door heights as to make them unusable. The later extensions to the station are at the higher level.

BROUGHTON-IN-FURNESS
Duddon Furnace (SD197884)
1 mile W of Broughton off A595
One of the most famous charcoal blast furnaces in the north of England, Duddon was erected in 1736 and finally abandoned in 1867. Situated just above Duddon Bridge and navigable water the furnace complex makes full use of the hillside to minimize lifting of raw materials. The floor levels of the charcoal barns and the ore store are at the same height as the charging platform of the furnace itself – some $28\frac{1}{2}$ ft above the casting floor. The bellows were worked by water power derived from a leat from the River Duddon augmented by a small stream through the site itself. The complex is unusually complete, the furnace retains its stack and there are adjacent workers' dwellings and stables.

BURNESIDE
Oak Bank Coppice Sheds (SD518964)
2 miles N of Kendal
This is one of the finest complexes of coppice sheds of its kind in Lakeland. These sheds were used to store and season coppice wood prior to its use in bobbin mills. The main shed with its round drystone pillars dates from 1847.

BURTON-IN-KENDAL
Holme Mill and Industrial Housing
(SD523780)
10 miles S Kendal off A6070
A flax mill was established at Holme in the late 18th century by the Quaker family of Waithman. The mill building was greatly altered but the count house and the adjacent rows of 3-storey workers' cottages survive as an example of early industrial colonization in a rural area.

CARLISLE
Shaddon Mill (NY395557)
$\frac{1}{2}$ mile W town centre
This superb 7-storey sandstone mill at Denton Holme, Carlisle, was built in 1836 by the firm of Peter Dixon. Sir William Fairbairn designed the iron framing and roof support

system of the interior and the building measures 224 ft by 58 ft and is over 80 ft high. The northern end of the mill has a tall narrow engine house which formerly contained a beam engine, its brick chimney is 350 ft high. Originally built as a cotton mill the building is still used for textile production albeit for woollen mule-spun yarn.

CLEATOR
Cleator Moor (NY395557)
3 miles SE Whitehaven on B5295
The settlement of Cleator Moor developed *c* 1840 as a direct response to the needs of the iron ore miners around Cleator for permanent dwellings and associated facilities. Within a few years there was a co-operative society, with its own flour mill, a commercial hospital, churches, chapels, public houses and even a small brewery, thus a genuine sense of civic pride had developed. The fine ironwork shop-front of the co-operative store of 1876 is an obvious indication of this.

CLIFTON
Wetheriggs Pottery (NY555263)
3 miles S Penrith off A6
This pottery still produces traditionally patterned Westmorland salt-glaze earthenware but now with modern machinery and kilns. However the old coal-fired kiln survives as does the pug mill, blunger, clay pit and tramway.

CONISTON
Coniston Mine (SD289987)
$\frac{1}{2}$ mile N Coniston
Situated at the southern extremity of the Borrowdale Volcanic Series this copper mine was not only a mine but a complete industrial colony with its own housing and services such as joiners shop. Most of the present remains date from post 1834 and include a series of huge waterwheel pits, evidence of the large waterwheels used to wind up the ore. Production fell drastically in the 1880s and the mine was virtually abandoned by the end of the century.

ELTERWATER
Elterwater Gunpowder Mill (NY326050)
3 miles W Ambleside on B5343
Throughout the second half of the 18th century, and the whole of the 19th century, the manufacture of gunpowder was an important industry in Lakeland. The area not only could provide charcoal, one of the main ingredients, but also had an abundance of water supply and the sites could be well isolated. The most extensive remains of the industry are at

Elterwater where incorporating pits of *c* 1823 with bedstones and crushing runners can be seen and some of the coppice stores have been converted into holiday accommodation.

FINSTHWAITE
Stott Park Bobbin Mill (SD373882)
1 mile N Newby Bridge off A590
Built in 1835 this mill is the most complete surviving bobbin mill in Lakeland and it is being preserved by the Department of the Environment. It contains much of its 19th-century equipment including lathes, polishing drums, saws and drying racks. Although the mill was latterly electrically driven most of the line shafting survives as does a small horizontal steam engine by Bradley of Brighouse and even the turbine it replaced. The coppice barns, with their square pillars are of a characteristic late 19th-century type.

GLEASTON
Corn Mill (SD260709)
3 miles E of Barrow-in-Furness
There are two watermills on this site and though each is of medieval origin the present fabrics are probably 17th century. The machinery of the northernmost mill building is fairly complete though the waterwheel is now in poor condition.

KENDAL
Elwood's Ropeworks (SD518932)
N of town centre
This small, late 19th-century, ropeworks still spins rope in the traditional way and contains several interesting old machines.

KENDAL
Kent Mills Carpet Manufactory (SD514933)
N of town centre
This fine pale limestone structure dating from *c* 1822 is a relic of the now defunct Kendal carpet industry. Once the property of the Quaker firm of Whitwell it was featured in a report on carpet making in Dicken's Household Words (*c* 1850).

KENDAL
Helsington Laithes Snuff Mill (SD513903)
1½ miles S town centre
This is one of two surviving water-driven snuff mills in Britain. A rather primitive heavy wooden undershot waterwheel provides all the necessary power to drive the 19th-century machinery, mainly mortars and grinding pans. The machinery is designed to avoid metal with metal contact to obviate the risks of sparks in a dust laden atmosphere and to minimize this dust is turned relatively slowly. The actual

mixing of the crushed tobacco leaf is a jealously guarded secret.

KESWICK
Millbeck Woollen Mill (NY257263)
1½ miles NW town centre
At Millbeck, to the north of Keswick, are the structural remains of a 18th-century woollen mill which operated from *c* 1760 to 1894. The original main mill has been converted into a large house and disguised by pepper-pot turrets though the structural layout is little altered. The former weaving sheds to the rear are little altered internally since the early 19th century. Indeed one room is papered with old newspapers of 1836.

MILLOM
Hodbarrow – Sea Barriers (NY180781)
1 mile S Millom
Hodbarrow mine is perhaps the most spectacular industrial relic in the region though many of its remains are fast disappearing. The site was intermittently worked since the 17th century but only became really important from the 1870s onwards and most of the present remains date from this latter period. Much of the history of Hodbarrow is of the fight to extend mining seawards necessitating a series of barriers. The first, built *c* 1885, was of timber but it was replaced in 1888–9 by a permanent wall built of stone and concrete on a deep clay embankment. This was replaced in 1905 by a much larger sea wall over a mile in length in the form of a girdle of limestone rubble and tumbled concrete blocks with a supporting heart of clay with steel or timber piling. This outer barrier has only recently been breached and much of the mine site is flooded though sections of the barriers can be inspected at either end.

MILLOM
Hodbarrow Mine – Engine houses
(NY108784)
1 mile S Millom
Near the eastern end of the Inner Barrier are a collection of engine houses the earliest being the limestone structure of the Annie Lowther pit *c* 1873. No.8 and No.10 engine houses nearby contained massive 70 in cylinder Cornish engines by Harveys of Hayle (1899) and Perran Foundry (1878) respectively. These engines worked until the early 1960s but have recently been scrapped.

MILLOM
Millom – Industrial Settlement (SD162802)
The town sprang up in the mid 1860s under the stimuli of iron mining and manufacture. It was

'planned' in so far as its houses and streets were laid out in a regular gridiron fashion. Other industrial housing developed at Haverigg e.g. communities such as Steel Green (SD170789).

NENTHEAD
Haggs Lead Mine (NY766451)
3 miles E Alston on A689

This mine adit, alongside the road from Alston to Nenthead, dates from the 19th century. Immediately behind the entrance grill a section of rail has survived complete with an ore truck. The neighbouring buildings are a smithy and candle house associated with the mine.

NENTHEAD
Reading and Public Fountain (NY781437)
$4\frac{1}{2}$ miles E Alston on A689

In the 19th century the London Lead Company, the most famous mining company in the area, built a planned village for its workers at Nenthead. This small building carries a tablet with the inscription 'London Lead Company's Workmen's Reading Room' while they also provided the adjacent public drinking fountain with its highly decorative cast-iron canopy.

NENTHEAD
Smeltmill (NY784433)
$4\frac{1}{2}$ miles E Alston on A689

Though in considerable decay in parts this is the most complete smelt mill in the North Pennines. Most of the processes can be clearly traced including furnace house, washing and dressing house and laboratory and the attendant maze of covered flues and watercourses. A collapsed 'horizontal chimney' led to a vertical stack on the hillside. On the hillside above the smeltmill is a huge wheel pit measuring some 50 ft by 7 ft which contained the waterwheel to drive the furnace bellows.

PATTERDALE
Hogget Gill Lead Smelter (NY389113)
10 miles N Windermere off A592

Very few traces of the early lead industry have survived in this area apart from the occasional level driven into the rock. This collection of ruinous walls represents a lead smelter that has been dated to *c* 1630 – a very rare survival.

PORT CARLISLE
Canal Entrance Lock (NY242642)
10 miles W Carlisle B5307

The $11\frac{1}{4}$-mile Carlisle Canal was opened in 1823. It allowed coasting vessels of up to 74 ft by $17\frac{1}{2}$ ft to reach Carlisle. The entrance lock at Port Carlisle became a transhipment point

for a newly developed steam packet service to Liverpool and the Solway Hotel was built to cater for this trade. The canal was converted into a railway in 1853 but the entrance lock survives in a ruinous state.

SATTERTHWAITE
Stony Hazel Finery Forge (SD336907)
4 miles NW Newby Bridge

The rapid introduction of the blast furnace process into Cumbria in the early 18th century caused a demand for forges to rework the brittle cast-iron into malleable wrought-iron. Stony Hazel finery forge is the most significant survivor of a constellation of forges serving ironworks such as Backbarrow and Duddon. The layout of this forge is remarkably complete in plan and the site has been leased to Lancaster University for research purposes and much, including the hearth, has already been cleared.

SHAP
Granite Quarries (NY563106)
2 miles S Shap off A6

These quarries only became practical to work with the coming of the railway in the 1860s. The pink granite, in a polished form, was widely used for monumental building at the turn of the century. At this time the quarries also diversified into pre-cast concrete and production has continued ever since.

STAVELEY
Elfhow Potash Pit (SD473997)
4 miles E Windermere off A591

This pit, which is rather more representative of the species than Winster (*q.v.*), is unusually complete for its early date – *c* 1694.

ULVERSTON
Newland Furnace (SD299798)
1 mile NE Ulverston off A590

This site was operated from *c* 1748 and was rebuilt by the Newland Company in 1770. Originally charcoal-fired the blast furnace continued in operation until the end of the 19th century though latterly using coke. The furnace and gear were finally dismantled in 1903. Much of the furnace structure remains as does the fine charcoal stove. There is a row of workers' dwellings built on to the charging ramp of the furnace and other associated housing up the Newland Beck – the stream which provided the necessary power.

ULVERSTON
Old Railway Station (SD285779)
NW town centre

This large functional building to the north of

the present station was indeed the original Furness Railway Ulverston Station built *c* 1855 before the Carnforth line was completed. This latter line caused the station to be moved to a lower level a hundred yards away.

ULVERSTON
Ulverston Station (SD284778)
W town centre
This station with its fine cast-iron platform canopies was completed in 1873 and replaced the earlier High Level Station. With the company's monogram F R in both stone and iron it exemplifies Furness Railway architecture at its best.

WHITEHAVEN
Candlstick Chimney and Wellington Terrace (NX968182)
W town centre
Cumbrian coal mining was dominated by a few large landowning families such as the Lowthers at Whitehaven. This gave rise to a concentration of the industry into a few, large, highly capitalized units. It also, in the mid-19th century, gave rise to a striking form of colliery architecture which perhaps reflected the almost feudal control of the families concerned. Whitehaven experienced the fullest development of this 'medievalization' of pitheads. The hillside to the south of the harbour was clad in an extraordinary array of keeps and towers disguising the mundane winding and pumping engine houses ventilation fans etc. These terraces have suffered severe delapidation since the pits closed and much has disappeared. However the candlestick chimney built in 1850 by Sydney Smirke has been restored as has one of the castellated gatehouses.

WHITEHAVEN
Duke Pit Fan Casing (NX969182)
W town centre
Duke Pit stood immediately east of Wellington Pit and its associated terrace (*q.v.*) and was similarly designed to resemble a medieval structure. In the course of demolition in 1969 a superb vaulted housing for a Guibal fan was revealed. Built *c* 1862 it originally housed a 36 ft (10.97m) wooden fan which ventilated the mine. The casing has now been consolidated and its surroundings landscaped.

WHITEHAVEN
Saltom Pit (NX964174)
1 mile SW town centre
At the foot of the cliffs in Saltom Bay on a ledge just above high water mark are the remains of Saltom colliery. This pit was the scene of the earliest experiments in through ventilation, piping of methane and use of atmospheric power with engines in dual operation. It was here that Cumbrian undersea mining was pioneered in 1731 with the aid of a Newcomen engine and its layout represents a typical 18th-century coal mine. On the top of the cliffs above is a horse gin circle used to wind coal up the cliff.

WINSTER
Potash Pit (SD412923)
4 miles S Windermere off A5074
Somewhat similar to small limekilns, but with important differences, potash pits were a vital ancilliary to the woollen industry in areas devoid of fullers earth. The potash was made by burning green bracken with charcoal, for subsequent use with lime and tallow to make soft brown soaps for washing and fulling in the Kendal cloth industry. This pit is one of the most impressive of the several hundred such pits that have now been identified.

WORKINGTON
Jane Pit Engine House (NX995277)
½ mile S town centre
This remarkable pit-head structure was the brain child of Henry Curwen and is a splendid example of castellated architecture which reflected the large landowner involvement in the Cumbrian coal industry. Apart from the two battlemented chimneys and the crennellated engine house which was built *c* 1843 there are also traces of a horse gin circle, a sealed shaft and remains of brick boiler vaults.

WORKINGTON
Pirt's Foundry (NX995290)
Town centre
This foundry, which has a long tradition of supplying mining machinery to an area famous for its pioneer ventures in mining, is housed in chapel-like building. This would seem to be a regional architectural quirk as there are foundries similarly embellished at Whitehaven and Cleator.

WORKINGTON
Schoose Farm Steading (NY014280)
1 mile SE town centre
Schoose Farm was built by John Christian Curwen, a famous liberal politician and agricultural innovator, in the early decades of the 19th century. The impressive battlemented steading and outbuildings which included a windmill were meant to symbolize agricultural leadership.

WORKINGTON: *Jane Pit engine house, typical of the high architectural finish of many of the colliery buildings in the Cumbrian coalfield.*

Derbyshire

The long N/S configuration of Derbyshire has given it a very diverse industrial heritage reflecting the quite different landscapes it embraces. There is a history of lead mining stretching back to Roman times in the Peak District while the NW of the county shares a textile background with neighbouring Lancashire and the NE of the county a common tradition of edge tool production with the neighbouring Sheffield region. The southern Pennine valleys witnessed the pioneer development of the textile factory system along the banks to the River

Derwent and its tributaries. To the S and E of the county extensive coal mining led to the construction of canals, tramways and railways and to the development of a important iron and steel industry. The SE of the county participated in the dramatic expansion of factory lace production in the late 19th century and huge tenement factories are to be found in Long Eaton, Draycott and Sandiacre. Finally in the S of the county a ceramic industry developed around Swadlincote. Superimposed on these developments were national and regional transport systems with centres such as Shardlow on the canal system and Derby on the railway system. Derbyshire has thus an outstanding legacy of industrial monuments. All the industries mentioned are represented.

Museums: Derby Industrial Museum is housed in a former textile mill on the site of the famous Silk Mill of 1721, a museum of lead mining has recently been opened in Matlock Bath and the Tramway Museum is housed in a quarry at Crich.

ALPORT
Smelt Mill (SK223648)
3 miles W Rowsley A524
On private land, but visible from road on other side of stream, are the extensive remains of mid-19th-century smelt mills. The flue makes 4 horizontal traverses of the lower hillside and culminates in a chimney stump which incorporated a scrubber.

ASHOVER
Stone Edge Smelt Mill (SK334670)
4 miles SW Chesterfield A632/B5057
Possibly the best preserved lead smelting site in Derbyshire, this cupola or reverberatory furnace dates from a rebuild of *c* 1811 on a site used since *c* 1770. The free standing square chimney is of this earlier period and is claimed to be the earliest industrial chimney in the country.

BELPER
(SK348478)
E of A6 to N of town centre
The Strutt family provided a high standard of accommodation for their employees as witnessed by the solidly built 3-storey cottages of North Row (1792–3) and even more so by the unique 'clusters' of William Street. The latter are blocks of 4 houses in pairs facing either way surrounded by generous gardens.

BELPER
North Mill (SK345481)
N of Belper town centre where A517 and A6 diverge
Built by William Strutt in 1804, North Mill is one of the most important 'fireproof' mills to survive. Strutt improved on the ideas demonstrated by Bage in his Shrewsbury Mill and North Mill is the model early 19th-century 'fireproof' structure with brick walls, cast-iron columns and beams supporting brick arches with wrought-iron tie bars and cast-iron framed roof. The cotton spinning machinery was housed on 5 floors and was driven by massive waterwheel, 18 ft in diameter and 23 ft wide, supplied with water by the prominent horse-shoe weir upstream from Belper Bridge.

BONSALL
Textile Workshops (SK274581)
2 miles W Matlock Bath off A5012
The small village of Bonsal was a major centre of domestic framework knitting. In 1844 there are said to have been 143 frames at work in the village. There is a stone-built workshop dated 1737 at SK274581 and a 19th-century brick and stone workshop at SK279583 which housed 6 frames in use into this century.

BUXWORTH
Canal Basin and Tramways (SK020822)
Beside B6062 1 mile E of its junction with A6
Extensive remains of basins and wharves at the terminus of a branch of the Peak Forest Canal. The basin is connected to extensive quarries by a system of tramways which incorporate very early examples of masonry skew bridges. The main tramway which retains much of its stone sleepers splits to allow one branch to serve the canal wharf and the other to gain sufficient height to cross the basins. The limekilns associated with the basins are very derelict.

CALVER
Calver Mill (SK247745)
2 miles N Baslow on A619
An impressive 7-storey cotton mill dating from 1803–4 on the site of a 1785 mill

developed by Gardom & Pares. The 20-bay masonry frontage has a pediment over protruding central 2 bays. It retains most of its original square-headed multi-paned windows. The staircase turrets are to the rear. It is still in use by Sissons.

CASTLETON
Oden Mine Crushing Circle (SK135835)
$1\frac{1}{2}$ miles W Castleton to the N of A625
The most complete crushing circle in Derbyshire. It was constructed *c* 1823 at a cost of *c* £40 and comprises an iron track 18 ft 2 in in diameter and 15 in broad with a crushing stone 5 ft 10 in in diameter with a 12 in broad tyre.

CHAPEL EN LE FIRTH
Tramway Tunnel (SK059815)
$\frac{1}{2}$ mile N Chapel en le Firth on A624 in grounds of Feroda Ltd
Claimed to be the oldest tramroad tunnel in the country, this 85-yard long tunnel at Chapel Milton is on the line of the Peak Forest Tramway which opened in 1796 from Buxworth (*qv*) to Dove Hole limeworks. The tunnel is now partially blocked.

CHESTERFIELD
Cannon Mill Foundry, Dock Walk (SK375708)
$\frac{1}{2}$ mile W town centre, S of A619

2-storey red brick building with an ornamented gable and blank Gothic arches. Oval cast-iron plaque with picture of cannon with cannon balls and dated 1816. Large overshot iron waterwheel. Modern plaque records that building was erected prior to 1788 as part of the Griffin Foundry of I & E Smith & Co (1755–1833).

CHURCH GRESLEY
Greens Pottery (SK305187)
5 miles SE Burton off A444
The Swadlincote area was a most important producer of pottery but the industry has witnessed a drastic contraction in recent years. Green's Pottery, however, which still has some of the traditional bottle ovens, flourishes as a manufacturer of kitchenware. There are plans to restore one of the kilns, which are of distinctive Derbyshire design, to provide a museum display of firing techniques.

CRESSBROOK
Cressbrook Mill (SK173726)
5 miles NW Bakewell off B6465
A most attractive cotton mill of 1815 in a delightful situation in Millers Dale, built alongside the remains of a small Arkwright

CRESSBROOK: *Cressbrook Mill of 1815.*

mill of *c* 1783. Unfortunately, the building is under used and not in the best of condition with only the uppermost storey windows retaining the original multi-panes. The main mill building is 12 bay, with the 4 central bays surmounted by a pediment with a dock, the hipped roof has a central bellcote. There are later single-storey sheds to the front of the mill and an apprentices' house behind.

CRICH
Quarry containing Tram Museum (SK351544)
2 miles W A6 (Whatstandwell) on B5035
A large disused quarry at Crich has been turned into the most extensive urban tramway museum in the country. There are workshops and ¾ of a mile of operating line with some 50 trams built between 1873 and 1953.

CROMFORD
Arkwright's Mills (SK298569)
2 miles S Matlock off A6
Nestling into a bluff above the junction of the Bonsall Brook and the River Derwent is one of the most significant industrial sites in the country. This is the location of Richard Arkwright's first water-powered cotton mills. The site was mainly developed from 1771–1791 in which period an extensive complex of stone-built mills and warehouses were built, deriving power from the Bonsall Brook and the Cromford Sough. The buildings have suffered damage over the years by fire and alterations for re-use, but remain almost original in plan if not in elevation.

CROMFORD
High Peak Junction (SK314559)
1½ miles SE Cromford A6
The eastern end of the Cromford and High Peak Railway built by Josias Jessop 1825–31. The railway shared a wharf with the Cromford Canal and besides the restored wharf shed there are several early railway installations, including workshops, offices, water tank, signal, stone sleepers, workers' bothy, and the lower pulley of the Sheep Pasture incline.

CROMFORD
Industrial Housing, North Street (SK295567)
2 miles S Matlock off A6
The village of Cromford is largely a product of Arkwright family's desire to employ well-housed, semi-dependent labour. Most of the houses date from their tenure, including the finest examples in North Street built *c* 1777 and comprising 2 rows of 3-storey stone

CROMFORD: *Leawood Pumping Station, an expensive solution to water supply problems.*

houses. Other structures include the Greyhound Inn (1788), the Church (1797), the School with its associated houses (1832) and at some distance removed, Willersley Castle, Arkwright's own residence.

CROMFORD
Leawood Pumping Station (SK315557)
2 miles SE Cromford on A6
A tall gritstone building at the northern approach to Wigwell Aqueduct housing a beam pumping engine built by Graham & Co, Milton Ironworks, in 1849. The engine has been restored to working order by enthusiasts.

CROMFORD
Wigwell Aqueduct (SK316556)
2 miles SE Cromford on A6
Built by William Jessop in 1792–3, this masonry aqueduct is one of the major engineering feats on the Cromford Canal. It has an 80 ft central span over the River Derwent flanked by cattle creeps. Before the canal opened, the original span collapsed and was rebuilt at Jessop's own expense.

DALE
Cat and Fiddle Windmill (SK438398)
2½ miles SW Ilkeston off A6096
A preserved post mill of *c* 1788 with a masonry roundhouse of 1844. It is in working order.

DARLEY ABBEY
Darley Abbey Mills and Housing (SK354386)
1½ miles N Derby, ¼ mile E A6
On the east bank of the River Derwent are the large cotton mills by Walter Evans and dating in part from a post-fire rebuild of 1788. A low wing nearest the river has been converted into a restaurant with views over the fine weir and toll bridge. On the other side of this bridge is the settlement of Darley Abbey with picturesque 18th-century brick housing, the earliest being a series of courts named The Square, Hill Square, etc. Further up the hillside are more conventional terraces, e.g. Brick Row.

DARLEY BRIDGE
Old Mill Close Mine Engine House (SK258618)
¾ mile W Darley Bridge by track off unclassified road.
The impressive ruins of an engine house built of massive ashlar blocks sited over Watts Shaft. Mill Close Mine itself was one of the most productive lead mines in the country.

DERBY
Railway Station Workshops etc (SK363356)
½ mile SE city centre

An extensive railway complex developed by the Midland Railway as the headquarters of their system. The centrepiece is Derby Station, itself much altered in 1892, but retaining some traces of Francis Thompson original of 1840–1. Close by there is the Midland Hotel, railway offices, an Institute of 1892 and some very early railway housing, some of which is being demolished. To the rear of the station are the locomotive workshops, built from 1840 onwards, including the famous roundhouse, 134 ft across.

DERBY
Rykeld Mills, Bridge Street (SK348365)
¼ mile W of city centre
Originally a silk mill, this imposing mill with its 7-storey and 5-storey blocks now weaves narrow fabrics. The earliest portions date from *c* 1825 and have small multi-paned cast-iron framed windows, circular section cast-iron columns, iron beams and brick jack arching.

DERBY
Silk Mill, Silk Mill Lane (SK354365)
NE of city centre
The Derby Industrial Museum is housed in a mill of 1910 built on the foundation arches of Lambe's Silk Mill erected in 1721 to the designs of George Sorocold. Silk-making at this site dates back to Crotchett's mill of 1702 also designed by Sorocold.

DRAYCOTT
Victoria Mill (SK445333)
3 miles W Long Eaton on A6005
Completed in 1907, Victoria Mill was one of the largest lace tenement factories ever built. Its decorative 4-storey, 5-bay street frontage surmounted by a clock is in fact the end elevation of a block 58 bays long.

DRONFIELD
Coke Ovens (SK369782)
1 mile SE Dronfield, 1/3 mile track off A61
A derelict bank of 2 by 24 coke ovens formerly served by a mineral railway line, and now much overgrown by vegetation. One of the largest such group of ovens to survive.

ECKINGTON
Seldom Seen Colliery Engine House (SK422800)
1 mile NW Eckington along track off unclass road to Mosborough
An exceptionally large brick built engine house some 75 ft high and 40 ft by 20 ft in plan. It was built to house a beam engine and is now in a ruinous condition.

GLOSSOP
Railway Station (SK035942)
¼ mile N town centre on B6105
Single-storey masonry station built in 1845 by Lord Howard and chiefly noted for the ornamental lion surmounting its main entrance. It is situated at the end of a spur of the Sheffield & Manchester Railway.

GLOSSOP
Cotton Mill (SK029924)
¼ mile W town centre on A57
The beginning of the 19th century witnessed a dramatic expansion of Glossop based primarily on cotton. By 1851 there were some 60 mills in the town but this century there has been an equally dramatic contraction and very little cotton spinning survives, though some firms have continued the textile tradition with man-made fibres. Huge complexes such as Wrens Nest are now occupied by a variety of industries.

HARTINGTON
Newhaven Railway Tunnel (SK151629)
9 miles SE Buxton on A515
Short tunnel under the Ashbourne-Buxton road. Fine masonry portals inscribed on the western side with Jessop Engineer and the coat of arms of the Cromford & High Peak Railway, and on the other with a waggon and the date 1825.

HAYFIELD
Weavers' Cottages (SK037871)
5 miles S of Glossop on A624
The village of Hayfield was an early centre of textile production. There are several examples of 3-storey cottages with workshop uppermost floors; one group high above the main road has a datestone inscribed 1780.

HEAGE
Morley Park Furnaces (SK380492)
2 miles SW Ripley, visible (though not accessible) from new A61 dual carriageway
This pair of fine masonry blast furnaces are all that remain of the important Morley Park Ironworks which operated from *c* 1780–1875. Erected by Francis Hunt in 1780 and 1818 respectively, these gritstone pyramids are some 36 ft high and square in plan with pointed arches.

IRONVILLE
Industrial Housing (SK438519)
Ironville before its drastic redevelopment by demolition and unsympathetic modernization was one of the best examples of company model towns in the country. It was mostly

developed from 1834–1860 by the Butterley Company around King William Street which led from a bridge over the Cromford Canal. Some earlier industrial settlement had taken place with Furnace and Foundry Rows of 1811.

LONGFORD
Cheese Factory (SK 220375)
10 miles E Derby off A52
A long low wooden building bearing a plaque with the inscription 'The first cheese factory built in England. Opened 4 May 1870, under the management of Cornelius Schermerhorn'. This structure is quite different from the traditional stone-built dairies of the Derbyshire uplands and displays American influences in its design.

LITTLE LONGSTONE
Monsal Dale Viaduct (SK 183716)
2 miles NW Ashford, ¼ mile W B6465
A spectacular masonry viaduct carries the now disused Midland Railway of 1862–63 over the ravine of the River Wye at Monsal Head.

LONG EATON
Leopold Street Lace Factories (SK 488336)
¼ mile W town centre
This street backing onto the Erewash Canal witnessed the most dramatic development of lace making premises in the last quarter of the 19th century. Its entire length of over 500 yards is lined by tall brick-built lace tenement factories. One block alone has some 50 bays and 6 turret staircases.

MATLOCK BATH
Masson Mill (SK 294573)
½ mile S Matlock Bath on A6
The highlighting of the windows in white together with the Venetian windows of the central protruding bays give the building a distinctive appearance unlike any others on the Derwent. To the rear of the mill a wide leat still feeds the waterwheel.

MATLOCK
Tramway Depot, Rutland Street (SK 303608)
⅓ mile N town centre
The Matlock Calbe Tramway, which played a significant part in the development of Matlock Bank was reputedly the steepest graded cable tramway in the world. The depot itself was designed by J Turner in 1893 and consists of a car shed, in which the pits and track remain, workshops, boiler house and winding house. There is also a waiting room.

MILFORD
Dyehouse (SK 351452)
6 miles N Derby, beside the bridge at Milford carrying A6 over the River Derwent
The Strutt family operated on an extensive scale at Milford as well as at Belper (*qv*). Indeed, from 1792 onwards Milford witnessed some of their earliest essays in the use of cast iron to enhance the fire resistance of their mills. Unfortunately, all the early buildings have gone but one of a pair of dyehouses built in 1832 incorporates the latest of Strutt's improvements in the design of the all important cast-iron beam itself. This building is to be restored by English Sewing Cotton Company Ltd – a firm whose constituent companies include the successors to both Arkwright and Strutt.

MILLERS DALE
Railway Viaducts (SK 128733)
2 miles NE of A6 on B6049
2 high railway viaducts carrying disused Midland Railway over ravine of River Wye. Both of metal spans on masonry piers, they provide a marked contrast to the masonry viaduct at Monsal Head 3 miles down the line. The earlier viaduct with curved spans dates from 1863, the later girder viaduct from 1903.

OVER HADDON
Mining Remains, Lathkilldale (SK 197661)
2 miles SW Bakewell by B5055 unclass road Over Haddon
Upstream of the ford on the River Lathkill below Over Haddon the dale is littered with mining remains, including the 19th-century Mandale Engine House, Mandale Sough *c* 1820, piers of an aqueduct of 1840 formerly carrying a wooden trough across the river, and numerous mine workings.

RIDGEWAY
Phoenix Scythe Works (SK 403822)
3 miles NW Eckington off A616/B6054
Ridgeway and nearby Ford (SK 398804) were important centres of sickle and scythe manufacture. The Phoenix works, makers of sickles and the 'Scythette' still use traditional methods of production. Long low stone buildings arranged in a courtyard and bearing inscription T & J Hutton 1812.

RIPLEY
Brittain Colliery Headgear (SK 415517)
1 mile NE Ripley off old Butterley toll road
A colliery headstock, partially encased in a round brick tower, has been preserved as a landscape feature along with its empty engine house.

ROWSLEY
Caudwells Mill (SK256657)
Centre of village S of A6
A commercial mill built 1875 with 8 pairs of stones powered by a breast shot waterwheel. It was re-equipped in 1885 with 8 sets of roller mills and a 48-in Trent turbine was installed 1887. The adjacent provender mill had its waterwheel replaced by a 33-in Little Giant turbine in 1898.

ROWSLEY
Railway Station (SK258660)
Either side A6 E end of Rowsley
The original station, a single-storey stone building with wide bracketed eaves, was built in 1849 to a design of Sir Joseph Paxton. It was the terminus of the Manchester Buxton Matlock & Midlands Junction Railway until the line was continued through to Buxton in 1863 when it was replaced by an equally attractive station on the other side of the road – now also disused.

SHELDON: *Magpie Mine, finest preserved site of the Peak District lead industry.*

SANDIACRE
Springfield Mills (SK480366)
¼ mile N town centre off B5010
Enormous lace factory built 1888 by Terah Hooley with a capacity of 160 lace machines. The 41 bay 4-storey frontage measures 350 ft and has unusually large cast-iron framed windows. Its central gable contains a clock. To the rear bordering the Erewash Canal is a fine chimney engine house and turret staircases.

SHARDLOW
Canal Port (SK443304)
6 miles SE Derby on A6
In the late 18th century a canal settlement was established near the Wilden Ferry bridging point of the River Trout a mile above the junction of the Trent & Mersey Canal and the Trent itself. Several Transhipment warehouses were built and associated industries such as rope making and malting developed. Many fine early warehouses have survived.

SHELDON
Magpie Mine (SK172682)
3½ miles W Bakewell by B5055 unclass road (Sheldon)

The most famous monument to the Derbyshire lead mining industry and the present remains display features of over 2 centuries of working. The most prominent structures are the engine house of 1869–70 and the chimney of 1840 alongside, but there are also several other buildings, including 2 winding houses (one of 1950s date), a boiler house and square chimney, agent's cottage and a power house. The presence of some 20 unfilled shafts in the area makes it advisable to stay to the well worn paths. The site is now under the care of the Peak District Mines Historical Society.

STANTON
Hillcarr Sough (SK259638)
1½ miles S Rowsley on the W bank of River Derwent
Started in 1766, this sough or drainage tunnel was to be the longest in Derbyshire with a length of 4½ miles. It was finished in 1787 and its outfall, a fine masonry arch in good condition, carries a considerable volume of water.

TICKNALL
Tramway Bridge, Calke Park Tunnel (SK355236)
½ mile E village on A514
The main road to the east of Ticknall is crossed by an elliptically arched stone-built bridge which carried a 1802 tramway from extensive limeworks to Ashby and Leicester. In the grounds of Calke Park to the south a tunnel 138 yards long was built by cut and cover merely to hide traffic from the drive to the house. There are remains of several lime-kilns alongside the embanked sections of the tramroad.

WHALEY BRIDGE
Warehouse (SK012816)
½ mile N of town centre beside A6
A most unusual canal/railway interchange warehouse built shortly after the horse-drawn Cromford & High Peak Railway of 1825 made connection with the Peak Forest Canal. The canal enters the gritstone warehouse by a central barge hole.

WHATSTANDWELL
Meerbrook Sough (SK325554)
1 mile N Whatstandwell on banks of River Derwent below A6
This sough makes its outfall in a fine dated and initialled arch in the grounds of a water supply station. Its completion in 1836 deprived Long Sough Cromford (SK295568) of much of its water with serious consequences for the cotton mills at Cromford (*qv*).

WIRKSWORTH
Middleton Top Winding Engine (SK275552)
1½ miles NW Wirksworth B5023
The Cromford & High Peak Railway was built 1825–31 from Cromford (*qv*) to Whaley Bridge (*qv*) and had 8 stationary winding engines to surmount inclines. The Middleton Top Engine is a double single-cylinder beam engine built in 1829 by the Butterley Company and is the only engine to survive on the line. The incline itself is 708 yards long at a gradient of 1 in 8. The bridge at its foot is one of the earliest cast-iron railway bridges in the country.

Devonshire

Devon displays a remarkable diversity and wealth of industrial monuments reflecting industries ranging from the metal mines of Tamar and Dartmoor to the cider industry of the south, from the lime burning on the north coast to the textile industry of the east. Transport systems have left a legacy of monuments including the river port of Morwellham with its canal incline plane, the harbours of Plymouth, the tramways of Dartmoor, the spectacular Meldon railway viaduct and the early concrete road bridge at Seaton.
Museums: Exeter Maritime Museum, The Quay, Exeter; Morwellham (*qv*); Tiverton Museum, St Andrews Street, Tiverton.

APPLEDORE
Richmond Dry Dock (SS466307)
3 miles N Bideford
Appledore has a long tradition of ship building and *c* 1850 Richmond Dock was constructed for James Yeo who sent ships built in Prince Edward Island, Canada to Appledore for finishing. It was also used extensively for overhauling schooners used in the fruit and cod trades. It could accommodate two schooners end to end and was claimed at the time to be the largest dry dock in England. The original caisson at the entrance has long since been replaced by dock gates.

BAMPTON
Suspension Bridge (SS938208)
2 miles W Bampton off A361
A neat 19th-century suspension bridge over the River Exe carrying a private road and belonging to the Stoodleigh Estate. It was substantially renovated *c* 1960.

BARNSTAPLE
Branham's Pottery (SS560349)
Town centre
Successors to a long tradition of pottery making, this firm produces the well-known Barium ware. A remarkable ornate Victorian tiled façade masks the works with its large circular beehive-shaped kiln.

BARNSTAPLE
Derby Lace Works (SS565336)
N of town centre
Erected 1796–1812, these works comprise a four-storey block of twelve bays with a copula in the centre. Inside cast-iron columns support shallow brick fireproof arches.

BERE ALSTON
Gawton Flue and Stack (SX456689)
3 miles SW Tavistock
This prominent stack, whose pronounced slant is said to be due to the cement on the south side drying out before that of the north when it was built in the 1890s, terminates the longest and most impressive arsenic flue in the county. It is several hundred yards long, in places over 6 ft high with 2 ft thick walls and winds up a near vertical hillside.

BERE ALSTON
Smelting Works, Weir Quay (SX435650)
5 miles SW Tavistock
Most of the local lead and silver areas of the Bere Alston peninsula were smelted in these works. The Tamar Smelting Works was built *c* 1820 and was re-equipped in 1845 and contained 18 furnaces which could deal with over 300 tons of ore a month. They closed *c* 1860. The nearby Union works were established *c* 1830 and have survived more completely with an assay house and count house projecting on either side of the smelter.

BOVEY TRACEY
Bovey Potteries (SX815773)
¾ mile S village on A382
Bovey Potteries were founded *c* 1750 and enlarged in the 19th century. Out of the total of 12 muffle kilns only 3 survive. These date from 1850 to 1900 and are reinforced with rails from the South Devon Railway. Although the pottery no longer operates the buildings are used for storage and most of the layout of the original works is traceable including the water supply system and the tramway.

BROAD CLYST
Windmill (SX991966)
5 miles NE Exeter on A30
This is the most complete of the 9 or so ruinous windmills in Devon. It was built in 1786 by Samuel Flood and bears the inscription 'Vive l'ingénie'. Disused since 1815, it was converted into flats in 1879 to house the homeless after a disastrous fire in the village. Three floors and a chimney were added at this time.

CHERITON BISHOP
Cheriton Cross Toll House (SX774929)
9 miles W Exeter on A30
A good example of a unpretentious two-storey toll house which retains its original door, porch and side windows.

DARTMOUTH
Newcomen Engine (SX879515)
Town centre
An original Newcomen engine is now housed in Coronation Park, Dartmouth. Originally used at Griff Colliery at Nuneaton in Warwickshire, it was re-erected by the Newcomen Society to commemorate the 300th anniversary of Newcomen's birth.

DAWLISH
Waterwheel (SX962767)
Town centre
This prominent 30 ft cast-iron pitchback waterwheel used to drive a mill. Of rather sophisticated late construction it was built by the Exeter foundry of A Bodley.

EXETER
Follett Buildings (SX919923)
City centre
Situated high above the River Exe this four-storey tenement block was opened in 1874 as

the first expression of the policies of the City of Exeter Improved Industrial Dwellings Company. This Company had been formed by a group of leading citizens a year earlier and the buildings were named after the mayor – their chairman.

EXETER
Iron Footbridge (SX924927)
City centre
This delicate little iron bridge carries a footpath over The Close, Exeter. Built in 1814 it retains its original iron lamp brackets.

EXETER
Quay Warehouses (SX924927)
City centre
These two impressive warehouses were originally bonded stores. The white limestone warehouse bears the date 1835 and was probably the work of Robert Stribling Cornish while the red stone warehouse seems to have been built at a similar date. Beyond these are a number of small bonded stores excavated into the sandstone cliff.

EXETER
Town Quay (SX920921)
City centre
The old quay at Exeter still has a fishmarket roofed over but with open sides and a King's Beam, an official weighing machine, with the inscription cast on it: A & W C Bodley Iron Founders Exeter 1838.

HAYTOR VALE
Haytor Quarries and Tramway (SX759775)
4 miles W Bovey Tracey
These granite quarries flourished in the first half of the 19th century supplying stone for many of the monumental buildings in London. To facilitate transport a 4 ft 3 in gauge tramway was constructed *c* 1820 from the quarries to Ventiford Wharf on the Stover Canal at Teigngrace – a distance of *c* 10 miles. The rails were made of granite blocks 12 in wide and 9 in deep and vary in length from 4 ft to 8 ft. These were laid longitudinally and had

EXETER: *Quay Warehouses with traditional ferry.*

LANDCROSS: *Hallsannery Limekiln, one of a series of fine limekilns on the north Devon coast.*

flanges on the inside. The wagons, made of iron with flangeless wheels, ran in trains of 12 drawn by 18 horses in single file. A section from Holwell Quarry (SX751778) to the Manaton road had much granite *in situ*, though the tramway has been disused for over a century.

HONITON
Copper Castle Toll House (ST172005)
¼ mile W Honiton
This toll cottage lies on the A35 out of Honiton and is the sole survivor of the toll houses which barred all entrances to Honiton. Single-storeyed, and battlemented it retains its wooden porch and wrought-iron toll gates. The other toll houses had only wooden bars.

HUNTSHAW
Hallspill Limekiln (SS470236)
3 miles S Bideford off A386
This kiln is older than most along the north coast of Devon being early 18th-century. It is shaped in a figure of 8 with 2 kilns.

LANDCROSS
Hallsannery Limekiln (SS461245)
2 miles S Bideford on A386
Situated 2 miles upstream from Bideford this two-welled, 19th-century limekiln presents a striking appearance with its crennellations and Gothic arches. A railed slipway gives access from the river and the charging ramp behind is intact.

LYNTON
Cliff Railway (SS721496)
¼ mile W town centre
Opened in 1890, Lynton Cliff Railway is the highest such railway in Britain. It is 900 ft long and surmounts a rise of *c* 500 ft. It was operated by water counterbalanced tanks slung below the passenger cars.

MARY TAVY
Wheal Friendship Arsenic Calciner (SX508796)
3½ miles NE Tavistock off A386
The production of arsenic at the end of the 19th century lessened the severity of the slump in mining. This calciner worked until 1925 and the condensing chambers and flue are still very prominent.

MARY TAVY
Wheal Friendship Count House (SX505794)
3½ miles NE Tavistock off A386
This building with its overhanging upper storey in the centre served as both the mine captain's house and the count house.

MERRIVALE
Blowing House (SX553753)
4 miles E Tavistock off A384
This is probably one of the least ruinous of the many Dartmoor blowing houses – primitive smelters. Many of the essential features are still discernible including the furnace and a mould stone with a sample mould cut in its rim. The dimensions of the house, *c* 32 ft by 15 ft, are comparatively large for its type.

MORWELLHAM
Morwellham Harbour (SX445695)
4 miles SW Tavistock
During the first half of the 19th century Morwellham was a very busy river port being served by the Tavistock Canal, via its incline, and by an incline from Devon Great Consols Mine. Its traffic was adversely affected by the opening in 1859 of the Tavistock–Plymouth railway and the closure in 1900 of the Devon Great Consols finished it. Now however it is being restored by a recreation and educational trust and the habours, the tiled quays, the inclined planes, the waterwheels, ore shutes and limekilns can be seen.

NEWQUAY
Limekilns (SX454697)
4½ miles SW Tavistock
Limeburning was one of the most important industries of the Tamar Valley in the 19th century. This elaborately constructed group of kilns still has its cone-shaped wells 20 ft deep and 10 ft across unfilled. A waterwheel worked incline was used to carry the stone from the barges.

OKEHAMPTON
Meldon Viaduct (SX565924)
2½ miles SW Okehampton off A30
This wrought-iron trussed viaduct, 540 ft long, was completed in 1874 across the valley of the West Okement. It has six girder spans, supported by lattice piers, the tallest of which is 120 ft high. The railway has been abandoned for several years but the viaduct had a further period of usefulness carrying contractors' lorries engaged in the construction of reservoir nearby.

OKEHAMPTON: *Meldon Viaduct, last of the high metal viaducts in the country.*

OTTERY ST MARY
Tumbling Weir (SY095953)
5 miles SW Honiton B3176
This unusual circular weir at Ottery Serge Mills fed the water not required to drive the mill's waterwheel, through a tunnel under the factory to rejoin the river.

PLYMOUTH
Sutton Wharf (SX483543)
½ mile SE city centre
Although Sutton Harbour has a mercantile past stretching back several centuries it was from the 19th century that most of the present installations date. Sutton quay dates from 1813–15 and contains what is reputed to be the last *in situ* length of broad-gauge rail in the century. There are also traces of three railway turntables and a cast-iron hand crane built by John E Mare of Plymouth in 1850.

PLYMOUTH
Smeaton's Tower (SX478538)
½ mile S city centre
When the present Eddystone lighthouse was built in 1882 the upper portion of the lighthouse built by Smeaton in 1759 was dismantled and re-erected on Plymouth Hoe as a memorial.

PLYMOUTH
Marshmills Tramway Bridge (SX520568)
3½ miles E Plymouth off A38
Situated at the southern end of the 2 mile Cann Quarry tramway which opened in 1829 the bridge still preserved a section of the 4 ft 6 in tramway. The tramway, designed by Mr Soper, operated until 1900.

SEATON
Concrete Road Bridge (SY252899)
½ mile E town centre
Built in 1877 this is reputably the earliest surviving concrete road bridge in Britain. The designer, as if unsure of the appearance of the novel material caused simulated joints to be cut to give the appearance of masonry. There is also an associated toll house built of the same material.

STARCROSS
Atmospheric Railway Engine House
(SX977817)
4 miles N Dawlish
Brunel's atmospheric railway followed the coast from Exeter to Teignmouth which it reached in 1847. The tube was evacuated by steam engines situated at intervals along the line and their engine houses are now the most significant survival of this ill-fated experiment

in transport. The Starcross engine house is the most complete and is built in an Italianate style, parts of other houses are to be seen in Exeter and Totnes. There is also a fairly complete engine house at Torre, Torquay (SX898663) on an extension line which was never operational.

STICKLEPATH
Finch Brothers' Foundry (SX639940)
3½ miles E Okehampton on A30
This water-power site on the River Taw originally consisted of a corn mill and a cloth mill. In 1814 the latter was converted by William Finch into an edge tool factory and in 1835 the corn mill was taken over to house the grinding shop. Besides standard agricultural tools such as scythes and billhooks special scoops for the china clay industry were made. The machinery includes a pair of water driven 'tilt' hammers, a water-powered fan while other exhibits have been added to form a museum of rural industry.

TAVISTOCK
Tavistock Canal Wharf (SX479741)
Town centre
This canal was built 1803–17 and is fed by a leat from the River Tavy. Much of the basin in Tavistock has been filled in but several early 19th-century warehouses and cottages remain.

TAVISTOCK
Canal Tunnel – N Portal (SX462723)
3 miles SW Tavistock
Although this portal has an impressive datestone bearing the date 1803 this signifies merely the commencement of tunnelling, the tunnel was not opened until 1817. In the course of the 14 years tunnelling tin lodes were intercepted and worked. The tunnel itself is over 2 miles long and emerges high on the hillside above the Tamar. An incline connected the canal to Morwellham quay 237 ft below. The water in the canal now powers a small hydro-electric generating station at Morwellham.

TIVERTON
Industrial Housing (SS958120)
Town centre
When John Heathcoat moved from the Midlands to Tiverton in 1816 and commenced lace making in a vacant cotton mill, he brought more than just lace making techniques, he brought an industrial life style. Around his new factory there developed rows of industrial housing more reminiscent of the Midlands than of a rural market town in Devon. Terraces such as Elm Terrace, St Pauls Street (SS950126) Melbourne Street (SS949127) and Loughborough Street (SS947133) date from this development.

TOPSHAM
Bridge Mill (SX971883)
4 miles SE Exeter on A377
This 18th-century tide mill was working until 1960 when the machinery and waterwheel were dismantled and the pool infilled.

TUCKENHAY
Cider Vaults (SX818563)
3½ miles S Totnes
Besides the paper mill (*qv*) Tuckenhay village also contained a corn mill, sailcloth mill, a cider factory, quarries and extensive quays. Of these the cider factory has survived. It was originally water-powered but although the wheel has disappeared some of the old machinery survives and the cellars themselves are intact.

TUCKENHAY
Tuckenhay Paper Mill (SX817558)
3½ miles S Totnes
This large derelict mill was converted from cloth to paper making *c* 1830. It was situated at a water-power site close to tidal water. Vessels of 160 tons burden could reach the river quay below.

TWO BRIDGES
Gunpowder Mill (SX628769)
3 miles NE Princetown off B3212
The Dartmoor Powder Mills were opened in 1855 and closed in the 1890s. For safety reasons the various buildings are well spread out. There are 3 substantial wheel houses built of massive granite blocks each with a central wheel pit and flanking grinding rooms. Two small chimney stacks connected by long flues to their respective buildings stand amid ruins of several buildings of lighter construction. Board of Trade safety regulations required destruction of gunpowder plant upon disuse hence the dereliction. Associated residential buildings are incorporated in Power Mill Farm and a testing mortar guards the drive.

UFFCULME
Fox Bros Textile Mill (ST062122)
7 miles E Tiverton off A38
This site comprises a variety of buildings dating from the late 18th century to the 20th century. Almost all the power is supplied by the waterwheel and the steam engine which are coupled to either end of the line shafting. The waterwheel is 15 ft by 18 ft and was probably installed in 1885. The steam engine is a 320hp Pollet & Wigzell horizontal cross compound engine of 1910.

WEARE GIFFORD
Beam Aqueduct (SS473206)
4½ miles S Bideford on A386
In 1825–7, Rolle, a local landowner, constructed a canal to link Bideford and Torrington. The most significant remains of this 6-mile canal are of the massive masonry aqueduct at Beam House. It now carries a private drive to the house.

Dorset

Dorset, with the exception of the Isle of Portland, has seen relatively little industrial development. Most of its industrial relics are associated with either agricultural processing, transport, or water supply. Portland presents a totally alien appearance to the rest of the county. Its landscape has been ravaged by centuries of extraction of vast quantities of building stone. Its villages are much more akin to mining settlements of northern England.

BRIDPORT
Palmer's Brewery (SY465921)
¼ mile S of town centre on West Bay road
Unusually, part of this working brewery is still thatched while a 16 ft by 4 ft low breast metal waterwheel installed by Helyear (Helier) of Bridport in 1879 drives the brewery 3-throw water pump. There is also a vertical steam engine by Bram & May of Devizes which does similar duty as well as driving the sack hoist.

BROADMAYNE
Brick kiln (SY735872)
5½ miles SE Dorchester off A352
Broadmayne is locally famous for its bricks and there were at least 6 kilns worked in the vicinity. This, however, is the only one not completely ruinous. It is an updraught 'Suffolk' kiln – the most primitive type found in Dorset. It worked until 1940, and indeed is still loaded with a charge of bricks.

CASTLETON
Merchants Railway Incline (SY686744)
¼ mile N Fortuneswell
The Portland Railway differs from most industrial mineral tramways in that it was built by a public company authorized by Act of Parliament. Opened in 1826 it ran on the level from Priory Corner to the top of the incline whence it descended to the quay at Castleton. Horses were used on the level stretch while the incline was self-acting. Stone sleepers can still be seen on this incline.

CHRISTCHURCH
Tuckton Tram Bridge (SZ149923)
½ mile W of town centre on B3059
Originally there was a toll footbridge across the Stour at this point and when the tramcar undertaking replaced it with their bridge they had to retain the toll. The fine cast-iron crests are a survival from the tram era.

CORFE CASTLE
Tramway Tunnel (SY946831)
1 mile NW Corfe Castle below A351
Benjamin Foyk opened clay pits at Norden in 1795, and in 1806–7 built a tramway to a quay at Middlebere on Poole Harbour – the first iron tramway in Dorset. It remained in use until the 1880s but much of it has now disappeared. The tunnel, however, which takes the tramway under the Wareham to Corfe Castle road is still in good condition. The western portal bears the inscription 'BF 1807'. Little remains of the quay at Middlebere apart from a few rotten timbers and some masonry.

LANGTON HERRING
Limekiln (SY622825)
5 miles NW of Weymouth off B3157
Dorset is characterized by small agricultural limekilns set into the hillside fields. This example is somewhat grander than the norm and has an unusual tunnel-like entrance which may have been designed to improve the draw!

LITTON CHENEY
Brewery (SY553906)
6 miles E of Bridport off A35

This small rural brewery has an associated cider house which is still in use. Brewing itself ceased in 1895 but the interior is virtually unaltered since then.

LYME REGIS
The Cobb or Harbour (SY339915)
Lyme Regis harbour was a very early anchorage and part of the present harbour is medieval and constructed of huge rounded stones. Much of the harbour was reconstructed in 1825 by the Royal Engineers, a fact which is chronicled on a very detailed commemorative plaque. There are several interesting buildings on the jetties and one of them bears a toll board of 1879.

MILTON ABBAS
Brewery (ST804016)
7 miles SW Blandford off A354
The exterior of this old farm brewery, which is now run as a private museum, is substantially intact, while the interior retains some of the original fixtures.

PORTLAND BILL
Navigation Aids (*c* SY677683)
Extreme S of Isle
The Bill has for many centuries been an important navigation sighting, as well as a shipping hazard. Clustered round the point is a selection of navigation aids including 3 lighthouses, 2 of which are disused, and disused coastguard station, a triangular sighting point dated 1844 and a modern radar station.

PORTLAND
Windmill Stumps (SY691713)
½ mile S Easton
These are reputedly the only 2 remaining windmill towers in Dorset. They are probably quite early in date and are located within 100 yds of each other. One has still some shafting left.

PORTLAND
Durdle Pier (SY705718)
1 mile E Easton
When Portland Stone was in great demand there were many jetties along the east coast of Portland but very few remain. This example is the only 18th-century quay that has survived. The present crane is 19th-century by Galpin of Dorchester but there are records of at least 2 earlier ones on the site.

SHERBORNE
Public Weighing Machine (ST638164)
Town centre

This machine, which is believed to be pre-1850, is housed in a self-contained structure in Half Moon Street, in front of the Abbey.

SHERBORNE
Waterwheel Pump, Castleton (ST647168)
½ mile E town centre
The local water board built this small classical pump house in 1868 to house a 25 ft diameter waterwheel. The wheel, which is 3 ft 9 in and pitchback, is supplied with water from two different sources – the nearby stream and Sherborne Lake, necessitating two penstocks. The wheel, by means of a geared ring on the rim, drove 3, 6-in vertical ram pumps in an adjoining room. The pumps have now disappeared.

STURMINSTER MARSHALL
White Mill (ST958006)
4 miles W Wimborne off A31
This mill, though derelict, contains the oldest mill machinery in Dorset. Most of it is contemporary with the 1,776 date-stone on the arch over the watercourse. There were two waterwheels and two separate sets of drives to the stones and most of the machinery is entirely of wood.

STURMINSTER NEWTON
Sturminster Mill (ST782135)
½ mile S of town centre off A357
The fabric of the building is probably 18th-century though the foundations are considerably earlier. The mill now contains a 45-in Armfield 'British Engine' turbine and contemporary (1904) hammer mills.

STURMINSTER NEWTON
Footbridge (ST782143)
¼ mile W of town centre
This graceful cast-iron footbridge was erected over the River Stour in 1841 and is still in very good condition.

SWANAGE
Water Tower, Taunton Road (SZ032780)
½ mile S of town centre
Elaborate efforts were taken to disguise the function of this water tower when it was erected in 1886. It was built to resemble a medieval keep and no hint of its function is apparent from its exterior.

THORNECOMBE
Sadborow Mill (ST371010)
6 miles W Dorchester off A356

This small rural corn mill has recently been restored to working order. The 20 ft diameter overshot wheel is fed from the pond behind the mill. There is also a miniature wheel, 4 ft in diameter, which is supplied by a separate pipe and is probably used to generate electricity.

TOLLER FRATRUM
Farm Wheel and Launder (SY577972)
7 miles W Dorchester off A356
This huge farm wheel, c 24 ft by 3 ft, is mostly below ground level and is contained with its associated machinery in a small outhouse built into the steading of Toller Fratrum farm. The drive from the wheel came off a ring positioned halfway up the spokes. The pond which fed water onto the wheel has been filled in but the launder which supplied the pond is extant. It had to cross a deep road cutting and did so by means of a cast-iron trough made by Spake of Bridport and dated 1832.

TOLLER FRATRUM
Water-meadows (SY581976)
7 miles W Dorchester off A356
Water-meadows were very important to Dorset agriculture from the 16th to the late 19th century. There were probably some 4,000 acres of meadow in 1800 but now little remains in use. These meadows at Toller Fratrum have been disused for several years but a fine set of iron sluices and hatch gates, manufactured by Galpin of Dorchester (1840–70), remain.

UPWEY
Upwey Mill (SY663851)
3½ miles N Weymouth
This large Georgian corn mill is still in regular commercial use. It is dated 1802 and is driven by a broad overshot wheel placed centrally in the complex.

WEYMOUTH
Sutton Poyntz Turbine Pump (SY706839)
3 miles NE Weymouth A353
In the grounds of Sutton Poyntz pumping station is a small stone building of 1856 which contains the survivor of a pair of jet reaction turbines installed in 1857 when Hawksley was consulting engineering to the water board. The installation was manufactured by Cook of Glasgow with 2 double-acting ram pumps supported by a classical cast-iron frame containing a vertical drive shaft and bevel gearing.

Durham

The new administrative county of Durham is only a rump of the former county, having lost most of its major maritime outlets on the Rivers Tyne, Wear, and Tees. Nevertheless, it retains many industrial monuments of the greatest significance associated with pioneer developments in lead and coal mining, steel manufacture and railways.

AYCLIFFE
Toll House (NZ285228)
5 miles N Darlington on A67
An early 19th-century toll house erected by the Boroughbridge and Durham Turnpike Trust. Very few toll houses now survive in County Durham, hence the significance of this modernized example.

BARNARD CASTLE
Demesne Mill, Grey Lane (NZ053158)
½ mile SE of town centre
A rubble-built corn mill on the River Tees utilizing a natural outcrop as a weir. Three-storey and rectangular in plan, it still houses a 15 ft diameter waterwheel and some iron gearing.

BARNARD CASTLE
Thorngate Mill (NZ049160)
¼ mile S of town centre
An early 19th-century weaving mill on the River Tees at the end of Thorngate – a street with 3-storey weavers' cottages with workshops on the uppermost floor. The mill building is a simple 4-storey stone rectangle of 10 bays with a projecting round staircase wing.

BEAMISH
North of England Open Air Museum
(NZ212549)
2 miles NE of Stanley
In the grounds of Beamish Hall is located one of the largest open air museums in the country. A fine farmstead with horse-wheel house

WEYMOUTH: *Sutton Poyntz Turbine Pump – unique installation by noted water engineer Hawksley.*

complete with rebuilt horse wheel is the only exhibit on original site but many notable monuments are being re-erected including Beamish vertical colliery winder, Rowley Station and a coal drop from Seaham Harbour.

BURNOPFIELD
Lintzford Paper Mill (NZ151571)
1 mile SW of Rowlands Gill on A694
A fine range of 19th-century industrial buildings on a site used for paper making since the end of the 18th century. Paper continued to be made until 1924. It is now a printing-ink factory and is reached by a graceful masonry bridge over the River Derwent.

BISHOP AUCKLAND
Newton Cap Viaduct (NZ206304)
N of town centre on the A689
This imposing stone-built viaduct over the River Wear with its 10 rough faced arches provides a fine contrast with the nearby medieval road bridge.

CASTLESIDE
Healeyfield Smelt Flues (NZ078485)
1½ miles SW Consett off A68
A very complex system of lead smelting flues winding across a small hill to the N of the site of the Healeyfield smelt mill which operated from 1805–1913.

COLD HESLEDON
Dalton Pumping Station (NZ411469)
2 miles SW Seaham on A19
Designed by Hawksley for the Sunderland & South Shields Water Company, Dalton pumping station is a handsome example of

Victorian industrial architecture though its prominent ornamental chimney has been truncated. The engine house contains a pair of 1877 Davy Bros Cornish beam engines.

CONSETT
Hounsgill Caves (NZ097490)
1 mile S Consett
These 'caves', a local curiosity, are in fact the product of sandstone quarrying, initially open and latterly underground by the pillar and stall method.

DARLINGTON
Coniscliffe Road Pumping Station
(NZ254139)
2½ miles W Darlington on A67
The Darlington Corporation Waterworks on Coniscliffe Road contain a series of engine houses dating back to 1849. A Teesdale Bros compound rotative beam engine of 1904 has survived and also a rare set of suction gas pumping plant installed by Hornsby & Sons.

DARLINGTON
North Road Railway Station (NZ289157)
½ mile N of town centre off A167
Built in 1842, this station though still in use has been partially converted into a museum to commemorate the 150th anniversary of the opening of the Stockton & Darlington Railway in 1825. It contains several notable locomotives including Locomotion No. 1 and a 46 ft landscaped layout of the original railway.

DARLINGTON
Skerne Bridge (NZ292156)
½ mile N of town centre off A167
Though in a setting scarcely recognizable from John Dobbin's famous painting of the opening of the Stockton & Darlington Railway in 1825, the elegant stone railway bridge over the River Skerne designed by Ignatius Bonomi is largely intact.

EAST HEDLEYHOPE
Coke Ovens (NZ166406)
3½ miles E Tow Law off B6301
A battery of mid-19th-century beehive coke ovens survive in good enough condition for their layout and construction to be studied.

EGGLESTON
Saddle House and Viaduct (NY988248)
5 miles NW Barnard Castle on B6278
This small stone building with its stone flagged roof is a rare survival from the days when pack horses were the only means of transporting ore from the lead mines to the smelt mills. Saddles and panniers were kept in this house which is alongside a viaduct constructed by the London Lead Co to improve access to a smelt mill.

FROSTERLEY
Bishopley Limekilns (NZ029360)
9 miles W Crook off A689
A range of a dozen mid-19th-century sandstone-built limekilns constructed for the Wear Valley Railway.

HAMSTERLEY
Derwentcote Cementation Furnace
(NZ131565)
4 miles N Consett off A694
A unique 18th-century cementation furnace survives in the Derwent valley – an area with a long tradition of iron working and sword making. The furnace itself is a stone-built conical hovel quite unlike the only other, but later, cementation furnaces that have survived in Sheffield. The path alongside the furnace and its associated building leads to a leat at the valley bottom around which there is fragmentary evidence of an extensive works.

HASWELL
Haswell Engine House (NZ374423)
6 miles E Durham off B1283
A massively built stone engine house probably once containing a Cornish pumping engine. The enormously thick bob wall with its beam arch are the most easily identifiable features of this impressive ruin.

SEAHAM
Londonderry Station (NZ413504)
1 mile N Seaham
A small station illustrating the immense influence and wealth of the aristocracy on whose land coal was mined. It was built for the private use of the Marquis of Londonderry on his privately promoted Londonderry Seaham and Sunderland Railway of 1854.

SEAHAM
Seaham Harbour (NZ435495)
A coal shipping harbour developed from 1828 onwards by the Marquis of Londonderry was entirely a creation of rail transport. Until a few years ago it contained the last coal drop – a massive counter balanced cast-iron beam which lowered coal trucks onto the decks of vessels in order to minimize coal breakage. This drop which dated from c 1850 has been dismantled for re-erection at Beamish Open Air Museum. The associated township was initially laid out by John Dobson, the Newcastle architect, and the harbour was enlarged progressively into the 20th century.

HAMSTERLEY: *Derwentcote Cementation Furnace, the only 18th-century cementation furnace in the country.*

SHILDON
Brusselton Incline, Sleeper Blocks and Bridge (NZ211256)
1 mile W Shildon off B6283
A fine masonry bridge of *c* 1825 carries the Brusselton Incline of the Stockton & Darlington Railway over the former access to a farm. The embankment still retains many stone sleeper blocks *in situ*.

SHILDON
Hackworth's House (NZ233258)
⅓ mile E of A6072 in Shildon
This pair of 19th-century cottages stand adjacent to the site of the Soho engine works where Timothy Hackworth did so much of his pioneering locomotive design and building. A plaque records that Hackworth himself lived in the building and it has been converted into a museum.

SOUTH HETTON
Railway Inclines (NZ382455–432494)
SW Seaham
Tandem gravity inclines survive on the South Hetton mineral railway of 1835 leading to Seaham Harbour. These were the last such inclines to work in the country and their future is in doubt.

STANHOPE
Snow Fence (NZ020451)
5 miles NE Stanhope off B6278
The Stanhope & Tyne Railroad opened in 1834 connecting Weardale to South Shields – a length of some 38 miles. It reached a height of 1445 ft AOD across the bleak moors and sections of its line were protected by a snow fence constructed of stone sleeper blocks. A section some 100 yards long has survived N of Waskerley reservoir.

TANFIELD
Causey Arch (NZ201559)
2 miles N Stanley off A6076
A spectacular monument to the prehistory of railways. The masonry Causey Arch was built by Ralph Wood in 1727 to carry a horse drawn waggonway from the collieries of Colonel Liddell to connect with the main system of waggonways which led to the Tyne. The arch has a span of 105 ft and now carries a footpath 80 ft above the Tanfield Beck.

WEARDALE
Kilhope Lead Mill (NY827429)
On B6293 12 miles W Stanhope, 7 miles E Alston

TANFIELD: *Causey Arch, the earliest major 'railway' bridge in the world.*

This crushing mill at the head of Weardale was built *c* 1860. Its most prominent feature is the 33 ft 6 in diameter waterwheel which originally drove 4 sets of crushing rollers. Although the site has been landscaped as a picnic site, workshop buildings and ore bins also survive.

WEST AUCKLAND
Gaunless Bridge Abutments (NZ186265)
¼ mile E village off A688
These abutments once carried the world's first iron railway bridge by which the Stockton & Darlington Railway of 1825 crossed the River Gaunless. The ironwork itself is now on display outside the National Railway Museum, York.

WHORLTON
Suspension Bridge (NZ107145)
4 miles SE Barnard Castle
An early suspension bridge over the River Tees below Barnard Castle. Built by Newcastle architect/civil engineer John Green in 1829–31, it has a span of 173 ft and carries a minor road 30 ft above the river.

Essex

Essex, with the exception of the south-western portion of the county absorbed by Greater London, is a county whose economy has been historically geared to supplying rural produce to the huge adjacent market of London. Hence it is natural that corn mills, whether wind, water or steam driven, should figure largely in the gazetteer. Even the heavier industries that did develop such as foundries, and there were some 25 foundries in Essex in 1850, concentrated on servicing this trade producing predominantly items of agricultural machinery. Firms such as Ransomes, Bentalls, Colemaud & Martans in the 19th century developed beyond the immediate local market and established Essex an important world supplier of all types of agricultural machinery.

The east coast of the county was favourably situated for both the export of malt to London and for the import of barley from north Essex and East Anglia. Hence, before railways provided greater flexibility of location, large complexes of maltings developed along estuaries such as that of the Stour. Many maltings, such as those at Mistley, successfully survived competition of the rail based maltings and indeed made use of railways themselves to the extent of building their own sidings.

In later years Essex was also to provide Londoners with leisure amenities and a rush of seaside resorts grew up typified by Clacton and Southend, with their famous piers.

ARDLEIGH
Spring Valley Mill (TM038277)
3 miles NE of Colchester off A137
Situated on the Salary Brook, this 3-storey mill dates from the late 18th century though much of the machinery is 19th-century. The overshot waterwheel, 13 ft 6 in diameter by 4 ft 9 in wide, is entirely of iron and drove 3 pairs of stones.

CLACTON ON SEA
Pier (TM179140)
Town centre
Designed by P Bruff, this pier was built in 1870 of memel and extended in 1890–3 in pine to a length of 1180 ft. The iron pavilion provided with these extensions was supplied by Murdoch & Cameron of Glasgow.

COGGESHALL
Abbey Mill (TL855222)
6 miles E of Braintree off A120
This splendid weatherboarded mill 100 ft long was built *c* 1600 on the site of an earlier monastic mill. Originally a textile fulling mill, it was converted to a flour mill in the mid-19th century and only ceased work in 1960. The machinery, which was driven by a 12 ft diameter 7½ ft wide waterwheel, is complete and the pit wheel is dated 1840. There is, however, little trace of the steam engine that was added soon after conversion to corn milling.

COLCHESTER
Bourne Mill, Bourne Road (TM006238)
½ mile S of town centre off B1025
The structure in which this corn mill is housed has a long history. It was built in 1591 by Sir Thomas Lucas, possibly as a fishing lodge and acquired in the 17th century by Dutch immigrants for a cloth mill. In the mid-19th century it was converted to a flour mill with 3 pairs of stones drive by a 22 ft diameter overshot wheel. The walls are built of freestone rubble and brick with stepped, Dutch style, gable ends and mullioned windows. The dormer windows and loading gantry were probably added in the 19th century. The National Trust now owns the mill.

COLCHESTER
Water Tower, Balkerne Hill (TL993252)
Town centre
Dominating the skyline of central Colchester this massive brick water tower is 105 ft high and was constructed in 1882.

GREAT BARDFIELD
Gibraltar Mill (TL680307)
7 miles NE of Great Dunmow off B1057
Reputedly this windmill started as a smock mill in 1680, was converted into a cottage in the early 18th century and in 1760 was heightened and reconverted into a tower mill. It has now been converted back into a house but much of the machinery has been incorporated.

HALSTEAD
Townford Mill (TL813304)
Town centre
In 1825 Samuel Courtauld and P A Taylor acquired the corn mill at Halstead and converted it to a textile mill for the production of mourning crape. The mill has 3 floors which contained different stages in the process viz

HARWICH: *Treadmill Crane re-erected from the naval dockyard.*

drawing, winding and 'silk mills' respectively. A beam engine replaced water power in 1824 and gas lighting in 1840. The mill has been frequently extended and modernized but the early core is still recognizable and an early Courtauld loom for weaving silk mourning crape has been preserved.

HARWICH
Navigation Light Towers, Dover Court (TM253308)
1 mile S of town centre
These lights which date from 1862 marked the approach to the Port of Harwich by a channel which has now been superceded. The shore light, supported by 6 iron columns, is 2-storeyed with an external iron stairway and galleried round the upper lamp room – some 50 ft in height. The off-shore light is smaller and supported by 2 V-shaped legs. Both lights are now in rather poor position but are at the southern end of a very interesting section of coastline which besides 2 further abandoned lighthouses and the dockyard crane (*qv*) has the remains of 19th- and 20th-century fortifi-

cations including a well preserved redoubt of the Napoleonic period.

HARWICH
Shipyard Crane (TM262325)
¼ mile S of town centre
This treadmill operated crane was installed in 1667 in the Harwich Navy Yard and was removed to its present site in 1928. The 2 wheels are 16 ft diameter by 3 ft 10 in wide on a common axle of 13½ in diameter which serves as the drum for the chains. The crane head consists of a horizontal beam fitted with pulley, the jib has a projection of 17 ft 10 in.

HEYBRIDGE
Bentall's Foundry (TL855081)
1 mile NE of Maldon B1022
Bentall's Trafalgar Engineering Works were probably established on this site to the S of the Chelmer & Blackwater Navigation *c* 1815. The works produced a great variety of agricultural machinery diversifying in the 20th century with engines and motor vehicles. Most of the 14-acre site is due to be cleared but the foundry is to be retained and a small museum is to be opened on the new site, across the Chelmer & Blackwater Navigation, to house such relics as

the early 19th-century Bentall plough and a restored Bentall motor car.

HIGH ONGAR
Braces Timber Yard (TL566037)
10 miles W of Chelmsford off A122
This sawmill is powered by a 1912 Garrat of Leiston steam engine with 2 cylinders and a 5 ft diameter flywheel. Transmission is by a 40 ft long belt and the engine is fuelled by offcuts from the saw. The sawmill is due to be electrified in the near future.

LITTLE DUNMOW
Parish Pump (TL656216)
1½ miles E of Great Dunmow off A120
This 7 ft cast-iron pump was erected in 1887 to mark Queen Victoria's Golden Jubilee. It was made by Warners of Cripplegate, London.

LANGFORD
Steam Pumping Engine (TL834088)
2 miles NW of Maldon off B1019
The Langford Waterworks retain a 400hp triple expansion vertical steam engine installed by the Lilleshall Co of Oakengates in 1927. Though the engine was superceded by electric pumps in 1966 it has been preserved by the water authority and there are proposals to convert the engine house into a museum of water supply and steam power.

MALDON
Beeleigh Steam Corn Mill (TL839083)
1 mile NW of Maldon
Situated on the site of a former watermill and served by the Chelmer & Blackwater Navigation, this mill has an 'A' frame steam engine of 1845 by Wentworth of Wandsworth which drove 5 pairs of stones on the floor above. The boiler would appear to be original – cylindrical, egg-ended made of overlapping iron plates. The engine which has a 10 ft 4 in beam is compound with cylinders of 15 in and 11 in outside diameters respectively and drove via a transmission room on the same level. The engine may be restored *in situ* by its owners, The Essex Water Co, or it may be moved to a projected museum at Langford Waterworks (*qv*) just across the Chelmer & Blackwater Navigation.

MALDON
Saltworks (TL854072)
NE of town centre
The River Blackwater is highly saline because of the great expanses of mudflats in the estuary. The works of the Maldon Crystal Salt Co draw water in at times of maximum salinity, filter it and heat it in 2 square stone 'baths' 10 ft by 10 ft with a furnace below. Evaporation is facilitated by the open nature of the roof tiling. Upon cooling large pyramidal crystals of salt are precipitated. Reputedly this is the only works of its kind producing salt by this traditional method. Recent archaeological investigations lend some support to the speculation that the present 18th-century works are on a site which the Romans may have used for saltworks.

MISTLEY
Maltings (TM117320)
1 mile E of Manningtree on B1352
The estuary of the River Stour at Mistley is lined by large late 19th-century maltings which are still in operation and make use of both water borne and rail borne supplies. These large maltings, utilizing a multi-storey design, huge kilns with wire mesh floors, mechanical rakes and wide germinating floors, contrast well with the early 19th-century maltings nearby (*qv*).

MISTLEY
Old Maltings (TM109319)
1 mile E of Manningtree on B1352
These maltings, adjacent to Mistley High Street, were erected between 1807 and 1828. Although most of them were in use until 1967 many still retain their original timber roof structure. They are characteristic examples of manually operated 19th-century maltings having only 2 storeys, small anthracite-fired drying kilns with perforated tile floors, open steeping tanks and narrow, tile surfaced germinating floors.

MOUNTNESSING
Post Mill (TQ635980)
3 miles NE of Brentwood off A12
This post mill stands in a public park by the old A12 and is owned by Essex County Council.

ORSETT
Baker Street Mills (TQ633813)
4½ miles N of Tilbury off A128
Adjacent to a dilapidated smock mill is quite a separate steam-driven flour mill. The 'A' frame beam engine, reputedly by Middleton of Southwark *c* 1840, has lost all its brass and even its beam but the cylinder, piston rod flywheel of 8 ft diameter remain. Steam was provided by a traction engine boiler.

ROYDON
Telephone Kiosk (TL403103)
3 miles W of Harlow
The telephone for the caravan site at Roydon

Mill is housed in a most unusual kiosk. Made in 1924 it was the Birmingham Civic Society's entry in a competition for cast-iron telephone kiosks. The competition was won by Sir Giles Gilbert Scott.

SHEERING
Maltings (TL489149)
3 miles NE of Harlow of B183
On the E bank of the Stort is a fine complex of maltings dating from the mid-19th century. Parts are still in use but the main range of 1865 with 6 pairs of circular brick kilns and cones is disused.

SOUTHEND
Pier (TL890830)
This, the longest pleasure pier of its kind, was built in 1889 to replace an earlier wooden structure of 1830 which with its 1846 additions stretched to $1\frac{1}{4}$ miles and was serviced by a horse tramway. The New Pier, on cast-iron piers, was designed by James Brunlees and built by Arrol Bros of Glasgow. It is 2360 yards long and carries an electric railway. The Prince George extensions of 1927 are of reinforced concrete. It has recently been badly damaged by fire and storm.

STANSTED MOUNTFITCHET
Drinking Fountain (TL520248)
9 miles S of Saffron Walden off A11
This beautiful canopy fountain was cast by Messrs Macfarlane & Co of Glasgow and fixed to its base by J L Glasscock, the Bishop Stortford builder. It was erected in 1871 at a cost of nearly £90 and, rather than the usual commemorative text, carries the admonition 'Keep the Pavement Dry'.

STANSTED MOUNTFITCHET
Tower Windmill (TL510248)
9 miles S of Saffron Walden off A11
Built in 1787, this 5-storeyed mill last worked *c* 1910 but has recently been restored. The machinery including 3 pairs of stones is comprehensive.

STOCK
Stock Windmill (TQ698989)
5 miles S of Chelmsford off B1007
A red brick tower mill with 5 floors owned and maintained by Essex County Council. It has a large, boat-shaped white painted cap but no fantail or stage. The drive to the 3 pairs of stones is by an iron upright shaft passing through 3 floors to a great spur wheel under driving the stones.

TERLING
Smock Mill (TL765150)
4 miles W of Witham
This windmill was moved from Cressing 4 miles away *c* 1832 and was worked until 1950 when the miller was killed by the machinery. The mill then became rather dilapidated but in 1973 underwent drastic reconstruction in conversion to a house. Some of the machinery has been retained for decorative purposes.

THAXTED
Tower Windmill (TL610309)
$7\frac{1}{2}$ miles SE of Saffron Walden on A130
Built in 1804 of local bricks, this mill has 4 floors and 3 pairs of stones. It has recently been restored and the machinery is virtually complete and it is hoped to have the sails turning within the near future.

THORRINGTON
Thorrington Tide Mill (TM083194)
7 miles SE of Colchester off B1027
Standing in a hollow at the head of the Arlesford Creek, this pine-built 3-storeyed white weatherboarded tide mill dates from 1831 and is in reasonable condition with its machinery fairly complete. However, only the ironwork of the 12 ft diameter waterwheel remains. The mill pond covers 10 acres and is occasionally used to sluice the channel leading to the mill.

WICKAM BISHOPS
Timber Trestle Viaducts (TL824118)
$1\frac{1}{2}$ miles S of Witham off B1018
The Maldon to Witham railway was constructed in 1848 and survived until 1965. These 2 viaducts were employed to cross the shallow Blackwater valley. Constructed of massive baulks of timber, the southern viaduct is 60 yards long and the northern 45 yards long.

WITHAM
Sauls Bridge (TL824139)
$\frac{1}{2}$ mile S of Witham on B1018
A single 18 ft span cast-iron bridge with Ransome & Sons Ipswich 1814 cast on E face.

Gloucestershire

Despite its rural image, Gloucestershire is rich in industrial monuments of a wide variety. These range from early iron working sites in the Forest of Dean to the woollen mills of the Stroud valleys, from derelict 18th-century canals to the ship canal connecting Gloucester and Sharpness, from the tramways of the Forest of Dean to the remains of one of the country's great estuarine railway bridges over the Severn. The Severn itself was a vital transport artery with several small harbours and river ports such as Lydney, Sharpness, Gloucester and Tewkesbury and a series of fine bridges such as those by Telford at Mythe and Over.

BIBURY
Arlington Mill (SP114068)
6 miles NE of Cirencester on A433
This water-driven corn mill is maintained privately as a museum of cornmilling and is open to visitors. Besides working cornmilling machinery from North Cerney there are collections of tools of rural trades and period furniture.

BREAM
Devil's Chapel Scowles (SO607046)
3 miles NW of Lydney off B4231
Iron ore has probably been dug from outcrops in the Forest of Dean since *c* 450 BC. Extraction was greatly expanded in the Roman period and continued until the outcrops were exhausted and underground techniques had to be developed. The worked out areas of outcrop are called scowles and present a fantastically contorted landscape of pits and intervening pillars. The Devil's Chapel is a very extensive area of such scowles.

BREAM
Flour Mill Colliery (SO606068)
4 miles NW of Lydney off B4234
This group of late 19th-century masonry buildings with red brick dressings is possibly the most complete complex of colliery buildings to survive in the Dean coalfield. They comprise offices, stores, workshops and an engine house; it is now a chemical works.

CAINCROSS
Ebley Mill (SO829046)
2 miles W of Stroud on A419
The Old and New Ebley Mills are some of the most impressive stone built mills in the country. They date from 1800 and 1823 respectively and replaced former corn and fulling mills on the site. The 5-storey New Mill has an impressive slate roofed turret designed by Bodley in the late 19th century and there is a slender hexagonal stone chimney. The mill was formerly powered by 5 waterwheels and a steam engine but the mill pond has been drained.

CAM
Cam Mill (ST754999)
1 mile N of Dursley off A4135
A very extensive site, still working, built mainly in red brick. Most of the buildings were rebuilt *c* 1815–18, and the main mill building was lowered from 5 to 4 storeys. A clock tower was added later, along with various other buildings. The mill is one of the few still weaving wool in Gloucestershire.

CANNOP
New Road Level 'Free' Mine (SO603114)
4 miles SW of Cinderford off B4226
This complex of corrugated-iron sheds by the roadside is probably the largest free mine still operating. These mines are typically transient in nature and leave very few traces other than spoil heaps when they cease operating.

CHALFORD
St Mary's Mills (SO886023)
3 miles SE of Stroud on A419
The water mill and one other building remain, along with an impressive clothier's house nearby. The mill itself is a simple rectangular four-storey building of 8 bays, the windows being divided by stone mullions as at Ebley There is an attic row of weaver's windows facing east, with a clock in the centre and a bell over. A 4-storey building at right angles to the mill and several outhouses remain. The mill is in local stone with stone slate roof.

CHELTENHAM
Electricity Sub-station, Clarence Road (SO947225)
¼ mile W of city centre
This attractive small three-storey brick building with its elaborate terracotta detail housed the transformer and distribution switchboards for the AC supply generated at the central station near the High Street. When it was opened in 1895 it was only of two storeys with a small arched construction parapet above and it also housed a testing room, a photometric room and stores. The present uppermost storey was added a little later to provide residential accommodation for the attendant.

CHELTENHAM
Penfold Pillar Boxes
Cheltenham has a wealth of ornamental ironwork including both fine wrought and cast-iron balconies and porches, 'Dragon, motif lamp posts and 'Penfold' pillarboxes. Eight of these Victorian pillar boxes remain in Cheltenham, each with slight variations in the design, particularly of the flap and in the presence or absence of the acorn on the top. All are octagonal with cast crests and other lettering.

Montpellier Walk	SO944218
Bayshill Road	SO944222
Pittville Spa	SO953237
Pittville Circus Road	SO960225
Lansdown Road	SO938217
St Pauls Road	SO948231
College Lawn	SO952213
Douro Road	SO220940

CHIPPING CAMPDEN
Old Silk Mills (SP150389)
S of town centre
This mid-18th century stone-built water-driven silk mill went out of use in 1880. A succession of occupants followed, the latest being craft workshops.

CINDERFORD
Guns Mills (SO675159)
2 miles NE of Cinderford

This monument, one of the finest remaining examples of an early charcoal blast furnace in the country, is in a rather dilapidated state. The furnace was in operation by 1635 and rebuilt in 1682–3 (the dates are cast on lintels). It was converted into a paper mill in 1743 and the furnace itself used as a stairwell – hence the openings cut in the walls. The hearth is missing but apart from the furnace tower the casting floor to the south, the bellows room and the wheel pit to the west have survived.

CLEARWELL
Clearwell Caves (SO587083)
3 miles S of Coleford off B4228
This commercial show mine is typical of old iron mines in the Forest of Dean prior to the Deep Phase of mining which began c 1800. These early mines started at the outcrop and followed the ore down, producing a series of caverns connected by narrow passages. Clearwell is now operated as a mining museum with laid paths and electric lighting.

COLEFORD
Whitecliffe Furnace (SO568103)
½ mile S of Coleford on B4228
Construction of this coke-fired furnace began in 1799 but a series of natural setbacks caused its original backer Samuel Botham to return to Uttoxeter before it was completed in 1804. In 1810 David Mushet, the noted Scots metallurgist, entered into the association of partners at Whitecliff and conducted some of his experiments at the site. The furnace was dismantled several years later after Mushet had withdrawn and all that remains is the free standing furnace with its membrane charging wall. The furnace is 40 ft high and 40 ft by 45 ft in plan, the hearth has gone but the composition of the shaft lining is clearly visible.

COATES
Eastern Portal Sapperton Tunnel (SO965006)
4 miles W of Cirencester off A419
Sapperton Tunnel is 2¼ miles long and was constructed between 1783 and 1789 to the design of Robert Whitworth. The eastern entrance is at the end of a deep cutting and is of a classical design with 2 attached Doric half-columns supporting a simple entablature. Niches on either side were apparently intended for statues but were never filled. The nearby Tunnel House was originally built for the workmen constructing the tunnel and is now an inn.

DRYBROOK
Fairplay Pit, Bull Engine House (SO659165)
2 miles SW of Mitcheldeam off A4136

This low massively built masonry engine house contained a 76 in cylinder bull engine with a 30 ft under beam. The cylinder was positioned directly over the dressed masonry lined shaft and had a stroke of 12 ft. The internal layout of the engine house is governed by this arrangement. While the engine was primarily used for pumping, the blocked up arch in the end wall has been suggested as possible access to winding, alternatively the balance tank of the underbeam may have been placed externally.

FRAMPTON-ON-SEVERN
Bridgekeeper's Lodge (SO746085)
10 miles SW of Gloucester off A38 on B4071
In the mid-19th century the Gloucester & Sharpness Canal Company built a series of lodges to house the bridge keepers in charge of their swing-bridge along the canal. The lodges, which are finished in stucco and have slate roofs, each have a classical portico supported by Doric columns, and with minor variations, conform to a standard pattern. The example at Frampton is illustrative of this pattern while other similar lodges can be found at Purton Bridge (SO692042), Ryalls Bridge (SO738050), Splatt Bridge (SO743067) and Parkend Bridge (SO778108).

GLOUCESTER
Docks (SO825185)
¼ mile SW of city centre off A38
When the Gloucester & Sharpness canal was finally completed in 1827 vessels of 750 tons could reach Gloucester but cargoes for further up the Severn had to be trans-shipped. This *entrepôt* trade caused a series of multi-storey warehouses to be built around the Docks. Many of these handsome warehouses were designed by Robert Mylne and almost all the buildings, including the flour mills, kilns and box factory are Listed as Buildings of Historic and Architectural interest.

GLOUCESTER
Over Bridge (SO816196)
1 mile W of city beside A40
This fine masonry bridge across the River Severn on the outskirts of Gloucester was designed by Telford in 1827 and opened in 1831. The body of the arch is an ellipse with a chord line of 150 ft and a 35 ft rise; but the stones of the external arch are set to segments of the same chord with a rise of only 13 ft producing a chamfered arch which eases the passage of flood water. In spite of the fact that the crown of the arch sank 10 ins on the removal of the centring the bridge carried

heavy traffic until recently when it was by-passed.

GLOUCESTER
Pillar Warehouse, Baker's Quay (SO826180)
¼ mile SW of city centre off A38
Built in 1849 on the side of the Gloucester and Sharpness Canal the salient feature of this double-span brick warehouse is that the upper 3 floors of the 2 western bays overhang the quayside and are supported on a colonnade of 7 large cast-iron Doric columns.

INGLESHAM
Canal Roundhouse (SU204988)
1 mile S of Lechlade off A361
It was common for canal companies to build lengthmen's cottages at suitable places along their waterways. The Thames & Severn Canal had a peculiar roundhouse variety. These circular towers contained 3 rooms one above the other, the 2 upper rooms being connected by a narrow curving stairway built into the thickness of the wall. In some cases the roof was an inverted cone for collecting rainwater.

KINGSWOOD
New Mill (ST737930)
1 mile W of Wooton under Edge on B4058
This fine brick-built, 5-storey mill is set in attractive grounds and fronted by a substantial mill pond. The main mill building itself, with its central staircase tower surmounted by a clock, is virtually empty – only the lower storeys are used for storage. The present offices, however, have incorporated the original wool stove, counting house and former dyehouses, many of which are older than the main mill.

LITTLEDEAN
Gaol (SO674137)
1 mile E of Cinderford on A4151
This model prison was built *c* 1790 to the designs of William Blackburn who followed the guide lines of the noted prison reformer Sir Onesiphorus Paul. The latter advocated a new type of prison building in which inmates were segregated according to age and sex. Littledean prison, apart from the removal of the tread wheel, remains much as it was when built.

LYDNEY
Lydney Harbour (SO633019–651014)
1 mile S of Lydney
Lydney was Bullo Pill's main rival as port to the Forest of Dean. The ancient harbour at Lydney was adversely affected by changes in the course of the River Severn and eventually

GLOUCESTER: *Pillar Warehouse Bakers Quay on the banks of the Gloucester and Sharpness Canal.*

the Lydney and Lydbrook Tramway cut a new canal to the river in 1813. A tidal basin was added in 1821 and this with the lower section of the canal, almost a mile in length, comprise the present harbour. Apart from the locks, which are still in use, there are the masonry foundations of coal shutes on the southern bank, a hand operated swing-bridge and harbour and shipyard offices.

NAILSWORTH
Egypt Mill (ST849999)
¼ mile N of Nailsworth on A46
This 2-storey, stone built, mill is an example of the larger kind of pre-factory mills. It consists of a single range of 2 sections, the western section with partially blocked horizontal headed windows may be older than the eastern section which has segmental headed windows. The site has been in use since the 17th century mostly as a woollen mill but for a time as a log mill then a corn mill. A handsome gabled clothier's house adjoins the mill.

NAILSWORTH
Dunkirk Mills (SO845005)
¾ mile N of Nailsworth on A46

A very fine range of mill buildings of various dates from the late 18th to early 19th centuries. The main range is 4 storeys high, flanked by several buildings of other dates, *viz* 1805, 1827, and 1855. Reputedly there are 3 waterwheels still *in situ*.

NEWNHAM
Bullo Pill (SO690099)
Bullo Pill is a tidal creek used until 1800 for boatbuilding. The Forest of Dean Tramroad developed it as their main outlet and the South Wales Railway and later the Great Western Railway followed suit and used it as a port until 1926. It was thus, despite its present desolation, of great historical importance in the development of the Forest of Dean coalfield. There are the remains of the tidal lock and the water storage basins at the creek head but little remains of the coal shutes which were once the *raison d'être* of the port.

NORTHWAY
Level Crossing Keeper's House (SO926342)
The Birmingham and Gloucester Railway built, *c* 1840, standard 2-storey lodges to their crossing based on a tollhouse model. To reduce the incidence of window tax all windows were narrow and on only 2 elevations – usually fronting the railway itself. The example at Northway fronts the lane but

otherwise conforms. It is brick built, with string coursing and 2 projecting bays.

NEWLAND
Redbrook Incline Overbridge (SO536103)
This steeply angled masonry structure straddling the Welsh/Gloucs border carried the incline of the Redbrook Tinplate Branch of the Monmouth Tramroad over the Coleford to Monmouth road. The tramroad was opened in 1812 to link Howler's Slade, Coleford and Monmouth. The eastern façade of the bridge presents a single arch over the road and a circular aperture to the north while the western façade, besides the road arch, has three blind arches to the south one of which spans the major mill leat of the valley.

RUSPIDGE
Lightmoor Engine House (SO641121)
In the mid-19th century the coal mine at Lightmoor had an impressive range of steam power. This fine masonry engine house contained one of the larger beam engines while there were also two A-frame beam engines and several horizontal steam engines. The engines were finally dismantled in 1934 hence the good state of preservation of the engine house. It is now used as a store.

KINGSWOOD: *New Mill, elegant monument to the final flourish of the Gloucestershire woollen industry.*

RUSPIDGE
Ventilation Chimney (SO652106)
2 miles S of Cinderford off B4227
This tall masonry chimney high up on a wooded hillside above the valley of the Cinderford Brook provided an updraught to ventilate the Findal Level of the 19th-century iron mine some 300 ft vertically below.

SAPPERTON
Frampton Mansell Viaduct (SO918028)
5 miles E of Stroud off A419
A fine red brick viaduct of 9 spans, 7 pierced. The line was the Cheltenham & Grand Western Union, authorized in 1836, which got into difficulties and was taken over and completed by the GWR from 1843. Brunel was involved in completing the line, but the attribution of the viaduct to him is not certain.

SAPPERTON
Western Entrance Sapperton Tunnel
(SO944033)
6 miles E of Stroud off A419

In contrast to the classical eastern portal (see Coates *qv*) this portal was Gothic in design. Although it is now much mutilated early prints show that the parapet over was battlemented, with a pinnacle at either end and in the middle. The tunnel entrance itself is semicircular with a massive keystone. Nearby, at Daneway (SO938035) is the inn built for the tunnellers.

SHARPNESS
Severn Railway Bridge Abutments (SO678034)
½ mile N of Sharpness along canal towpath
The Severn Railway bridge opened in 1879 providing the shortest route to Wales until the Severn Tunnel was driven. It remained in operation until 1962 when it was damaged by a river barge and it was demolished in 1969. On the eastern bank only the abutments of the swing section over the Sharpness & Gloucester Canal have survived. The circular pier on which the section pivoted and which contained the steam driven machinery is particularly fine.

SHARPNESS
New Dock (SO657022–664028)
By 1869 the congestion in the original Sharpnesss basin was such that a larger dock was essential. This was opened in 1874 and comprised a tidal basin and a larger section at canal level and accommodates ships of up to 7000 tons. The canal itself can only take vessels of up to 750 tons and their multi-storey warehouses were built on the eastern dock side to facilitate transhipment. Besides 2 of these fine warehouses there are various original dock offices, quaint weatherboarded shops and 2 swing-bridges.

SHARPNESS
Old Dock (SO670031)
¼ mile NW of Sharpness Docks
Designed by Telford and opened in 1827 this dock is at the original entrance lock from the Severn to the Sharpness & Gloucester Canal. The basin is small and was never intended as a commercial dock. Besides the tidal basin and handsome Dock Office there is a stable for the towing horses.

STAUNTON
Chartist Housing and School (SO792290)
7½ miles N of Gloucester A417
The Chartist Co-operative Land Society was formed in 1845 to attempt to reverse the drift of population to the industrial towns. The Society established three colonies in NW Gloucestershire at Snigs End, Staunton and

Lewbands. Many of these neat, single-story, brick-built cottages with a central gable have survived and the handsome school building at Snig's End has been converted into a public house – The Prince of Wales.

STINCHCOMBE
Stancombe Park Weighbridge (ST738975)
3 miles NW of Wooton under Edge on B4060
A weighbridge in local stone by the side of the road. The balance itself is in a small chamber, which is open to the sky, and the arch of which is in poor repair. The machinery, however, is in working order, despite some rusting. Built by Bartlett & Son of Bristol, it was tested by Parnell & Sons Ltd, Narrow Wind St, Bristol, to Class 3, to weigh 4 tons. Registered ER 408 A1.

STONEHOUSE
Stanley Mill (SO813043)
2½ miles W of Stroud off A419
This brick-built mill at Kings Stanley is famous for its internal structure of cast-iron double columns down each floor, supporting traceried cast-iron arches which incorporate dove tail for the line shafting. The stone-paved floors rest on brick arches on iron beams and the brickwork is so constructed to give a sand sprinkler effect in case of fire. The mill was rebuilt in this form 1812–13 and is thus one of the earliest fireproof mills to survive. Originally it was powered by 5 waterwheels giving a reputed 200hp and a 40hp steam engine was added in 1820.

STOW-ON-THE-WOLD
Donnington Brewery (SP174272)
2 miles NW of Stow off B4077
This attractive complex of 18th- and 19th-century masonry buildings is built round the nucleus of a former corn mill. Thomas Arkell bought the premises in 1827, a date recorded on one of the outbuildings, and the Arkell family have owned it ever since. In 1865 the mill was converted into a brewery and considerably extended to the rear. Until 1959 all power was supplied by 2 waterwheels fed from the extensive mill pond but since then they have been supplemented by a small diesel engine.

STROUD
Butterow Toll House (SO856042)
1 mile S of Stroud
Built in 1825 this octagonal, 2-storey, stone house has 4 pairs of Gothic windows. Although converted to a shop its toll board is still in position above the door.

SYMONDS YAT
Limekiln (SO564161)
4 miles N of Coleford
The design of this typical Dean limekiln with its single well placed centrally between the arches allows the kiln to be considerably lower than the more normal arrangement whereby the well is behind and above a single arch. On the inner side of each arch there are rake holes a few feet from the ground.

TEDDINGTON
Teddington Hands (SO963339)
5 miles E of Tewkesbury on A438
A stone pillar with 6 arms at a junction of 6 roads. The inscription records, in verse, its erection in 1676 and its repair a century later.

TETBURY
Brewery (ST887935)
½ mile NW of town centre off B4014
A fine Victorian brewery. The firm was established in 1800, a date recorded on the building. Built of local stone with slate roofs ornamented by red tiles along the ridges, the brewery is notable for its central 4-storey block with pediment of exaggerated height and hipped roof. The windows have elegant semi-circular heads. This block is flanked by 2 others of 3 and 2 storeys, topped with Chinese-influenced louvred structures. There is also a tall engine house in stone, with a slim red brick chimney with ornamental top.

TEWKESBURY
The Mythe Bridge (SO889337)
1 mile N of Tewkesbury on A438
This handsome cast-iron bridge was designed by Telford and erected in 1826. Build of cast-iron sections supplied by Hazledine of Shrewsbury, it was strengthened in 1923 with reinforced concrete slabs over the decking. The

Gothic toll house at the eastern end was also designed by Telford.

ULEY
Sheppards Mill (ST794984)
2 miles E of Dursley off B4066
Great Mill or Sheppard's Mill (after the owner, Edward Sheppard), was one of the most important cloth mills in the county. Built up during the early 19th century, at its peak in the 1830s, the mill consisted of over 30 buildings, and possessed 3 steam engines and an iron foundry. All aspects of the manufacture of cloth were combined on this one site. In 1837 the business failed, and the mill was sold. All that remains today is the Great Mill building itself, now in use on the farm, and the 2 other buildings, which were the press shop and the agent's house.

WINCHCOMBE
Tan Yard (SP027284)
6 miles NE of Cheltenham off A46
The tannery consists of a central block of 4 storeys, with windows on the ground and first floors, and vertical slats on the top 2. It is constructed in stone, with slate and stone roof. Other adjacent buildings include an estate office with delicate latticed ground floor windows and an isolated weatherboarded house of 2 storeys, the lower being given over to stalls.

WOODCHESTER
Frogmarsh Wool Stove (SO841018)
2 miles S of Stroud off A46
This circular masonry roundhouse opposite Frogmarsh Mill is the most complete surviving example in the country. There are several in the Stroud area and they are to be found as far S as Frome in Somerset. They were used for drying cloth and were superseded by single-storey ranges with ventilated walls and steam pipes.

Hampshire

Hampshire is a predominantly rural county whose agricultural resources have long been commercially exploited to provision its major ports and dockyards and to supply hops and beer to the London market. The surviving monuments are thus associated with these activities, with corn mills, hop kilns, breweries, prominent along with the transport systems that served them. The naval dockyards of Portsmouth and Bucklers Hard also encouraged an iron industry to briefly develop and it was at Funtley near Havant that Cort made his vital advances in the puddling of iron.

ALTON
Crowley's Brewhouse Tower (SU718391)
SE of town centre
Alton is one of the most famous brewing towns in southern England. This brewhouse tower, completed in 1902, is of exceptional height and is built in alternating bands of red and yellow brickwork with a ventilated slate roof. The original brewery on this site was established in 1763 and brewing finally ceased in 1970.

ANDOVER
Town Mill (SU363454)
Town centre
A 2-storey brick-built mill with mill house attached and one external hoist in the loft floor. A plaque on the mill records that it was rebuilt 1764. Originally powered by the River Anton this mill was in use up to 1968 using electricity.

ARLESFORD
Arlesford Toll House (SU580324)
7 miles E of Winchester on A31
This 2-storey toll house is rather more substantial than the norm. Classically designed in brick, it is fortunate to have survived alongside the busy A31.

BINSTEAD
West Court Hop Kilns (SU765412)
4 miles NW of Alton off A31
There were a large number of hop gardens in north-east Hampshire concentrated mostly around Alton. The village of Binstead has several kilns, these at West Court being well preserved.

BINSTEAD
Telegraph House (SU785414)
5 miles NE of Alton off A31
This house was built in the early 19th century as one of a chain to relay messages visually between the naval dockyard at Portsmouth and the Admiralty in London. It is probably the most complete such house in Hampshire.

BUCKLERS HARD
Naval Shipyards (SU409001)
3 miles SE of Beaulieu
These rather insignificant stake-lined depres-
sions are all that remains of the once flourishing dockyard that produced many famous naval ships-of-the-line from the 1740s–1840s. The most illustrious being Nelson's HMS *Agamemnon*.

EASTLEIGH
Conegar Lock (SU467186)
½ mile E of Eastleigh off B3037
The most complete lock on the old Itchen Navigation from Southampton to Winchester. Most of the locks were turf-sided but this example is masonry and brick. The structure also incorporates sluices for the adjacent water meadows.

FAREHAM
Cort's House (SU550081)
3 miles NW of Fareham
This timber-framed house, with its E-shaped extensions was occupied by Cort in the last quarter of the 18th century while he conducted his famous experiments in the adjacent iron mill. It has been extensively renovated and only the exterior is original. The farmhouse on the west side of the valley was originally built for Samuel Jellicoe, Cort's partner.

FAREHAM
Funtley Iron Mill (SU550082)
3 miles NW of Fareham
This early 18th-century forge site assumed historical significance in 1775 when it was acquired by Henry Cort as it was here that he developed his crucial 'dry puddling' process for the manufacture of wrought iron. It was at this site that he also pioneered the use of grooved rollers in the production of bar iron. Very little remains above ground to give witness to these important developments but some of the original layout was determined by excavations in 1964–5. The rolling mill itself was water driven and there are extensive remains of the complicated water supply system.

HAYLING ISLAND
Brickyard (SU717033)
3 miles S of Havant off A3023
This family brickyard unusually still employs the clamp method of making bricks. This technique does away with the need for a kiln

altogether and is dependent on the constituents of the bricks themselves being combustible. There are therefore very few installations on the site – just brick making machines and drying racks.

HEADLEY
Headley Mill (SU813357)
8 miles NE of Petersfield off A325
Drawing water from the River Way for its picturesque pond, this large watermill still has its machinery in perfect order. The breast shot wheel, working 4 pairs of mill stones is still used for milling flour and provender.

HEADLEY
Passfield Hop Kilns (SU824344)
7 miles NE of Petersfield off A325
An interesting group of 4 disued oasts built in local sandstone. Three are conical and one rectangular – reflecting slight variations in process.

HURSLEY
Village Smithy (SU428253)
4 miles SW of Winchester on A3090
This working smithy has changed little over the last century. Its forge and bellows are intact and horse shoes litter the floor.

LANGSTONE
Windmill Tower (SU720049)
1 mile S of Havant off A3023
Only some 5 windmills survive in Hampshire

HEADLEY: *Passfield Hop Kilns.*

whereas there are traces of over 150 watermills. This stone-built tower mill has lost its sails and has been converted to a dwelling.

LYMINGTON
Salterns (SU328940)
2 miles S of Lymington
Salt was almost certainly produced in the Lymington area from prehistoric times onwards but production reached a peak in the 18th century and by 1800 Lymington's trade of 149,839 bushels was second only to Liverpool's. However the raising of the duty on salt had disastrous effects on the south coast industry by 1825 when the duty was lifted few salterns remain. Today very little remains other than embanked pools and a few undistinguished brick buildings.

PORTSMOUTH
Eastney Lock (SZ677998)
2 miles E of town centre off A288
This decrepit lock was the entrance to the Portsea Canal – a canal that has long since disappeared. It was the last link in an inland navigation route from London to Portsmouth Dockyard by way of the Wey & Arun Canal, the Portsmouth and Arundel Canal. This route was popular only during wars with France.

PORTSMOUTH
Eastney Pumping Station (SZ674993)
2 miles E of town centre off A288
The sewage pumping station at Eastney, Portsmouth is a most interesting site and much of it is open to the public under the auspices of the city museum service. A complete sequence of pumping over the last 100 years is represented. There are only slight remains of a pair of Clayton beam engines in the 1867 engine house but James Watt, Woolf compound rotative beam engines of 1887 are preserved in splendid condition. The next stage in the sequence was the installation of Crossley horizontal opposed gas engines in 1904 – a type of engine virtually extinct. These engines are now preserved along with a later diesel engine and are also on exhibit. The sequence is continued on the working part of the site by standby low tension electric pumps of the 1930s and modern high tension electric pumps.

PORTSMOUTH
Fort Widley (SU656065)
4 miles N of town centre
The Portsdown Hill forts were planned in the 1850s in answer to a supposed French invasion threat. Usually called Palmerston Forts the threat had passed by the time they had been completed in the 1860s. They were designed to defend the naval harbour against a landward attack from the north and Fort Widley, which is open to the public, is a good example of these massively constructed forts most of which are in fact underground.

PORTSMOUTH
Naval Dockyards (SU628006)
NE of town centre
This, one of the main dockyards in the country, has many buildings of industrial interest including Ship Shop No. 3, a great, prefabricated iron-framed building of *c* 1849, the cast-iron framed fire station of 1843 and the Block Mill built *c* 1800 by Samuel Bentham to house Marc Brunel's block making machinery. However, most of the dockyard with the exception of access to HMS *Victory* is not normally open to the public.

RINGWOOD
Generating Station (SU145035)
1 mile SW of Ringwood off B3347
This building, on an island site on the River Avon, was purpose-built as a low head hydroelectric generating station in 1924. The building has recently been gutted but it formerly contained 2 turbines installed by Armfields of Ringwood.

SHERFIELD ON LODDON
Longbridge Mill (SU683582)
4 miles NE of Basingstoke off A33
Situated on the River Lodden this brick, half-timbered and weatherboarded mill has a cast-iron undershot wheel and most of its machinery *in situ* though it now uses electric drive.

SOUTHWICK
Golden Lion Brewhouse (SU627085)
7 miles W of Havant on A333
This is an excellent example of a 19th-century brewery purpose-built to supply one village inn and a certain amount of off-licence trade. Built of brick with timber ventilating louvres, the brewhouse still contains its original brewing equipment including a small horizontal steam engine.

SWAY
Peterson's Folly (SZ279969)
1½ miles S of Sway
A very early mass concrete tower built 1886–91 by the landowner to alleviate local unemployment. Almost 200 ft high, it has reputedly 365 steps in the spiral staircase housed in an external tower. Many of the nearby houses date from this period and are also of concrete.

SWAY
Holmesley Station (SU232007)
4 miles NW of Sway
A good example of the domestic style of architecture employed in stations on the Southampton & Dorchester Railway. Built in 1847, the station has been converted into a private residence while the track has been utilized for the alignment of a new road.

TOTTON
Eling Tidemill (SU365125)
½ mile S of Totton off A35
This disused brick tidemill is built on the seaward side of a causeway across the mouth of the Bartley Water. It has 2 waterwheels placed side by side on different shafts in the middle of the building driving 2 pairs of stones. The causeway itself is a toll road complete with cabin and toll board.

TWYFORD
Water Pumping Station (SU493249)
4 miles S of Winchester off A333
This installation is a typical medium sized, early 20th-century, steam driven, water supply pumping station. Its engine is an inverted vertical triple expansion of 1913 made by Hathorn Davey with large wooden connecting beams to the well pumps some 20 ft away. The

building also houses diesel and electric pumps which provide dramatic comparison to the steam engines in terms of size and efficiency. Within the grounds of the pumping station is a water treatment plant complete with quarry, water engine operated tramway, limekilns and pugmill.

WEST WORLDHAM
Hartley Maudit Toll House (su734366)
3 miles SE of Alton off B3006
A neat, 2-storey, brick toll house which has suffered very little alteration. Its location at a very minor junction partly explains its survival.

WHITCHURCH
Silk Mill (su463479)
S of town centre off A34
This extremely fine red brick 3-storey mill is dated 1815. It has 5 bays, a steep one-bay pediment, bell tower and clock. The water-wheel is enclosed in a wooden lean-to and, with its associated machinery, is intact. Silk is still woven but with electric power.

WINCHESTER
City Mill (su487294)
¼ mile E of town centre
This small brick-built corn mill with tile hung gables dates *c* 1744 and still has one wheel in position. It is now used as a Youth Hostel.

WINCHESTER
Hyde Brewery (su480299)
¼ mile W of town centre
Brewing has ceased at this 19th-century complex and it is now merely a distribution depot. The main office building has a stone marked 'Hyde Brewery Rebuilt 1821' and has frosted glass windows, one marked 'Counting House'. The yard is characteristically paved with granite sets.

Hereford and Worcester

The new county was a product of the 1974 local government reorganization which brought together 2 counties with dissimilar industrial backgrounds. Worcestershire had shared in the general industrial expansion in the West Midlands and its industrial monuments are reminiscent of this, e.g. significant canal monuments at Stourport, Worcester and Tardebigge, metal working industries at Redditch and Belbroughton and potteries at Worcester.

Hereford on the other hand was isolated from these developments by the Malvern Hills and its industrial monuments are typically those of a rural county such as watermills, hop kilns, and a fine series of bridges over the Wye, it has also relics of 2 canals which with limited success tried to penetrate to Leominster and Hereford respectively.

ARLEY
Victoria Bridge (so767792)
4 miles NW of Bewdley off B4194 (Arley) footpath to bridge
A dramatic single arch cast-iron bridge of 200 ft span over the Severn built in 1862 by Brassey to a design by Fowler and cast at Coalbrookdale. It now carries the steam hauled Severn Valley Railway which runs from Bewdley to Bridgnorth.

ASTLEY
Yarranton's Furnace (so805668)
4 miles S of Stourport off B4196
A very early blast furnace site which has been investigated by excavation to reveal its 17th-century configuration is situated beside the Dick Brook ½ mile above its confluence with the River Severn. The furnace takes its name from the period in the mid-17th century when it was operated by Andrew Yarranton.

BELBRCUGHTON
Nash's Scythe Works (SO919772)
6 miles E of Kidderminster A456/B4188
The largest of a chain of former edge tool sites in the parish of Belbroughton. It ceased operation several years ago and the brick forge buildings, offices and warehouses are now in a variety of unrelated uses. There are several other sites on the same small stream, some only now traceable by their hammer ponds. Significant remains can be seen at Galtons Mill (SO933774) and Drayton Mill (SO906763).

BEWDLEY
Station and Viaduct (SO793754)
3 miles W of Kidderminster on A456
Bewdley station is a single-storey brick built station with a 2-storey station house attached and is the southern terminus of the preserved Severn Valley Railway. It is at the end of a viaduct built in 1862 of large sandstone blocks which have weathered badly and now appear to be much more ancient. The station has a fine covered passenger overbridge and an original signal box perched on the viaduct approach embankment.

BISHOPS FROME
Hop Kilns (e.g. SO684467)
5 miles S of Bromyard off B4214
The central part of the county is one of the great hop producing areas in the country and although the processing in this industry is now highly centralized there are still numerous hop kilns attesting to the former local scale operations. Several brick-built 18th-century examples occur in the Bishops Frome area, e.g. Leadon Court (SO684467), Paunton Court (SO670500), Upper Venn Farm (SO665514).

BLAKEDOWN
Churchill Forge (SO883795)
4 miles NE of Kidderminster off A456
North Worcestershire has shared a metal working tradition with the neighbouring Black Country since the 16th century. Edge tool mills are to be found at Belbroughton (*qv*) and Churchill. The Churchill forge, although dilapidated, still contains 2 overshot water-wheels and a unique range of water-driven machinery which was in use until recently in the manufacture of spades and shovels. Originally a corn mill, it was converted to a blade mill in the late 16th century.

BLAKEDOWN: *Spring Oliver, Churchill Forge, – unique survival in an historic edge tool manufacturing area.*

BRIDGE SOLLARS
Metal Bridge (SO413425)
6 miles W of Hereford off A438
Constructed by public subscription in 1896, the bridge has 3-span lattice girders supported on 4 circular metal piers.

GOODRICH
Huntsham Bridge (SO568182)
4 miles S of Ross-on-Wye off B4229
A 3-span Warren girder bridge supported by 2 pairs of cylindrical metal piers with oval heraldic devices above each pier. The sides of the bridge are arched lattice girders 6 ft high.

GREAT MALVERN
Railway Station (SO783456)
Great Malvern station is justly famed for its array of platform ironwork. Built *c* 1859 at the time when the town was being developed as a spa resort the pillars on the platform have capitals with cast-iron foliage of astonishing realism.

GREAT WITLEY
Shelsley Beauchamp Toll House (SO754633)
2 miles S of Great Witley on B4197
Attractive white-washed semi-hexagonal fronted 2-storey cottage with Gothic windows and central porch.

HAY-ON-WYE
Tramway Bridge (SO230428)
$\frac{1}{4}$ mile NE of Hay – just within Hereford and Worcester
Small masonry tramway bridge of 1816 which carried the Hay Tramroad over the Dulas Brook. The tramroad operated for some 50 years.

HEREFORD
Victoria Bridge (SO513394)
E of town centre
Attractive suspension bridge linking Castle Green with George V Park was erected by public subscription in 1897 in memory of Queen Victoria's Diamond Jubilee. It has ornamental lamp posts on the abutment pillars and lattice pylons.

HEREFORD
Wye Railway Bridge (SO503394)
$\frac{1}{2}$ mile W of city centre
The GWR built an impressive 3 span cast-iron bridge across the Wye in 1853. The arched ribs were replaced by steel replicas this century but the structure is none the less imposing. The embanked approaches are pierced by flood relief arches.

HEREFORD
Jubilee Cider Works (so516420)
1½ miles N of city centre on A4103
A small works on the outskirts of Hereford typical of the type of works which were transitional between the farm-based industry and the large modern complexes such as Bulmers Cider Works. It is housed in a group of red brick buildings erected in 1897 and there are still examples of hydraulic presses as well as the more traditional horse-driven edge runner mills.

HEREFORD
Broomy Hill Pumping Station (so496394)
1 mile W of city centre Breinton Road
A water supply complex being conserved as the Herefordshire Waterworks Museum. There are 2 main parts to the complex – the upper site which includes 2 filter beds of 1856, a prominent brick water tower of 1883, and a superintendent's house of 1856 and the lower site which is based round a pumping station of several periods (1850/1862/1895/1906). The lower pumping station houses 2 steam engines – a vertical triple expansion engine of 1895 (the oldest of its type in the country) and 2 cylinder vertical engines of 1906 both by Worth Mackenzie & Co, Stockton.

HOLT FLEET
Bridge and River Lock (so821633)
4½ miles W of Droitwich A4133
This large single-span cast-iron bridge with sandstone abutments was built by Telford in 1826. Although it has been strengthened and widened, it retains much of its original appearance. The large masonry lock with its large 2-storey lock-keeper's house and pair of 19th-century cottages forms an attractive complex.

KIDDERMINSTER
Brinton's Mills (so831764)
¼ mile SW of town centre
Kidderminster is one of the main centres of carpet production in the country and the mills dominate the town. Brinton's Mill occupies a large site between the Staffs & Worcs Canal, Corporation Street and Exchange Street. Built typically of Worcestershire soft red brick with yellow and blue brick dressings, it has pedimented end elevations and prominent cornices. A similarly built tall square plan chimney has lancet-type false windows.

KINGS CAPLE
Hoarwithey Bridge and Toll House
(so548295)
8 miles S of Hereford unclass road E of A49

Built in 1876, the bridge is constructed of a single pair of continuous Warren girders supported by intermediate stone piers to give 3 equal spans of approximately 85 ft. The toll house at its western end is most unusual. It rises 3 storeys from the river bank but only 1½ from the bridge level and has a steeply pitched roof.

LEOMINSTER
Putnal Field Tunnel (so500663)
6 miles N of Leominster off A49
Tunnels were to be the undoing of the abortive Leominster Canal, of the 3 commenced, only 2 were finished and only one, the 330-yard long Putnal Field, opened to navigation *c* 1796. The canal never achieved its junction with the River Severn and trade was restricted to the Leominster end. It was closed in 1859 and partially used for the line of the Tenbury Railway. The portals of Putnal Field tunnel have survived as has a short watered stretch leading S from the southern portal.

MONKHIDE
Priory Bridge (so612440)
7 miles E of Hereford off A4103
Brick built bridge carrying minor road over the section of the Hereford & Gloucester Canal which was opened in 1843. The bridge is built of sharply angled skew requiring tortuous brick courses.

MORTIMERS CROSS
Watermill (so426637)
7 miles NW of Leominster off A4110
Small rural watermill restored to working order and under the guardianship of the Department of the Environment.

POWICK
Hydro-electric Power Station (so835525)
2 miles S of Worcester on A449
This was the first major low-fall hydro-electric generating station to be built in the country and is hence a most important monument. The river frontage has a tall single-storey brick façade built on a series of blue engineering brick arches which would originally have been outfalls for the turbines. The complex is no longer producing electricity but its pedigree has been fully established by Prof G Tucker in *Industrial Archaeology Review* Vol 1, No 2, 1977.

POWICK
New Bridge (so836524)
2 miles S of Worcester A449
Cast-iron single-span bridge of 1837 with massive sandstone abutments pierced by 2

small iron framed accommodation arches. A short distance upstream is a bridge of Civil War fame.

REDDITCH
Washford Mills, Ipsley Street (SP045674)
E of town centre
The largest needle works in Redditch with buildings displaying a variety of periods and building styles. Originally established in 1730 by the Millward family, most of the buildings are 19th-century or later. The main 3-storey block has a handsome central projecting bell tower behind a screen of trees. A somewhat later 3-storey block has narrow brick buttresses running the height of the building and cast-iron window detailing on 1st floor. Washford Mills was one of the first sites to employ water power in needle production, doing so as early as 1780.

REDDITCH
British Mills, Prospect Hill (SP043681)
½ mile N town centre on A441
Georgian-style, 2-storeyed, stuccoed façade with 2 large entrance arches leading to courtyards around which are the workshops. Originally produced needles and fish hooks but now in a variety of unrelated uses.

POWICK: *Hydro-Electric Generating Station – the first major low head installation in the country.*

REDDITCH
Forge Mill (SP045685)
1 mile N of town centre off A441
Situated on the N bank of a large pond on the River Arrow is the most important monument to the needle industry – an industry on which the prosperity of Redditch was based. The water-powered site dates from monastic times and was converted to needle scouring in the 1730s and the W wing is of this date. A wheel house with a 1910 waterwheel is between the 2 buildings and drives various scouring and polishing machinery. The needle scouring finished commercially on this site in 1958 and the buildings were partially restored as a private museum. Access is restricted but possible by permission.

SELLACK
Suspension Bridge (SO565280)
4 miles NW of Ross, 9 miles S of Hereford unclass road off A49
Constructed in 1896 by Lewis Harper, Aberdeen, this suspension footbridge has a central span of 190 ft. The pylons are braced tapered

iron columns surmounted by ball and spike caps. A few miles downstream is the slightly smaller and later (1921) Foy suspension bridge constructed by Rowell & Co, Westminster, with a span of 142 ft.

STOURPORT
Canal Basins (SO820730)
S of town centre
An extensive system of canal basins developed from 1768 onwards with the construction of Brindley's Staffs & Worcs Canal. The Middle (Upper) Basin was designed by Thomas Dadford and completed in 1771 by which time the canal was open to Wolverhampton. This was followed by Clock Basin and the 2 lower basin in 1781. The famous clock warehouse is early 19th-century, the clock tower itself being 1812. No. 3 basin built with a separate connecting basin to the Severn in the early 19th century has been infilled.

STOURPORT
Canal Toll House, York Street (SO812714)
Town centre
Tiny, picturesque, single-storey cottage dated 1853 beside narrow lock leading to canal basin. Slightly further up the canal is an attractive 2-storey premises with cast-iron framed windows and 2 large cart entrances. Iron winch on wharf side.

STOURPORT
Tontine Hotel (SO811710)
¼ mile S of town centre on bank of River Severn
A large commercial hotel built *c* 1770 to cater for the passengers using the flyboat service and for merchants attracted to the business generated by the adjacent canal basins. In the 19th century business declined to such an extent that the once sumptuous hotel was converted into apartments with only a public house retaining a link with the past. This inn which faces the Middle Basin is well worth a visit.

TARDEBIGGE
Canal Locks and Engine House (SO988689–SO956672)
3 miles SE of Bromsgrove on A448
Thirty narrow locks comprising the longest flight in the country. Opened in 1815, they raise the Worcester & Birmingham Canal some 217 ft. The summit lock is unusually deep (14 ft) – it replaced an abortive lift. A massive beam engine house whose steam pumps returned water up the flight has now been converted into a plush night-club retaining some of the original ironwork. N of the

locks the Lickey ridge is pierced by a tunnel 580 yards long and a canal depot with some early canal housing is sited at its southern portal.

WHITNEY
Whitney Bridge (SO259474)
4½ miles N of Hay on Wye B4350
A most unusual bridge with 2 masonry spans bracketing a central wooden lattice section of 3 spans carried on 2 wooden piers. The bridge was rebuilt in 1802 and from 1817 to 1860 it also carried the Hay Tramroad. The single-storey toll house at the northern end is still in use and appropriate toll boards are displayed. Three miles to the SW is a neat single-storey toll house on the same road (SO235437).

WORCESTER
Diglis Canal Basins (SO851539)
½ mile S of city centre
The southern terminus of Worcester and Birmingham Canal, there are 2 entrance locks from the River Severn with a large lock-keeper's house and a range of single-storey workshops with round headed cast-iron framed windows. The upper basin has an early dock office and swing-bridge.

WORCESTER
Fownes Gloves, Talbot Street (SO853546)
On inner city centre by-pass
A large late 19th-century 3-storey brick building of 27 bays with a pediment over central 3 bays and 2 wooden belfries on its hipped slate roof. It closed for glove making in 1972.

WORCESTER
Porcelain Works (SO852544)
¼ mile S of city centre
The Royal Worcester Porcelain factory was started on a riverside location in 1749 and the earliest parts of the present premises in Severn Street date from 1792. The fine Georgian building fronting the yard serves as a 'seconds' sales department and the adjacent Dyson Perrins Museum contains the finest collection of Royal Worcester in the world.

WORCESTER
Railway Bridges (SO844550 etc)
W and N of city centre
The Worcester Malvern & Hereford branch of the GWR has several interesting structures on its length within the city. It crosses the W & B canal at Lowesmoor (SO854554) by an unusual brick bridge with a large circular hole piercing the spandrel. A metal bridge decorated with heraldic devices crosses Foregate and an im-

posing brick viaduct traverses the flood plain of the Severn with a 2-span metal girder section over the river itself.

WORCESTER
Shrubhill Engine Works (SO855553)
½ mile E of city centre
A very large works established 1864 and built in a typically Worcester style in red brick decorated with yellow brick around windows and piers. The classically designed central portion of the main façade masks a large erecting shed. At the foot of Shrubhill there is

an impressive clock tower. Latterly occupied by Heenan and Froude.

WORCESTER
Vinegar Vat Hall, Lowesmoor (SO854551)
¼ mile E of city centre
Huge late 19th-century red brick structure with yellow brick dressings and stone cornice. The main elevation is 13 bays long with 2 tall storeys of metal-framed windows. The end elevation is pedimented. The interior is a huge open hall built to hold large vats and used in the preparation of vinegar.

Hertfordshire

A rural county whose economy was geared to supplying London with produce. Its industrial monuments reflect this bias being mainly associated with milling, brewing and transport. Further evidence of this London orientation is provided by the New River, built originally in 1608–13 to supply potable water to the capital and subsequently improved several times.

ARDELEY
Cromer Windmill (TL300286)
5 miles NE of Stevenage off B1037
The only surviving post mill in the county, Cromer windmill ceased operation c 1930. It has been restored as a landmark and fitted with plain sails.

BALDOCK
Seven Roes Maltings (TL246337)
Off High Street
This is one of at least 7 maltings that were in operation in Baldock last century. Dating from c 1826 the 2-storey yellow brick range has an anthracite kiln with an oven built by H S King of Nailsworth, Gloucestershire.

BERKHAMSTEAD
Horse Wheel, Ashridge House (SP994123)
3 miles N of Berkhamstead on B4506
This wheel, which was probably built in 1808, is located in the cellars of the house. It is an extremely complex cast-iron structure which raised water by means of pumps at 6 ft 6 in, 165 ft and 194 ft below the surface. It fell out of use c 1860 when the house was supplied with water from the nearby village waterworks.

BISHOPS STORTFORD
Maltings (e.g. TL491206)
S of town centre
Bishops Stortford was formerly a major centre of malting with as many as 20 identifiable maltings. In the last few years only 2 sites have remained in operation in South Mill Road, 3 buildings dating from 1843, 1856 and 1897 and in Station Road (TL489210) 2 modern units and an early 19th-century maltings.

BROOKMANS PARK
London Coal Duty Boundary Marker (TL243028)
4 miles S of Hatfield off A1
This graceful stone obelisk some 12 ft high alongside the railway is perhaps the most striking of the some 44 coal duty markers in Hertfordshire. They were originally erected in the mid-19th century alongside railways, waterways and roads 20 miles from the General Post Office in St Martin's-le-Grand to delineate the area within which the City Corporation could levy duty on incoming coal. In 1861 they were re-erected to demarcate the Metropolitan Police District and with the repeal of Duty Acts in 1889 ceased to have a function.

BROXBOURNE
Brick Kiln and Clay Mill, Station Road (TL373071)
5 miles SE of Hertford off A10
James Pulham established a terracotta and artificial stone works *c* 1845 in Broxbourne and its products quickly achieved a national reputation. Most of the factory was demolished for a car park but one bottle kiln *c* 9 ft square and 6½ ft high surmounted by cone 11 ft high survives and a clay mill with 2 edge runners 4 ft 6 in in diameter on a concrete and granite bed. The horse beams and yoke also survive.

CHESHUNT
Turnford Pumping Station (TL364049)
6 miles SE of Hertford on A10
The water board have preserved the steam engine which drove the No. 1 pump. It is a Boulton & Watt 90hp single cylinder, jet condensing lever paddle type marine beam engine with a cylinder diameter of 28 in. It was first installed in 1848 at the Hempstead Road Well and was transferred to do duty at Turnford in 1871.

COLLIERS END
Kiln (TL370202)
5 miles N of Ware off A10
An unusual underground circular kiln *c* 25 ft in diameter possibly of late 18th-century date with a central firebox. The nearby brickfield worked until *c* 1920 but the kiln was more likely to have been for burning chalk.

HARPENDEN
Donkey Wheel, Annables Manor (TL101156)
7 miles NW of St Albans off A6
This large, oak donkey wheel dates from the 17th century and drew water from a well 146 ft deep. The wheel itself is 13 ft 6 in in diameter by 3 ft 4 in wide and is composed of 2 sets of 4 main spokes with 8 sub-spokes between the main rim and a small inner ring.

HEMEL HEMPSTEAD
Gadebridge Park Bridge (TL051082)
W of town centre off A4146
This graceful iron footbridge in Gadebridge Park was built *c* 1840 by John Cromstone, a local craftsman. It has stone abutments, an iron girder deck with segmented arch bracing and decorative spandrels and elaborately decorated iron side rails splayed at each end of the bridge to 2 terminal pillars.

HERTFORD
Fulling Stocks, Horn's Mill (TL321117)
SW of town centre
Fulling stocks are a very rare survival even, in a case such as this, where they have been put to a use that is not the original use. The installation comprises a battery of 5 stocks now used to impregnate sheep skins with cod liver oil in the production of chamois leather but almost certainly designed to work broadcloth.

HERTFORD
Maltings, West Street (TL320120)
SW of Hertford town centre
Hertford was an important centre for malting and in 1970 at least 9 sites were readily identifiable. There are no operating maltings left in the town but the unit in West Street has been converted into a youth centre. It dates from *c* 1852 and was originally part of Nicholl's Brewery.

HERTFORD
New River, Chadwell Spring (TL350137)
2 miles NE of town centre off A119
The New River, constructed by Hugh Middleton 1608–13, was designed to supply London with potable water from the abundant Chadwell Spring between Hertford and Ware. The River was some 40 miles long and 15–20 ft broad terminating in a reservoir at Clerkenwell known as New River Head. By the 18th century Chadwell Spring was not only inadequate to supply demand but its flow diminished. It is now dry though its site is demarcated by 18th-century boundary stones.

HERTFORD
New River, Intake Gauge (TL340138)
1½ miles NE of town centre off A119
By the early 18th century the Chadwell Spring was becoming inadequate to meet the London demand and the New River Company promoted a Bill in 1738 to allow them to abstract a measured volume of water from the River Lea. They made a cut from the Lea to the New River and erected a gauge over the cut. This gauge was replaced in 1770 by a larger one designed by Robert Mylne and enclosed in a massive marble chest. The present gauge alongside the Lea itself was built by William Mylne in 1856 and comprises 2 iron chambers 15 ft long floating at Lea level and joined by a semi-elliptical iron beam 28 ft long. This beam therefore reacts to the river level and partially controls the fall of water over the sluice.

LEMSFORD
Lemsford Mill (TL220124)
1 mile W of Welwyn Garden City
A large 4-storey brick and weatherboarding watermill with a central hoist and lucan dates from *c* 1838 but partially rebuilt 1863. It worked until *c* 1905 and has an interesting

internal structure of cast-iron columns and a queen post trussed roof. The overshot water-wheel has gone.

ST ALBANS
Abbey Mills (TL142068)
S of town centre
A complex of 19th-century buildings at an ancient milling site. The mill itself has gone but the 2 dark red brick 3-storey blocks and the associated mill house date from the period when the site was a silk mill.

TRING
Silk Mill, Brook Street (SP925118)
5 miles NE of Berkhamstead
At the end of the 18th century and throughout the 19th century silk manufacture flourished in Hertfordshire and indeed some firms operated until *c* 1938 and the tradition is maintained in nylon manufacture at Baldock. The former silk mill in Brook Street, Tring, started as a water-powered corn mill and was operated by the firm David Evan & Co from 1828–1887. Silk throwing ceased on this site

c 1898 but 2 truncated brick-built ranges of the 19th-century mill survive with a disused waterwheel 22 ft by 6 ft.

WARE
Maltings (e.g. TL360140)
S of town centre
Ware was formerly a major centre of malting and there are several 19th-century disused malting buildings with one site – Victoria Maltings, Amwell End, still in operation. The 5-storey brick building with 3 kilns dates from a rebuild of 1907 with alterations in 1936 and 1948. A further steel-framed building was added 1964–66.

WATFORD
Grove Park Bridge (TQ087988)
1½ miles NW of town centre
An elegant early 19th-century stuccoed brick bridge with a very wide segmental arch carries the drive to the Grove, seat of Lord Clarendon, over the Grand Union Canal. The main arch is

HERTFORD: *Fulling Stocks, Horns Mill.*

flanked by narrow matching arches and the parapet is balustraded. The canal in this section has been widened out as an ornamental water feature of the Park.

WELWYN GARDEN CITY
Welwyn Viaduct (TL242145)
2 miles N of town centre
Designed by Lewis Cubbitt and built by Thomas Brassey 1848–50 of local blue brick, Welwyn Viaduct is over 1600 ft long. It has 40 arches of an average span of 40 ft and carried the Great Northern Railway some 90 ft above the River Maron.

WELWYN GARDEN CITY
Toll House, Ayst Green (TL223130)
1½ miles S of Welwyn
The only toll house to be firmly identified as such in the county. It is a half-timbered cottage built *c* 1728 – before the typical toll house design had evolved.

Humberside

Humberside is a creation of the 1975 local government reorganization and comprises the portions of Yorkshire and Lincolnshire bordering the Humber estuary.

With the notable exceptions of its major ports of Hull, Goole and Grimsby and the modern ironworks of Scunthorpe, most of the county's industrial monuments are derived from a rural economy and the transport services built to serve such an economy, e.g. wind and watermills, maltings, turnpike roads and rural canals.

BARTON-UNDER-HUMBER
Brickworks (TA035234)
¾ miles N of town centre
From the late 18th century the advantages for brickmaking of the southern bank of the Humber began to be recognized. The large reserves of good quality clay coupled with the river and canal links with rapidly expanding industrial areas led to a great expansion in the 19th century – from 5 brickworks mentioned in Kelly's Directory in 1826 to 32 in the 1896 directory in the riverside parishes alone. Barton was the centre of this industry and although brickmaking has now ceased a few works still produce clay pantiles and the remains of many small rectangular kilns survive.

BARTON-UPON-HUMBER
Ferriby Sluice, South Ferriby (SE974211)
3½ miles W of Barton-upon-Humber on A1077
At the junction of the New River Archolme with the Humber is a sea lock around which has developed a small industrial complex including boat repairing and brickworks. The 18th-century lock is still in regular operation necessitating the bridge on the main road being swung.

BEVERLEY
Crane, Beverley Minster (TA038392)
¼ mile S of town centre
This vertical tread wheel crane was rebuilt in 1716 to replace a medieval machine. Situated above the Tower crossing, it is 15 ft 6 in in diameter and enables one man to lift ¼ ton.

BRIGG
Wrawby Windmill, Mill Lane, Wrawby (TA035087)
2 miles NE of Brigg off A18
The last post mill in the region, Wrawby windmill was restored as a museum in 1965. It was built *c* 1760 and has 4 spring sails driving 2 pairs of stones, is turned into wind by tail pole and has a brick roundhouse. It is open to the public certain holidays.

BROOMFLEET
Weighton Lock (SE874256)
8 miles W of Hessle off A63
Constructed under an Act of 1772, the Market Weighton Canal sought to provide a naviga-

tion and a drainage channel – uses which were difficult to reconcile. The fine masonry lock at the entrance was opened in 1776 and was built by either John Smith or his successor Grundy. Virtually in its original condition, it has to combine the function of tidal lock and sluice.

CLEETHORPES
Pier (TA318090)
Built in 1875 by the famous firm of Head, Wrightson & Co of Stockton, this pier was originally 1200 ft long, extending from the pier gardens themselves on a landward elevated section. When in 1903 the pierhead pavilion was destroyed by fire, cafés and booths were erected on the site and the new pavilion erected at midpoint. The pier was breached by the military in 1940 and subsequently the severed section was demolished to reduce the pier length to its present 335 ft, the elevated section having been already demolished *c* 1938.

FLAMBOROUGH
Old Lighthouse (TA250708)
4 miles NE of Bridlington off B1255
Built by Sir John Clayton in 1674, this octagonal stone-built tower stands to its full height of 4 storeys. It is the only intact coal light in England.

GOOLE
Company Town (SE748234)
SE of town centre
Goole was a creation of the Aire & Calder Navigation which in 1825 opened a dock basin (SE748231) at the junction of their new cut with the River Ouse. From 1825 they initiated a controlled development of a settlement comprising terraces of small houses designed for labourers, larger houses for the professional classes, pubs, shop etc. An imposing hotel named Banks Arms on completion in 1825 but renamed the Lowther *c* 1835 was built privately but bought by the company in 1827. Extensive redevelopment has largely destroyed the red brick uniformity of this part of Goole.

GREAT DRIFFIELD
Riverhead Buildings (TA028573)
¼ mile S of town centre
At the head of the Derwent Navigation there is a fine complex of late 18th-century and early 19th-century brick-built industrial buildings including a mill, a row of warehouses and a terrace of cottages.

GRIMSBY
Hydraulic Tower, Grimsby Docks (TA280116)
1 mile N of town centre

The floating dock system at Grimsby is very much a creation of the railways. Indeed in 1847 the Grimsby Docks Company merged with a consortium of railways to form the Manchester Sheffield & Lincolnshire Railway and the foundations of a new dock were laid. The railway reached Grimsby in 1848 and the Dock (later called Royal Dock) was opened in 1852. A dramatic feature of the docks is the red brick tower 309 ft high built in 1852 by J W Wild on the model of Palezzo Pubblico at Siena. It was originally to power the docks hydraulic system. It is now used to sluice out the docks.

HORKSTOW
Suspension Bridge (SE973190)
4½ miles W of Barton-upon-Humber off B1204
Built in 1835 to the designs of Sir John Rennie, this elaborate suspension bridge is one of the oldest in the country. The ironwork was forged by John and Edward Walker at Gospel Oak ironworks near Birmingham and the 2 suspension cables on each side support a span of 130 ft 9 in.

HULL
Ferro Concrete Building (TA096295)
¼ mile NW of City Centre
In 1900 the long established engineering firm of Rose Downs & Thompson & Co Ltd constructed, for their own use, at their Caroline and Cannon Street premises a ferro concrete building which was the first of its kind in England. To do so they had to obtain a licence to use the techniques developed by Monsieur Hennebique.

HULL
Humber Dock (TA098282)
½ mile S of city centre
The evolution of the floating dock system in Hull is a complicated story. The earliest Queens Dock of 1779 was built off the River Hull itself at the N end of the medieval river wharves. It was not until the 19th century that the potential of the Humber estuary was developed by the opening in 1809 of Humber Dock. Engineered by John Rennie and William Chapman, Humber Dock eventually gave access to Princes Dock (1829) and Railway Dock (1846). Swing-bridges were therefore necessary, one of which bears the cast legend 'Haigh Foundry Company, Wigan, 1804'.

HULL
Paragon Station (TA082287)
W of city centre

HORKSTOW: *Elegant suspension bridge now serving merely a farm track.*

The original entrances to the station and the Station Hotel were built *c* 1848 and the Italiante south façade was the work of G T Andrews. The train shed and booking hall are considerably later.

HULL
Springhead Pumping Station (TA042295)
3 miles W of city centre
The city of Hull, being so very flat and low lying has had a long history of organized water supply. Much of the water was conducted in open leats from sources at Springhead and in the 19th century a large imposing pumping station was built on the site. Besides being the local headquarters of the present water authority this building houses a small museum devoted to the history of water supply. The central feature of the museum is the exceptionally finely made 1876 Cornish beam engine manufactured by Bells Lightfoot & Co of Tyneside.

MELBOURNE
Church Bridge, Thornton (SE758444)
5 miles SW of Pocklington off Melbourne road

This bridge over the Pocklington Canal was constructed between 1814 and 1818. Built of brick with a dressed stone parapet, coursing and arch facing, the bridge is of a most unusual but graceful curved and buttressed design.

NAFFERTON
Nafferton Mill (TA058589)
2 miles NE of Great Driffield off A166
This 5-storey, brick and slate watermill was built *c* 1840 as a corn mill and malting. In this century it was used solely as a maltings until its disuse in 1966. The breast shot waterwheel survives as does a corn dressing machine.

NEW HOLLAND
Manchester Square (TA083237)
5 miles NE of Barton-under-Humber on A15
New Holland owes its existence to its pier from which the main ferry across the Humber plied to Hull. The ferry was operated by the railways and continued in operation until the Humber Road Bridge made it redundant. Manchester Square was constructed *c* 1898 by the GCR to house some of its employees.

PAULL
Lighthouse (TA166262)
6 miles E of Hull off A1033
This attractive river light was built in 1836 but was abandoned in 1870 and converted into a dwelling.

POCKLINGTON
Devonshire Mill (SE801478)
1 mile S of town centre
A 4-storey brick and tile building with a loft built on a virgin site in 1808. The breast shot waterwheel, which was augmented in 1893 by a steam engine and in 1905 by an oil engine, survives being built mainly of iron with a diameter of 14 ft and a width of 7 ft. Although the building has been disused for several years, much of the machinery and 2 pairs of stones have also survived.

POCKLINGTON
Railway Station (SE803487)
¼ mile S of town centre
A handsome brick-built station with stone dressings and a 5-arch collonade on frontage. Since the closure of the railway it has been converted into a school sports hall for which purpose the rare overall roof was admirably suited.

SKIDBY
Skidby Windmill (TA021333)
6 miles NW of Hull on A164
Prominent 6-storey brick-built galleried tower mill of 1821 with 4 patent sails and white metal cap with fantail. Preserved by the local authority, it is open to the public at weekends in the summer and its associated brick-built outbuildings include a barn, granary, and cart shed.

SPURN HEAD
Smeaton's Light (foundations) (TA400111)
11 miles SE of Patrington off B1445
The ever changing spit of sand at the mouth of the Humber posed a threat to shipping and a problem to light builders. Smeaton erected a pair of temporary lights in 1769 and commenced building 2 brick towers 90 ft and 50 ft shortly afterwards. The low light was washed away *c* 1779 some 3 years after both had first been lit, but the high light survived until 1894 when it was demolished. Only the other circular protecting wall some 90 ft in diameter marks the site.

STAMFORD BRIDGE
Stamford Bridge Mill (SE713556)
8 miles NE of York on A166
This large corn mill astride the River Derwent originally contained 2 waterwheels and 5 pairs of stones. The 5-storey building has been converted into a public house and restaurant but retains as a showpiece one of the waterwheels which is undershot and made of iron by Hawkswell of Yarm in 1921 with a diameter of 16 ft and a width of 7 ft. Two of the 3 pairs of stones it drove are also preserved *in situ*.

Isle of Wight

Agriculture and tourism have been the major industries of this small county. The former was developed commercially at an early date to provision the fleet off Portsmouth dockyard while the latter was essentially a railway age phenomenon. Both have left a variety of monuments which are supplemented by others relating to navigation and salt production.

BEMBRIDGE
Bembridge Windmill (SZ640875)
½ mile SW of village off B3395
This prominent landmark on an exposed site on the eastern end of the Isle of Wight has been substantially restored and is in the guardianship of the National Trust. Built of local stone, the tapered tower is 38 ft high and is weatherproofed on one side with Roman cement. The cap is a simple one with a double pitched roof and a hipped gable at the rear and a front panel to the plane in which the common, or

cloth sails, rotate. The 2 pairs of stones are located on the second floor and are driven from underneath. The mill would seem to date from 1746 and is a typical example of an 18th-century corn mill prior to the sophisticated developments of the East Anglian windmills.

CALBORNE
Upper Mill (sz414869)
½ mile W of village off B3401
This mill consists of 2 buildings, the original watermill and a roller mill which was added on the downstream side in 1894. The 2 pairs of stones of the watermill itself were latterly powered by a 20 ft diameter overshot wheel made in 1881 by the firm of J Dyer of Newport. The plant in the roller mill could be driven by the waterwheel but also had auxiliary power to drive it. Originally this power was supplied by an oil engine, then a steam engine but these have been replaced by a Rushton producer gas engine installed in 1920. Both the producer and the engine survive and make this a most interesting complex.

CARISBROOKE
Carisbrooke Castle, Donkey Wheel (sz487877)
1 mile SW of Newport off B3401
This famous donkey wheel and its well house in the castle bailey were rebuilt in 1587 over a well which was sunk to a depth of 161 ft in 1150. The wheel has a diameter of 15 ft 6 in with the 4 main spokes of each set arranged tangentially about the shaft with subsidiary framing at right angles to these main spokes. The wheel is put to work with donkeys for the benefit of visitors.

COWES
Warehouse, Medina Road (sz498955)
¼ mile S of town centre
The early shipyards, warehouses and wharves along the Medina at Cowes suffered from extensive wartime bombing and from continuous redevelopment. This stone-built, 3-storey warehouse on the road leading to the floating bridge is one of the few survivors.

HAVENSTREET
Gas Retort House (sz556989)
3½ mile SW of Ryde
Very little of the gas industry has survived on the Island, this retort house, dated 1886, in Havenstreet railway yard is the most significant monument. It is merely a shell having been gutted many years ago.

BEMBRIDGE: *Bembridge Windmill, typical primitive 18th-century design.*

NEWPORT
Broadlands Lace Factory (sz505895)
½ mile NE of town centre off A3054
This massive 3-storey yellow brick building with its 3 projecting gable hoods on its frontage and projecting wings to the front and rear was built by the firm of Freeman & Nunn in the second quarter of the 19th century. They moved from the East Midlands to the Isle of Wight in 1826–7 and brought with them an adaptation of the traversing bobbin machine which had been patented by John Heathcot in 1808. Indeed they were involved in extensive litigation with the patentee for several years but this did not prevent there being 80 bobbin net machines on the Island by 1831. The factory closed in 1877 and is now Government offices.

NEWPORT
Toll House, Fairlea Road (sz570907)
1 mile NE of town centre on A3054
A small octagonal 2-storey toll house, known as the Round House. Built in red brick with a tiled roof and casement windows it has been extended to the west.

NEWPORT
Warehousing, Sea Street (*c* sz501895)
¼ mile N of town centre
The NE side of Sea Street contains 2 main blocks of warehouses from the mid-18th century. They vary between 2, 3, or 4 storeys, in painted or red and purple brick with either old tile or slate roofs, central hatches and windows with ornamental cast-iron grills. Some have original hatches on their river frontage.

NEWTOWN
Salterns (sz418911)
5 miles E of Yarmouth off A3054
Until the early 19th century there were quite extensive salterns on both sides of the Solent. Those at Lymington were regionally important but are now almost obliterated. Those at Newton on the Isle of Wight, though only of local importance, have survived remarkably well. The low stone revetted banks are now in a National Trust Nature Reserve and are well maintained but the associated brick structure is extremely disappointing.

NITON DOWN
Old Lighthouse (sz494773)
5½ miles W of Ventnor off A3055
This 2-storey circular tower structure is the remains of a lighthouse begun by Trinity House in 1785 but abandoned before completion owing to the mists that veiled the hill.

Some·150 yards to the NW of this structure stands the old medieval pharos attached to St Catherine's Oratory.

RYDE
Pavilion, Melville Street (SZ595927)
Town centre
This late 19th-century timber structure, which is used as a dance hall by the associated hotel, is raised off the ground on short piers and is designed in a pier head style. It has a hipped slate roof with bands of scalloped slates, spike finials and a fretted valance. The walls are of grooved planks with a band of octagonal windows.

RYDE
Pier (SZ594930)
¼ mile N of town centre
The original pier at Ryde was built in 1813–14 and was the forerunner of the phenomenon of the Victorian pleasure pier. The present pier has been extended several times to almost twice its original length of 1250 ft and in 1879–80 a pier was built alongside to service rail ferries. Between the pedestrian way and the railway there is the disused track of the earlier tramway.

ST CATHERINE'S POINT
Lighthouse (SZ497754)
4½ miles W of Ventnor off A3055
This lighthouse, designed by Walker & Burgess, was built in 1838–40 following the wreck of the Clavendon in Chale Bay in 1836. Originally the stuccoed octagonal tower was 120 ft high with 3 storeys diminishing by stages with the lantern above. In 1875, however, on account of mist the height was reduced to 86 ft by the removal of the upper 1½ storeys. The lantern is set within a castellated parapet and was one of the first in the world to be illuminated by electric light being fitted with it in 1888. The lighthouse keeper's houses are contemporary with the original structure and the second, lower 2-storey tower, was added in 1932.

ST HELENS
St Helens Fort (SZ647898)
3½ miles SE of Ryde, ½ mile offshore
One of the 4 circular island bastions of stone and brick in the Solent forming part of Lord Palmerston's scheme of 1860 against the threat of French invasion. The other forts are No Man's Land Fort (SZ640938), Horse Sand Fort (SZ655949) and Spit Sand Fort (SZ636972).

ST HELENS
Tidemill (SZ632887)
4 miles SE of Ryde on A3330
This mill at the head of Bembridge Harbour is one of at least 6 tidemills that once operated on the Isle of Wight and was built (*c* 1780) at a time when the Island was an important victualling centre for the fleets assembling in the Solent. The structure became very ruinous after disuse and only the shell of the present converted building is original.

SEAVIEW
Cottages, Salterns Road (SZ625917)
2 miles E of Ryde
This group of cottages, some of which have been much altered, date back to the 16th century and were originally inhabited by those that worked the salt flats. They bear names such as Old Salterns Cottage, Salterns Cottage and Saltmeads Cottage.

SHANKLIN
Pier (SZ586814)
¼ mile SE of town centre
Built in 1891 with an overall length of 1200 ft, this pier is one of 6 on the Isle of Wight that are still in use. A fire destroyed the concert pavilion in 1927 but this was rebuilt and a new landing stage was added in 1935.

SHANKLIN
Railway Station (SZ581819)
¼ mile W of town centre
The Isle of Wight Central Railway ran from Ryde to Ventnor via Brading Sandown and Shanklin, now only the section as far as Shanklin is open. The latter station is possibly the most attractive of the Island stations and has been comparatively little altered. It is built in a vernacular style with numerous gables, a steeply roofed tower and prominent chimney stack. It is fronted by a long veranda.

YAFFORD
Yafford Mill (SZ446822)
1½ miles E of Brighstone off B3399
A small rural corn mill which would have catered for only local needs in contrast to the large trading mills elsewhere on the Island. The mill is in working order and the 2 pairs of stones are driven by an overshot wheel 13 ft 6 in wide fed by a pipe and tall box from the dam of a long narrow mill pond.

YARMOUTH
Tidemill (SZ356894)
¼ mile S of town centre
This mill stands on a dam at the point where

the Thorney Brook enters the estuary of the River Yar. Built in 1793 it is a 3-storey brick building with an additional roof store. The southern portion of the building was the millers house while the stump of a chimney to the north-east marks the site of a single-storey extension which housed an auxiliary steam engine. The pond has now silted up but the tide flaps are still *in situ* on the dam.

YARMOUTH
Old Boathouse (SZ351897)
¼ mile W of town centre off A3054
An attractive, L-shaped, single-storey range of boathouses attached to a maintenance yard. The masonry walls have a distinct batter and hence the wide access doors are similarly inclined. The gable ends are highlighted in brick and the seaward end has a stone filial.

Kent

Kent is a large rural county whose stock of industrial monuments mainly derives from its many ports and from agricultural processing. The economy of the county has long been geared to serving London and the naval dockyards with commodities such as grain, hops, paper and gunpowder. Its northern coast has not only dockyards at Chatham and Sheerness, which contain pioneer examples of building construction, but also transport monuments such as the Strood Tunnel and Gravesend Pier. The S coast has the important channel ports of Dover and Folkestone with some interesting installations and rail links.

ALLHALLOWS
London Stone (TQ861786)
2 miles NE of Grain
At the mouth of the Yanlet Creek in the Isle of Grain stands a stone obelisk marking the limit of the authority of the Port of London over the River Thames. Nearby is an iron beacon, one of many erected in Elizabethan times to warn of impending invasion.

APPLEDORE
County Boundary Stone (TQ940253)
2½ miles SW of Appledore beside Royal Military Canal Road
The boundary stone between Kent and Sussex is situated at the point where the Kent Ditch intersects the Royal Military Canal and was erected in 1806 at the time of the cutting of the Canal. It comprises a stone pillar with hemispherical top and stepped base set on a brick plinth.

CANTERBURY
Tyler Hill Tunnel (TR143597)
1¼ miles N of city centre
The Canterbury & Whitstable Railway opened in May 1830 and its tunnel through Tyler Hill ranks as one of the earliest railway, as distinct from tramway, tunnels in the world. Although somewhat shorter than the contemporary tunnel on the Liverpool & Manchester Railway, it is possibly a few months senior in terms of traffic worked through and here too cable haulage was employed. It is now blocked at both ends.

CHATHAM
Dockyard Saw Mills and Ropery (TQ7669)
Naval Dockyard 2 miles N of town centre
These Saw Mills were erected between 1810 and 1813 and were equipped by Marc Brunel. An underground canal allowed logs to be brought from the Mast Pond to the sawmill to be cut into planks by steam saws. The stock brick façade hides an internal construction which relies heavily on the use of cast iron in an attempt to improve the fire resistance of the building.

CHESTFIELD
Oast House (TR134658)
2 miles SE of Whitstable

A rather imposing example of an oast house long since converted for residential use.

CHILHAM
Chilham Castle Horse Wheel (TR065534)
6 miles SW of Canterbury off A252
This horizontal gear turning wheel works a 3-throw pump and is housed under a tiled roof attached to the keep of this castle. The 6 ft diameter overhead wooden-gear wheel no longer connects with the vertical iron-gear wheel but otherwise the wheel is substantially intact.

CHILLENDEN
Chillenden Windmill (TR268543)
4 miles SW of Sandwich off A256
This open trestle post mill was built in 1868 – one of the last of this type to be built. The tail pole is carried on a wheel and although the mill is no longer worked the machinery is intact.

CRANBROOK
Union Windmill (TQ779359)
Town centre
This imposing smock mill in the care of the county council is some 75 ft high and is possibly the finest smock mill in England. Built in 1814 with common sails by James Humphrey of Cranbrook, its present double shuttered patent sweeps are to a design of 1840 and have a span of 68 ft.

DOVER
Fairbairn Jib Crane (TR319410)
¼ mile S of town centre
This crane in the old Dover Harbour was built to a 1868 patent by the Fairbairn Engineering Company Ltd of Manchester. Hand operated and with a lifting capacity of 20 tons, it is still in use. It is one of the very few surviving relics of a very famous engineering firm.

DOVER
Shakespeare Cliff Railway Tunnel (TR296394–TR308399)
2 miles SW of town centre
1392 yards long, this tunnel was completed in 1844 by William Cubitt for the main line of the South Eastern Railway. There are 2 single-line bores in the form of tall Gothic arches spaced some 10 ft apart and horizontal galleries from the cliff face were used in its construction as well as the more usual vertical shafts.

DOVER
Water Pumping Station (TR322422)
½ mile N of town centre
Two Worthington Simpson inverted vertical triple expansion engines are in operation at the Dover pumping station. The engines were installed in 1939 and are thus notable for their late date.

FAVERSHAM
Chart Gunpowder Mills (TR009613)
½ mile W of town centre
For 3 centuries Faversham was a major centre of gunpowder manufacture with half a dozen mills in operation. Most of the evidence for this activity has disappeared but within the site of the Home Works, the oldest of all and once the Royal Gunpowder Factory, the Chart mills have been preserved by the Faversham Society. They comprise 2 pairs of gunpowder mills; each pair worked in tandem off a single large waterwheel. The site is now enveloped by a modern housing estate, yet remains one of the most complete survivals of the gunpowder industry in the country.

FOLKESTONE
Cherry Garden Pumping Station (TR210380)
2 miles NW of Folkestone off A260
The local water authority have preserved a duplex non-rotative triple expansion horizontal Worthington-type engine installed by James Simpson of London in 1889. It was the first such engine to be built in Britain and has thus an important niche in the history of steam technology. There is also a pre–1870 single-cylinder vertical steeple engine and also a 2-cylinder vertical donkey engine of pre–1880 preserved.

GRAVESEND
Canal Basin and Lock (TQ656743)
½ mile E of town centre off A226
The entrance lock and basin of the Thames & Medway canal are still in use for pleasure boating though most of the canal itself has disappeared. Opened in 1824, the canal was superseded by a railway in 1845.

GRAVESEND
Town Pier and Light (TQ648745)
¼ mile N of town centre
This cast-iron lighthouse at the end of the pier dates from *c* 1834 and is the earliest cast-iron light in the south of England. The pier itself is supported by massive cast-iron Doric columns and there is a twin pier belonging to the Thames navigation service, some 250 yards to the east (TQ651745).

HERNE
Herne Windmill (TR184665)
1½ miles S of Herne Bay off A291
This octagonal smock mill was built *c* 1781

and has a brick roundhouse and derelict stage. Its cap is shaped like a small post mill with curved gables and is in reasonable condition, but it has recently lost its sails.

HERNE BAY
Pier (TR173683)
The first pier was built in 1831–2 nominally by Thomas Telford and was constructed of oak and memel. Although 3613 ft long and massively built it suffered extensive damage by marine burrowing animals and much of it was replaced in cast iron. It was finally demolished in 1870 and iron piled pier built in 1873. This in turn was incorporated into the present pier built 1896–9, the iron pile carrying steel girders. The present pavilion dates from 1910 and is undergoing modernization.

HIGHAM
Strood Tunnel (TQ738711)
2½ miles NW of Rochester off A226
Originally constructed for the Thames & Medway Canal, this tunnel, 3946 yards long, was completed in 1824, and 20 years later the canal was converted into a railway and the tunnel, whose dimensions were unusually large for a canal tunnel, was able to be used by the railway.

GRAVESEND: *Town Pier, early use of cast iron in pier construction.*

HYTHE
Royal Military Canal (TR189348)
1½ miles E of Hythe on A259
The Royal Military Canal, which was constructed by 1806 as a defence ditch against an invasion of the Romney Marshes, runs from Winchelsea in Sussex to Hythe. At the latter end it terminates in a sluice through the sea wall. Although the canal had some commercial use and is still used for pleasure boating in Hythe itself, there is no communication at this end with the sea.

LOOSE
Wool House (TQ755521)
3 miles S of Maidstone on A229
A 15th-century half-timbered house formerly used for the cleaning of wool and now owned by the National Trust.

MAIDSTONE
Hayle Paper Mill (TQ756538)
1 mile S of town centre off B2010
Maidstone is an important centre of the Kent paper making industry. Most of the historically famous mills have been enlarged and

modernized, but some on restricted sites have been bypassed by this expansion. Hayle Mill is such a one with a mill pond fronted by a range of 2 and 3-storey weatherboarded and louvred dry lofts. The hipped slate roof is carried on a kingpost framework while between the lower floors a waterwheel *c* 1878 provided the power for making the paper.

There is a fine example of an 18th-century dry loft at **Turkey Mill** (TQ773556) on the Ashford road, while at **Springfield mills** (TQ756566) the rag room is dated 1806 and a cast-iron beam of 1805 steam engine by Boulton & Watt has been preserved. Springfield Mill was reputedly the first paper mill to operate solely on steam.

OTTERDEN
Otterden Place Horse Wheel (TQ946542)
3 miles N of Charing
This is reputably the finest of all the rope winding horizontal animal engines for raising water. Situated in a courtyard to the rear of this Elizabethan house, the drum is some 17 yards from the well-head and a tiled roof extends for all this length. This arrangement is necessitated by the confined space around the well itself.

PEMBURY
Oast Houses (TQ644399)
1¼ miles E of Pembury
A group of several oast houses near Kippings Cross have not been converted for residential purposes and one is complete with white painted cowls. The lower storey is brick and the upper storey weatherboarded, the 2 kilns themselves are conical.

RAINHAM
Mierscourt Horse Wheel (TQ813645)
4 miles SE of Gillingham off A2
Housed under a small thatched roof, this horse wheel is essentially very primitive. The horse arm drives the upright shaft by a simple claw clutch and hence the 3 ft 6 in diameter wooden drum at the top of the shaft revolves and winds the rope which is led over a pulley to the well. A simple brake arrangement is activated when the horse stops.

ROLVENDEN
Rolvenden Windmill (TQ838316)
½ mile W of Rolvenden on B2086
This fine example of a post mill was partially restored some years ago. The buck is black weatherboarding and is supported on a brick base.

ST MARGARET'S AT CLIFFE
St Margaret's Bay Windmill (TR363436)
3½ miles NE of Dover off B2058
This smock mill dates from 1929 and is thus one of the last windmills to be erected in the country.

SHEERNESS
Archway Block, Dockyard (IL911752)
Sheerness Docks, ½ mile W of town centre
A 3-storey brick building some 450 ft long of Georgian proportions. The internal construction displays the fire resisting features that Edward Holl, architect to the Navy until 1824, employed so dramatically in the recently demolished Quadrangle, viz cast-iron columns supporting cast-iron beams with slotted cast-iron filler beams and floors of York stone slabs. The Archway block seems to have been used as an adjunct to the saw mill.

SHEERNESS
Boatstore (TQ910753)
Sheerness Docks, ½ mile W of town centre
Designed by Col GT Greene, Director of Engineering and Architectural Works to the Admiralty, this surprisingly modern looking multi-storey iron-frame building was constructed 1858–60. The Naval Dockyards with their prefabricated Ship Shops of *c* 1849 at Chatham and Portsmouth were pioneers of building techniques and the Boatstore at Sheerness is a prime example of this tradition. Sheerness Dockyard itself was relinquished by the Navy in 1960 and is now being developed commercially.

SISSINGHURST
Oast Houses (TQ807384)
2 miles NE of Cranbrook off A262
At Sissinghurst Castle there is a particularly fine group of oast houses. The 2-storey red brick range has 2 large kilns and 6 smaller ones, all complete with white painted wooden cowls. The kilns and roof are tiled with red tiles. The main range of the oast house is now used as a tea room.

SITTINGBOURNE
Dolphin Barge Yard (TQ910643)
½ mile NE of town centre
The old barge yard on the banks of the Milton Creek at Sittingbourne comprises a set of barge repair blocks, sail loft, carpenter's shop, forge and a small area of saltings. The salt loft is 2-storey and built of ship's timber while the forge is supported by ancient sailing barge tillers and is complete with large leather bellows. The site is being restored by a charitable trust.

SHEERNESS: *Revolutionary metal-framed Boatstore in Sheerness Dockyard.*

Lancashire

As an industrial county the new administrative county of Lancashire is only a shadow of its former self. It has lost its major cities – Liverpool and Manchester in the S and the Furness area in the N. Its character has been changed from an industrial giant to a relatively minor county, one of whose main industries is tourism centred on the resort of Blackpool. It still contains the pioneer area of textile production in the valleys around Blackburn and Burnley and some notable canal monuments associated with the Leeds & Liverpool and Lancaster canals. The former maritime tradition is reflected by structures at Lancaster, Glasson Dock and Fleetwood.

BARNACRE-WITH-BONDS
Forge (SD505459)
3 miles NE of Garstang
Small 2-storey stone-built water-powered forge on tributary of the River Wyre. Now used as a joinery, it still has a 20ft high breast waterwheel.

BLACKBURN
Eanam Wharf (SD689282)
NE of town centre on A677
The Leeds & Liverpool Canal in Blackburn runs beside a small group of early canal buildings which have been relatively unaltered since they were built in the first quarter of the 19th century. They comprise a long range of stone warehouse buildings with small-paned windows, hoists and an old flag roof, an office, 2 houses and the base and iron column of a wharf jib crane.

BURNLEY
Leeds & Liverpool Canal (e.g. SD843320)
Periphery of town centre
The Leeds & Liverpool Canal almost encircles the centre of Burnley. It comes in from the N then E to cross the River Brun on a masonry aqueduct, then S on a massive embankment ³/₄-mile long over the valley of the River Calder, then NW to the ornamental portals of the 559-yard long **Gannow Tunnel** (SD827330–SD824325). There is a canal house and boatyard at **Finsley Gate** (SD843320), warehouses at Manchester Road, a ground floor warehouse with formerly 10 cottages above at Sandygate and a yard in Yorkshire Street with a pair of limekilns built into the base of a massively buttressed retaining wall. This section of canal was opened in 1796 and became a focus for steam-powered mills in the expanding cotton industry.

CLITHEROE
Industrial Community, Low Moor
(SD730418)
1 mile SW of Clitheroe off B6243
A fine example of an early compact and isolated industrial community associated with a single mill. The mill itself, Garnett & Horsfall's Low Moor Mill, has gone but several streets of early stone-built cottages, 2 chapels, a village school and co-operative store survive.

DARWEN
Tram Triangle, Whitehall (*c* SD698204)
1 mile S Darwen, E of A666
At the terminus of the former steam tramway of 1881 is the only remaining example of a steam-tram reversing triangle. East Lanca-shire had an extensive system of 4ft-gauge steam tramways before the advent of electric trams.

ELLEL
Galgate Silk Mills (SD485557)
5 miles S of Lancaster off A6
Started in 1792 by W Thompson, J Noble and J Armstrong, the present buildings are of 3 main dates – a 3-storey stone-built single aisle mill of 1792 with staircase tower, a 3-storey stone-built mill of *c* 1830 with cast-iron columns but timber beams, a 5-storey brick-built mill of 1851 also with cast-iron columns and timber beams and water tank on roof for sprinkler system.

FLEETWOOD
Lower Lighthouse, Esplanade (SD337486)
N town centre
This striking red sandstone 3-stage light was built 1836–41 and was probably designed by Decimus Burton who was responsible for planned settlement of Fleetwood. The first stage is a Tuscan colonnade with balustrade above, square plan middle stage carries a bracketed balcony with cast-iron railings and the third stage is octagonal surmounted by a dome and drum. The complementary **Upper Lighthouse** in Pharos Place (SD339484) was also almost certainly designed by Burton and is equally striking.

GARSTANG
Wyre Aqueduct (SD491448)
W of village
A graceful 54 ft-span single-arch masonry aqueduct carrying the Lancaster Canal over the River Wyre. Built *c* 1796 its gracefully curved retaining walls and deep cornice have all the hallmarks of Rennies mastery of stone as a building material.

HASLINGDEN
Higher Mill, Holcombe Road, Helmshore
(SD780210)
1½ miles S of Haslingden off B6235
A water-powered woollen finishing mill built 1789 as a woollen fulling mill. Now maintained as a museum, it contains early fulling stocks and finishing machinery and an 18 ft waterwheel. Some of the finest examples of early cotton machinery including Arkwright's water frame and a spinning jenny and a small 1846 beam engine by Peel Williams & Peel are housed in the building.

HEYSHAM
Sunderland Point (SD426560)
4 miles S of Heysham

In the early 18th century the Lune estuary was developing trade with the West Indies and at Sunderland Point an outport for Lancaster was developed by Robert Lawson, a local merchant, to allow ships too large to reach Lancaster to moor and be unloaded. After a short period of prosperity this trade ceased but the 2 terraces of houses still survive accessible by a causeway submerged by the tide twice daily.

LANCASTER
Glasson Dock (SD445562)
5 miles S of Lancaster off A588
Sunderland Point in the Lune estuary was rather an exposed mooring and at a more sheltered anchorage across the river another outport for Lancaster developed. In recognition of this in 1751 the port commissioners put down a large mooring stone and chain for the ships to tie up. In 1791 Glasson wet dock capable of accommodating 25 vessels was completed. In 1826 Glasson Dock was linked with the Lancaster Canal and a larger inner basin constructed. In 1836 a patent slip and grid iron were constructed and in 1838 a graving dock was opened. Most of these features as well as a swing-bridge, small light and the contemporary housing survive though now mainly servicing pleasure craft.

LANCASTER
Lune Aqueduct (SD484639)
1 mile NE of town off A6
Built by John Rennie with Alexander Stevens as architect and contractor, the Lune Aqueduct was completed in 1797 and is possibly the finest masonry aqueduct in the country. The Lancaster Canal is carried 51 ft above the river by 5 arches – each of 70 ft span and 39 ft height. The rusticated stone is surmounted by a typically Rennie deep cornice and Doric entablature.

LANCASTER
Skerton Bridge (SD479623)
Town centre
This 5-arch masonry bridge which carries the A6 over the River Lune was designed by Thomas Harrison and built 1783–1788. It is supposedly the first bridge of any size in England to have a level roadway from end to end.

LANCASTER
Warehouses, St George's Quay (SD474623)
W town centre
In the 18th century Lancaster developed as a prosperous port with Sunderland Point (*qv*) and later Glasson (*qv*) as outports to accom-modate vessels too large for the River Lune. Several fine mid-18th-century stone-built warehouses of 4 and 5 storeys, their gable walls complete with wooden hoists. The classical Customs House designed by Richard Gallow in 1764 bears witness to the former importance of the port.

LYTHAM ST ANNES
Windmill, East Beach (SD371270)
Eastern end of town on A584
White-washed brick 3-storey tower mill built *c* 1804 as corn mill and in use until *c* 1926. Recently restored with boat-shaped cap, shuttered sails and fantail.

ORMSKIRK
Water Tower, Scarth Hill (SD429066)
$1\frac{1}{2}$ miles SE of Ounskirk off A570
Circular 19th-century iron water-tank with panelled sides and low conical roof on brick base of 8 tall open arches. Another prominent water tower was built E of Tower Hill in 1850 by the Ormskirk Local Board of Health. This is a tall square red brick tower surmounted by a stone-coloured tank portion with pyramidal roof.

OSWALDTWISTLE
Hargreaves House (Stanhill Post Office) (SD728277)
3 miles E of Blackburn off A679
The house in which James Hargreaves lived and invented his spinning jenny in 1764. According to the commemorative plaque 'he was compelled to leave Stanhill because of the persecution of the local spinners and others who feared the invention would deprive them of their livelihood. Hargreaves went to Nottingham where he died AD 1778'. Nearby at **Peel Fold Farm** (SD717280), a 17th-century stone-built farmhouse, Robert Peel (1723–1795) carried out his early experiments in calico printing.

OSWALDTWISTLE
Coke Ovens (SD736285)
4 miles E of Blackburn off A679
In the early 19th century beehive coke ovens were typically built at either a pithead or by a canal. Those at Oswaldtwistle are an example of the latter and were formerly served by a basin off the Leeds & Liverpool Canal. There were 3 ranges of ovens at this site built at right angles to the canal but only the range adjacent to the basin survives in fairly complete form. It comprises 18 brick-built ovens arranged back to back enclosed in rubble with masonry and walls.

PRESTON
Centenary Mill, New Hall Lane (SD551297)
E town centre
An example of late 19th-century cotton mill incorporating the most modern structural techniques available. It was built by Horrockses in 1895 and has steel beams and concrete floors giving much greater freedom of movement and also permitting most of the walls to be devoted to windows. In the weaving sheds steel lattice girders allow bays to be 90 ft square instead of 10 ft by 12 ft, common early in the century.

QUERNMORE
Castle Mill (SD520609)
3 miles SE of Lancaster
A water-powered corn mill built 1818. It has an unusual stone wall and roof cladding protecting a 36 ft diameter overshot waterwheel though this wheel which drives through a rim gear is almost certainly not original.

RAWTENSTALL
Whitehead's Mill, New Hall Hey (SD810225)
S of Town Centre on A56
Large 4-storey stone-built mill dating from 1862. Its crenellated cornice and projecting stair wings contrast with some of the more austere examples of mill building nearby.

THORNTON CLEVELEYS: *Marsh Mill.*

Square free standing chimney and lodge in same style.

RIBCHESTER
Oaks Bar Toll House (SD670335)
8 miles E of Preston on A59
Comparatively few toll houses survive in Lancashire. This single-storey stone-built cottage is at the Ribchester crossroads on the Whalley Preston road.

THORNTON CLEVELEYS
Marsh Mill (SD335426)
4 miles S of Fleetwood on A585
The low-lying district of Fylde had to rely on wind power rather than water power for conventional milling. Marsh Mill is a late 18th-century 5-storey tower mill some 50 ft high with staging at third floor level, a boat-shaped cap, common sails and fantail. The mill has been restored by the local authority.

WHALLEY
Whalley Viaduct (SD728363)
7 miles NE of Blackburn off A666/A59
This 680-yard long brick viaduct over the River Calder was built by the Bolton Blackburn Clitheroe & West Yorks Railway in 1851. It cost £35,000 and has 48 spans rising to some 70 ft above the river. Where one arch frames the gatehouse of Whalley Abbey the adjacent arches have echoing Gothic infill.

Leicestershire

Leicestershire is a county of 2 quite different portions – to the N and W of Leicester itself is an area with a long tradition of coal mining and textile production with several significant monuments associated with these including the Moira blast furnace, to the E of Leicester it is predominantly rural. It also has several canal monuments most notably the Foxton incline and some lesser railway monuments.

ASHBY
Railway Station (SK355163)
¼ mile S of town centre
A graceful building of 1849 in Greek Doric style possibly by architect Robert Chaplin. Built by Midland Railway to be in keeping with the aspirations of Ashby as a refined spa resort. After several years of disuse the station

has now been restored and converted to offices. With its approach flanked by a high rusticated wall it is now one of the most handsome buildings in NW Leicestershire.

AYLESTONE
Packhorse Bridge (SK567007)
3-miles S of Leicester off A426

A long narrow packhorse bridge and causeway dating, in parts, from the 15th century. Some 270 ft long and only 4 ft wide it crosses a minor stream and low swampy ground by means of 11 irregular arches, some of which are pointed *à la Gothique*. Some of the piers have projecting cutwaters and refuges above. The canal bridge which gives access over the Grand Union Canal to the packhorse causeway has the same very narrow roadway.

BAGWORTH
Railway Incline (SK446090–453086)
4 miles S of Coalville off B585
One of the major engineering works of the Leicester & Swannington Railway which was surveyed by George Stephenson and built by Robert Stephenson in 1832. This cable worked incline necessitated the unhitching of a locomotive and the trucks were hauled to the top by a stationary steam engine housed in a 2-storey hexagonal building. The engine house survives but the engine itself has gone. The incline which is some 800 yards in length was disused from *c* 1848 when the Midland Railway acquired the Leicester & Swannington Railway and by-passed this section.

CASTLE DONNINGTON
Kings Mills (SK417275)
1 mile W of Castle Donnington
An important early water-powered industrial site on a cut-off from the River Trent. It has been variously used for corn grinding, fulling, papermaking, gypsum grinding and button working. The mill buildings which were originally quite extensive have almost entirely disappeared but parts of 3 iron waterwheels, numerous watercourses and a gypsum kiln survive.

CLAYBROOK MAGNA
Watermill (SP499892)
4 miles SE of Hinkley off A5
Three-storey brick-built watermill on River Soar in use until recently as a grist mill though latterly worked by electricity. Twelve foot diameter waterwheel in repositioned wheelhouse.

COALVILLE
Elastic Webb Factory, Belvoir Road (SK424137)
¼ mile S of town centre B585
A 3-storey, 16-bay factory built in brick in 1878. The gable over the 2 central bays and the terra cotta ornamentation of the round headed windows gives it some distinction.

COALVILLE
Signal Box (SK427144)
Town centre on A50
An unusually tall 19th-century signal box in a very prominent situation controlling the crossing on the main road in Coalville. The box itself is bracketed out beyond its 2-storey base. Both box and base have fine window detail. The nearby Railway Hotel was built *c* 1833 and served as a station for the Stephensons' Leicester & Swannington Railway. The stabling at the rear was used by carriers for the later Midland Railway.

EARL SHILTON
Hosiery Workshops (SP453971)
3 miles NE of Hinckley on A47
Earl Shilton was an important knitting village with 650 machines recorded in a survey of 1844. Most of the workshops have disappeared. This terrace of 6, 2-storey cottages has long workshop windows on the rear ground floor and a row of small brick outhouses which may have housed additional machines. An example of a 3-storey cottage with top floor workshop can be seen in Wood Street (SP460976).

FOXTON
Canal Incline and Locks (SP693897)
The 10 narrow locks at Foxton on the Leicester line of the Grand Union Canal were opened in 1812 and were always a bottle neck on the through route from Leicester to London. In 1896 it was agreed to construct an incline plane to surmount the 75 ft difference in height and after testing with a large scale model the plane was built between 1898–1900. Foxton Plane was 307 ft long and occupied 2 parallel planes each carrying an 80 ft by 15 ft by 5 ft tank in which the boats could be floated. The incline was steam powered and could pass a pair of boats in as little time as 5 minutes in contrast to the some 70 minutes required to navigate the locks. However the capacity of the incline was never fully utilized due to a general decline in traffic and the incline was officially closed in 1910 though was operable until *c* 1914. It was finally dismantled *c* 1926. The concrete planes are much overgrown.

GLENFIELD
Glenfield Tunnel – Western Portal (SK544065)
2½ miles NW of Leicester off A50
When this tunnel was built by the Stephensons in 1832 on their Leicester & Swannington Railway it was the longest such tunnel in the world. It was abandoned in the 1960s and blocked at each end. The eastern portal lies

beneath a housing estate while the western survives as one of the earliest railway tunnel portals in the country. The opening itself is horse-shoe shaped flanked by brick pilasters with a large masonry cornice.

HINKLEY
Hosiery Workshops, Lower Bond Street (SP428943)
Town centre
These fine, reconstructed, examples of framework-knitters' cottages contain some 19th-century machinery, including a stocking frame, and are maintained as a museum by Messrs Atkins whose premises are opposite.

KEGWORTH
Hosiery Workshop, Brittania Inn (SK488264)
½ mile S of village on A6
Built in the late 19th century for hand operated machines, this 2-storey framework-knitters' workshop was used for this purpose until the 1950s. It has typically long ranges of multi-paned workshop windows and an external stair giving access to the upper floor. It

GLENFIELD: *Horseshoe-shaped portal of historic railway tunnel before its disfiguration by recent sealing.*

is one of the best examples to survive of a typical frameshop of the Leicestershire hosiery industry.

LEICESTER
Abbey Lane Pumping Station (SK589067)
1 mile N of city centre
Built in 1891 as the sewage works pumping station, this is now the site of the Leicester technological museum collection. It is centred round the imposing brick engine house which contains 4 large beam engines by Messrs Gimson of Leicester. These engines with their associated decorated massive iron columns are fine examples of the ultimate stage in beam engine technology. The outbuildings house an interesting collection of historic vehicles and machinery. The tall detached octagonal brick chimney with its decorated stone cornice and pedestal is a conspicuous landmark.

LEICESTER
Donisthorpes Factory, Bath Lane (SK580045)
¼ mile W of city centre
Parts of these textile works and especially some of those fronting Bath Lane probably date from the late 18th century. The main 3-storey brick-built pedimented mill building with its slate hipped roof, wide eaves, hexagonal lead-domed cupola and weather vane is probably early 19th century. The site is very cramped and it is difficult to obtain a clear view of any of the main buildings.

LEICESTER
Frisby Jarvis Factory, Frog Island (SK581053)
¼ mile NW of city centre on A50
A large late-19th-century hosiery works displaying more architectural pretension than was the norm in Leicester at this date. The 20-bay frontage of the brick 4-storey main building has a 3-bay section slightly protruding and surmounted by a heavy pediment and clock. This, along with the wide bracketed eaves and fine window proportions and detail, combine to make it a handsome building.

LEICESTER
West Bridge (SK582043)
¼ mile W of city centre
One of a series of bridges over the canalized section of the River Soarall dating from 1890 or 1891. The others are at Mill Lane, the Newarke and Upperton Road. West Bridge has 2 cast-iron arches obscuring iron girders with stone abutments and elaborate cast-iron detailing of spandrels and parapet. At either end are masonry octagonal turrets with ogee shaped domes.

LOUGHBOROUGH
Taylors Bell Foundry, Cobden Street
The famous Oxford bell founders of John Taylor & Co established a branch in Loughborough in 1859 and subsequently moved their entire operation to the town in 1884. Most of the buildings on this sprawling site are late-19th-century, the testing tower was rebuilt in 1898 after a fire. In 1887 the firm cast Great Paul which at 17 tons was the largest in the country.

LOUGHBOROUGH
Towles Factory, Queen Street (SK544201)
½ mile NE of town centre
Parts of this large textile complex date from Cartwright & Warners original spinning factory of 1790 which fronted the Leicester Navigation. Pedimented mill building can be seen from old entrance in Mill Street. Still in use as a hosiery factory with main building fronting Queen Street.

LOUGHBOROUGH
Workers' Housing and Workshops, Pinfold Gate (*c* SK540198)
Pinfold Gate contains a terrace of exceptionally fine workers' houses built *c* 1860 for the neighbouring William Cotton's Hosiery Factory. The houses have elaborate lattice-pattern cast-iron windows with terra cotta panelled lintels. A large cart entrance in the original centre of the row gave access to the rear. Across the road is a 3-storey house with top-floor workshops, 2 of the 4 windows on the top floor have their original sliding casements.

MARKET HARBOROUGH
Railway Station (SP742875)
¼ mile E of town centre on A427
Although there was a station on this site before 1860 the present imposing main building dates from 1885 and was built as a joint station for LNWR and LMR. A covered ramp leads from the entrance building to the platforms which are at a considerably higher level.

MEASHAM
Brick Drying Sheds, Bosworth Road (SK337121)
4 miles SW of Ashby off A453
Measham was locally famous for large bricks – the so-called Wilkes Gobs (11½ in by 5½ in by 4½ in). Little remains of the brickworks itself but this 3-storey terrace of *c* 1800 has been converted from drying sheds with residential accommodation in the upper 2 floors and garages in the original arched bays on the ground floor. The structure is largely built of gobs.

MEASHAM
Canal Warehouses (SK333121)
4 miles SW of Ashby on A453
Fine pair of matching canal warehouses on either side of the turnpike bridge over the Ashby Canal in Measham. Built of the oversize Wilke's gobs both warehouses were served by bargeholes for direct loading. The elevations at right angles to the main road have tall blind recesses.

MOIRA
Blast Furnace (SK314152)
3 miles SW of Ashby off B5003
Built *c* 1804 by the Earl of Moira, Moira Furnace is one of the finest industrial monuments in the East Midlands. It was built

alongside the newly opened Ashby Canal with an arched ramp across the canal for conveying the raw materials to the furnace top. The canal section of this ramp has been demolished but a section is preserved behind a cladding of dwellings immediately adjacent to the furnace. The massive brick built stack is square in plan and has 3 pairs of recesses above the main arches on each open face. The furnace seems to have gone out of use in the mid-19th century.

MOIRA
Engine Cottage (SK313150)
3½ miles SW of Ashby off B5003
This tall narrow brick-built cottage with its unusually few and irregularly spaced windows was in fact an engine house for a beam pumping engine. It was built in 1805 to pump a local colliery – the date is recorded on the massive spring beam inside. The bricked up beam aperture can still be seen on the bob wall. The engine house was converted in the 19th century to a workers' hostel and is now a single cottage.

MOIRA: *Moira Blast Furnace.*

MOUNTSORREL
Railway Bridge (SK579154)
4 miles SE of Loughborough off A6
A graceful red brick structure built 1860 to carry a mineral line from the granite quarries at Mountsorrel to the main line. The span over the River Soar is a wide low segmental arch of outstanding design.

OAKHAM
Railway Station (SK857090)
¼ mile W of town centre off A606
A dignified 2-storey brick station of the late 19th century. The projecting wings are connected by a prominent square columned porch. The slate roof has wide bracketed eaves and prominent bargeboards to the gables.

REARSBY
Rearsby Mill, Ratcliffe Road (SE642149)
¾ mile NW of Rearsby
Early 19th-century mill and house in a red brick 3-storey range. The mill has a weather-

boarded lucan and retains its machinery with an undershot wheel of 1907 driving 2 pairs of stones.

SHACKERSTONE
Railway Station (SK378067)
3 miles NE of Market Bosworth
A neat single-storey red brick station with stone window surrounds, bracketed eaves and a hipped slate roof. The platform side has a delicate cast-iron 5-bay colonnade between the wings of the main building. This feature recurs on other stations on the same line such as Measham (SK332119). Shackerstone Station is now the base of a steam locomotive preservation society. The approach to the station passes an early canal aqueduct over the River Sence and a cast-iron parallel-rail bridge.

SHEPSHED
Windmill (SK462181)
1 mile SW of Shepshed off A518
A fine 4-storey red brick tower mill with ogee cap, fantail and 2 sails beautifully maintained as an adornment to a private house which has been built against the mill.

WIGSTON
Hosiery Workshop, Bushloe End (SP604987)
¼ mile W of town centre on A5096
One of the most remarkable survivals of the domestic system of hosiery manufacture occurs in Wigston. The unit comprises a master's house, seaming room, workshop and shop and is arranged along a street frontage and around a rear yard. The contents of the 2-storey workshop have survived intact since its closure in 1952 and include 8 knitting frames in the ground floor and 5 sock-making machines in the upper floor. Although the house itself is earlier the complex as it now appears is a monument to late 19th-century domestic industry.

WIGSTON
Railway Housing (SK595985)
½ mile W of town centre off A5096
The Midland Railway provided a considerable amount of accommodation for its employees. A typical example is Midland Cottages, a terrace of 20 identical houses off Station Road, Wigston. They have distinctive pointed windows usually in pairs. Similar cottages can be seen in Knight on Lane, Leicester SK590017).

Lincolnshire

Lincolnshire is a rich agricultural county whose prosperity has traditionally been in produce exported from the many small ports of its inland waterways and from its major port of Boston. Indeed Boston was second to London in port dues in the 13th century. Most of the county's industrial monuments are related to those themes of agriculture and waterways.

ALVINGHAM
Alvingham Watermill, Church Lane (TF368920)
3 miles NE of Louth
18th-century corn mill on the River Ludd with breast shot waterwheel driving 2 pairs of Peak stones. Operates most summer Sundays.

ALFORD
Alford Windmill, East Street (TF455761)
Town centre
A 5-sail tower mill built 1813 and open to the public on certain holidays.

BOSTON
Boston Dock (TF333431)
½ mile SE of town centre
The opening of this dock in 1884 transformed Boston's declining trade and within 12 years trade had increased eightfold. The entrance lock is 300 ft by 50 ft and can take vessels of up to 3000 tons and gives access to a basin 7 acres

BOSTON: *Lincoln's Granary Packhouse Quay – now a music centre.*

in extent. Shortly after the opening of the dock the first of the 2 large granaries was built measuring 220 ft by 52 ft and some 57 ft high. The second slightly larger granary was added in 1891.

BOSTON
Hospital Bridge (TF331449)
½ mile N of town centre
This cast-iron bridge over the Maud Foster Drain has an extremely low arch. Although it has a span of 67 ft 9 in it rises only 2 ft 6 in. It bears the inscription 'Cast at Butterly 1811'. A similar footbridge with an identical inscription and similar dimensions was erected at Cow-bridge (TF328471).

BOSTON
Lincoln's Granary (TF237438)
Town centre
This large warehouse block to the S of Pack-horse quay has a complicated structural history. The original block was built prior to 1741, parallel to the river, but 2 large wings were added in the late 18th century at right angles reaching down to the river. By 1811 the space between these wings had been built up to

give the present 6-bay river frontage. This evolutionary sequence can best be discerned from the roof lines. The building is occupied by T L Lincoln & Sons, seed growers.

BOSTON
Van Smirren's Warehouse (TF237437)
Town centre
This tall conspicuous warehouse on Doughty Quay was built c 1810. Its narrowness, only 3 bays wide, though 5 storeys high, is accentuated by prominent stone pointing and tall round headed windows on the ground floor. Its low pitched roof has wide projecting eaves giving the warehouse a rather exotic appearance.

GAINSBOROUGH
Toll Bridge (SK814891)
¼ mile SW of town centre
In 1791 a bridge was built to replace the chain ferry which had formerly been the only means of crossing the Trent at Gainsborough itself. The 3-arched bridge had side spans of 62 ft and a centre span of 70 ft and, being erected by a

turnpike trust, had a pair of single-storey toll houses. Although the bridge itself was widened in 1964 and considerably modified, the toll houses on the eastern approach have survived.

GAINSBOROUGH
Warehouses (SK814892)
¼ mile SW of town centre
There is a series of early 19th-century warehouses in Bridge Street, many of which have access to the river. Typically they have centralized hatches and hoists and most of them were used in connection with the grain trade.

GRANTHAM
Londonthorpe Mill (SK924381)
1 mile N of Grantham off A607
The fronting of this mill, with its twin gables separated by a semi-circular pediment, is rather Dutch looking – a characteristic shared by some of the domestic architecture in nearby Manthorpe. Brick-built, with an adjoining mill house, it probably dates from the 19th century. The waterwheel measuring 16 ft by 6 ft 7 in is high breast shot and was installed by Wakes & Lamb at Newark-on-Trent in 1914. It powers 3 pairs of stones: French, Peak and composition respectively.

HALLTOFT END
Barkers Bridge (TF362459)
3 miles E of Boston off A52
One of a series of attractive, small, brick bridges over the Cowbridge Drain, this example is at the junction with Hobhole Drain.

HEAPHAM
Windmill (SK873887)
4 miles SE of Gainsborough off A631
This 4-storey brick tower mill dates from *c* 1878 and although it has lost its sails and fantail, it retains most of its original milling machinery. The mill itself is 43 ft high and 19 ft diameter.

HOLBEACH
Wool Barn (TF358269)
N of town centre
This barn in Boston Road, Holbeach, dates from *c* 1795 and has staggered flues at each end for wool drying.

HORNCASTLE
Canal Basin (TF260695)
Town centre
The Horncastle Navigation was completed in 1802 with a small terminal basin at Horncastle. This basin has largely disappeared as the navigation through the town has been converted into a conduit. However, contemporary warehouses remain as witness to the location of the basin.

LINCOLN
Central Station (SK975709)
½ mile S of city centre
Built in a Tudor-Gothic style by the Great Northern in 1848, this station contrasts strongly with the earlier classical St Marks Station (*qv*). In many ways it is more in harmony with its surroundings echoing, if not copying, local styles.

LINCOLN
St Marks Station (SK973707)
¾ mile S of city centre
This rather austere but elegant neo-Greek station built by the Midland Railway in 1846 has been partially demolished by British Rail. The canopies over the platform and most of the appointments, other than those of the main block, have gone.

LINCOLN
The Glory Hole (SK973711)
½ mile S of city centre
The Glory Hole is the colloquial name for Brayford Basin where the River Wilham Navigation meets the Fossdyke which connects Lincoln to the River Trent. The basin had many interesting old warehouses which are fast disappearing. An early brush factory has so far survived.

LINCOLN
Tower Mill (SK971723)
½ mile NW of city centre
This tower in Mill Road is the last surviving mill on Lincoln Edge and as such is of historic interest even though it has lost its cap and sails. Dating from *c* 1840, it has 3 storeys and is built of tarred brick with a modern felt-covered conical roof.

LONG SUTTON
Windmill Tower (TF435243)
4 miles E of Holbeach off A17
There are remains of 3 windmills at Long Sutton – all beside the old sea bank itself. It has lost its sail and cap.

LOUTH
Crown Mill (TF333876)
NE of town centre
One of the 12 Domesday corn milling sites on the River Ludd. Dated 1716, it was enlarged in the mid- and late 19th century and is now worked by a turbine.

LOUTH
Louth Station (TF332878)
NE of town centre
Built by the Great Northern Railway in 1854, Louth Station with its round arched *porte-cochère* is a prominent example of the neo-Jacobean style so favoured by stations in the mid-19th century.

LOUTH
Ticklepenny Lock (TF351890)
1½ miles NE of Louth
The Louth Navigation was opened in stages from Tetney Haven to Louth in 1767 and 1770. It has rather unusual locks with arched sides – presumably intended to resist inward thrust from the land. Ticklepenny is a typical example – 88 ft 7 in long and 15 ft 6 in wide with a fall of 7 ft.

PINCHBECK
Spalding Marsh Pumping Station (TF262262)
4½ miles NE of Spalding off A151
One of 2 small, steam-driven, drainage pumping stations to survive in Lincolnshire. It belonged to the Deeping Fen, Spalding and Pinchbeck Internal Drainage Board and until recently was maintained as stand-by. The engine itself is an 1833 single-cylinder rotative A-frame, beam engine and is the earliest such engine *in situ*.

SKEGNESS
Skegness Pier (TF572634)
Built in 1881 this pier is some 1800 ft long with a large T-shaped head 222 ft long and 122 ft wide supporting a theatre and elevated promenading deck. The pier neck is generally 20 ft wide and 2 pairs of shelters, one at the

landward end, the other mid-way along. The structure is supported by pairs of cast-iron columns on cast-iron screw piles and although it has suffered from ship collision it appears largely as built.

SLEAFORD
Bass Maltings (TF074452)
SE of town centre
This range of maltings is one of the largest ever built in England and dates from the turn of the century. They are no longer used as maltings and are occupied by several unrelated firms – forming a small industrial estate. The engine house contains 2 horizontal tandem compound steam engines installed by Tobey & Co, Lincoln, *c* 1904 and 2 single-cylinder horizontal rotative pumps.

TATTERSHALL
Dog Dyke Pumping Station (TF206558)
9 miles S of Horncastle off A153
Dog Dyke is one of only 2 small steam-driven drainage pumping stations to survive in Lincolnshire. Prior to recent reorganization it belonged to Witham 3rd District Internal Drainage Board but has been disused for many years. The building contains its original 1855 single-cylinder rotative beam engine and scoop wheel and there are plans to preserve it.

TEALBY
Tealby Thorpe Watermill (TF150900)
2 miles E of Market Rasen off B1203
This watermill is maintained by its owners as a museum of milling bygones. The mill with its '10 o'clock' wheel, can be worked for demonstration purposes.

Greater London

Though London lacks the foundations usually associated with industrial development such as fossil fuels or metal ores, it has nevertheless as great a range of industries as any comparable area in the country. It has been, since Roman times, the major British market and has attracted industries to serve this market. Thus although most of London's industrial monuments are associated with service industry or transport, others reflect its former varied industrial history, e.g. bell foundry, Whitechapel, pottery, Fulham, textile mills, Morton, copper mills and small arms works, Enfield.

Transport dominates London's stock of industrial monuments, its function as a port has left London with one of the finest collections of dock, warehouse and riverside monuments in the country though the future of many of them must be uncertain. Parts of St Katharines Dock complex have been restored but fine installations at East and West London docks and the Royal Docks are not yet so secure. Railways have contributed a magnificent series of terminal stations including Paddington, Kings Cross, and St Pancras, and associated monuments such as Camden Round House, Wharncliffe Viaduct and Primrose Hill Tunnel. Canals, though not quite so prominent have also left significant structures including the fine bridges in Regents Park. London has also a unique series of coal duty boundary marks on lines of communication approaching the historic city.

Most notable among the monuments belonging to service industries are the exceptional collection of installations for water supply and sewage disposal including the New River Head, and steam pumping stations at Kew Bridge, Kempton Park and Crossness. London has also 3 of the finest brewery sites in the country at Chiswell Street, Brick Lane and Wandsworth and numerous windmills and watermills, including the tower mill at Brixton, the smock mill at Upminster and the post mill at Kelston Common, the tide mills at Bromley-by-Bow and the watermills at Ponders End.

BARBICAN
Whitbread's Brewery, Chiswell Street (TQ326819)
One of London's most famous breweries with buildings dating from the early 18th century. One of the first sites in London to adopt steam power on a large scale – a famous painting of 1792 shows horses in the brewery yard against a background of smoking chimneys. The immense Porter Tun Room of 1784 has a fine King Post timber roof with a clear span of 65 ft while the early 19th-century Tun Room retains its original timber Queen Post roof. The tapestry commemorating Operation Overlord is on public display in the Porter Tun Room.

BATTERSEA
Conduit Tramway Track, Battersea Bridge (TQ271773)
On the W of the approach to Battersea Bridge is a small landscaped open space in which is preserved a short section of conduit tramway track. The conduit tramway came into use in the inner London area in May 1903 to spare the disfigurement of the central area by overhead wires. It had only a short life due to operating problems.

BETHNAL GREEN
Bethnal Green Museum, Cambridge Heath Road (TQ350828)

An outstation of the Victoria & Albert Museum, the conventional red brick façade hides a spacious cast-iron framed interior of 3 bays. These are re-erected parts of the original temporary structures erected at South Kensington to house exhibits from the Great Exhibition and popularly known as Brompton Boilers.

BOW
Fairfield Match Works, Fairfield Road (TQ374832)
Founded 1861, Bryant & Mays match factory was noted for its good working conditions. The red brick boundary wall with its blind Gothic arches incorporates several attractive cottages as well as a gatehouse with large terracotta arched doorway with bas relief of boat on sea.

BRENTFORD
Kew Bridge Waterworks, Kew Bridge Road (TQ188780)
The most important *in situ* group of beam pumping engines in the world. Now run as a museum by a trust. The engines include a Boulton & Watt of 1820, a Maudsley of 1838, a 90-in Cornish Engine of 1871 and an 1859 Bull engine by Harvey. The 200 ft high stand pipe was built 1867, disguised as a campanile.

BRENTFORD
Gallows Bridge (TQ163783)
Single-span iron footbridge with yellow brick abutments over the Brentford Canal. Built by Horseley Iron Works, Birmingham, and dated 1820. The Brentford Canal connected the Grand Junction Canal to the River Thames.

BRIXTON HILL
Brixton Windmill, Blenheim Gardens (TQ305744)
Brick-built tower mill of *c* 1816, some 50 ft high with boat-shaped wooden cap. Internal machinery from a dismantled Lancashire mill. Preserved by GLC and open to the public.

BROMLEY
Shortlands Pumping Station, Valley Road (TQ395692)
Earlier pumphouse built late 19th century by Kent Water Works Co in Kentish ragstone rubble in Gothic style. Later pumphouse built early 20th century of squared Kentish ragstone by Metropolitan Water Board.

BROMLEY-BY-BOW
Three Mills Conservation Area, Three Mill Lane (TQ383828)

BROMLEY-BY-BOW: *House Mill, Three Mills Lane – an 18th-century tidemill.*

One of the most important water-powered sites in the country with 2 tidemills surviving virtually intact. House Mill dates from 1776 with a 10-bay brick southern façade and a weatherboarded northern façade encasing a timber-framed mill with 4 undershot waterwheels of *c* 20 ft diameter. The nearby Clock Mill is dated 1817 with a clock tower of *c* 1750. It is 5 storeys high with cast-iron columns and wooden beams and it contains 3 undershot wheels. It has a pair of oast houses abutting its western side.

CAMDEN TOWN
Round House, Chalk Farm Road (TQ283843)
Designed as an engine shed for the London & North Western Railway by R Stephenson's drawing office, this magnificent structure was completed in 1847. Now used as a theatre, the fine conical roof of 180 ft diameter is carried on 24 tall cast-iron Doric columns and a framework of curved ribs. The turntable machinery has mostly gone but the fine undercroft vaults are accessible by appointment.

CHINGFORD
Humphrey Gas Pumps, King George's Reservoir (TQ373979)
These pumps were installed in 1913 to lift water against a head of only 5 ft. There were 5 of the Humphrey pistonless gas pumps driven by producer gas. Four of the pumps had 7 ft 8 in diameter combustion chambers each capable of lifting 40 million gallons a day and the 5th with a chamber 5ft in diameter with a 20 million gallon capacity. These engines were very economical when the circumstances permitted. Now disused.

CHISWICK
Tramway Sub-station, Chiswick High Road (TQ215787)
Monumental classical building of red brick with stone dressing of *c* 1900 built for London United Electric Tramways Co. Company crest and initials in sculptured panel over one entrance. Interior has fine iron staircase and colonnaded gallery.

CITY
Central Meat Market, West Smithfield (TQ318818)
Large single-storey structure screened by walls in red brick and Portland Stone but notable for its fine cast-iron interior. Designed by Sir Horace Jones in 1866 it has a central covered roadway 50 ft wide with elaborate screens of open metalwork as its main feature.

CITY
Cannon Street Station Towers, All Hallows Lane, Cousin Lane (TQ326806)
Terminal station of the South Eastern Railway designed by Hawkshaw & Barry 1865-6, now largely rebuilt but the monumental yellow brick towers fronting river remain.

CROYDON
Water Tower, Park Hill (TQ330650)
Norman style brick water tower built *c* 1860 with an early (*c* 1851) circular covered brick service reservoir.

DEPTFORD
Power Station, Deptford Green (TQ375779)
The first electric generating station in the world to transmit an extra high tension was built at Deptford in 1888 by the London Electricity Supply Co under the direction of Sebastion De Ferranti. The original massive plain brick-built engine halls are incorporated into the present Deptford East Power Station.

DEPTFORD
Railway Incline, Deptford Station, Octavius Street (TQ372774)

The London & Greenwich Railway was built in 1833-36 entirely on a viaduct 3¾ miles long. As it was divorced from the surrounding land surface, all rolling stock had to be manoeuvred up and down inclines from their depots. There were originally 3 inclines of which only the example at Deptford survives, now relegated to stepped ramp with a variety of uses under its arches. On the same railway there are 2 fine road bridges retaining their original 1836 fluted Doric cast-iron columns at Spa Road and Abbey Street.

ENFIELD
Clarendon Arch, near Bush Hill (TQ324951)
Tunnel conveying the Salmons Brook under the New River and called the Clarendon Arch after the coat of arms and inscription 'This arch was rebuilt in the year 1682 Honorable Henry Earle of Clarendon being Gov'. However a further stone records 'This bank of earth was raised and formed to support the Channel of the New River. And the frame of timber and lead which served that purpose 173 years was removed and taken away. MDCCLXXXVI Peter Holford Esquire, Governor'. It would seem, therefore, that the tunnel was rebuilt in 1786 - 173 years after the New River's creation in 1613.

ENFIELD LOCK
Royal Small Arms Factory, Ordnance Road (TQ372983)
Some custom-built mid-19th-century buildings survive of this historic works where mass production techniques were first applied to the manufacture of small arms.

EUSTON
Euston Station Lodges, Euston Square (TQ296823)
The magnificent terminus of the London & Birmingham Railway, with its famous entrance arch of 1838, was swept away in the 1960s. All that remains of the formal layout are 2 stone lodges designed by J B Stanley *c* 1870 and the statue of Robert Stephenson erected 1871. The lodges bear panels inscribed with the names of stations served by the Railway.

FINSBURY
New River Head, Rosebery Avenue (TQ313828)
The headquarters of the former Metropolitan Water Board are at an historic site off Rosebery Avenue. The site contains the roundhouse of a windmill and horse mill of *c* 1708 used to pump water, Smeaton's engine house of *c* 1768, the 14th-century Devil's Conduit House

re-erected from Queen's Square, Bloomsbury, and the revetment of the Round Reservoir of 1609–13. The 20th-century buildings are also of distinction and incorporate features from the 17th-century Water House of the New River Company.

FULHAM
Fulham Gasworks, Sands End Lane, Michael Road (TQ260768)
London has a very distinguished history of gas manufacture and supply with the first public lighting in 1807 at Carlton House and the formation of the Gas Light and Coke Co in 1812. The gasworks at Fulham have the earliest surviving gasholder built 1830 and one of the finest ever built – No. 3 'The Regent'.

FULHAM
Fulham Pottery, 210 New Kings Road (TQ244761)
Little survives of the famous pottery founded by John Dwight in the late 17th century. A 19th-century bottle oven incorporated into workshops is the most significant relic.

GREENWICH
Blackwall Road Tunnel, Tunnel Avenue (TQ390796)
Ornamental 2-storey turreted and gabled entrance built by T Blashill prior to the opening of the tunnel in 1897.

GREENWICH
Pedestrian Tunnel, Cutty Sark Gardens (TQ383781)
Circular red brick lodge with glass domed roof built 1902 to house lift shaft and entrance to 9-ft bore subway to Isle of Dogs. Tiled interior and mahogany panelled lift.

GREENWICH
Water Tower, Shooters Hill (TQ437766)
Octagonal polychrome brick water tower built 1910, some 8 storeys high with a pointed swept tiled roof with gabled dormers.

HAMPSTEAD HEATH
Toll House, Spaniard's Road (TQ266872)
Single-storey 18th-century brick-built toll house with hipped tiled roof and shuttered windows. Its juxtaposition with 18th-century Spaniards Inn still forms a 'gateway' at the spot where the road entered the Bishop of London's estate.

HANWELL
Wharncliffe Viaduct, near Uxbridge Road (TQ150804)
Named after, and bearing the arms of, Lord Wharncliffe, this superb 8-arched brick-built viaduct carries the GWR across the valley of the River Brent. Built by Brunel in 1836–37 it is 900 ft long and its massive square pillar piers which have been likened to Egyptian pylons are in fact hollow to lessen the load of the structure.

HANWELL
Windmill Bridge, Windmill Lane (TQ143796)
The Brentford Branch of the GWR was planned by Brunel and opened in 1859. It passed under both Windmill Lane and the Grand Junction Canal at the same spot necessitating a complicated intersection with the canal carried in an iron trough.

HANWORTH
Kempton Park Waterworks, Hanworth Road (TQ110709)
Housed in a monumental engine house of 1928 are the 2 largest triple expansion vertical steam engines in Europe. Built by Worthington Simpsons, they produce over 1000hp each. Formerly they supplemented a hall of 5 large Lilleshall triple expansion engines of 1906.

HOLBORN
Holborn Viaduct, Farringdon Street (TQ316815)
Famous road viaduct some 1400 ft long and 80 ft wide built by William Heywood 1863–9. 107-ft cast-iron span over road carried on granite piers, pavilions house stairs between the 2 levels. The ornate decoration to the balustrades includes statues, winged lions and the City arms.

HOLBORN
Kingsway Tram Tunnel, Southampton Row (TQ305817)
An ambitious tram underpass some 1100 yds long was constructed in the first decade of the 20th century to take trams from Theobalds Road to Victoria embankment. It was largely rebuilt in 1931 to accommodate double decked cars and remained in operation until 1952. Parts of the tunnel have been utilized by a motor underpass but the original incline at Theobald's Road survives.

KENSINGTON
Electricity Generating Station, Kensington Court (TQ258797)
Very early 3-storey red brick generating station, possibly designed by J J Stevenson and equipped by Col Compton – a pioneer in the field. Operated from 1888–1900. Stone plaque over the entrance inscribed 'Electric Lighting Station'.

HOLBORN: *Kingsway Tram Underpass Tunnel, Southampton Row.*

KESTON
Keston Windmill, Heathfield Road
(TQ415640)
A weatherboarded post mill of *c* 1716 with a tarred brick roundhouse. The shutters of the sweeps and the fantail are missing but otherwise the machinery is fairly complete.

KEW
The Palm House, Royal Botanic Gardens
(TQ187769)
Experience gained in erecting horticultural glasshouses led directly to such ambitious constructions as the buildings for the Great Exhibition of 1851. The Palm House dating from 1844–8 and designed by Decimus Burton and Richard Turner is one of the finest surviving essays in iron and glass.

KINGS CROSS
Kings Cross Station, Euston Road (TQ303830)
Fine double train shed built 1850–2 by William and Lewis Cubitt for the Great Northern Railway and fronted by stock brick façade with massive plain towers. Hailed as an early forerunner of 'functionalism'. The train sheds'
71 ft-spans were originally of laminated timber but replaced by wrought iron 1869–87. Extensive mid-19th-century goods depot to the rear originally with interchange facilities with a basin of the Regent's Canal.

KINGS CROSS
Gasholders, Goods Way (TQ300833)
Impressive group of very fine 19th-century gasholders with ornate cast-iron framework.

LIMEHOUSE
Railway Lookout Tower, Mill Place
(TQ364814)
At the junction of the Fenchurch Street and Blackwall railway lines, an octagonal stock brick tower with stone dressing dating from the early days of signalling.

MERTON
Merton Abbey Works, Station Road
(TQ264698)
A silk printing works of Liberty & Co Ltd established in 1885 in an 18th-century former calico manufactory. The wheelhouse contains large iron undershot waterwheel.

MORDEN
Morden Hall Park Mills, Morden Hall Road
(TQ262686)

The River Wandle between Croydon and Wandsworth was formerly lined by watermills. 2 snuff mills survive at Morden on either side of the river, the earlier on the east bank being 18th-century and the later *c* 1860. One large undershot wheel survives but little of the snuff grinding machinery.

PADDINGTON
Paddington Station, Praed Street (TQ266813)
Magnificent train shed of 1855 built by Brunel and Matthew Digby-Wyatt as terminus of the Great Western Railway. Recent painting has highlighted the fine ironwork of the 3 great naves and 2 transepts and has revealed the detailing on features such as the Directors' Balcony above Platform 1.

PENGE
Croydon Canal, Bett's Park, Anerley Road (TQ346696)
The 9½ mile long Croydon Canal was opened in 1809 at a cost of £127,000 with 28 locks. It was bought by the London & Croydon Railway in 1836 and part of the line built over the railway. A section has survived as an ornamental water garden in a park near Anerley Station.

PENGE
Crystal Palace Low Level Station, Anerley Road (TQ341705)
Though the street façade has lost some of its grand appearance by the demolition of northern pavilion, the large sweeping staircases from the platform level are a reminder of the prestige of this suburban station when it catered for visitors to the Crystal Palace.

PENTONVILLE
Islington Canal Tunnel, Vincent Terrace (TQ317833)
The eastern portal to the major tunnel on the Regent's Canal was designed by John Nash *c* 1820. The round-arched brick opening is flanked by pilasters carrying a parapet.

PONDERS END
Wright's Flour Mill, Lea Valley Road (TQ362956)
A traditional flour milling complex comprising mill, miller's house and barn – a rare survival in London. The mill itself has 3 storeys and attic with a brick ground floor and weatherboarded upper part with projecting sack hoist. Electric power installed 1909 as water was diverted for reservoir.

PRIMROSE HILL
Railway Tunnel Eastern Portal, Primrose Hill Road (TQ275843)

Originally opened in 1837 on the London & Birmingham Railway, this tunnel was the first on a London Railway. It was doubled in 1879 but is still most attractive with massive stone-dressed piers with hipped capitals imitating lead roofs.

REGENT'S PARK
Macclesfield Bridge, North Gate, Regent's Park (TQ275834)
Built originally *c* 1816 over James Morgan's Regent Canal, this brick arch bridge with its cast-iron Doric columns achieved fame by its destruction in a gunpowder accident in 1874. It was rebuilt using the same Coalbrookdale columns.

ROTHERHITHE
Engine House and Shaft, Tunnel Road (TQ352798)
Close to the famous Mayflower Inn are the remains of the engine house in which the Brunels, Marc and Isambard, housed their steam pumps when constructing the first tunnel below the Thames. Driving commenced in 1825 and after many years of vicissitudes including disastrous flooding, the tunnel was finally opened in 1843. Though a financial flop and never a success as a pedestrian tunnel, the tunnel with its 38-ft bore was converted to railway operation in 1865 and is still a most important part of the London Underground system.

ST PANCRAS
St Pancras Railway Station, Euston Road (TQ301828)
Magnificent terminus of the Midland Railway. The train shed with its single span roof of 243 ft was designed by W H Barlow and built 1868–74. It is fronted by Sir George Gilbert Scott's monumental Gothic masterpiece, originally the Midland Grand Hotel, but now relegated to office use.

SOMERS TOWN
Polygon Buildings, Polygon Road, Pheonix Road (TQ295830)
Grim 4-storey tenement blocks built by the Midland Railway *c* 1870 to house 288 families.

SOUTHALL
Water Tower, Gasworks Road (TQ125798)
Octagonal red brick water tower with battlemented top built *c* 1895 by South West Suburban Water Company. Now disused.

SOUTHWARK
Kirkcaldy's Testing Works, 99 Southwark Street (TQ318804)

Moved from the Grove, Southwark in 1873 into a 4-storey building designed by T R Smith, the Testing Works were established by David Kirkcaldy in 1864 as the world's first commercial mechanical testing works. The building houses a massive Patent Testing Machine capable of exerting huge pressures on materials being tested to destruction and designed by Kirkcaldy in 1864 and manufactured by Greenwood & Batley of Leeds.

SOUTHWARK
Hop Exchange, Central Building, Southwark Street (TQ326801)
Impressive building by R H Moore constructed 1866 with 3 giant external storeys concealing 6 internal storeys. The large Corinthian half-columns are cast-iron and a pedimented entrance has details of brewing in the typanum. The galleried court has iron balustrades decorated with hop plant designs. Suffered from extensive fire damage in 1920.

SPITALFIELDS
Cutler Street Warehouses, Middlesex Street (TQ335815)
The largest complex of land-locked warehouses in the country, this site was developed from 1768 onwards, though most of the buildings date from 1793–1801 and are the work of Richard Jupp and Henry Holland. S P Cockerall added a final group in 1819–20. The warehouses are surrounded by a monumental panelled brick wall on a stone plinth. The warehouses have mostly timber-framed interiors with some fire resisting features in the staircases. The site is due to be extensively redeveloped and it is uncertain how much will survive.

SPITALFIELDS
Eagle Brewery, Brick Lane (TQ338820)
Truman's Brewery in Brick Lane is an attractive complex of 18th- and 19th-century stock brick buildings, some with classical detailing. The Wilkes Street façade dates from 1756, the Brick Lane façade from 1837.

SPITALFIELDS
Liverpool Street Station, Liverpool Street (TQ333817)
Built 1872–75 by Edward Wilson, engineer to the Eastern Counties Railway Company, the western bays of the vast train shed have fine cast-iron columns supporting wrought-iron trusses with cast-iron detailing. Fronted by asymmetrical Gothic-styled yellow brick buildings.

SPITALFIELDS
Weavers' Houses, Fournier Street (TQ338818)

An area formerly renowned for its silk weaving, many of the 18th-century 3-storey houses in Fournier Street have an additional attic storey with large workshop windows.

STRAND
Floral Hall, Covent Garden Market (TQ303808)
Designed by Frederick Pye *c* 1860, reputedly utilizing materials left over from the Crystal Palace when it was moved to Sydenham from Hyde Park.

STRAND
Sewer Gas Lamp, Carting Lane (TQ305806)
An unusual type of gas lamp patented by Webb in 1895 to extract and burn sewer gases as well as providing street lighting by town gas. The example in Carting Lane is particularly handsome with a fluted iron column and ornate lantern.

THAMESMEAD
Crossness Pumping Station, Belvedere Road (TQ484811)
White brick engine house with magnificent interior of elaborate cast-iron work to central octagonal frame which supports the beam floor of 4 rotative beam pumping engines. Installed by J Watt & Son in 1865, the engines were converted to triple expansion by Goodfellows in 1899 and are rated at 210 hp. Crossness was part of Bazalgette's grand scheme for the Metropolitan Board of Works and pumped from the Southern Outfall.

TOTTENHAM
Pumping Station, Markfield Road (TQ344888)
Small former sewage pumping station now incorporated into a children's playground. The engine house contains a compound beam engine of 1886 by Messrs Wood Bros, Sowerby Bridge. The engine which is free standing on its 8-column frame is the last such engine *in situ*.

TOWER
St Katherines Docks (TQ339805)
The 23-acre dock system on the site of St Katharines was built by Telford 1825–28. Since their commercial closure in 1968, they have been developed as a hotel and trading centre with a marina with the loss of most of the fine 1828 warehouses by Hardwick. The later Peninsular Warehouse survives as do many of the original dock fittings including a movable footbridge of unique design.

WANDSWORTH: *Ram Brewery Engine.*

TOWER
Tower Bridge (TQ337802)
London's most famous industrial monument built 1888–1894 to architectural designs of Sir Horace Jones and engineering designs of Sir John Wolfe Barry. It consists of 2 steel towers encased in a sheathing of granite and Portland stone worked to resemble a French chateau with a suspension span on either side. One of the steam engines with its hydraulic pumps was preserved *in situ* when the 1040 ton bascules were converted from hydraulic to electric operation in 1976–77.

TWICKENHAM
Shot Tower, Crane Park (TQ128728)
between Hounslow Road and Great Chertsey
The major survival of the powder mills is a tall brick-built 18th-century shot tower with a conical cap. The tower is one of the earliest in existence.

UPMINSTER
Upminster Windmill, St Mary's Lane
(TQ557868)
A large galleried smock mill dating from *c* 1803 with most of its machinery complete. The windshaft came in 1899 from a post mill at Maldon. Preserved by Havering LB.

WALLINGTON
Surrey Iron Railway, Public Library,
Shotfield (TQ288637)
In the grounds of Wallington Library are re-laid sections of tramway plates from the Surrey Iron Railway which was incorporated in 1801 as a public railway. Engineered by Jessop, the horse-drawn tramway ran originally to Croydon from whence an extension, the Croydon, Merstham & Godstone line continued to lime works at Mertsham.

WALTHAMSTOW
Old Coppermill, Coppermill Lane (TQ351883)
A large 2-storey brick building with a hipped pantile roof so constructed with massive timbers to provide as much clear space as possible with no internal divisions is the major relic of the copper rolling mill that operated from 1808. The site was acquired by the East London Waterworks Company in 1854 and the waterwheel adapted to drive pumps supplemented by a Bull steam engine housed in a 3-storey Italianate tower. A 19th-century wooden jib crane also survives on a disused wharf.

WANDSWORTH
Ram Brewery (TQ256747)
Brewery of Young & Co still making traditional ales and noted for its stable of Shire horses and continuing use of very early steam engines. Both engines are Woolf compound rotative beam engines by Wentworth & Sons, Wandsworth, and are dated 1835 and 1867. Some interesting 18th- and 19th-century buildings also survive.

WAPPING
Hydraulic Pumping Station, Wapping Wall
(TQ353805)
The last of the London Hydraulic Power Company's pumping stations to contain equipment. Built in 1892, the steam pumps were replaced by electric pumps in the 1950s but the station with its tanks and accumulator tower is otherwise complete. Engineer's cottage is same ornate red brick.

WAPPING
London Docks and Warehouses (TQ345806)
The London Docks were developed from 1802 onwards with John Rennie as engineer and Daniel Alexander as surveyor and architect. They comprised 2 main docks – Eastern and Western and 4 small basins – Hermitage, Wapping, Tobacco and Eastern. The fine range of massive 4-storey brick-built warehouses on the North Quay were noted for their ventilated vaults containing immense quantities of wine and also for the liberal hospitality of the wine merchants. The docks were closed in 1969 and some demolition and infilling has taken place. They are due to be redeveloped as part of the larger Dockland scheme.

WAPPING
Skinfloor Warehouse, London Docks
(TQ346806)
The unprepossessing corrugated-iron clad single-storey building occupying the corner between the East and West London docks is in fact one of the most significant industrial monuments in London. Dating from *c* 1804 and attributed to Rennie, the roof supports are ingeniously designed to provide as little restriction on internal movement as possible. The rows of cast-iron columns have Y-shaped branches connecting to the next column and they support timber-framed aisles of queen post construction.

WEST HAM
Abbey Mills Pumping Station, Abbey Lane
(TQ388832)
Venetian-Gothic style pumping station built 1865–8 by Bazalgette and Cooper to house 8 beam engines arranged 2 to each arm of a cruciform. The steam engines have been replaced by electric pumps but the station is still

an important monument on account of its magnificent interior of stone columns and cast-iron balconies.

WHITECHAPEL

Whitechapel Bell Foundry, Whitechapel Road (TQ339815)
Famous Church Bell Foundry in 18th-century premises with an interesting old jib crane beneath a bracketed canopy. The firm is noted for its traditional techniques with most of its production by hand.

WIMBLEDON

Artesian Wellhouse, 21 Arthur Road (TQ246715)
Dating from 1798, this domed structure is built over one of the first deep wells to be sunk in the outskirts of London. The well itself is now sealed but was 563 ft deep.

Manchester

The metropolitan county of Manchester includes Manchester itself and the major industrial towns of Stockport, Salford, Bolton, Bury, Oldham and Wigan and thus displays one of the most dense concentrations of industry in the country. Based originally on coal and textiles, almost every industry is now to be found. This area saw the 2 pioneer transport developments, viz the Bridgwater Canal and the Manchester & Liverpool Railway, both of which have left major industrial monuments – Worsley Basin and Liverpool Rd Station respectively. The early lead in canal construction was followed up by the Manchester, Bolton & Bury Canal, the Ashton Canal, the Rochdale Canal and the Peak Forest Canal, all of which have left significant monuments. Further railway development bequeathed a magnificent series of railway warehouses to central Manchester.

ASHTON-UNDER-LYME

Dunkinfield Canal Basin and Bridge (SJ935984)
5 miles E of Manchester off A635
At the junction of the Peak Forest and Ashton Canals is a small basin with semi-derelict warehouses served by barge holes. The most prominent feature is a fine towpath bridge of 1835 to carry the towpath of the Ashton Canal over the later Peak Forest Canal. The bridge parapets are constructed of vertical stone slabs.

BOLTON

Bank Top Industrial Community (SD722122)
2 miles N of town centre off A666
Developed by the Ashworth family of New Eagley Mill between 1835 and 1855, this early factory community consists of the terraced stone cottages of Ashworth Lane, Eleanor Street and Hugh Lupus Street, church, school, farm and even a tennis club. There are further planned industrial communities at Barrow Bridge (*qv*) and Halliwell Road (SD7011), the latter developed by J H Ainsworth in 1847 and consisting of terraced cottages (some formerly back to back), a church, school and public house.

BOLTON

Barrow Bridge Industrial Community (SD689116)
2 miles NW of town centre off A58
A model village was developed on the outskirts of Bolton based on employment at Dean Mills which were built by Gardner and Bazley *c* 1837. Under the general heading of Bazley Street are 7 ranks named First Street, Second Street, and so on. The houses perched on the side of the hill, are sturdily built in stone with the first 4 tanks being 2-storey, the others 3-storey – being graded for different classes of workers. There is an Institute built 1846 and original stone footpaths with gas lamps while,

in the valley below, are a mill manager's house and shops. Only the mill pond of the mill itself survives.

BOLTON
Swan Lane Mill (SD708079)
1 mile SW of town centre on A579
Large brick-built multi-storey cotton mill typical of a late Victorian spinning mill. Built for 196,420 mule spindles it had separate sections for Sea Island cotton and carded Egyptian cotton. It has a projecting twin-engine house and a tall circular brick chimney.

BURY
Bury Bridge Canal Basin (SD797109)
¼ mile W of town centre on A58
One of the termini of the Manchester, Bolton & Bury Canal built under an Act of 1791, completed in 1808, and abandoned in 1961. The Bury end in fact opened some years earlier and then the through route carried some coal traffic until 1968. There is a 3-storey brick-built warehouse with a barge hole in its end elevation allowing direct internal loading. It may date from 1797.

DELPH
Weavers' Settlements (e.g. SD974093)
1½ miles NW of Delph off A6052
The valley of the W tributary of the River Tame from Delph to Denshaw is littered with the remains of early textile works. The river itself has been repeatedly dammed to provide power for a series of mills, most of which have now gone. The hillsides above have scattered settlements of stone-built houses with weavers' attics. A small group of 10 such houses lies just off the A6052.

ECCLES
Barton Aqueduct (SJ767976)
5 miles W of Manchester off A57
Completed in 1894 to designs of Leader Williams, the Barton Swing Aqueduct carries the Bridgwater Canal over the Manchester Ship Canal and replaces Brindley's famous masonry aqueduct of 1761 which crossed the River Irwell at a point immediately to the W. Operated hydraulically, the steel trough 235 ft long, 19 ft wide and 6 ft deep can be swung, full of water, through 90 degrees to allow ships to pass. The trough weighs 1400 tons when full of water and is swung on roller bearings. Sharing the same pier is a swing-bridge carrying the B2511.

HORWICH
Wallsuches Bleachworks (SD653118)
5 miles W of Bolton off B6226

Established in 1777 by J & T Ridgway to exploit the newly discovered bleaching properties of chlorine, this bleachworks was also pioneer in its use of 1798 Boulton & Watt engine to drive its machinery. The 4-storey stone-built main block has some small-paned windows and may be 18th-century. The smaller block with bellcote is also early.

LITTLEBOROUGH
Early Textile Mills (e.g. SD932176)
4 miles NE of Rochdale off A6033
Littleborough is a good example of the early type of Lancashire textile town – based on water power and with woollen mills giving way to cotton mills in the 19th century. The typical mill e.g. the 2-storeyed stone-built Clough Mill was small and entirely dependent on water. They could not compete, in the late 19th century, with steam-driven mills of the coalfield.

MANCHESTER
Barton Arcade, Deansgate (SJ837985)
N of city centre
Built by Corbett, Raby, and Sawey in 1871, this is the finest shopping arcade in the city. Its exterior gives little idea of the adventurous and elegant structure, of the iron and glass vaulted roof and the 3 storeys of iron railed balconies inside.

MANCHESTER
Castlefield Basin (SJ831975)
S of city centre
This was developed as the Manchester terminus of the Bridgwater Canal from 1764 onwards as an open wharf. The first warehouse (the Duke's) was built in 1789 followed by a succession of multi-storey warehouses, most of which were served by barge hole branches. Only Middle and Merchants warehouses now survive. By 1810 most of the development was complete and a connection had been made with the Rochdale Canal.

MANCHESTER
Central Station, Lower Mosley Street (SJ837977)
S of city centre
Built by the tripartite Cheshire Lines Committee in 1880 as a terminus of the Midland expresses to London and of the regional lines to Liverpool and Chester, Central Station has a magnificent iron arch roof of 210 ft span. 90 ft high and constructed by Andrew Handyside of Derby, it covers an area of 4 ½ acres. It is second in size only to St Pancras. It is, however, fronted by only mean wooden buildings meant to be temporary but never re-

placed. The station closed in 1969 and its future is still uncertain.

MANCHESTER
Dale Street Canal Basin (SJ847982)
E city centre
The entrance to the former basin of the Rochdale Canal in Dale Street is by a crenelated arch with canal company offices alongside. In the infilled basin itself is a fine, stone-built, pre–1805, 4-storey warehouse with barge holes beneath. It is carried on a vaulting of square stone pillars with huge wooden beams.

MANCHESTER
Liverpool Road Station (SJ830978)
W city centre
The original 1830 terminus of the Liverpool & Manchester Railway relegated to a goods station in 1844 when the line was extended to Victoria. The modest 2-storey frontage on Liverpool Road contrasts strongly with the later palaces of the railway age and the internal appointments to the track, which is at first-floor level, are equally modest. After years of neglect this, the earliest main line

MANCHESTER: *Central Station Train Shed, magnificent roof span now relegated to use as a car park.*

passenger station, is to be restored to celebrate the 150 years of passenger traffic. The station-master's house and early goods warehouses adjoin the station.

MANCHESTER
Railway Warehouses, Ducie Street
(SJ848981)
E city centre
A series of massive warehouses were built in the latter part of the 19th century by rival railway companies. They each incorporated the latest technical designs of their day and are thus an interesting civil engineering sequence. The earliest was built in 1867 by the MS & L railway in Ducie Street, 7-storeys high with massive cast-iron pillars supporting wrought-iron beams. The second was in Watson Street (SD835975), built in 1881 by the Cheshire Lines Committee, and the third was in Deansgate (SD834975), built in 1898 by the GWR – a massive 5-storey structure with steel box girder

pillars, steel box girder lengthwise beams and rolled steel crosswise beams supporting a brick arched floor.

MANCHESTER
Soho Foundry, Pollard Street (SJ856983)
1 mile E of city centre
Established in 1800 by David Whitehead beside an arm of the Ashton Canal, this foundry was taken over by W W Williams and G Peel *c* 1810. Throughout the 19th century the firm of Peel, Williams & Peel had a reputation for fine gearwork and they proudly exhibited a gearwheel pattern in the pediment of the 3-storey Pollard Street façade which also proclaims their name in carved stone. The foundry, forge and erecting shops are long derelict.

MARPLE
Aqueduct (ST955901)
½ miles N Marple by canal towpath.
A magnificent masonry aqueduct carrying the Peak Forest Canal some 100 ft above the valley of the R. Goyt. Opened *c* 1799 the aqueduct has 3 arches with pierced spandrels and is the work of Benjamin Outram, the canal and pioneer railway engineer. Outram was able to use his expertise with tramways to connect the canal basin at Bugsworth to the famous limestone quarries at Doveholes.

OLDHAM
Cotton Mills (e.g. SD927027)
1½ miles S of town centre on A627
Oldham is the archetypal late 19th-century textile town. Until recently there were over 100 cotton mills, very few of which will survive in the textile industry. Most of them are comparatively late. Indicative of this is that none of them are recognized as Historic Buildings. Typical examples are the late 19th-century Bell Mill (SD927027), 5-storey with ornamental top storey and water tower and Glen Mills, Greenacres, 1904 with yellow brick decoration and ornamental water tower.

RADCLIFFE
Steam Crane, Little Lever (SD768068)
1 mile W of Radcliffe
On the bank of the Manchester, Bury & Bolton Canal overlooking the Mount Sion works is a small steam crane built by Smith & Sons of Rodley near Leeds. Although it has been disused for many years, it is still substantially intact and there are plans to restore it during the present canal 'clean-up campaign'.

RADCLIFFE
Waterwheel Pump (SD767066)
1 Mile W of Radcliffe, S of river

On the far side of the River Irwell from Mount Sion Bleach (now paper) works is a water-driven beam pumping engine of *c* 1830. Reminiscent of Rennies Claverton Pump (*qv* Avon) it has 2 cast-iron beams on masonry columns driven by 12 ft diameter by 5 ft wide iron waterwheel.

REDDISH
Houldsworth Mill, Houldsworth Street (SJ892933)
2 miles N of Stockport off B6167
Built 1863–65 by Henry Houldsworth, this mill is a good example of the very large Lancashire textile mills of the latter part of the 19th century. Consisting of 2, 4-storey blocks linked by a 5-storey central element containing clock feature and flanked by Italianate staircase towers, the mill has an internal structure of large cast-iron pillars, cast-iron beams and brick arches. A tall octagonal tapering chimney with ornamental cap rises from the centrally positioned engine house at rear. The Houldsworths developed an area E of the mill for employees' housing complete with church, school and club designed by Alfred Waterhouse.

ROCHDALE
March Barn Bridge, Castleton (SJ886111)
2 miles S of Rochdale off A664
A fine masonry skew arch bridge built *c* 1800 carrying a cobbled path over the Rochdale Canal. It is reputedly the first skew arch to be built in stone with winding courses. William Jessop was the consulting engineer for the canal at the time with Thomas Bradley of Halifax and Thomas Townsend the resident engineers, and to this team must go any credit for this pioneer structure.

ROYTON
Diamond Rope Works Mill Engine (SD929080)
2 miles N of Oldham off A663
In a tall red brick engine house attached to an earlier mill is a 1912 inverted compound engine by Scott & Hodgson. With 14 in high pressure cylinder and 30 in low pressure cylinder, the engine developed 250 hp at 90 rpm. The rope works itself is now closed.

SADDLEWORTH
West Portal, Standedge Canal Tunnel (SE007081)
1 mile NE of Saddleworth off A670
(See West Yorks – Marsden for details)

SHAW
Dee Mill, Mill Engine (SD944090)
4 miles NE of Oldham off A663

The preserved engine at Dee Mill is a good example of the ultimate in reciprocating steam mill engines. A horizontal twin tandem compound engine built by Scott & Hodgson in 1907, it developed 1500 hp at 60 rpm. With high pressure cylinders $18\frac{1}{2}$ in in diameter and low pressure cylinders 42 in in diameter, it used steam at 160 psi. It is housed in a red brick tall single-storey engine room attached to a 4-storey mill building. The interior of the engine house is light and airy with fine tile work on the walls.

STOCKPORT
Mersey Railway Viaduct (SJ890906–893901)
W of town centre
Dominating the centre of Stockport is the huge brick viaduct of the Manchester & Birmingham Railway built by G W Buck and opened in 1842 at a cost of £70,000. Over 110 ft high and 1780 ft long, some of its arches, most of which are 63 ft span, actually straddle 6-storey mills. It was widened in 1888–9. The slight difference in brick colouring being still quite obvious.

REDDISH: *Houldsworth Mill, typical late 19th century mill.*

TYLDESLEY
Astley Green Colliery Winding Engines (SD705999)
3 miles W of Worsley off A580
The prominent engine house at Astley Green Colliery contains one of the largest steam winding engines ever built. A horizontal twin tandem compound engine, it was erected by Yates and Thom in 1912 and developed c 3,000 hp from its 35 in and 60 in cylinders.

WESTHOUGHTON
Incline, Embankment and Crossing House (e.g. SD674061)
4 miles SW of Bolton off A6
There are slight traces of the Chequerbent incline (SD670048/678068) of the Bolton & Leigh Railway built in 1828 by George Stephenson. It was originally powered by a stationary engine and some stone blocks survive as this section was by-passed when the track was realigned for locomotives. The

crossing house (SD674061) on the A6 in Chequerbent also survives in an altered form.

WIGAN
Canal Wharves, Wallgate (SD577053)
½ miles W of town centre
The heavily locked Leeds & Liverpool Canal rises some 200 ft in 23 locks from Wallgate Basin in Wigan to Aspull – a distance of just over 2 miles. At Wallgate basin a derelict 18th-century stone-built 2½-storey warehouse has 2 barge holes. There is a proposal to reduce it in height and to landscape the surrounding area.

WIGAN
Haigh South Outfall, Haigh (SD591072)
1½ miles N of town centre
The Haigh Sough drainage system was started by Sir Roger Bradshaigh in 1653 and was extended in the 19th century. It is thus one of the oldest colliery drainage systems in the Lancashire coalfield. It was travelled annually for maintenance purposes until 1929. This outlet is to the Yellow Brook in Haigh Lower Plantations, Bottling Wood and still has a flow of water.

WORSLEY
Canal Basin, Worsley Delph (SD749006)
N of town on B5211
Worsley was very much the source of the Bridgwater Canal as it was from here that the Duke of Bridgwater shipped coal to Manchester in 1761. The surface canal made connection with navigable adits driven into the sandstone to exploit the Middle Coal Measures. This system of underground canals on 4 different levels was developed by James Brindley and John Gilbert and by 1840 had reached 46 miles in extent. At Delph 2 entrances to the Main Level can still be seen. The system ceased operation in 1887.

Merseyside

Merseyside, a production of the local government organization of 1974, comprises most of the Wirral peninsula and the northern bank of the Mersey estuary. It is dominated by the port of Liverpool which contains most of its significant industrial monuments. Others are to be found at St Helens, the famous glass-making town with its former link to the Mersey – the Sankey Canal, the first true canal in England.

BIRKENHEAD
Port Sunlight Community (SJ3484)
4 miles S of Birkenhead off A41
Started in 1888 by Messrs Lever Brothers in association with their soap works, this was one of the most ambitious model settlement-sevelopments to precede the garden city movement. According to contemporaries the housing conditions were 'virtually ideal' with generous bedroom and bathroom provision in attractive gabled houses in a spacious setting – all quite different from the regimented terraces of earlier model settlements such as Saltaire.

BIRKENHEAD
Windmill (SJ287894)
2 miles W of town centre off A5027

A much restored late 18th-century tower mill with cap and sails.

LIVERPOOL
Cooling Towers, Lister Drive Power Station (SJ383917)
3 miles E of city centre off A57
These 5 cooling towers were the first ferro-concrete hyperbolic cooling towers to be built in Britain. They were built in 1924 by L G Mouchel & Partners to a Dutch patented design of 1916. These are substantially smaller than later towers and have wide base tapering sharply to a neck two-thirds of the way up and

LIVERPOOL: *Albert Dock, masterpiece of fire proof enclosed dock.*

the tops have a pronounced flare with a prominent lip round the rim.

LIVERPOOL
Docks
Jesse Hartley, Liverpool's dock engineer from 1824–1860, left as his monument an unsurpassed series of massive dock structures. These now comprise the finest series of closed docks in the country and the following entries are only a sample of the industrial archaeological gems to be found.

Albert Dock, Canning Place (SJ341898)
¼ mile S of Pier Head
Possibly Hartley's finest work, built 1841–45 and loosely modelled on St Katharine's Dock, London, this 7-acre dock is surrounded on all sides by 5-storey brick fireproof warehouses on colonnades of massive cast-iron Doric columns each 12½ ft in circumference and 15 ft high. A cast-iron swing-bridge of standard Hartley design and dated 1843 and cast by the Haigh Foundry, Wigan, lies across the passage into the dock.

Dock Traffic Office, Canning Place (SJ341899)
¼ mile S of Pier Head
In the NE corner of Albert Dock is a remarkable cast-iron building in the style of a classical stone temple designed by Philip Hardwick in 1846–7. Its Tuscan portico has a remarkable 36 ft long architrave which is a single casting with an iron cornice and frieze welded on. The columns 17 ft 8 in high are cast in halves and welded together. The top storey was added by Hartley in 1848.

Dock Wall, Regent Road (SJ3392)
1 mile N of Pier Head
Hartley enclosed his docks with huge walls embellished with fortress features. The stretch in Regent is typical, built in 1848, it is 18 ft high of large granite blocks with entrances composed of 3 gate piers, the centre forming a watchman's hut, the gates sliding back through enormous side piers into the thickness of the masonry. Large carved plaques proclaim which part of the dock system is being entered.

Stanley Dock (SJ335922)
1 mile N of Pier Head
This dock has typical Hartley features such as octagonal dock tower, massive gated wall and 4-storey brick warehouses on unfluted Doric cast-iron columns. At the eastern end of the dock a connection was made with the Leeds & Liverpool Canal. Four **Canal locks** (SS340922) in Lightbody Street.

Victoria Tower, Salisbury Dock (SJ333921)
1 mile N of Pier Head
A fanciful octagonal hydraulic tower which opened the sea passage into Salisbury Dock

constructed by Hartley in 1848. Built of irregular shaped stone blocks, it repeats the fortress-like appearance of many of the dock structures by having a bracketed stone balcony at the second floor, narrow slits and a corbelled parapet. Eight massive clock faces are placed half way up.

LIVERPOOL
Hartley's Jam Factory, Hartley Avenue (SJ369969)
5 miles NW of city centre off A59
W P Hartley factory of 1886 was embellished with medieval-castle details such as a turretted entrance gateway complete with portcullis. Hartley Village was developed as model housing from 1888 onwards and had a dining hall as part of the amenities.

LIVERPOOL
Oriel Chambers, Water Street (SJ341904)
City centre
Completed in 1864, this is a superb example of the constructional use of cast iron by local architect Peter Ellis junior (1804–1884). The outer façades have stone mullions separating delicate cast-iron framed oriel windows individually cantilevered 2 ft 6 in out from stanchions of the main skeleton which is constructed of cast-iron beams on cast-iron columns with shallow brick arches supporting the floor. Inside is a courtyard with stanchions set in from the façade making it an early example of curtain walling. A similar example of Ellis's work dating from 1866 is No. 16 Cook Street (SJ343904).

LIVERPOOL
Royal Liver Building, Pier Head (SJ338904)
City centre
An early example of reinforced-concrete construction built 1907–1911 by E Nuttall & Co, Manchester, to the designs of Walter A Thomas. The pioneer use of concrete in this 8-storey building is obscured by the dark stone cladding and conventional architectural detailing such as the semi-circular Ionic portico.

LIVERPOOL
St George's Church, St Domingo Road, Everton (SJ355925)
1½ miles NE of city centre off A59
St George's Church, designed by Thomas Rickman and John Cragg, was built between 1812 and 1814. It is important as one of the earliest buildings incorporating prefabricated

LIVERPOOL: *Oriel Chambers, Water Street, pioneer metal-framed building.*

components, the whole of the interior structure being of cast-iron sections enclosed within stone external walls. Columns, vaulting, ceiling panels, balcony rails and window frames were all made to a standard design and erected as complete units on site. As an example of Gothic architecture, it is exceptionally fine but its real significance lies in the principles which were established here and which led to the growth of a thriving export trade in prefabricated iron buildings from Liverpool. The horizontal iron ties within the church are later additions designed to prevent the walls of the nave from bulging. Iron was used even more extensively in the construction of St Michael-in-the-Hamlet Church, St Michael's Road, Aigburth (SJ369871) by the same architects in 1815.

LIVERPOOL
Stanley Park, Kirkdale (SJ359937)
2½ miles NE of city centre off A580
Stanley Park has a collection of cast-iron structures of *c* 1870 by E R Robson. They include 5 cast-iron bridges, a bandstand, 2 pavilions and shelter. A later conservatory with delicate ironwork was added by Mackenzie and Moncur in 1899.

LIVERPOOL
Train Sheds, Lime Street Station
(SJ352905)
½ mile E of city centre
A segmental arch screen at street end of perhaps 1836 fronts a graceful glass-roofed shed of 1867 with a span of 200 ft supported on double Doric iron columns. A parallel shed was added to the S in 1874–9 on square piers.

LIVERPOOL
Ventilating Shaft, Edgehill Tunnel
(SJ363903)
1½ miles E of city centre off A5080
From the opening of Lime Street station in 1836 until 1870 trains were hauled up a 1 in 97 gradient by stationary engines at Edge Hill. When locomotives worked this section smoke pollution in the 2,025-yard tunnel became a problem and a brick chimney rising to 198 ft above rail level was built. Its base housed a steam-powered fan of 29 ft 4 in diameter which was connected to the tunnel by a horizontal gallery. The machinery has gone but the chimney which tapers from 54 ft at its base to 23 ft at the top survives.

NEWTON-LE-WILLOWS
Huskisson Memorial, Parkside (SJ606955)
1 mile E of Newton-le-Willows of A573

William Huskisson (1770–1830), a Liverpool Member of Parliament, was run down here on Wednesday 15 September 1830 by the locomotive 'Rocket' driven by Joseph Locke. The occasion was the opening of the Liverpool & Manchester Railway. Trains stopped at Parkside for the locomotives to take on water and to pass in 'review' before the Duke of Wellington. Huskisson, walking across the tracks to speak to the duke, was struck by 'Rocket'. Badly injured he was rushed to Eccles by George Stephenson driving 'Northumbrian', but he died the same evening.

RAINHILL
Railway Station (SJ491914)
2 miles SE of Prescot off A57
The site of the trials held on the Liverpool & Manchester Railway in October 1829 to find a satisfactory form of motive power. A notice on the station commemorates the winning of the trials by George Stephenson's 'Rocket'. One of the 2 cylinders of another contender 'Novelty' is displayed in the booking hall. To the W of the station is a single-span masonry skew bridge designed by Stephenson with an angle of 34 degrees. The stone post milestone on the bridge may be contemporary.

ST HELENS
Old Double Locks (SJ536961)
1½ miles E of St Helens off A58
The St Helens Canal is generally accepted as being the first typical English canal and the staircase pair of locks known as Old Double Locks are the first staircase locks in the country. They were built in 1758 and their plan displays a barrel shape typical of very early locks. The New Double Locks (SJ519962) one mile W date from *c* 1772 and are not barrel shaped.

ST HELENS
Pilkingtons Ravenhead Glass Works (SJ5094)
1 mile SW of town centre off A58
St Helens is synonomous with glass making. A 19th-century print shows numerous glass cones in a landscape criss-crossed by canals and railways. However, rationalization of the glass industry has led to its concentration in large, relatively modern factories such as that of Pilkingtons. Little of the casting hall of the Plate Glass Works of 1773 now exists. When it was built the original casting hall was reputedly the largest factory under one roof in the country. Manager's house, stable and some associated cottages also survive. The modern museum opened by Pilkingtons in 1965 is the finest display of the history of glass making in the country.

SOUTHPORT
Seaside Shelters and Pier, Promenade
(SJ3317)
NW town centre
On the promenade there are 3 good examples of Victorian iron and glass seaside shelters with typical pagoda shaped roofs. Southport Pier (SJ335176) was built 1859–60 primarily for promenading as distinct from landing and it is thus one of the earliest true pleasure piers. In 1868 it was lengthened to 4,380 ft but after storm damage it was shortened to its present length of 3,650 ft.

WALLASEY
New Brighton Pier (SJ312941)
Northern tip of peninsula
Short pier designed by Eugenius Birch and built by J E Dowson of London in 1866–7 on the rocks at tip of Wirral. Cast-iron columns carry wrought-iron superstructure and attractive pavilion.

Norfolk

Norfolk is mainly an agricultural county and its industrial monuments reflect this bias with wind and watermills predominant. It contains however the earliest large industrial site in the country viz. Grimes Graves flint mines (Fig. 45). These underground galleries at Weeting (TL817898) date from neolithic times and flint knapping has survived in the area until the present century. However, the county town of Norwich and the port of Kings Lynn offer some diversity while Great Yarmouth with its smoke houses, Melton Constable with its former railway workshop settlement, and Fakenham with its early 19th-century gasworks contribute less usual monuments. Indeed the gasworks at Fakenham is the only example of a horizontal retort to be preserved in England. In the late 19th century the Norfolk coast was developed as a holiday playground with resorts such as Hunstanton, Cromer and Great Yarmouth.

ASHILL
Chalk Pit & Limekiln (TF783043)
5 miles SE Swalfham B1077
Mid-19th-century limekiln which survived in use, with alterations until mid-20th century. Lime was extensively burned in Norfolk as a fertilizer from early 19th century onwards.

BILLINGFORD
Windmill (TM167786)
3 miles E Diss A143
This brick tower mill was built in 1860 to replace a post mill that had been blown down. The mill still has its sails and fan tail and has been restored by Norfolk Windmills Trust.

BURNHAM MARKET
Burnham Overy Mills (TF836436)
Beside A149 5 miles W Wells-next-the-Sea
This red brick, long range of buildings on the River Burn originally comprised a mill, mill house and maltings. The mill was restored in 1960 after a fire the previous year, so little original machinery survives. Prominent Lucans project either side of the roof. The nearby 6-storey tower mill was erected by John Savary in 1816 as an additional unit to the watermill. It was severely damaged in a storm in 1914 and subsequently converted to a dwelling.

CROMER
Pier (TG219424)

NORFOLK: *Grimes Graves Flint Mines – the earliest large industrial monument in the country.*

This pleasure pier was built in 1900–1 and this was one of the very last of the genre of Victorian pleasure piers. Rather shorter than most, only 500 ft it was built on cast-iron columns supported by wrought-iron piles but the substructure has undergone considerable repair and modification including in 1930 the encasement of many of the piles in concrete. The pier suffers periodic storm damage but is still in use.

DENVER
Denver Mills (TF605013)
1 mile S Downham Market W of A10
6-storey restored tower mill of *c* 1835 in care of Norfolk Windmills Trust with 2-storey steam mill attached.

DILHAM
Tonnage Bridge and Toll Cottage (TG347261)
5 miles SE North Walsham E of A149

This small brick bridge spans the disused North Walsham & Dilham Canal and dates from *c* 1811. To the south, facing the canal, is a brick cottage wth a pantiled roof. This may have been the toll cottage.

DISS
Bevin's Maltings (TM115802)
Town centre ¼ mile N A1066
This fine range of old, 2-storey maltings in Victoria Road bear a circular stone with an inscription dated 1788. There is a further range of old maltings in Vince's Lane.

DOWNHAM MARKET
Cast-Iron Clock Tower (TF612032)
Town centre
This memorial clock is a replica of the clock on the Bund at Shanghai. It was cast by W Cunliffe of London and erected in 1878 by J Scott.

DOWNHAM MARKET
Eagle Mills (TF603032)
¼ mile W town centre S of A1122

Large 5-storey steam mill built 1854 and converted, along with later adjacent maltings, to roller milling in 1888. Still in use.

FAKENHAM
Fakenham Gasworks (TF919293)
$\frac{1}{3}$ mile S town centre beside A1065
This is the last English example of the small, horizontal retort, hand-fired gasworks and although it ceased production in 1965, it is being preserved as a monument to the gas industry. The works originally opened in 1825 but the present retort house dates from 1846 – the year street lighting was introduced to Fakenham. Although the works illustrate typically 19th-century scale of production, most of the present machinery is 20th century. The 2 retort beds themselves were rebuilt in 1907 and 1910 respectively. The exhausters and purifiers are of similar date, the station meter and the Livesey washer are of the 1920s, while the condenser is as late as 1953. The earlier gasholder is single-lift and dated 1888, while a second holder of complete riveted steel design was added in 1924. A showroom and offices complete the complex.

FRITTON
St Olave's Bridge (TM457994)
5 miles SW Great Yarmouth A143
Very early Bow string girder bridge with cast-iron bow segments composed of 2 by 45 ft ribs bolted at centre and wrought-iron rods. Opened in 1847, the bridge has a clear span of 80 ft. The original cast-iron framed deck was replaced in steel in 1959.

HALVERGATE
Stracey Arms Drainage Mill (TG442090)
5 miles W Yarmouth on A47
This 3-storey brick tower windmill has been preserved by Norfolk County Council. It has a white weatherboarded ogee cap, 4 sails and an 8 sail fantail and bears the inscription 'R Barnes, Engineer, Gt Yarmouth 1883'.

HOLKHAM
Holkham Hall Estate (TF884436 etc)
2 miles W Wells-next-the-Sea
Monuments adorned with agricultural subjects erected to memory of Thomas Coke, the pioneer agriculturalist. The estate has many sites of interest, including Longlands Farm (TF880400) with its former foundry, forge, sawmill and model farm, former gasworks (TF878430), brickworks (TF862428) and lime-kiln (TF869436).

HORSEY
Horsey Mere Windpump (TG453222)
8 miles N Caister-on-Sea on B1159

This drainage windmill was built in 1912 by Dan England of Ludham on the foundations of an 18th-century mill. The present mill ceased to work in 1943 when it was struck by lightning. It is owned by the National Trust and has been restored though it no longer works the pumps.

KINGS LYNN
Bentink Dock (TF617209)
$\frac{1}{2}$ mile N town centre
Throughout the Middle Ages Kings Lynn was one of the most important ports in England and even in 1784 its custom dues were the fifth highest in the country. Although Lynn lost this eminence in the 19th century, a flourishing trade continued with north west Europe and 2 docks were built to accommodate vessels of 3,000 tons carrying capacity. The later of these docks, the Bentink was opened in 1883 and still has some of its original warehouses. It is interconnected with Alexandra Dock (1861) and 2 swing-bridges span this connection.

KINGS LYNN
Hanseatic Warehouse (TF617197)
S of town centre
Half-timbered structure with brick nogging. Built in 15th century and used by Hanse until 1751 but considerable modern work.

MELTON CONSTABLE
Railway Workshops (TG043330)
10 miles E Fakenham on B1354
This site, in the heart of rural Norfolk, was rather improbably developed as a railway workshop by the Midland & Great Northern Railway. Between 1885–1910 the company built *c* 100 houses for its workers along with a school and institute and even had a gasworks to serve the workshops and dwellings The settlement is now totally severed from the railway system and British Rail have sold their interests. The station itself was noted for having a detached private waiting room for Lord Hastings.

MUNDESLEY
Brick Kiln (TG311376)
7 miles SE Cromer off B1159
This kiln at Kiln Cliffs now forms the focus of a caravan site. The updraught kiln, which has a tall cone and is built into a bank, has been much altered having had windows inserted, a new doorway and even a clockface. One of the nearby brickmaking sheds has been converted into a shop.

NORWICH
Anchor Brewery (TG228088)
NW town centre

Bullards Brewery, on the banks of the River Wensum in Norwich, dates mainly from the latter half of the 19th century. Closest to the river and fronting onto Coslany Street is a charming courtyard of offices. Next to this is the fine fermenting block of 1864 with its rows of tall cast-iron, fanlighted windows, decorative brickwork and cast-iron columns and spandrels. The basement is covered by shallow brick arches carried on cast-iron columns which bear the legend 'Bullard & Sons 1864'. The brewery is now disused.

NORWICH
Coslany Bridge (TG227088)
NW of town centre
This small cast-iron bridge which carries Coslany Street over the River Wensum is dated 1804 and is thus one of the earliest surviving iron bridges in the country. Besides some fine early masonry bridges, Norwich has several other 19th-century iron bridges, including Station Road Bridge (TG226093) and Foundry Bridge (TG238085).

NORWICH
Earlham Hall Horse Pump (TG193080)
1 mile SW town centre
In one corner of the courtyard of Earlham Hall is a tile and brick building housing a horse wheel. This wheel which dates from *c* 1775 is constructed of wood with a 10 ft diameter gear wheel connecting with a 2 ft diameter spur wheel driving a crank for a 3 throw pump.

NORWICH
Jarrold's Works, Cowgate (TG235093)
N of town centre
This handsome 6-storey brick-built mill was originally constructed in 1839 as a yarn mill to the design of Richard Parkinson. Its long, 20-bay, frontage overlooking the river, its spectacular rounded end turret and the narrow arch motif of the first 3 floors, combine to make this visually one of the most impressive industrial buildings in the country. For most of its life this building has been occupied as a warehouse by Jarrold's, the printers.

NORWICH
New Mills Air Compressing Station, off Westwick Street (TG226091)
NW of town
This station, built in 1898 astride the River Wensum, used to supply the compressed air to operate sewage ejectors situated at various points in the city. The pumps, which were driven by horizontal water turbines powered by the river, operated at a pressure of 30 psi. Now redundant but hopefully to be preserved.

NORWICH
Panks Showroom Castle Hill (TG233083)
Town centre
Remarkable cast-iron and glass-fronted showroom built *c* 1868 and one of the earliest examples of modern curtain wall construction.

REEDHAM
Berney Arms Drainage Mill (TG465049)
4 miles NE Reedham. Accessible from Berney Arms Halt or by water. No road access
This 7-storey, brick-built mill stands over 70 ft high and was built by the Yarmouth mill-wrights in 1840. At the 3rd-floor level there is an external iron stage and there is also an iron gallery round the cap. The 24-ft diameter scoop wheel is situated away from the mill itself and is driven via a horizontal shaft. Originally the mill also ground cement. The mill is in the guardianship of the Department of the Environment and is open to the public.

SETCHEY
Toll House (TF636138)
4 miles S Kings Lynn on A10
Relatively few toll houses have survived in Norfolk. This single-storey cottage with projecting bay is in local Carr stone and has Gothic windows.

SHERINGHAM
Railway Station (TG147410)
4 miles W Cromer A149
Headquarters of the North Norfolk Railway – a preserved 3 miles of line to Weybourne. Fine ridge and furrow roof awning on cast-iron columns. Otherwise a rather plain station.

SUTTON
Windmill (TG396239)
8 miles SE North Walsham, 1 mile E A149
Reputedly the tallest mill in the country with 9 floors and cap totalling almost 80 ft in height. Four pairs of stones on 6th floor, 4 patent sails and 10 bladed fantail. Originally built 1789, rebuilt 1857 after a fire and now being completely restored.

THETFORD
Cast-Iron Bridge (TL868831)
NW of town centre
Single-span cast-iron bridge dated 1829, gas standard lamps in centre of parapets.

WEST NEWTON
Appleton Pumping Station (TF707273)
2 miles SE Dersingham B1440
The carstone pumphouse contains a recently restored single cylinder Pratchitt horizontal

engine of 1877 driving 3 pumps via a crankshaft. Octagonal chimney. Fine Italianate Victorian water tower nearby (TF705278) was converted into holiday home of the Landmark Trust.

WOLFERTON
Railway Station (TF660286)
5 miles N Kings Lynn, 1 mile W A149
Station for Sandringham Estate, the 1898 half-timbered building with royal retiring rooms is now a museum. Original stone-built station of 1862 converted to waiting rooms when new half-timbered station was built.

YARMOUTH
Smoke House (TG527060)
½ mile S of town centre

This is one of the few surviving smoke houses in commercial use. The building presents a variety of gables to the street. The lower sections contain the washing and steeping pits while the tall narrow gable is the smoke house proper with its blackened perpendicular racks from top to bottom. The roof is now surmounted by cowls but these are a later feature. A more traditional smoke house survives to the west of the range.

YARMOUTH
Icehouse, Haven Bridge (TG521074)
Town centre
A rare survival of commercial icehouse. Brick-built with massive buttresses, this example has a hipped thatched roof and characteristically few windows.

Northampton

Northamptonshire displays two quite different trends in its industrial development. It has developed a shoe industry reminiscent in its organization of Leicestershire to the N while in most other ways it resembles the Home Counties to the S. Thus its transport system, which contributes most of its notable industrial monuments such as Stoke Bruerne canal complex and Kilsby Tunnel, is primarily part of a national not local network, it merely passes through the county and is not generated by it.

BLISWORTH
Blisworth Tunnel (SP729529–739503)
5 miles SW of Northampton off A43
The 3,056-yard-long tunnel on the Grand Union Canal N of Stoke Bruerne was one of the great engineering feats of the canal builders. Its construction which started in 1794 was plagued by difficulties and especially by the amount of water that was encountered. For several years a tramway over the hill allowed traffic to be conveyed on either side of the unfinished tunnel. Eventually the tunnel was opened in March 1805 and is a vital part of the cruising network today.

BRACKLEY
Railway Viaduct (SP595371)
½ mile E of town centre
This 756-ft-long viaduct was built in 1899 on the line of Watkin's ill-fated Great Central Railway. It crosses the valley of the Great River Ouse on 19 brick arches. The Great Central was of historical importance as the first large scale civil engineering project carried out with mechanical as opposed to manual methods of excavation.

BRAUNSTON
Canal Basin and Bridges (SP540659)
4 miles NW of Daventry off A45
The Grand Junction Canal met the Oxford Canal at Braunston half a mile W of the Braunston Tunnel which was completed in 1796. The original junction was 300 yards E of the present junction and it was close to this former site that basins and repair facilities developed. When the new straighter course of the Oxford Canal was cut it necessitated

several new bridges including the elegant cast-iron double bridge erected by the Horseley Ironworks. There are also remains of reservoirs and their attendant engine houses as witness to the water supply problems besetting the Braunston Summit.

COSGROVE
Cosgrove Canal Bridge (SP793427)
1½ miles NE of Stony Stratford off A508
The Grand Junction Canal at Cosgrove is spanned by an unusually ornate masonry bridge probably designed to be in keeping with the nearby Priory. The low arch is pointed in the Gothic fashion and there are numerous blank niches and ornamented buttresses. The bridge is quite unlike most contemporary canal bridges and is remarkably similar in its treatment to that given by Brunel to structures on the Great Western Railway some 40 years later. A little way to the S the village street pierces the canal embankment with a passage-way too narrow for vehicular traffic.

HARDINGSTONE
St Peters Bridge (SP778594)
1½ miles SE of Northampton on A428
A single-span cast-iron bridge built in 1843 to carry the Northampton–Bedford Road over the River Nene. It has 6 cast arched members with lattice work in spandrels and was cast by Barwell at the Eagle Foundry, Northampton.

HARLESTONE
Watermill (SP707646)
5 miles NW of Northampton off A428
A corn mill being restored by local enthusiasts. Its machinery is virtually complete and it is hoped to return it to full working order.

KETTERING
Railway Station (SP864780)
½ mile SW of town centre
Built by the Midland Railway in 1857 on its new line to London, Kettering Station was designed by C H Driver. It retains one of his distinctive multi-ridged canopies of transverse greenhouse-type supported on bracketed columns with elaborate tracery in the spandrels.

KILSBY
Kilsby Tunnel (SP565715–578697)
5 miles N of Daventry off A361
The 1½-mile-long Kilsby Tunnel was possibly the greatest engineering feat on Stephenson's London & Birmingham opened in 1838. Its construction has been immortalized by lithographs by J C Bourne, one of which shows the interior of the tunnel lit by a working shaft. The brick towers capping these shafts, the largest of which was 60 ft in diameter, now provide ventilation for the tunnel. The driving of the tunnel was greatly complicated by an extensive quicksand which, according to Smiles, required 8 months incessant pumping at the rate of 2,000 gallons per minute.

NORTHAMPTON
Billing Watermill (SP815615)
4 miles E of Northampton off A45
A corn mill restored as a museum of milling complete with waterwheel and machinery. Operated in conjunction with the Billing Aquadrome.

NORTHAMPTON
Brown & Pank's Warehouse, Bridge Street (SP755596)
¼ mile S of town centre
This rather strange-looking but most impressive building rises directly from the river and was built in 1887. Its exaggerated architectural details, including a projecting suspended rectangular tower with louvred window, bracketed eaves and concave lead covered spire, give the 4-storey brick building an Italian Renaissance appearance.

NORTHAMPTON
Hunsbury Hill Ironstone Quarries (SP738584)
2 miles SW of Northampton off A43
An extensive area of ironstone workings dating from the late 19th and early 20th centuries. The south pits (SP742575) closed 1921 and show shallow depth of overburden and heaped spoil – a consequence of the trestle and barrow method of removing overburden. The track-bed of an ironstone tramway serving Hunsbury furnaces is the projected site for a museum of mineral railway exhibits to be operated by the Northamptonshire Ironstone Railway Trust.

NORTHAMPTON
Manfield Building, Campbell Square (SP755609)
¼ mile N of town centre
Three-storey cement-rendered brick show factory built *c* 1857 for Moses P Manfield in a modified classical style. The ground floor of rusticated semi-circular headed windows sits on a half cellar storey lit by street level 'lights' in a typical feature of Northampton shoe factories. A campanile-styled tower rises 2 storeys above the rear of the building.

TOWCESTER: *Stoke Buerne Waterways Museum.*

NORTHAMPTON

Manfield Shoe Factory, Wellingborough Road (SP772614)
1 mile E of town centre on A45
Designed by Charles Dorman in 1890, this single-storey shoe factory building is in marked contrast to the mid-19th-century multi-storey factories of the town centre. It was one of the earliest factories (other than weaving sheds) in the country to be consciously arranged on one floor. The Jacobean style red brick building has stone dressings and stone capped gables, those on the projecting 2-storey centre with stone finials.

OUNDLE

Maltings, North Street (TL044885)
¼ mile NE of town centre
Two-storey 18th-century stone-built maltings range with a hoist and central double carriage doorway.

ROADE

Roade Cutting (SP750525)
5 miles S of Northampton on A508
Stephenson's insistence on gentle gradients (less than 1 in 330) led to an impressive series of engineering works on the line of the London & Birmingham Railway, some of which might have been avoided or at least significantly lessened had he adopted steeper gradients. The 65 ft deep cutting through the Northamptonshire hills at Roade is a case in point, 1½ miles long, 800 navvies were employed on its cutting which was seriously hampered by waterlogged shale beds.

TOWCESTER

Stoke Bruerne Canal Locks and Warehouse (SP745500)
6½ miles S of Northampton off A508
A most attractive canal-side complex a few hundred yards S of Blisworth tunnel (*qv*) on the Grand Junction Canal. It is now the site of the Waterways Museum housed in a former

warehouse and one of its double locks has been converted to display a barge-weighing machine. The nearby road bridge had a second arch added in 1835 when the locks were doubled. A canal-side inn and shop complete the complex.

WEEDON BEC
Heyford Ironworks (SP654580)
6 miles NW of Towcester off A5
Between the canal and railway are the remains of 3 blast furnace hearths started in 1857 and closed in 1891.

Northumberland

Despite losing Newcastle, and hence most of its population, in the local government reorganization of 1974 Northumberland has still an impressive stock of industrial monuments. These range from lead mining remains in the W to limekilns and coal shipping facilities of the coast and include significant transport relics such as Keilder and Lambley viaducts and the Union suspension bridge.

ACKLINGTON PARK
Dam on River Coquet (NU203029)
3 miles SW of Amble on B6345
This beautifully proportioned dam across the River Coquet was probably designed and built by John Smeaton in 1776 and is possibly the dam featured in his collected 'Reports' of 1837. The dam powered an ironworks which failed and was converted to a blanket mill in 1791 and continued intermittently as such until the 1930s.

ALLENDALE
Blackett Level Portal (NY837560)
N of village
This stone faced portal draining into the River East Allen is the entrance to a drainage level which takes water from several mines in the East Allendale Valley. When construction started in 1854 it was intended to be $7\frac{1}{2}$ miles in length but when work was abandoned in 1903 only $4\frac{1}{2}$ miles had been completed.

ALLENDALE
Smelt Mill and Flues (NY832567–814538)
W of Allendale village
Established by 1692 this smelting site was greatly extended in the 19th century with long horizontal flues being added in 1808 and 1845–50. Three flues some miles in length lead from the smelt mill site to terminate in 2 chimneys on the open moorland above.

ALLENHEADS
Industrial Settlement (NY860454–850464)

7 miles S of Allendale on B6295
Allenheads and the neighbouring settlement of Dirt Pot are largely the creation of the Blackett–Beaumont lead mining enterprise in the early 19th century. Apart from the mine and smelt mill there is a planned industrial village with school, shop, public house and dwellings for workers, foremen, manager etc.

ALLENSFORD
Allensford Furnace (NZ079503)
2 miles SW of Consett off A68
On the N bank of the River Derwent below Allensford Bridge are the remains of a 17th century blast furnace. The furnace itself has survived to a height of some 14 ft and as it seems to have gone out of blast by the middle of the 18th century it is a most significant survival of early blast furnace technology. On the hillside above the furnace a calcining kiln has also been recently excavated.

ASHINGTON
Woodhorn Colliery (NZ289884)
5 miles E of Morpeth off A197
This colliery contains the last operating steam winding engine in the North East coalfield. The horizontal duplex engine was built by Grant Richie & Co of Kilmarnock in 1900 but its future, and that of the pit itself, is uncertain.

BAMBURGH
Castle Windmill (NU182352)
5 miles E of Belford on B1342
The shell of this pre 1800 tower mill to the N of

BEADNELL: *Impressive group of early limekilns.*

the castle itself has been preserved with a conical slate roof. Originally a corn mill, none of the machinery or sails have survived.

BARDON MILL
Tileworks (NY779647)
6 miles E of Haltwistle on A69
These works originally produced brick and tiles but later diversified into the production of ornamental pottery garden ware and chimney pots. The firm of Errington Ray & Co still produce a little 'artistic' pottery, and reproduction 'Roman' Ware. An old kiln is sited prominently beside the A69.

BEADNELL
Limekilns (NU238285)
10 miles N of Alnwick off B1340
This group of 18th century kilns by the small harbour of Beadnell represent several periods of construction. The kilns, though vulnerable to sea damage, have been consolidated by the National Trust and their openings are used for the storage of fishermen's gear. Built of dressed rubble, they are strictly functional in appearance and display none of the architectural embellishments which became popular in the 19th century.

BELFORD
Goods Shed (NU126337)
14 miles S of Berwick-on-Tweed off A1
Masonry goods shed originally spanning 2 tracks. The fine stone details include ball finials on gable ends, buttresses at each corner and dressings to all openings. Seven bay front elevation has large arched doorway.

BELFORD
Warren Mill (NU147344)
14 miles S of Berwick on B1340 off A1
This site 2 miles to the E of Belford has a long tradition of malt production, some of which is chronicled on a slate slab with the heading 'Warren Mill 1925'. The 2-storey building is now run as an adjunct to a Tweedsmouth mill and the original water-driven machinery has been replaced by electrically driven equipment.

BERWICK-ON-TWEED
Icehouse (NT997529)
W of town centre
Built into the hillside of Bankhill is an example of a commercial icehouse used to store ice collected during the winter for use in the salmon netting industry. Commercial icehouses, as distinct from those of private large houses, are comparatively rare.

BLYTH
Staiths (NZ306830)
N of town centre
Coal staiths, once such a familiar sight on the

coast of North East England, are now disappearing rapidly. Blyth still retains some large wooden examples, the North Side Staiths of 1896 are now disused but the later West Staiths of 1928 are in partial use.

BROOMHAUGH
Horse-Wheel House, Riding Mill (NZ014616)
3 miles SE of Corbridge on A68
One of the very many circular horse-wheel houses in Northumberland dating from introduction of the threshing machine in the early 19th century. The slate roof is supported by 6 pillars.

CAPHEATON
Tilery (NZ027815)
10 miles SE of Otterburn off A696
This works, which probably dates from *c* 1800 is the best preserved of some 40 such works in the county. Despite some recent demolition, most of the kilns, clay pits and coal workings can be seen and numerous ancillary buildings.

CHOLLERTON
Farmstead (NY933720)
6 miles N of Hexham on A6079
An early 19th-century steading with remains of both a windmill tower for a threshing mill and the later steam engine house, boiler house and chimney for the engine that replaced it. Northumberland has a large number of fine stone-built farmsteads of this period reflecting the activities of the wealthy agricultural improvers.

CORBRIDGE
Farnley Toll House (NZ001629)
1 mile SE of town
Few turnpike toll houses have survived in Northumberland. This example, which stood on the Gateshead to Hexham Turnpike of 1777, is of unknown date but has survived road widening.

CORBRIDGE
Pottery (NY992652)
½ mile N of town centre
The substantial remains of Walkers Pottery comprise 2 bottle kilns, some 30 ft in diameter, a circular downdraught kiln and 2 rectangular Newcastle kilns. The firm produced sanitary and domestic ware.

FORD
Ford Forge (NT933384)
8 miles NW of Wooler off A697
This small industrial hamlet, a mile from the parent village of Ford, located to take advantage of water power, has several extant buildings of 1800. The corn mill, which contains 2 undershot waterwheels 16 ft by 5 ft and 16 ft 6 in by 5 ft 4½ in respectively has its machinery intact and is currently being restored. The remainder of the buildings are used as an estate timber yard.

HAYDON BRIDGE
Farm Wheel House, Fourstones (NY892680)
4 miles NE of Haydon Bridge on B6319
The farm buildings in this village contain a wheel house for a horse wheel for threshing and, built on to it, the chimney and associated buildings of the steam engine which replaced it.

KIELDER
Railway Viaduct (NY632924)
12 miles NW of Bellingham off Kielder road
This stone-built viaduct carries the Redesmouth to Riccarton line of the North British Railway over the valley of the Kielder Burn. Opened in 1862, it employs a skew arch construction with each block of masonry shaped using a geometrical technique developed by a Newcastle mathematician, Peter Nicholson. The branch closed in 1956 but the viaduct has been preserved because of its importance in the study of civil engineering.

LAMBLEY
Railway Viaduct (NY675584)
6 miles SW of Haltwhistle (9 miles NE of Alston on A689)
This magnificent stone viaduct of 1852 carries the Alston Branch of the Newcastle & Carlisle Railway some 110 ft above the River South Tyne. It has 9 semi-circular arches of 58 ft span.

LOAN END
Union Suspension Bridge (NT933510)
5 miles SW of Berwick off A698
Designed by Captain Samuel Brown and built across the River Tweed in 1820, this was the earliest large suspension bridge in Britain. The dressed stone monumental pylons carry 3 sets of chains on each side with iron rod suspenders to the wooden deck. The chains themselves are composed of Browns patented wrought links. A wire rope cable was added in 1902–3 to each side by way of strengthening the structure.

NEWTOWN
Ewart 'Station Hotel' (NT968318)
3 miles NW of Wooler off A697
This fine building, some 3 miles N of Wooler, was a speculative venture intended for travel-

lers on a railway line which, in the event, was never built. The plan of the building emphasizes its projected railway use with windows to the S sides only as sidings were to be to the rear of the building.

OTTERBURN
Tweed Mill (NY888928)
18 miles SW of Newcastle on A696
This early milling site, with its collection of buildings dating from the late 18th to early 20th centuries, was adapted for woollen manufacture in 1821. The traditional methods of woollen manufacture were practised until recently.

RENNINGTON
Little Mill Lime Kilns (NU228173)
3 miles NE of Alnwick off B1340
These extensive lime workings contain 2 sets of kilns. The older, possibly dating from the late 18th century, has a single kiln and 3 drawholes on a semi-circular plan. The 19th-century group comprise 8 kilns with an impressive central Gothic arched access way.

RIDSDALE
Ironworks (NY909848)
14 miles NW of Corbridge on A68
Established *c* 1836, this ironworks only operated into the 1860s and has thus left in plan the layout of a small mid-19th-century ironworks unadulterated by later developments. The engine house, built to contain 2 beam blowing engines, is the most substantial relic but traces of coke ovens, the furnace yard and the servicing tramway can also be discerned.

SEATON
Seaton Sluice (NZ339769)
4 miles S of Blyth on A193
The small natural harbour at the mouth of the Seaton Burn was inadequate to cope with the potential traffic from the nearby collieries and an artificial harbour was constructed 1761–64. This involved cutting, much of it out of solid stone, a deep water dock 800 ft long, 30 ft wide and 52 ft deep which would be capable of operating at all states of the tide. By 1777 some 48,000 tons of coal were shipped from this harbour. Industrial development, including a glassworks of 1763 and copperas beds, was fostered by Thomas Delaval, the promoter of the harbour scheme. Seaton Sluice had a working life of just one century and the glassworks closed in 1870.

SLAGGYFORD
Burnstones Viaduct (NY676543)
5 miles NW of Alston on A689
This low, stone-built viaduct on the 1852 Alston Branch of the Newcastle & Carlisle Railway is rather unusual in having 6 arches on the W side and only 5 on the E. This is because the southern part of the viaduct crosses the Thinhope Burn on a skew while the arch over the road is at an opposing skew. The effect is to pinch out one arch on the E side. The extra arch on the W side is therefore blind with converging piers.

Nottinghamshire

Nottinghamshire has a wide variety of industrial monuments reflecting two quite different themes – agriculture in much of the N and E and industry, notably coal mining and textiles, in the W. Agricultural processing is represented by wind and watermills and by a selection from the *c* 50 recognizable maltings. The coal industry has Bestwood steam winding engine and bellpits at Strelley while the textile industry has mills in Beeston, workshops in Ruddington and Stapleford and the Lace Market warehouses of Nottingham. The River Trent provides a waterborne outlet to the sea and is the focus of several canals including the Beeston, Nottingham, Chesterfield and Grantham canals. The county has unfortunately lost several magnificent steam pumping stations such as Elkesley but retains Papplewick whose interior decoration is unsurpassed anywhere in the county.

AWSWORTH
Bennerley Viaduct (SK471437–476441)
4 miles S of Eastwood off A6096
Built 1876–7 to carry the Great Northern Railway across the valley of the Erewash, Bennerley Viaduct is one of the 2 great surviving metal viaducts in the country. It is 484 yards long with a maximum height of 60 ft and comprising 15 wrought-iron piers between massive brick abutments, each pier being a cluster of wrought-iron columns. The columns rest on cast-iron base plates and have cast-iron saddles carrying girders of the spans. It is usually ascribed to the famous firm of Handyside & Co, Derby, though Eastwood Swingler & Co, Derby, would seem to have been joint contractors.

BEESTON
Anglo Scotia Mills (SK525373)
Wollaton Road, ¼ mile N of town centre
A 4-storey lace factory of *c* 1870 of quite exceptional architectural treatment. The 12-bay façade on Wollaton Road has tall Gothic windows, crennellated parapet and narrow hexagonal turrets the full length of the corners and bracketing the central 2 bay section. The rear sections of the mills are also treated with architectural extravagance.

BEESTON
Canal Entrance Lock, Rylands (SK536353)
1 mile S of Beeston
The Beeston Canal was constructed under a Trent Navigation Act of 1794 and opened in 1796. The masonry broad lock (63 ft by 14½ ft) would have been constructed at this time. The disused, partially infilled masonry lock bypassing the weir may be earlier. There is a small complex of cottages including a modernized lock-keeper's house and toll booth.

BESTWOOD
Colliery Winder (SK557478)
5 miles N of Nottingham off A611
A fine 3-storey winding engine house with its associated headstocks on the No. 2 Shaft, Bestwood, has been preserved by the county council. It contains a vertical twin cylinder steam engine of 1873 possibly by Worsley Mesnes.

CALVERTON
Framework Knitters' Cottages (SK621491)
7 miles NE of Nottingham of A614
Hailed as the birthplace of the mechanized hosiery industry because it was here that the Rev William Lee invented the stocking frame in 1589. Calverton had indeed by the mid-19th century become a 'knitting' village par excel-
lence, when the population of some 1350 supported over 400 machines. There are several surviving examples of knitters' cottages including a portion of Windles Square.

CARLTON-IN-LINDRICK
Carlton Mill (SK588838)
3½ miles N of Worksop off A60
A 2- and 3-storey stone-built watermill and mill house. The waterwheel is visible from the road bridge while some machinery is maintained as a museum exhibit.

GONALSTON
Smithy (SK679475)
7 miles NE of Nottingham off A612
Neat brick smithy dated 1843 with a low relief ornamental horseshoe of black painted bricks framing the gable doorway. The board above the doorway has the following verse.

Gentleman as you pass by
Pray on this shoe cast your eye
If it is too tight, we'll make it wider
Twill ease the horse and please the rider
If lame by shoeing (as they sometimes are)
You can have them eased with the greatest
care.

LITTLEBOROUGH
Toll House (SK814831)
8 miles E of East Retford, unclass road
Very few turnpike toll houses have survived in Nottinghamshire. The example at Littleborough is the most unaltered. Built of pale orange brick, it is a half hexagonal, 2-storey cottage with some original windows and a central porched doorway. It is situated on a very minor road which was originally the Retford Littleborough turnpike connecting Retford to the River Trent.

MANSFIELD
Kings Mills Viaduct (SK520598)
1½ miles W of town centre off A615
A very significant monument to the pre-locomotive era of railway transport. Built in 1817, as part of a horse-drawn railway from Mansfield to Pinxton, it carried a double track railway on 5 arches across a small valley. The piers have shallow pillaster buttresses and the whole is given added strength by symetrically spaced circular iron ties. It is now unused and the track lifted after many years as a railway siding.

MANSFIELD
Midworth Street Maltings (SK540610)
E of town centre
One of only 2 stone-built maltings in the

county, these are also probably the oldest. The foundations appear to be very early and much of the structure dates from the 18th century when it was one of the largest malting units in the county. Only 2 storeys high, it is some 250 ft long with a slate roof and 4 gables on the Gilcroft Row elevation.

MANSFIELD
Railway Viaduct (SK540610)
E of town centre
The centre of Mansfield is dominated by curved railway viaduct some 40 ft high. Built of squared rubble with ashlar dressings and brick linings under arches, it has 13 arches most of which are round but these over Church Street and Market Street have pointed *voussoirs*.

MANSFIELD
Textile Mill (SK548617)
½ mile NE of town centre off B6033
Mansfield was a major centre of the cotton industry in the early 19th century with many large mills powered by the River Maun. This large 4-storey stone-built mill was erected *c* 1800 but since 1880 it was operated by Messrs Goldie Wade & Goldie as a hosiery factory.

NEWARK
Brewery and Maltings, Northgate (SK800544)
¼ mile N of town centre on A46
A range of ornate red brick offices with terra cotta dressings dating from 1890 front a brewhouse of 1882. Somewhat older maltings are to be found on either side of the brewery complex.

NEWARK
Great North Road Viaduct (e.g. SK790555)
1 mile NW of Newark on A6065
The former main road to the N crossed a large low lying island formed by 2 branches of the River Trent. This island was subject to flooding and in 1768 John Smeaton produced a report for the construction of an arched causeway. The scheme was completed *c* 1770 at a cost of £12,000 and carried modern trunk road traffic until 1964 when the Newark by-pass was built.

NEWARK
Peach's Maltings (SK802547)
½ mile N of town centre off A46
Newark was a very important centre of malting based initially on the water-borne trade on the River Trent and also in rail transport in the later 19th century when there were 26 maltings in the town. Peach's Maltings

is a typical 19th-century brick-built maltings with 4 hipped-roofed kilns. On the same site is Bairds Maltings, a large red brick range of 3 storeys and 2 loft storeys and 1 visible kiln.

NEWARK
Railway Station (SK796543)
¼ mile N of town centre on A6065
A dignified single-storey station with subdued classical details dating from 1838. It is built in a pale brick with stone window surrounds, quoins and cornice. The central doorway is flanked by pairs of low relief pilasters and is set in 3-bay protruding section surmounted by a small masonry pediment.

NORTH LAVERTON
North Laverton Windmill (SK776820)
5 miles E of East Retford (North Laverton road)
A 3-storey tower mill dating from 1813 built of brick weather-proofed with tar with a typical East Midland ogee-shaped cap and 4 patent sails. It was used, with repairs and modifications, continually from 1813 to 1956 under the control of a Subscription Mill Company of local farmers. In 1956 a limited company was formed and with the help of various official bodies the mill has been able to continue to operate.

NOTTINGHAM
Lace Market, Stoney Street (e.g. SK576397)
¼ mile E of city centre
A spectacular mid-19th-century commercial precinct developed around Stoney Street, St Mary's Gate, Broadway and Barker Gate based on the lace industry – an area now popularly known as the Lace Market. A distinctive, heavily ornate monumented building style was adopted with the architect T C Hine being the leading protagonist. The Thomas Adam's warehouse in Stoney Street of *c* 1855 is a magnificent example of an E-shaped plan.

NOTTINGHAM
Fellows Morton and Clayton Warehouse, Canal Street (SK573393)
¼ mile S of city centre
Late 19th-century complex with a private wharf and crane alongside Nottingham Canal. The main warehouse is an elegant 4-storey, 2-gable building in pinkish grey brick with barge hole covered access. The premises on Canal Street comprise ornate brick offices, cobbled yard and stables.

PAPPLEWICK: *Papplewick Pumping Station in a setting befitting to its magnificent interior.*

NOTTINGHAM
Warehouse, Arkwright Street (SK572392)
¼ mile S of city centre
Imposing late 19th-century 7-storey brick-built warehouse separated from the canal by a wall which is pierced by the tunnel of a private branch canal. Originally a grain store, the stack has small square-headed windows and loading doors on each floor.

PAPPLEWICK
Grange Farm Outbuildings (SK547502)
7 miles N of Nottingham on B683
The stream draining S from Newstead Abbey is the unlikely setting for a chain of cotton mills which witnessed the first use of steam power in the textile industry. George Robinson was established in the cotton industry near Papplewick in the 1770s and by the 1780s had a chain of mills on the Leem, including one at Grange. In 1784 Robinson commissioned a steam engine from Boulton & Watt and the 10 hp engine was at work by 1786 followed by a second engine in 1790. Very little survives of these historic sites other than outbuildings and cottages at Grange Farm.

PAPPLEWICK
Papplewick Pumping Station (SK582522)
8 miles N of Nottingham off A60
The fine ornate Victorian engine house in its most attractively landscaped setting contains 2 James Watt & Co single cylinder, rotative beam engines of 1884. The interior of the engine house is exceptional for the wealth of ornamentation including stained glass windows and filigree decoration on the columns which support the engine beams. The pumping station is preserved by a Trust and is open to the public summer weekends.

RATCLIFFE-ON-SOAR
Redhill Tunnel, northern portal (SK496308)
7 miles SW of Nottingham of A648
The northern portal of the 1840 Midland Counties Railway tunnel through Redhill on the southern bank of the River Trent is elaborately castellated. A vantage point to view the portal can be gained on a track from Trent Lock on the opposite bank of the River Trent.

RUDDINGTON
Framework-Knitters' Shops, Chapel Street (SK571320)
4½ miles S of Nottingham off A60
A small museum comprising a group of early

19th-century workshops and cottages has been established as a monument to the domestic framework knitting industry. One frameshop has been restored with 11 hand frames, winding wheels etc and a display of products, documents and photographs. The cottages are being restored to present period displays of 1850 and 1900.

SOUTHWELL
Fiskerton Mill (SK742516)
3 miles SE of Southwell
A large corn mill on the River Greet ¼ mile before it joins the River Trent. At the end of the 18th century it was seemingly used as a cotton mill and its main elevation, with its numerous windows would suggest such a use.

STAPLEFORD
Lacemakers' Cottages, Nottingham Road (SK506379)
5 miles W of Nottingham on A52
A group of mid-19th-century red brick, 3-storey cottages with distinctive workshop windows in uppermost floor.

STRELLEY
Bell Pits (SK505417)
5 miles Nottingham off A609
In the grounds of Bilborough College alongside the B6004 is a fine group of bell pits. The central depressions surrounded by mounds of spoil show up clearly in the well-cared for parkland and are the surface evidence of a mining technique practised for centuries. This group probably dates from the 17th century.

TROWELL
Swansea Canal Bridge (SK490394)
1½ mile N of Stapleford off A6007
Situated on an abandoned but water-filled section of the Nottingham Canal of 1796, this masonry bridge is the best preserved on the canal. The elliptical arch is braced by 3 metal ribs of early date. There is a pair of stop gates just N of the bridge and stop grooves and planks under the bridge.

WISETON
Lady's Bridge (SK715903)
5 miles SE of Bawtry off A631
Surveyed by James Brindley in 1769, the Chesterfield Canal was completed by Hugh Henshall in 1777. The western end was closed in stages from the late 19th century but the section E of Worksop is a designated cruiseway. Some 20 bridges are at least partly original. Lady's Bridge at Wiseton is noteworthy in having ornamental railings instead of parapets and carved stone heads at the keystones. The nearby Drakeholes Tunnel (SK706905) 154 yards long is the main engineering feature on the open section and is one of the earliest broad canal tunnels in the country.

WORKSOP
Canal Depository (SK586792)
Town centre
A small canal-side complex dating from the second quarter of the 19th century. The enclosed yard with Georgian looking gatehouse and office buildings gives access to a 3-storey pale brick depository which spans the Chesterfield Canal by means of a low, wide, stone-faced segmental arch. Although many warehouses have barge holes allowing covered access, this is usually provided by canal offshoots. It is rare to find a warehouse over the main line as in this case.

WORKSOP
Railway Station (SK586797)
¼ mile N of town centre
An attractive low mid-19th-century range of stone buildings grouped on the S side of the track. Mostly single-storey with a 2-storey central section abundant use is made of curved Dutch gables both on the front elevation and high lights breaks in the roof line.

Oxfordshire

The impression of Oxfordshire is of a predominantly rural county though there have been long industrial traditions in brick making and the woollen industry. These have left monuments such as the brick kiln at Nettlebed and the blanket mills of Witney and Bliss Tweed Mill, Chipping Norton. Most of the county's monuments are focussed, however, on Oxford and the River Thames. The

Thames was the region's major highway and in the late 18th century canals were built to link it with the Midlands (Oxford Canal), the River Severn (Thames & Severn Canal), and Somerset River Avon (Wilts & Berks Canal). Much of the industrial expansion in Oxford itself is relatively recent and most of its monuments are transport related. Exceptionally fine traditional breweries survive at Hook Norton and Henley.

ABINGDON
Cast-Iron Bridge (SU495970)
¼ mile S of town centre

This attractive small cast-iron bridge has the inscription 'Erected by the Wilts & Berks Canal Company AD 1824/ Cast by Acramans Bristol' on outer cast-iron rib facing the River Thames. The Wilts & Berks Canal was opened in 1810 and closed in 1906. Very little of significance survives despite its length of 59 miles.

ABINGDON
Pumping Engine, Town Hall (SU498971)
Town centre

In the basement of the Town Hall are 2 small late 19th-century Crossley gas engines which were installed in 1906 to drive water supply pumps. These are a rare unaltered survival of house-type installation which could be used to service an individual building from either a shallow well or from low head supply.

BANBURY
Boatyard (SP459406)
½ mile E of town centre

This barge building yard dates from *c* 1790 when the dock was constructed off the Oxford Canal by the Evans family who then operated the yard until 1850. Many of the workshop buildings are very early and relatively un- altered. The yard was bought by George Tooley in 1900 and the business was carried on by Herbert Tooley.

CHIPPING NORTON
Bliss Tweed Mill (SP293268)
1 mile W of Chipping Norton off A44

One of the finest textile mill buildings in the country. It was built in 1872 by George Woodhouse on the site of a mid-18th-century mill which had burnt down. From the centre of the 4-storey mill rises a large dome enclosing the lower part of the tall mill chimney. The rest of the mill is in keeping with corner towers, urns and a balustraded para- pet.

DIDCOT
Engine Shed (SU525906)
½ mile N of town centre

The headquarters of the Great Western Society is an engine shed behind Didcot Station where they have assembled a large collection of GWR steam locomotives and rolling stock. Didcot was at a point where wide gauge and standard gauge met and the wooden goods transfer shed has different sized arched entrances for the different gauges.

EYNSHAM
Eynsham Flash Lock (SP446089)
5 miles NW of Oxford off B4044

Most remaining flash locks are decayed and ruinous but a fine and nearly complete beam and paddle type can be seen on a small tributary of the Thames just below Eynsham lock. Although traffic on this ½ mile navi- gation to Eynsham Wharf ceased in 1925, the beam still survives bolted to the stop-post and supporting a foot-bridge.

GARFORD
Venn Mill (SU430949)
4 miles W of Abingdon on A338

A 2-storey and attic rubble-built watermill dating from the first decade of the 19th century. Central loading door on first floor. The mill retains most of its 19th-century machinery including an undershot iron water- wheel and 2 pairs of stones.

HENLEY
Brakspear's Brewery (SU763827)
Town centre

Henley Brewery is mainly late 19th-century but Old Brewery House is mid-18th-century and there are several 20th-century additions including engine houses. There is a long 2- storey pedimented block of 1897, a louvred tower with cast-iron columns dated 1892, early brewing coppers and a single cylinder vertical steam engine of 1880 by Riley Manu- facturing Co.

HENLEY
Grey's Court Donkey Wheel (SU724834)
2 miles W of Henley

The 19 ft-diameter donkey wheel at Greys Court dates from the 16th century and until *c* 1914 raised water from a well 200 ft deep by means of 2 buckets acting on the arrangement one-up-one-down. The nearby horse engine in its octagonal cast-iron columned wheelhouse

CHIPPING NORTON: *Bliss Mill with its extraordinary domed chimney.*

to the W of the donkey wheelhouse was re-erected from Shabden Park, Surrey.

HENLEY
Nettlebed Brick Kiln (SU703868)
5 miles NW of Henley off A423
A most unusual conical brick kiln over 30 ft high with a base 20 ft in diameter tapering to 3 ft diameter at top. Possibly 17th-century, the kiln is entered by a brick arched door on NW side.

HOOK NORTON
Brewery (SP349332)
5 miles NE of Chipping Norton off A361
A stone and brick-built brewery given a whimsical appearance by the use of half-timbering in certain features, most prominently in a suspended sack hoist tower attached to the main tower which itself is surmounted by a ventilated water tank. A small horizontal steam engine of *c* 1890 by Buxton & Thornley is still used to pump the liquor and power to the hoist. This is a fine example of a typical late 19th-century vertical brewery producing traditional ale.

OXFORD
Canal Bridges (e.g. SP506066)
Canal lies to W of city centre
A fine series of canal bridges are to be found within the city. The red brick examples (e.g. SP494098, SP495096, SP504073) with stone or blue brick dressings were probably designed by James Brindley's office though their construction *c* 1790 was some years after his death. There are also 3 counter weighted wooden draw bridges (e.g. SP502088) reputedly of the same date and a cast-iron roving bridge at Isis Lock (SO506066) which is probably 19th century.

OXFORD
Folly Bridge and Toll House (SP514054)
¾ mile S of city centre on A4144
Rusticated stone bridge of 3 main arches rebuilt on an ancient bridging site in 1826. The iron girder bridge over the S stream was built 1888.

OXFORD
LMSR Railway Station Yard, Park End Street (SP506063)
½ mile W of city centre off A420
This cast-iron structure, now occupied by a tyre firm, was built *c* 1852 and may be

constructed of re-used parts of the Great Exhibition building. Clad in weatherboarding on a brick plinth, the central 6 bays of the 12-bay structure have a projecting canopy.

OXFORD
Old Iffley Lock and Roving Bridge
(SP525036)

2½ miles SE of city centre off A4158
A very early navigation site with a pound lock in use by 1632 but present stone-built structure much later and heavily repaired. Early 19th-century elliptically arched masonry roving bridge upstream from lock.

OXFORD
Toll House, Banbury Road (SP504107)

2½ miles N of city centre on A4165
An attractive stone-built early 19th-century 2-storey turnpike cottage with a semi-hexagonal projecting central bay containing the doorway. Stone mullion windows with drip mouldings above, a wide eaved hipped slate roof and central chimney stack all give the cottage distinction.

MINSTER LOVELL
Chartist Village, Brize Norton Road etc
(SP3110)

2½ miles W of Witney on A40
The Land Company, an offshoot of the Chartist Movement, bought some 300 acres at Minster Lovell in 1847 as part of their scheme to provide the working classes with land and hence a political base. The land was distributed by ballot in 1, 2, and 3 acre lots with standardized cottage; 62 of the original 78 cottages survive but only a few resemble their original plan of 3-bay bungalow with kitchen, sitting room and bathroom with courtyard outbuildings. A putative school building for the Charterville Allotments is situated in upper crescent.

WITNEY
Blanket Factories (SP355103)
Town centre

Witney has long been famous for its blankets with Early's Blanket Mills and Smith's Blanket Mills carrying on the tradition. The former, in Mill Street, is largely 20th-century but with an early 19th-century mill beside the river. Smith's premises in Bridge Street are also *c* 1900.

WOODSTOCK
Combe Saw Mill (SP418150)

2½ miles W of Woodstock off A4095
A fine range of stone buildings comprising an estate saw mill, joinery and smithy. At one end of the building is a 12 ft diameter by 8 ft wide low breast shot waterwheel which drove, via overhead shafting, a variety of machinery and blowers. This lay shaft could also be driven by a small single cylinder rotative beam engine *c* 1852 with 18 in by 2 ft 8 in cylinder.

Shropshire

Shropshire has perhaps the richest stock of industrial monuments of any county. The gorge of the River Severn at Ironbridge has valid claims to be considered the birth place of the Industrial Revolution. Besides the Iron Bridge itself there is Darby's historic furnace and the Hay Incline (the greatest tub boat incline in the country) and lesser monuments such as Coalport China Works, Bedlam and Blists Hill furnaces, Coalport Bridge, Severn Wharf Warehouse and tramway track, the tar tunnel, Maw's tileworks and the Albert Edward railway bridge. All these monuments are described in a section under Ironbridge Gorge. Within a few miles of Ironbridge there is Longdon-upon-Tern Aqueduct, the first significant cast-iron aqueduct, the unique guillotine canal lock gates at Hadley Park and Bage's Mill, Shrewsbury, the first major iron framed fireproof building in the country.

Besides the pre-eminent monument the county has much to offer – a fine series of structures on the Shropshire Union Canal system, the lead mining relics of south Shropshire, an early charcoal furnace at Charlcote, railway sites in Shrewsbury and Bridgnorth (terminus of the restored Severn Valley Railway) and the toll houses and milestones of Telford's Holyhead road.

ATCHAM
Berwick Tunnel (SJ538114)
4 miles SE of Shrewsbury off A5

The 970-yard long Berwick Tunnel opened in 1797 and was the first long canal tunnel to incorporate a tow path. Although the Shrewsbury Canal is now closed the elegant masonry-faced southern portal of the tunnel is still accessible. It bears the date 1797 on the keystone.

BERRINGTON
Cantlop Bridge (SJ517063)
4½ miles SE of Shrewsbury off A458

A 4-rib cast-iron bridge of 32 ft span erected in 1812. It was probably cast at Coalbrookdale and carried traffic until it was by-passed in 1975.

BRIDGNORTH
Cliff Railway (SO717929)
Connecting Low Town and High Town, Castle Hill Railway of 1892 is the only inland funicular railway. Originally water balance operated the 2 cars which are now wound by electric motor.

BRIDGNORTH
Railway Station (SO715926)
SW of town centre

Northern headquarters of the preserved Severn Valley Railway. Built originally in 1863, Bridgnorth Station is an attractive single-storey masonry building with projecting Dutch gables on its long façades. It has a wooden signal box on a brick base at the northern end of the platform.

CHIRK
Chirk Aqueduct (SJ287372)
5 miles N of Oswestry off A5

The success of the cast-iron trough at Longdon-on-Tern (*qv*) encouraged Jessop and Telford to employ the same technique in their great aqueducts on the Ellesmere Canal. Chirk aqueduct across the River Ceiriog is less well known than its great neighbour in Wales the Pont Cysyllte aqueduct but is nevertheless most impressive. Built 1796–1801 it has 10 masonry arches each of 40 ft span carrying the canal 70 ft above the river. Encased in the masonry superstructure is a cast-iron trough whose rigidity does away with the need for massively thick masonry.

CLEOBURY NORTH
Charlcote Furnace (SO638861)
7 miles SW of Bridgnorth off B4364

A 17th-century blast furnace built of thin sandstone blocks standing in isolation on a remote farm. Dating from *c* 1760 the furnace which has an almost complete lining has been partially shored up to take some of the weight off the iron lintels of the tapping arch and tuyère arch.

CRAVEN ARMS
Milepost (SO433827)
9 miles NW of Ludlow on A49

An obelisk, opposite the old coaching inn, gives distances to London and 35 other towns and is evidence of the former importance of this turnpike route.

DITTON PRIORS
Brown Clee Hill Tramway (SO602878)
10 miles SW of Bridgnorth off B4364

The Clee Hills have been mined and quarried for hundreds of years for coal, limestone, copper and dhustone. The surface is littered with abandoned workings and their associated tramways. On Brown Clee Hill a long incline connected these workings with the Cleobury and Ditton Priors Light Railway.

EARDINGTON
Eardington Forges (Upper SO725897 Lower SO734895)
2½ miles S of Bridgnorth

In 1778 a mill on the Mor Brook at Eardington was converted to a forge for working charcoal iron and 4 years later a second forge was established on the banks of the Severn. The forges were linked by a ½-mile long underground canal and they continued in operation until 1869. A curved stone weir is the most prominent feature of the Upper Forge site while at the Lower Forge there is a jumbled complex of walls and caves.

EYTON UPON THE WEALD MOORS
Wappenshall Junction (SJ664146)
2 miles NE of Wellington off A442

The Newport Branch opened in 1835 to connect the Shrewsbury and Shropshire Canals to the Birmingham and Liverpool Junction Canal. The junction at Wappenshall is notable for its fine masonry skew roving

bridge and the 3-storey warehouse with internal wharf.

HADLEY
Guillotine Locks (SJ672133)
1 mile NE of Wellington off A518
The Shrewsbury Canal, engineered by Clowes and latterly Telford, opened in 1797 and was distinctive in its use of guillotine lock gates. Much of the canal has disappeared following its abandonment in 1944 and the best surviving examples of the locks are at Hadley Park on the Trench branch. In a distance of 200 yards both an original 'balance box counter weight' pattern of lock and the modified version with side weights are to be seen.

HOPE
Roman Gravel Mine (SJ334000)
4 miles SE of Minsterley beside A488
The lead mines of Shropshire are concentrated in a small area some 12 miles SW of Shrewsbury. Although lead was mined from Roman times onwards, most of the remains of numerous engine houses and ancillary buildings date from the 19th century. Mention is made of only 3 mines in this gazetteer, for more details refer to specialist guides such as *The Shropshire Lead Mines*, Brook and Allbutt (1973). Roman Gravel Mine was worked, as its name suggests, in Roman times and then again from the 1780s. It was second to only Snailbeach Mine (*qv*) in its output in the late 19th century. The surviving remains are of this period, including, on the hilltop, an engine house built in 1878 for a 60 in Cornish engine by Harvey of Hayle.

IRONBRIDGE GORGE
Most of the sites in the Gorge are being preserved by the Ironbridge Gorge Museum Trust and are accessible to visitors to the museum. The Trust publishes a fine series of guides to the monuments in their care and therefore only the briefest details are given here.

BUILDWAS
Albert Edward Bridge (SJ661038)
Designed by John Fowler, this graceful cast-iron railway bridge was manufactured by the Coalbrookdale Company and erected in 1863.

COALBROOKDALE
Darby Furnace (SJ667047)
Originally built as a charcoal-fired furnace in 1638, adapted in 1709 by Abraham Darby for his historic smelting of iron using coke as a

HADLEY: *Guillotine Locks' evidence of Telford's ingenuity in water conservation.*

fuel. Subsequently used for casting the members of the Ironbridge itself.

COALBROOKDALE
The Great Warehouse (SJ667046)
A 3-storey brick building with many cast-iron features such as window frames, lintels and sills and cast-iron columns built by the Coalbrookdale Company in the 1830s. The prominent clock was added in 1843.

COALBROOKDALE
Rose Cottages (SJ668042)
A group of wooden-framed buildings dating from *c* 1642 and associated with the boring mill to the rear. Restored by the Trust.

COALPORT
Coalport Bridge (SJ702021)
Built originally under an Act of 1777, this was commonly referred to as the Wood Bridge although the wooden superstructure was supported on iron ribs. The present structure bears the date 1818 and may incorporate iron members from the earlier bridge.

COALPORT
Coalport China Works (SJ695024)
Established by John Rose 1794–5, the Coalport Works became famous for its exceptionally fine porcelain. The works were purchased by Staffordshire manufactures in 1923 and closed in 1926. Now restored, they are part of the Ironbridge Gorge Museum.

COALPORT
Hay Inclined Plane (SJ695028)
The collieries of the Shropshire coalfield, and its associated ironworks, were served by a system of tub boat canals developed from the 1760s onwards. A series of inclined planes overcame the differences in height and the most spectacular of these, the Hay Incline, has been restored by the Museum Trust. Opened in 1793, the incline has a vertical rise of 207 ft.

COALPORT
Tar Tunnel (SJ694025)
Driven in 1787 as an access and drainage adit to the coal workings under Blists Hill, the Tar Tunnel, as it was to become known, accidentally tapped a spring of natural bitumen. This tar was exploited commercially until *c* 1843. Visitors are admitted to the first 300 ft of the 3,000-ft long tunnel.

IRONBRIDGE
Bedlam Furnaces (SJ677034)
Built specifically for coke smelting 1757–58 these furnaces were superseded in the 1840s by the furnaces at Blists Hill, Madeley. The blast

COALBROOKDALE: *Darby Furnace.*

was provided by waterwheel-driven bellows with a steam engine returning the water to the reservoir.

IRONBRIDGE
Free Bridge (SJ681033)
Built in 1909 to ease the traffic on the Iron Bridge, this is one of the earliest reinforced-concrete bridges in the country.

IRONBRIDGE
Iron Bridge (SJ673034)
Probably the most famous industrial monument in the world, the Iron Bridge was erected in 1779 and was the first civil engineering work in the world constructed entirely of iron. Its 100 ft span is supported by 5 cast-iron rib members.

IRONBRIDGE
Wharf Warehouse (SJ667036)
An attractive Gothic brick warehouse and counting office built in the 1840s by the Coalbrookdale Company and now an interpretive centre for the Gorge.

JACKFIELD
Maw's Tilery (SJ692026)
This enormous range of brick-built tileries was built by Maws and Co who had been established in 1852 at Bethnall further up the Gorge and moved to Jackfield in 1883. By the end of the 19th century they were the largest tile producers in the world.

LONGDON-UPON-TERN
Longdon-upon-Tern Aqueduct (SJ617156)
$3\frac{1}{2}$ miles NW of Wellington off B5063
Following the collapse of Clowes conventional masonry aqueduct carrying the Shrewsbury Canal over the River Tern Telford decided to experiment with the use of a cast-iron trough. Although a minor aqueduct in this material was opened merely a month before on the Derby Canal, Longdon-upon-Tern aqueduct when it was completed in 1796 was the first important cast-iron aqueduct in the country. As well as a 187 ft cast-iron trough constructed

IRONBRIDGE: *The Iron bridge.*

of *voussoir*-shaped sections bolted together it had a partly cantilevered tow path outside the trough and cast-iron supporting legs. It was very much a pioneer structure and many of the design faults were not to be repeated in the many later cast-iron aqueducts.

MADELEY
Furnace Bases and Blowing House, Blists Hill (SJ694031)
The site being developed as an open-air museum by Ironbridge Gorge Museum is itself of considerable interest. The Madeley Wood Company built 3 blast furnaces in the 1830s and in 1851 a brick and tile works was established. The foundations of the furnaces can be seen and the huge blowing house which now contains an 1886 vertical blowing engine from Priorslee.

MAMBLE
Wharf House (SO672705)
9 miles SW of Bewdley off A456
Just inside the county boundary is a fine 3-storey brick house with a projecting circular

bay. This was the wharf house and offices at the canal/tramway interchange at the end of the uncompleted Leominster Canal. It dates from *c* 1796.

MARKET DRAYTON
Tyrley Cutting (SJ693315)
2½ miles SE of Market Drayton off A529
One of the most impressive civil engineering features on Telford's Birmingham & Liverpool Canal is the 2-mile-long cutting S of Market Drayton. Completed in 1835, this canal represents the ultimate in English summit canal engineering. Its constructional techniques resemble much more closely those of the railways than those of Brindley 60 years before.

MINSTERLEY
Snailbeach Lead Mines (SJ375022)
2 miles S of Minsterley off A488
A very rich lead mine worked in Roman times and again from 1784 until 1911. An extensive

and complicated site with several engine houses, including the massive New Engine House of 1856 built for a 61 in Cornish engine, at least 5 shafts and numerous ancillary buildings such as ore dressing sheds, a compressor house and a locomotive shed of 1877.

MONTFORD
Montford Bridge (SJ433153)
4 miles NE of Shrewsbury on A5
Built by Telford, in his capacity as county surveyor, in 1792 in red sandstone with 3 segmental arches, Montford Bridge and its associated toll house predate Telford's up-grading of the Holyhead road by some 25 years.

OSWESTRY
Milestones (e.g. SJ299309)
Telford's Holyhead road, unlike the present A5, passed through Oswestry. A reminder of this is the series of 'Holyhead' milestones on the present A4083 and A483 such as that below Old Oswestry hill fort.

PANT
Incline and Brake Drum (SJ273218–274218)
5 miles S of Oswestry off A483
The Montgomeryshire Canal was opened in 1797 and from the start lime and limestone was the major commodity carried. The extensive quarries at Pant were connected to the canal by a tramway which had a self acting incline to overcome the final 75 ft drop to the canal. A large wooden winding drum supported by masonry walls survives at the top of the incline and there are limekilns at the foot beside the canal.

PENNERLEY
Tankerville Mine (SO355995)
4 miles S of Minsterley off A488
Worked in second half of 19th century with most of the remains dating from a re-equipping in the 1870s. 3 masonry engine houses of this date, the largest built to hold a 40 in engine of 1876. Closed *c* 1891.

SHREWSBURY
Bage's Mill (SJ499139)
½ mile NE of town centre on A49
Jone's maltings at Ditherington incorporate the first major attempt at an iron-framed fireproof building in the country. The large 4-storey brick range was originally built in 1797 as Benyon Marshall & Bage Flax Mill with cast-iron columns supporting cast-iron beams and brick-jack arching. There are, however, no longitudinal beams and the walls are load bearing. The distinctive multi-ridged roof is also iron-framed.

SHREWSBURY
Coleham Sewage Pumping Station (SJ496121)
¼ mile SE of town centre
Two-storey red brick engine house with stone dressings built 1898–1900 to house 2 compound rotative beam engines by W R Renshaw of Stoke on Trent. Engines now turned by electric motor for visitors on Wednesday and Friday afternoons.

SHREWSBURY
Howard Street Warehouse (SJ495130)
NE of town centre behind railway station
A most imposing building erected in 1835 by Fallowes & Hart of Birmingham as the terminal warehouse of the Shrewsbury Canal. Its tall single-storey façade has a massive Doric portico while its interior is designed to give a lofty and spacious area to accommodate its second function as a market for perishable commodities carried on the canal. The internal structure is composed of tall cast-iron columns supporting a massive timber-framed roof. There is a former covered wharf to the side of the warehouse but the canal basin itself has long since been converted into a car park.

SHREWSBURY
Railway Station, Castle Gates (SJ494129)
NE of town centre
An impressive 3-storey sandstone building in a collegiate Jacobean style originally designed by T. K. Penson in 1848 and subsequently reconstructed in 1903–4 in the same idiom.

WEM
Starks Lift Bridge, Whixall (SJ492346)
4½ miles NW of Wem
A wooden counterbalanced drawbridge carrying Windmill Lane over the Ellesmere Canal. There is a series of these fine relatively cheap accommodation bridges along the Ellesmere canal.

Somerset

Even in its post–1974 much reduced size Somerset presents a wide variety of industrial monuments ranging from the typically West-of-England woollen mills in the NE of the county to the iron ore mining remains of Brendon, from the leadmines of Mendip to the pumping stations of the Somerset levels. It has seen several novel attempts to overcome problems of water transport in hilly districts and canals such as the Grand Western, Chard and Dorset & Somerset have left a legacy of lifts, incline planes, tunnels and aqueducts. Following the lead of Bath to the N turnpike systems of great complexity were developed in the 18th century round each of the local centres such as Frome, Shepton Mallet, Wells and Bruton leaving fine series of milestones, boundary posts and toll houses. Railway penetration was fairly late but has left rare survivals in the overall wooden roof at Frome Station and the traversing bridge at Bridgwater.

BRADFORD-ON-TONE
Canal Lift and Aqueduct (ST144218)
1½ miles N of Wellington off A38
The Grand Western Canal was promoted at the end of the 18th century to link the Bristol and English Channels. However, only the central section from Taunton to Tiverton was ever built. This comprises a summit level from Lowdwells to Tiverton and an eastern section rising from Taunton with the aid of 2 locks, 8 lifts and an inclined plane. Some of the masonry of the lift at Nynehead has survived as well as 2 cast-iron trough aqueducts – Nynehead Court Aqueduct (ST143217) and Tone Aqueduct (ST147224).

BRIDGWATER
Barham Brothers, Brick And Tile Works
(ST300376)
¼ mile NW of town centre
This large brick and tile works on the East Quay is now largely disused and very dilapidated. There are several kilns of the bottle oven type i.e., the kilns themselves are housed in a conical hovel. The lower part of each hovel is encased in a rectangular building which acts as a final drying shed utilizing heat from the kilns. The drying sheds are more substantial than usual, being constructed on brick piers with sophisticated wooden shuttering between and substantial pantile roofs.

Bridgwater bricks and especially pantiles achieved a high reputation and were transported all over Somerset.

BRIDGWATER
Docks (ST297376)
¼ mile NW of town centre
In 1841 the Bridgwater & Taunton Canal was extended to terminate in docks in Bridgwater itself rather than at Huntworth as formerly. There is an inner and outer dock with a large red brick warehouse along one side of the inner dock. Between the docks is a lock and the connection with the river is made by both second barge lock and a single pair of gates. The docks which have been disused and formerly belonged to British Rail are now owned by the local authority and are to be preserved as an amenity area.

BRIDGWATER
Glass Cone (ST298374)
¼ mile NW of town centre close to docks
Built in the early 18th century by the Duke of Chandos as one of his speculative ventures this cone was originally one of the largest in the country. It was converted for pottery making after a few years and finally demolished in 1943. It was recently excavated to reveal the early 18th-century furnace hearth and foundations and may possibly be preserved.

Bridgwater Docks, the presence of a steam dredger attributed to Brunel attests the former importance of these docks. The dock is now disused and the dredger displayed at Exeter maritime museum.

BRIDGWATER
Railway Traversing Bridge (ST300374)
¼ mile NW of town centre
A single line traversing railway bridge with a separate pedestrian walk incorporated in the structure. It was designed in 1869 to carry a branch line of the Bristol Exeter Railway over the River Parret to the Bridgwater Docks. Originally there were 2 movable sections and a fixed portion on the western bank. The easternmost section could be moved on rails to one side to allow the main bridge section itself to be pulled back to give 100 ft clearway on the river. The main section was operated by a steam-driven chain and drum mechanism but the steam engine which also drove the rack and pinion movement of the offsetting section has been destroyed.

BRUTON
Gants Mill (ST675342)
¾ mile SW of town centre off A359

A 3-storey and attic stone-built watermill with a history of varying uses. It was converted from a grist mill to a fulling mill in medieval times then to a silk throwing mill in the late 18th century. It is now an animal foodstuffs mill and store, the waterwheel having been replaced by a turbine in 1870.

BUCKLAND DINHAM
Wool Stove and Packhorse Bridge (ST756509)
2 miles NW of Frome on A362
Virtually hidden in the vegetation beside the road is a stone-built wool stove some 20 ft high rising from the banks of a small stream. It has one doorway and a grate-like opening at its base. Immediately to the rear is a packhorse bridge.

BURNHAM-ON-SEA
Navigation Light (ST298504)
1 mile N of town centre off B3139
The low light of the pair of navigation lights just N of Burnham was built in 1832 and is the only surviving pilelight of J Nelson. It is a 2-storey clapboard structure supported by 9 tall timber piles with access by wooden stairway. Its partner light is a conventional tower lighthouse 800 yards (ST304505) inland.

BURROW BRIDGE
Pumping Station (ST357305)
10 miles SW of Street on A361
Housed in the original pumping station is the
museum of land drainage of the Wessex Water
Authority (from whom permission must be
obtained to view). An Easton & Anderson
steam engine and pump of 1869 are preserved
in situ along with a replacement boiler of 1924.
There is also a collection of small pumps from
some of the Authority's other stations.

CASTLE CARY
Higher Flax Mills (ST635323)
8 miles S of Shepton Mallet off A371
In the 19th century the town was a centre for flax
production and one of the mills Torbay, or
Higher Flax Mills, still produces webbing. The
3-storey block with iron hoist is dated 1870 but
the mill pond has been filled in. Other
premises originally connected with textiles are
the former Boyd's mills in High Street
(ST644325) and Florida Works (ST640325).

CHAPEL ALLERTON
Ashton Windmill (ST414503)
4 miles SW of Cheddar off B3151

CHARTERHOUSE: *Lead condensing flues
dating from the last main period of working.*

This, the most complete windmill in the
region, was restored by its previous owner, Mr
C C Clarke, and presented in 1966 to Bristol
City Museum. It is a cylindrically shaped
tower mill built of local lias stone with a
wooden cap which can be moved by hand with
a chain drive. The mill last operated in 1927
and used common sails to the last.

CHARD
Holyrood Mill (ST323085)
S of town centre on A358
Gifford Fox's works were established by
entrepreneurs from the Midlands seeking a
less militant workforce for the introduction of
machinery. The main block is brick-built, 5
storeys, with a lucan on the N end elevation
and dates from the second quarter of the 19th
century.

CHARTERHOUSE
Lead Works (*c* ST507561)
4½ miles NE of Cheddar off B3371

The dry valley at Charterhouse together with its continuation, Velvet Botton (ST503555) displays a large variety of lead working remains. The site is overlooked by the traces of a Roman settlement attesting to the antiquity of the workings in this area. Most of the visible remains, however, date from the last period of exploitation viz the operations of the Mendip Mining Company from the 1850s to the 1880s. In the latter part of this period material was merely dressed and sent to Bristol for smelting. There are significant remains of a fine set of 4 parallel flues at ST507561 and a large quantity of black slag, scanty remains of a Pattinson silver extraction plant at ST506557 and sets of buddle pits at ST504556 and ST501553.

COLEFORD
Canal Aqueduct (ST684487)
5 miles NE of Shepton Mallet off A367
This was the largest and most expensive engineering work on the Nettlebridge branch of the Somerset & Dorset Canal. Built *c* 1800 it must have originally been quite a handsome structure but it has now been robbed of its parapets.

CRANMORE
East Somerset Railway Station (ST665430)
4 miles E of Shepton Mallet off A361
The attractive, small, stone-built station is the headquarters of a railway preservation society who have restored the station and a short section of track to steam locomotives at weekends. The signal box has been converted into an art gallery and a fine cast-iron urinal and telephone box/letter box have been erected on the platform.

CREECH ST MICHAEL
Chard Canal Aqueduct (ST271253)
3 miles E of Taunton off A358
The northern section of the short-lived Chard Canal was opened in 1840 to join the Bridgwater & Taunton Canal at Creech St Michael. This necessitated crossing the River Tone and traversing its flood valley. A fine masonry aqueduct was constructed with a stone-faced embanked approach pierced by flood arches. The embankment and some of the aqueduct have survived over a century of dereliction; the canal having closed in 1867.

CREWKERNE
Viney Mills (ST449091)
SE of town centre off A356
Crewkerne shares with many other small Somerset towns a textile tradition, in this case specializing in canvas and webbing. The older

stone-built premises at Vineys date from 1800 onwards. Sailcloth is still produced.

EAST HARPTREE
Smitham Chimney (ST555546)
7 miles E of Cheddar off B3135
The most visually dramatic relic of local mining in Mendip, this stack was built *c* 1867 by the East Harptree Lead Works Co Ltd. This short-lived venture reworked old waste and constructed a reservoir, buddles, furnaces, flues and the chimney. The pond still survives as do traces of the flue system in the woods to the NE of the chimney. The company was liquidated in 1875 and all the buildings except the chimney pulled down. The chimney itself is characteristically 'Cornish' in construction i.e. the upper third is brick, the lower portion being masonry with a bottom diameter of 12 ft.

FROME
Housing, Trinity Street (ST772484)
W of town centre off A362
The streets around Trinity Street to the W of Frome town centre are an example of one of the earliest major suburban developments of workers' housing outside London. It would seem the area was laid out in the last decades of the 17th century to cater for the housing demand caused by the expanding woollen industry. Though much of the area has recently been cleared, several of the original streets of small terraced houses remain.

FROME
Railway Station (ST784476)
E of town centre off A362
Built *c* 1850 this station has been relatively little altered and thus assumes a significance beyond its function as an occasional halt for local trains on a loop off the main SW line. Its main buildings are of timber in an austere functional classical style that has been attributed, with no certainty, to I K Brunel. Its overall roof, constructed of heavy timber beams, is now a very rare survival for a rural station although the single track it now spans looks rather forlorn.

FROME
Wold Stoves (ST777483, 778483)
Town centre
Frome was an important centre of the West of England Woollen industry throughout the 17th, 18th and 19th centuries. Although most of the mills have been converted to other uses, there are still many relics of the industry. Two roundhouses or woollen stoves have survived, one easily viewable just off the agricultural

market in Justice Lane the other in the grounds of the new telephone exchange. The latter can be viewed through a gap in the buildings 200 yards along Willow Vale from the Town Bridge.

GLASTONBURY

Abbey Barn (ST504385)
E of town centre on A361
The magnificent tithe barn of Glastonbury Abbey has been restored by the county council as a Museum of Rural Life and houses a fine collection of agricultural and rural crafts.

GREAT ELM

Murtry Aqueduct (ST764498)
1½ miles NW of Frome off A362
Built *c* 1800 this handsome stone structure was one of 2 major aqueducts on the Nettlebridge branch of the abortive Somerset & Dorset Canal. The main line of the canal never held any water but the branch did so for a short period though, as the patent lifts were never in full operation, no traffic could navigate the canal.

HIGH HAM

Stembridge Windmill (ST433308)
4 miles NW of Somerton off B3153
This prominent mill is one of 2 substantially complete windmills in the SW. (see Chapel Allerton) A stone-built tower mill with an unusual thatched cap, it dates from *c* 1820 and was worked into the present century. Though the sail blocks survive, some of the milling machinery has gone. It belongs to the National Trust.

KILVE

Shale Retort and Limekiln (ST145444)
4 miles E of Watchet off A39
This retort which dates from *c* 1920 is one of the last relics of the Somerset shale oil industry. An industry which early this century seemed to have such a promising future. Closer to the beach (ST145444) is a large limekiln in which local limestone was burnt with fuel from South Wales.

LUXBOROUGH

Gupworthy Chapel and Settlement (SS967354)
10 miles SW of Watchet off B3190
This modest cottage-like building served as a Baptist Church from *c* 1860 until a few years ago. Most of the other buildings in this small mining colony have virtually disappeared, only the footings of the walls are traceable. The area in front of the chapel itself was the pithead of Gupworthy Mine while nearby is an adit entrance to this extensive mine.

LUXBOROUGH

Ventilating Chimney, Chargot Wood
(SS974358)
8 miles SW of Watchet
A datestone, with 1867 incised, has recently been removed from this small squat chimney midway up the hillside in Chargot Wood. A fire was lit in a grate at the base of this chimney causing air to be drawn up the flue from the mine below, hence causing a current of air in the mine itself.

MARTOCK

Parrett Works (ST446187)
6 miles SW of Ilchester off A303
An unexpectedly large industrial complex in a now very rural setting on the River Parrett. It is, however, sited in a central situation as regards the Somerset local agriculture-based textile industry. The Parrett Works serviced these industries by producing a wide range of machinery and also took part directly with rope and twine manufacture. The present buildings include an impressive stone-built, 4-storey fireproof mill of the 1850s with a large derelict waterwheel, a splendid Italianate 70 ft-high square chimney decorated with blind arcading, a manager's house, foundry outbuildings, ropewalks, and a terrace of employees' housing.

MELLS

Fussell's Ironworks (ST737488)
3 miles W of Frome off A362
This is the most important of at least 6 sites operated by the Fussell family in this part of Somerset for the manufacture of edge tools. There would seem to have been a metal working site at this location, where the Mells Stream enters a gorge, since early in the 18th century but this site was greatly expanded in the mid-19th century. Besides the 3 massive arches built to house water-driven tilt hammers there were numerous hand forges and at least 6 waterwheels, one of which has survived. The site would also seem to have had its own gas supply at an early date and the offices and storerooms have also partially survived. At the time of its closure in the 1890s this was certainly one of the most extensive edge tool factories anywhere in the country.

PRIDDY

St Cuthbert's Lead Works (*c* ST545505)
3 miles N of Wells
Extensive remains of foundations and flues are to be found on the E side of a shallow valley marking the site of the last lead works to operate on Mendip. Major reworking of slag on this site dates from 1857 and continued

intermittently under various proprietors until final closure in 1908. The plant, which once included a tall engine house, 5 furnaces, and at least 8 buddles, was dismantled in 1910. Entrances to 3 flues can be seen at ST545506 while a further flue system can be examined some 100 yards to the S.

RODE
Rode Bridge Woollen Mill (ST802543)
4 miles N of Frome off A36
A 3-storey rubble-built mill of *c* 1800 is the only survival of a small woollen complex which included besides the present building a fulling mill and a dyeworks. Fulling on this site has been practised since at least the 16th century and continued to the mid-19th century when the site reverted to corn milling. Rode was an early centre of the woollen industry with at least 5 mills in operation in the 18th century.

SHEPTON MALLET
Anglo Bavarian Brewery (ST616437)
W of town centre
Highly ornate 4-storey stone-built brewery with 3-storey maltings. It originally produced IPA when it was built in 1872 but changed to lager production when bought by the Garton family. To the rear is a fine red and yellow brick chimney with bracketed cornice.

SHIPHAM
Calamine Mining (ST445574)
3 miles NW of Axbridge off A38
The Mendips beside being mined for lead were from the 16th century also the source of the zinc ore, calamine. Mining of this reached its peak in the late 18th and early 19th centuries. Very little survives to witness the production of this essential ingredient for the local brass industry other than a stone chimney some 20 ft high in a field to the E of Shipham church, and the gated entrance to the nearby Singing River Mine.

STREET
Clarks Factory (ST483368)
Town centre
For 150 years the shoe manufacturers C & J Clark have virtually controlled the development of Street, building terraced houses for their employees e.g. Wilfred Road and civic buildings for the town. Their original factory is now a Museum of Shoemaking and most of the other industrial buildings in the town are leather related.

TAUNTON
Canal Lock, Firepool (ST232253)
½ mile N of town centre

The Bridgwater & Taunton Canal was opened in 1827 and connected with the River Tone at Firepool. Remains of the top lock survive and the channel is kept in good condition. Two truncated limekilns surmounted by a water tank serving the adjacent railway stand alongside the canal.

TREBOROUGH
Brendon Incline (ST023344–029352)
5 miles SW of Watchet off B3190
This incline was constructed by the West Somerset Mineral Railway Company in 1857–8 to provide access to the mines on the Brendon Hills. It is over ¾ of a mile long at a gradient of 1 in 4 and was self acting on the principle of loaded trucks on the downward run pulling up empty trucks. The winding pit, just below the crest of the incline, held 2 massive 18 ft diameter iron drums and originally incorporated a house for the operator. The present fanciful façade replaced this cottage in the 1920s and was built to house a barn by a local farmer.

WELLINGTON
Tone Mills (ST126219)
1 mile NW of town centre
Parts of the Tone Mills works of Fox Bros & Co Ltd date from 1754 and have thus over 200 years use in the woollen industry. Fox's also took over the nearby Tonedale flour mill in 1800 (ST128215) though the present fire-resisting buildings date from a rebuild after a fire in 1821.

WESTONZOYLAND
Pumping Station (ST340328)
5 miles SE of Bridgwater off A372
The most complete of a series of steam driven pumping stations which reclaimed the wet moors bordering the River Parrett. The 2-storey red brick building houses an Easton & Ames engine of 1861 and an Appold pump. Disused since the 1950s, it is being restored by volunteers in collaboration with Wessex Water Authority.

WESTPORT
Canal Warehouse (ST385198)
4 miles N of Ilminster on B3168
At the terminus of the Westport Canal is a square plan warehouse with a stone ground floor and a brick second storey formed of 5 tall blind arches. There is a loading door in the central arch on the canal elevation. The 2 mile canal was completed in 1840 but was disused from *c* 1875 though still kept clean for drainage purposes.

WITHIEL FLOREY
Burrow Farm Engine House (ST009345)
7 miles SW of Watchet off B3190
This mine was first opened *c* 1860 in the peak period of the Brendon Hills iron ore production. The mine was connected to the western extension of the West Somerset Mineral Railway in 1863 but closed soon after 1867. It was reopened *c* 1880 and the impressive engine house of characteristically Cornish style may have been built at this time to the designs of Captain Henry Skewis. It housed a 25 in Cornish rotary beam engine which did both pumping and winding duty and is the better preserved of the 2 remaining engine houses on Brendon, the other is Kennesome Hill. The stone structure alongside was a miner's drying shed.

WOOKEY HOLE
Paper Mill (ST532477)
1½ miles NW of Wells off A371
It is reputed that paper has been made at this site since before 1610 and certainly the Wookey Hole watermark was registered in 1783. Originally the waterwheels were fed by mill leats on the western side of the valley but in 1852 the present leat on the E side was constructed. Production was greatly expanded when the duty on paper was repealed in 1861, there being 10 vats in use in 1876 as compared with only 2 some 30 years earlier. Most of the present buildings date from the second half of the 19th century. The mill is now occupied by Madame Tussauds and is open to the public with demonstrations of hand making of paper. Wookey Hole village itself is almost entirely a creation of the Hodgkinson family's enlightened paternalism; under their direction the village school, church, club and many of the cottages were built.

WOOLVERTON
Shawford Mill (ST793534)
3½ miles N of Frome on A36
The present 2-storey early 19th-century stone building is the truncated remains of a 4-storey woollen mill which is the most significant survival of the largest dyeworks in the district which had at one time 16 vats and 10 furnaces. One of the 2 water courses under the building still drives a turbine connected to a DC generator. The bridge over the River Frome at this point has an elegant bow-fronted 2-storey toll house (ST793535) erected by the Black Dog (Warminster & Frome) Trust before the construction of their major new route to Bath in 1834 when a toll house was built some distance to the N.

YEOVIL
Leather Factory, Eastland Road (ST561162)
N of town centre off inner ring road
Yeovil's main industry until recently was the dressing of leather and the manufacture of leather goods. The premises of Perrin Leather Co in Eastland Road are a good example and comprise 2 stone-built 4-storey buildings with louvred top floors for drying skins and a covered yard between. The large block is dated 1855. A 3-storey brick extension to the N has perforated walls as well as louvres on the upper floors. The steam plant has gone but the engine house and chimney remain.

Staffordshire

Despite losing the Black Country to the West Midlands in 1974 local government reorganization, Staffordshire has an extremely large stock of industrial monuments. It has numerous canal monuments displaying both early canal technology in Brindley's Trent & Mersey Canal and late canal technology in Telford's Birmingham & Liverpool Junction Canal. It encompasses the Potteries, the most important region of ceramic production in the country, with notable monuments such as Gladstone Pottery and Shirley Bone Mill and the Staffordshire Coalfield with the prominent remains in the vicinity of Stoke on Trent. The railways have also left their mark, Winton

Square, Stoke on Trent, is one of the finest railway developments in the country, while the architectural standard of some local stations and embellishments to some bridges and tunnels are exceptional. The water-powered industries of the valleys in the E of the county have left monuments such as Cheddleton Flint Mills and the textile mills of Leek. The county is also notable for its group of steam-driven water pumping stations and for the maltings and breweries of Burton on Trent.

BREWOOD

Avenue Bridge, Chillington (SJ888075)
6 miles W of Cannock off A5
This bridge over the Shropshire Union Canal in Brewood Park was designed by Thomas Telford. Built of rusticated stone in classical style with a turned balustrade, the bridge spans a deep cutting and carries a former avenue to Chillington Hall.

BURSLEM

Longport Potteries (SJ857494)
4 miles NW of Stoke Railway Station
Along this section of the Trent & Mersey Canal is a collection of potteries including Price's Teapot Works and Arthur Wood's Teapot Works. They display some bottle ovens once such a prolific feature of the Potteries but now becoming rather rare.

BURTON ON TRENT

Bass Brewing Museum (SK247234)
N of town centre off Horninglow Street
A most attractive museum has recently been established in the former 19th-century 3-storey joinery of the Bass brewing complex. Although concentrating primarily on the Bass company and Burton on Trent, the history of brewing in the country in general is well demonstrated. External exhibits include a compound steam engine, model brewery and the Bass steam locomotive and directors' coach.

BURTON ON TRENT: *Bass Brewing Museum in a former joinery in their extensive 19th century brewery.*

BURTON ON TRENT
Clay Mills Sewage Pumping Station
(SK263258)
3 miles N of town centre off A38
The original installation of 1885 at this works has recently been superseded by a modern sewage plant and there are plans to preserve one of the 2 engine houses with its contents. The 4 compound rotative beam engines were built by Gimson & Co and there are numerous other smaller engines of *c* 1885 on the site.

BURTON ON TRENT
Maltings (*c* SK235230)
NW of town centre
Burton is the centre of the British brewing industry and obviously most of the breweries have been extensively modernized. However, the huge ranges of maltings with their distinctive kilns produce much of the earlier atmosphere of the town. A fine panorama of these maltings is obtained from the embanked section of A38 by-pass.

CHEDDLETON
Brewhouse (SJ973525)
3½ miles S of Leek on A520
Adjacent to the flint grinding mill is a small porter brewery long since disused. It is mentioned in detail in an advert of 1815 being occupied by Messrs Joul and comprising brewery vaults, storeroom, cooper's shop and malthouse.

CHEDDLETON
Cheddleton Flint Mill (SJ972526)
3½ miles S of Leek on A520
Crushed flint is an important raw material for the pottery industry and in the 18th century many water-powered crushing mills were established in the valleys to the E of the Potteries. Cheddleton Mill, on the River Churnet, is served by the Caldon Canal and has been restored by a voluntary trust. The site comprises a canal wharf and crane, calcining kilns, slip kilns, a plateway and the 2 grinding mills. The North Mill is powered by a 22 ft diameter low breast waterwheel and has been restored to its early 19th-century state. It contains a 14 ft diameter underdrift grinding pan with cast-iron sweep arms and oak hanging arms with ancillary pumps, hoists etc. The South Mill is maintained as a museum and besides the original machinery there are exhibits representing most of the techniques in the preparation of the raw materials of the pottery industry.

CHESTERTON
Springwood Furnace (SJ822499)
4 miles NW of Newcastle under Lyme off A52
Built against the hillside overlooking Apedale are the remains of an 18th-century blast furnace. It was reputedly erected in 1768 by John Parker and certainly in use by the 1780s. Although the 40 ft furnace is built almost entirely of brick, the hearth itself is masonry. A terrace of 19th-century cottages almost obscure the furnace and the nearby engine house has been converted into dwellings. A series of dams can be traced in the fields above the furnace.

COLWICH
Lichfield Drive Railway Bridge (SJ997211)
5 miles SE of Stafford off A513
This splendid bridge in Shugborough Park was built in 1847 in a classical style and with elaborate heraldry to satisfy the tastes of the local landowner – the Earl of Lichfield. It carries the railway over one of the main approach drives to the house.

COLWICH
Shugborough Railway Tunnel (SJ981216–988215)
5 miles SE of Stafford off A513
The portals of this tunnel through Shugborough Park were heartily decorated to appease the Earl of Lichfield, owner of the Park. The western portal is castellated while the eastern portal is in an Egyptian style.

DRAYCOTT-IN-THE-MOORS
Cresswell Pumping Station (SJ974395)
8 miles NW of Uttoxeter off A50
This water pumping station which belonged to the Staffs Potteries Water Board still operates 2, 1932-vertical triple expansion steam engines by Hathorn Davey as well as an economiser engine by E. Green & Sons.

ECCLESHALL
Millmeece Pumping Station (SJ830339)
3 miles S of Eccleshall of A519
This water pumping station, which is built of rather striking orange-red bricks, has a rather unusual arrangement of pumping assembly. The 1926 horizontal tandem compound Hathorn Davey steam engine has a piston rod extension through the end wall of the engine house to operate the well pumps outside. The similar 1914 Ashton & Frost steam engine is also still working as are an economiser engine and steam winch.

FROGHALL
Limekilns (SK028476)
3 miles N of Cheadle off A521
An extensive bank of well-preserved limekilns are to be found at the terminus of the Caldon Canal. Froghall itself was the focus of a system

HANLEY: *Etruscan Bone and Flint Mill with its narrow Dutch gabled engine house.*

of tramways serving both iron ore mines and stone quarries.

GAILEY
Canal Wharf (SJ920104)
4 miles W of Cannock on A5
There is a small canal complex dating from *c* 1772 at Gailey Lock on the Staffordshire & Worcestershire Canal, some 3 miles S of Penkridge. Besides the basin, wharf and lock, there is a warehouse, a toll office, the toll clerk's house, a tower-like lengthsman's cottage with Gothic windows and a small lockkeeper's cottage. Across the bottom of the lock the canal is spanned by a brick-built stone-faced bridge with 2 bridge holes – over the canal and tow path respectively.

HANLEY
Deep Pit (SJ885484)
2 miles N of Stoke on Trent Railway Station

This former coal mine forms part of the Hanley Central Forest Park – an ambitious land reclamation scheme involving landscaping the coal tips and converting railways into footpaths. The engine house of Deep Pit is preserved though the engines themselves have been scrapped.

HANLEY
Etruscan Bone and Flint Mill (SJ872478)
1½ miles NW of Stoke-on-Trent town centre
The bone works, adjacent to the summit locks of the Trent & Mersey Canal, were erected in 1857 and have an unusual Dutch gabled engine house which still contains its small beam engine. The works which processed an essential raw material for the manufacture of fine china may be preserved as a museum.

HANLEY
Twyford's Works, Cliffvale (SJ873464)
1½ miles NW of Stoke-on-Trent town centre
These works, famous for the sanitary ware

produced, back on to the Trent & Mersey Canal and contain 2 ovens and a warehouse dated 1891. The red brick frontage on the main road characteristically masked the industrial nature of the site.

KIDSGROVE
Harecastle Tunnel Portals (SJ837541)
½ mile S of town centre
These 2 portals some 50 yards from each other provide a fine contrast of the building scales and techniques of Brindley and Telford. The former drove his 2,897-yard tunnel at a time when engineering techniques were in their infancy and although the bore was only 9 ft the task took 11 years to complete. Telford, on the other hand, built his slightly longer tunnel (2,926 yards) on a much larger bore (15 ft) but by sinking 15 shafts took only 2 years. Brindley's tunnel has long since been disused and Telford's tunnel is at present closed due to roof falls. However, as it is on the line of the Trent & Mersey Canal – a major arterial waterway – British Waterways are resolved to reopen it.

LEEK
Brindley's Mill (SJ979569)
½ mile NW of Town Centre on A523
This small 2-storey building which has been somewhat mutilated over the years, was designed and built in 1752 by James Brindley, the noted canal engineer. Brindley's early training was as a millwright and some of the machinery, including the upright shaft, is original but much is 19th century.

LEEK
Hazelhurst Locks and Aqueduct (SJ948538–951537)
2½ miles SW of Leek off A53
The junction of the Leek and Caldon Canals is effected by an attractive aqueduct (SJ954536) and a flight of 3 locks. The aqueduct is dated 1841 and the locks themselves with their associated side pounds, footbridges, accommodation bridges, and roving bridge are constructed in the finest tradition of canal engineering.

LEEK
Milestone (SK006592)
2 miles NE of Leek on A53
Between Leek and Buxton there is a fine series of circular column cast-iron milestones. This example gives the distances to Buxton 10 miles and Leek 2 miles.

LEEK
North Portal, Leek Railway Tunnel (SJ973565)
½ mile W of town centre
The portal of this tunnel was designed to give the appearance of a natural cavern in the rock.

LICHFIELD
Railway Bridge (SK118091)
½ mile S of town centre on A51
This bridge in St John's Street is constructed of built-up wrought-iron girders on brick abutments and has a cast-iron parapet. It incorporates a stone-built pedestrian way in a Gothic style.

LICHFIELD
Sandfields Pumping Station (SK112084)
1 mile S of town centre off A5127
The original installation at Sandfields was built in 1856 alongside the Wyrley & Essington Canal and comprised 3 single-cylinder, condensing, rotative beam engines made by James Watt & Co, originally for South Devon Atmospheric Railway but remodelled for pumping duty at Sandfields. In 1873 a Cornish-type beam engine was installed by J Davies of Tipton to augment capacity. In 1922, 2 Sulzer Bros uniflow steam engines replaced the earlier beam engines and continued in operation until electrification in 1966 when all the steam plant, with the exception of the Cornish engine, was scrapped.

LONGTON
Gladstone Pottery (SJ914433)
3 miles SE Stoke on Trent Railway Station
Pottery making on this site dates back to 1787 though the present appearance of the works dates from the mid-19th century. The premises have been owned by a long succession of firms and the name Gladstone is derived from the famous politician and not a china manufacturer. The works are now being restored as a working museum and comprise 4 bottle ovens, an engine house and slip house, clay preparation rooms, casting shops, saggar makers' shop, showrooms and offices. In addition there is a museum of history of pottery manufacture and a ceramic tile gallery.

MODDERSHALL
Ivy Flint Mill (SJ923368)
3 miles NE of Stone off A520
One of the numerous water-driven stone-grinding sites in the Moddershall Valley, Ivy Mill had a high breast wheel 19 ft in diameter by 6 ft broad powering 2 grinding pans 6 ft and 14 ft diameter respectively.

NORBURY
Canal Junction (SJ793228)
5 miles SW of Eccleshall off A519
This basin, which was formerly the junction of the Shropshire Union and the Newport Branch Canals, has developed as a popular pleasure cruiser marina based on the British Waterways depot. It has thus recovered its busy appearance reminiscent of when it was one of the main outlets for the tub-boat canal system of the Shropshire coalfield.

ROCESTER
Cotton Factory (SK113394)
4½ miles N of Uttoxeter off B5030
Part of the textile complex at Rocester now operated by Courtaulds is the original water-driven cotton mill erected by Richard Arkwright in 1781–2.

STOKE
Eturia (SJ867475)
1½ miles NW of Stoke-on-Trent Railway Station
Josiah Wedgewood moved his factory from Burslem to Eturia in 1769 but unfortunately his famous workshops were needlessly demolished a few years ago. However, a somewhat mysterious structure known as the Roundhouse has survived from the original development. Across the Trent & Mersey Canal is the grand hall built by Wedgewood to replace his house in Burslem. The mansion has been greatly modified and is now the offices of the Skelton Ironworks.

STOKE
Railway Station and Hotel (SJ879456)
Town centre
The North Staffordshire Railway developed Stoke, the focal point of their system, as their headquarters and as the town had not yet established an urban character they built a handsome square in Jacobean style to complement their station. The North Stafford Hotel, opposite the station, is designed as an early Jacobean manor house while the sides have 2-storey houses in simpler versions of the same style. The station itself dates from 1848 and was reputedly designed by R A Stent. The façade has 3 Dutch-style Jacobean gables fronted by a single-storey round arched colonnade which supports the enormous oriel window of the company's boardroom in the central gable.

STONE
Joules Brewery (SJ901339)
Town centre
Occupying what is possibly a medieval brewing site, Joules Brewery is named after John Joule, son of Francis Joule who in 1795 bought an existing brewery in Stone. It passed out of the family in 1870 and now belongs to Bass Charrington. Although much of the brewery is modern, the offices fronting onto High Street are early while the cooperage and bottling plants are 19th-century.

STONE
Railway Station (SJ896346)
½ mile NW of town centre
This handsome station was built in 1848 by the North Staffordshire Railway Company in their characteristic Jacobean style. It is very similar in style to Stoke-on-Trent Station with the same patterned brickwork and stone dressings and 3 Dutch gables.

STONE
Rockwood Pumping Station (SJ914353)
1½ miles NE of Stone on A520
This ornate 2-storey pumping station visible from the Longton road was built c 1890 to supply Stone with potable water. It is now disused and the steam pumps long since scrapped.

TAMWORTH
Hopwas Pumping Station (SK172050)
2 miles W of Tamworth off A51
A South Staffordshire Waterworks Company station containing 2 disused single-cylinder rotative beam engines installed in 1880 by Gimson & Co.

TUNSTALL
Chatterley Whitfield Colliery (SJ885534)
2 miles NE Tunstall off A527
An extensive colliery with several distinct pitheads only recently ceased production. Its name dates from its takeover by the Chatterley Company in 1872 and it achieved fame as one of the first mines to produce over one million tons. A museum has now been established on the site with access to the underground galleries at the foot of the Winstanley shaft. Eventually several other features on the site will be restored including the horizontal twin cylinder steam winding engine of 1914 by Worsley Mesnes.

WOMBOURN
Botterham Staircase Locks (SL860913)
5 miles W of Dudley off B4176
These are probably the oldest unaltered pair of staircase narrow locks on the canal system.

TUNSTALL: *Wynstanley Pithead, Chatterley Whitfield Colliery.*

This stretch of the Staffs & Worcs Canal was open by 1770 and the locks at Botterham with their fine circular weir overflow may possibly indicate what the more celebrated 3-lock rise at Bratch (SJ867938) looked like before it was altered.

Suffolk

The industrial monuments of Suffolk are dominated by its wind and watermills of which it has some of the finest in the country including Saxtead Green post mill in the guardianship of the Department of the Environment, Harringfleet smock mill and Woodbridge tidemill. Other monuments such as the maltings of Ipswich, Oulton Broad and Stowmarket typify this rural county.

BARNINGHAM
Aldred's Steam Mill (TL971776)
11 miles NE of Bury St Edmunds
A143/B111
The exterior of this mill is typical of the traditionally built steam-power mills which, though once fairly common, are now quite rare. The interior, however, has been completely modernized, the necessary power now being provided by electricity.

BRENT ELEIGH
Cast-Iron Bridge (TL934482)
6 miles NE of Sudbury off B1115
This bridge on the road from Lavenham to Monks Eleigh is dated 1813. Fortunately, it has now been by-passed and no longer has to carry heavy traffic.

BURY ST EDMUNDS
Westgate Brewery (TL956638)
Town centre
Founded by Benjamin Greene in 1799 the buildings to the N of Westgate Street are mostly mid-19th or early 20th-century in an Edwardian Tudor style. The brewhouse of 1910 has timber clerestory roof and cast-iron columns.

COMBS
Model Farm (TM041566)
$1\frac{1}{2}$ miles S of Stowmarket off A45
Built *c* 1865 by Lancaster Webb as a complete unit, this farm steading is still in use. The open axial passage is flanked by buildings for livestock while the storage barns comprise the entire width at the rear. The open-sided covered yards are supported by wooden pillars on truncated conical cast-iron bases.

DALHAM
Dalham Windmill (TL720617)
8 miles W of Bury St Edmunds
This octagonal smock mill which probably dates from *c* 1800 stands some 50 ft high. The cap has a rear gable and is surrounded by a gallery while the wooden portion of the mill itself is covered in protective tar sheeting. The assembly stands on a tarred base of red brick. Although the 4 patent sails are in poor condition, they are likely to be restored and the mill put into working order.

DRINKSTONE
Drinkstone Windmill (TL964622)
$7\frac{1}{2}$ miles E of Bury St Edmunds off A45
This mill, which dates from 1685 and is one of the oldest post mills in the country, is still worked and has 2 cloth-spread common sails and 2 shuttered-spring sails. These latter sails replaced 2 common sails last century.

EAST BERGHOLT
Flatford Mill (TM077332)
$1\frac{1}{2}$ miles SE of East Bergholt
Large attractive mill complex once belonging to John Constable's father and the subject of some of Constable's most famous paintings. Now a National Trust field centre.

FELIXSTOWE
Dock Office (TM281329)
SW of town centre
The only remaining building of the original

Felixstowe Docks, this timber-built 2-storey building in a Swiss chalet style probably dates from *c* 1880.

FRAMSDEN
Framsden Windmill (TM192597)
9 miles E of Stowmarket off A1120
Originally built in 1769, this post mill has been greatly modified over the years. The present roundhouse was added *c* 1840, the mill having hitherto an unprotected base. The fantail which turns the mill runs on a stone track. Much of the machinery, which drove 2 pairs of stones, is complete and is currently being restored.

FRITTON
Priory Mill (TM458998)
7 miles NW of Lowestoft off B1074
This small 4-sided smock mill was built in 1910 and was thus one of the very last such mills to be built. It stands only 25 ft high and has a tiny white cap and the vestiges of a fantail. It is constructed on 4 solid tarred brick piers and retains 2 of its complement of 4 patent sails while the one-piece casting of the 8 ft diameter scoop wheel also survives.

GLEMSFORD
Silk Mill (TL825465)
6 miles NW of Sudbury
Glemsford in the 19th century developed as a small industrial colony set in a rural context. A silk throwing mill was established *c* 1830 and was followed by a horsehair factory and a horsehair cloth factory with associated industrial housing. The horsehair cloth factory in Brooks Street was partially turned into dwellings many years ago but the silk factory, though it has lost its overshot waterwheel and auxiliary beam engine and has been extensively modernized, has survived.

HERRINGFLEET
Herringfleet Windmill (TM466976)
6 miles NW of Lowestoft off B1074
This octagonal smock mill with its black painted weatherboarding is preserved and maintained by the county council. It was built in 1823 as a drainage mill and is one of the few mills in working order retaining only common sails. The mill is winded by a prominently braced tailpole with winch. The scoop wheel consists of a central iron frame carrying wooden blades – in all some 16 ft in diameter. The marshman for whom a couch and fireplace are provided in the ground floor sets the mill going occasionally.

HIGHAM
Toll House (TL746662)
7 miles W of Bury St Edmunds on A45
A pleasant, stone-built slated octagonal toll house with Gothic detailing standing on the Newmarket to Bury St Edmunds road.

HOXNE
Hoxne Watermill (TM189778)
4 miles E of Diss off B1118
Built in 1747 as a flax factory, this fine weatherboarded watermill on a brick base was later converted to corn milling. It is probable that the lucan was added at this time. Machinery, including iron undershot wheel, survives.

IPSWICH
Fore Street (TM169441)
Town centre
Timber-framed warehouse outbuilding at S of wing of Nos 80 and 80a Fore Street – may be as early as 15th century in origin. Exposed timber framing with bricknogging. A central cart entrance leads to the rear which extends to the dock front. There are unglazed mullioned openings. Tiled roof – very picturesque.

IPSWICH
Maltings, Dock Street (TM167437)
Town centre
These maltings with their massive range of kilns give an indication of the importance to Ipswich of the water-borne trade in grain and its associated products. The tiers of dormer windows on both the kilns and the maltings are a rather unusual feature. All now out of use.

IXWORTH
Pakenham Windmill (TL931694)
6 miles NE of Bury St Edmunds off A143
This 5-storey brick-built tower mill was erected in 1821 and is one of only 3 windmills still in miller's hands and in working condition. The mill has been much restored since the war, the timber cap having been replaced by an aluminium one with a gallery and yet a further set of sails.

LEISTON
Garretts Long Shop (TM444625)
4 miles E of Saxmundham
Main survival of Garrett's engineering works, this large erecting shop has a fine queen post roof and open framed gallery. Some of the cast-iron trusses linking the timber uprights are dated RG 1853.

LOUND
Lound Waterworks (TG503006)
5 miles NW of Lowestoft off A12
These waterworks supply a third of Lowestoft's water and use the spring-fed Fritton Lake and a series of excavated ponds, totalling some 190 acres in all, as the source. Water is pumped through the various stages of treatment then repumped to Lowestoft. In the mid-19th century some of this pumping duty was performed by a pair of single cylinder grasshopper beam engines installed *c* 1854 by Easton and Amos.

LOWESTOFT
Reynold's Fish Curing House, Raglan Road (TM547931)
Town centre
The last of several such processing structures to remain to use, this example is typically 2-storey with shuttered first floor and roof vents.

MILDENHALL
Staunch (TL708743)
11½ miles NW of Bury St Edmunds off A1101
Before the pound lock was introduced on English waterways flash locks, or staunches as they were called in East Anglia, were employed as a means of allowing the passage of boats while at the same time maintaining sufficient depth for navigation. They usually consisted of a weir with a section which could be removed to pass a boat. Timber staunches survived in use in East Anglia until quite recently but have now all disappeared, the masonry or brick walls, however, survived in places. In this case the staunch was by-passed by a mill stream so no weir was necessary. The date 1832 is inscribed on the stone coping.

NEWMARKET
Old Station (TL649634)
¼ mile E of town centre
Opened in 1848 at the end of a branch line which only lasted 2 years, this station was superceded by another on the line from Cambridge and was relegated to use as a goods station. Its striking façade, with pairs of Ionic columns supporting a turreted entablature, is now rather decayed.

NEWMARKET
Southfields Pumping Station (TL620639)
1 mile W of Newmarket
The steam engine house at this pumping station contains a 1912 Hathorn Davey vertical triple expansion steam engine which drove 3 underfloor force pumps. It is one of the smallest waterworks triples to survive and it is hoped that it may be preserved.

OULTON BROAD
Swannell's Maltings (TM522935)
2 miles W of Lowestoft off A1144
A picturesque block of maltings overlooking Oulton Broad and dating from *c* 1900. Besides the 2 main blocks of 4-storey maltings there are massive drying kilns and many outbuildings.

PAKENHAM
Watermill (TL937695)
5 miles NE of Bury St Edmunds
An early 19th-century brick Georgian façade to earlier timber-framed weatherboarded mill of 1754. The 3-storey mill with its 16 ft wheel has all its machinery and is being restored The 5-storey windmill nearby (TL931694) is also in working order.

SAXTEAD
Saxtead Green Mill (TM253645)
15½ miles E of Stowmarket on A1120
This typical late 18th-century East Suffolk post mill is in the guardianship of the DOE and has been extensively restored. It is now in working order and open to the public. The white painted buck of 3 storeys stands on a 2-storey brick roundhouse – a total height of some 46 ft. The 4 double-shuttered patent sails have a span of 54 ft 7 in and drive 2 pairs of stones on the 2nd floor of the buck. The mill is winded by a fantail mounted on the ladder.

SNAPE
Maltings (TM393575)
4 miles S of Saxmundham on B1069
Extensive 19th-century maltings complex, some converted into concert hall (rebuilt after fire) and associated uses. Others still in commercial operation.

STOWMARKET
Maltings (TM051587)
Town centre
These maltings in Station Road are a most attractive group of buildings, some of them dating from the late 18th century. The varying dates of construction are reflected in the use of varying materials, most notably pantiles and slates.

WOODBRIDGE
Buttrum's Windmill (TM264494)
W of town centre
This tower mill, with its fine ogee cap, is the last surviving windmill built by the noted firm

of Whitmore & Binyon of Wickham Market. The cap contains sophisticated windmill machinery including an endless chain used to operate the striking rod controlling the shutters.

WOODBRIDGE
Woodbridge Tidemill (TM275488)
S of town centre
When, in 1957, the main wheel shaft of this tidemill broke it brought to an end an era in English milling. Woodbridge mill had been the sole working survivor of once numerous tidemills round our coasts. The mills were powered by tidal water, impounded in a large

SNAPE: *Snape Maltings, now a famous concert hall complex.*

pound at high tide, being sluiced through the mill when the tide fell. The sluices at Woodbridge allowed the 20 ft diameter wooden waterwheel to be either breast shot or under shot depending on the level of water in the pond. By following the former method by the latter, efficient use could be made of all the water impounded. The machinery at Woodbridge is very sophisticated for a tidemill driving 4 pairs of stones with automatic tentering. The mill after a period of deterioration following disuse has been restored.

Surrey

This small county is dominated by the proximity of London and most of its industrial monuments relate to communications or service industries. Among the former are structures on the Wye Navigation, the Wey & Arun and Basingstoke canals, the Surrey Iron Railway and the Admiralty semaphore towers linking London with Portsmouth. Service industry sites are typified by the water pumping stations and reservoirs around Walton and the corn grinding mills of the rivers Mole and Wey.

ADDLESTONE
Coxes Lock Mill (TQ061642)
2 miles SE of Chortsey off A317
The premises of Allied Mills Ltd beside Coxes Lock have some early buildings on this ancient milling site. The River Wey still powers a turbine housed in an 18th-century building while the 19th-century eastern block is monumental in size and design being 7-storey with a gabled attic.

BETCHWORTH
Limekilns (TQ208514)
4 miles W of Reigate off A25
Extensive chalk workings have removed much of the end of a ridge of North Downs. In one of the quarries several kilns survive displaying a variety of shapes, some circular, and one square tower-like split shaft limekiln *c* 70 ft high.

BUSBRIDGE
Water Tower, Munstead Heath Road (TQ987428)
1½ miles SE of Godalming off B2130
Late 19th-century octagonal brick tower some 100 ft high in 3 distinct stages. Uppermost stage corbelled out from lower stages. Cylindrical taller stair turret on upper part of E side.

COBHAM
Telegraph Tower, Chatley Heath (TQ089585)
1½ miles SW of Cobham
5 storeys high, this brick-built tower was erected in 1823 as a semaphore telegraph station to relay Admiralty messages from Portsmouth to London.

DORKING
Old Castle Mill, Reigate Road (TQ180502)
½ mile E of town centre off A25
Early 19th-century brick and weatherboard 4-storey mill with mansarded slate roof. Although now a private dwelling the mill retains its iron breast shot wheel.

EPSOM
Epsom Well, Well Way (TQ192502)
1 mile SW of town centre off A24
This is the well that gave Epsom its fame as a spa when the 'beneficial' effects of drinking the mineralized water were first recognized in the early 17th century. The well head now consists of a square hollow pedestal of flint with cement angles.

ESHER
Mile Post (TQ147655)
1 mile NE of town centre on A3
Prominent stone cylinder 6 ft high on 2 ft plinth and surmounted by stone ball. Gives distances to Hyde Park Corner, Westminster Bridge, Portsmouth, Hampton Court and Walton-on-Thames.

EWELL
West Ewell Station, Chessington Road (TQ214627)
1½ miles N of Epsom
An attractive almost unaltered 2-storey brick-built station of *c* 1847 with stationmaster's house attached. Original canopy on 4 iron columns with ornamental barge boards and shelter with waiting room on opposite platform.

COBHAM: *Telegraph Tower, Chatley Heath.*

FARNHAM
Willey Mill, Alton Road (SU816452)
2 miles SW of Farnham off A31
Brick-built 18th-century mill with mill house attached. Reputed to be still in working order.

FARNHAM
High Mill, Moor Park Lane (SU857471)
1¼ miles W of town centre off A31
18th-century mill building and house on River Wey. The mill itself is weatherboarded with a half hipped mansard tiled roof and retains some of its machinery.

FARNHAM
Bourne Mill, Guildford Road (SU852474)
1 mile E of town centre on A325
Farnham was one of the great corn markets of South England and still has an impressive array of watermills although most of these date from the 18th century when the town's prosperity has passed its peak. Bourne Mill, however, has some 17th-century features. Now an antique shop, it is a fine 3- and 4-storey block, brick on the ground floor and partly tile-hung and partly weatherboarded on the upper floors.

GODALMING
Water Tower, Frith Hill Road (SU969447)
½ mile NE of Godalming
Fine late 19th-century water tower built of coursed ragstone with brick dressings. Unusual plan, basically square but with curved central sections to each side with slit windows and mock castellation.

GUILDFORD
Semaphore House, Pewley Hill (TQ002492)
½ mile SE of town centre off A281
Square 3-storey tower built *c* 1800 as a semaphore telegraph station relaying Admiralty messages between Portsmouth and Whitehall. Flanked by 2-storey wings. Further towers at Claygate (TQ158647) and Chatley Heath, Cobham (TQ089585) (*qv*).

GUILDFORD
Water Mill (SU996493)
W of town centre
This prominent watermill in Millbrook is now used as the scenery workshops of the Yvonne Arnaud Theatre. Most of the 3-storey and attic red brick mill with its half-hipped roof dates from the 18th century but a 2-bay extension with larger windows but under the same roof bears a datestone 1896.

GUILDFORD
Wooden Crane (SU994495)
W of town centre
An 18th century timber-framed and weatherboarded cranehouse with a plain tile roof enclosing 19 ft diameter treadwheel. The wheel wound a chain attached to a jib crane on the wharf outside. A much smaller version of the Harwich dockyard crane, this is probably the only treadmill powered crane still *in situ* in the country. The jib has a nominal safe load of 2 tons but has not been used since 1908.

OUTWOOD
Windmill (TQ328455)
5 miles SE of Reigate off A23
Built in 1665, this is the oldest post mill in working order. The brick roundhouse, 22 ft internal diameter, is later as is much of the machinery. Much of the latter is 19th century and the mill is fitted with patent sweeps. It is open to the public at weekends.

PIRBRIGHT
Canal Locks (SU943569–911565)
5 miles W of Woking A324/B3012
The Basingstoke Canal rises *c* 95 ft by 14 locks to the N of Pirbright Common. This stretch of the canal is parallelled by L & SWR railway's Southampton line and the railway company had to erect a high wall to prevent horses on the adjacent tow path being frightened.

PURLEY
Surrey Iron Railway Track, Rotary Field (TQ316622)
1½ miles S of Croydon off A235
The horsedrawn Surrey Iron Railway was built under an Act of 1803 and a re-erected part of its track has been laid down in its original alignment in Purley.

REIGATE
Wray Common Windmill (TQ269511)
½ mile NW of town centre (off A242)
Handsome brick-built 4-storey tower mill erected 1824 and partially restored with ogee metal cap, fantail and shutterless sails. Disused since *c* 1895 and now converted into residence.

REIGATE
Reigate Heath Windmill (TQ235501)
2 miles W of town centre off A25
Built in 1765, this post mill with its boat-shaped top and restored sails is now used as a church. To this purpose the upper walls of tarred weatherboarding have been extended at the bottom to fit over the roof of the brick-built roundhouse and so prevent movement and a small bell added to the N side.

SEND
Worsfold Gates Navigation Lock (TQ016557)
2 miles SE of Woking off A247
The Wey Navigation was constructed by Sir Richard Weston under an Act of 1651 and extended in 1760. Until recently several of the locks were of the early turf sided pattern but now only Worsfold Gates and Walsham Lock (TQ578050) resemble the original configuration. Both locks retain the peg-and-hole paddles though Walsham Lock has concreted wings. Worsfold Gates is a flood lock and is thus normally left open with no fall to surmount.

SHALFORD
Watermill (TQ001476)
1½ miles S of Guildford off A281

Restored 3-storey 18th-century mill on River Tillingbourne in the care of the National Trust. Brick ground floor with timber-framed upper floors contains 12 ft by 8 ft breast shot iron wheel driving 3 pairs of stones.

STAINES
West Station, Wraysbury Road (TQ033718)
½ mile W of town centre off B376
Unusual occurance of a private residence being converted into a railway station. The dwelling, known as Moor House, was built *c* 1820 and enlarged in 1885 when it was opened as Staines West Station. It still retains many pre-railway features.

East Sussex

East Sussex shares with its neighbour, West Sussex, a great industrial past which has left but scant trace. There are very few physical remains above ground, other than hammer ponds, to witness the importance of the Wealden iron industry. Although the pages of the Bulletin of the Weald Iron Research Group record many iron working sites from Roman date onwards and chronicle numerous excavations of these sites few sites exhibit even the scanty remains of Ashburnham furnace (*qv*) which, when it ceased operation in 1820, was the last smelting works of the once paramount Wealdon iron industry. Of the products of that industry somewhat more survives. Perhaps most obvious are the iron tombstones such as those at Wadhurst Church (*qv*)

The most abundant industrial monuments in E Sussex therefore derive from industries other than iron. The importance of agriculture is witnessed by the large number of substantial wind and watermills that have survived while the role of the south coast as a pleasure ground for London is emphasized by the splendour of the prestige railway links typified by the magnificent train shed of Brighton Station and by the extravagance of the pleasure piers themselves.

The provision of an adequate supply of drinking water to settlements built on chalk has always posed a problem and the solutions to this problem have left numerous monuments. The massive beam engines of Goldstone Pumping Station (*qv*) are hence in a direct line of descent from the animal driven pumps of Stanmer Park (*qv*)

BATTLE
Old Workhouse (TQ732159)
½ mile W of town centre on A2027

Built in 1841 as one of the large Union Workhouses created by the 1834 Poor Law, this impressive stone building is typical in

appearance and layout of these erstwhile forbidding institutions.

BEACHY HEAD
Belle Tout Lighthouse (TV563955)
5 miles SW of Eastbourne off B2103
Mist frequently obscured Stevenson's cliff top light of 1831 and it was replaced by the present foreshore Beachy Head lighthouse this century. The original granite lighthouse has lost its lantern and is now incorporated into a dwelling.

BREDE
Brede Pumping Station (TQ814178)
7 miles N of Hastings off A28
Built in 1903, the main pumphouse now contains one of a pair of 410 hp Tangye triple expansion vertical steam engines of 1904 and, in an annex, a similar 1941, Worthington Simpson engine – the latest surviving in a pumping station. The complex was originally supplied with coal by an 18 in-gauge steam tramway from a wharf on the River Brede. River traffic ceased in 1920 but the tramway was not abandoned until 1933.

BRIGHTLING
Brightling Sawmill (TQ686201)
5 miles NW of Battle off B2096
This single-storey brick and timber building was purpose built as a sawmill although the water-powered site is more ancient. Basically intact, though disused for many years, the iron overshot wheel belt drove a circular saw.

BRIGHTON
Palace Pier (TQ314037)
S of city centre
Built 1891–9, this pier was one of the last great Victorian Amusement piers to be constructed. Some 1760 ft in length, it is 45 ft wide across the neck with a 189 ft wide 'head'. During its construction the nearby Chain Pier which it was to replace was finally destroyed by a storm after a precarious life of 73 years. The Palace Pier was itself damaged by a vessel collision in 1973 but is being repaired. It carries an extraordinary variety of architecture from the low iron and glass dome of the Palace of Fun to the onion domes of the Theatre.

BRIGHTON
Volks Electric Railway and Seashore Electric Tramway (TQ316038–335033)
SE of city centre
Opened in 1883, from the Swimming Arch to the Old Chain Pier, Volks Electric Railway was the first such line in Britain. It was

BEACHY HEAD: *Former lighthouse built 1831.*

extended in 1894 and 1901 to Black Rock (1¾ miles) on a 2 ft 9 in gauge. Originally only 2 rail, a third rail supply system was introduced c 1893. Much of the permanent way dates from 1947–8 but most of the cars, through successive rebuildings, are of 1897 to 1901. The steel and timber viaduct beyond Banjo Groyne was the terminus from 1896–1901 of Volks Seashore Electric Tramway which ran along the foreshore to Rottingdean 2¾ miles to the E. All that is left of this extraordinary venture are lines of concrete blocks morticed into the chalk 100 yards S of the Undercliff Walk, these were the sleepers for the 2 railroads 2 ft 8½in gauge and 18 ft apart which carried the 'Daddy-Long-Legs' railcar.

BRIGHTON
West Pier (TQ303037)
SW of city centre
One of the classic piers designed by Eugenius Birch. Opened in 1866, it was subsequently extended in 1893 and is now 1115 ft long with a head measuring 310 ft by 140 ft. Its buildings epitomize late Victorian and Edwardian amusements architecture.

EASTBOURNE
Eastbourne Pier (TV617988)
E of town centre
Designed by Eugenius Birch, this pier was completed in 1872 but subsequent to storm damage the shoreward end was raised in 1877. It is some 1000 ft in length and supports a concert hall, pavilion and 2 games saloons.

HASTINGS
East Hill Lift (TQ828096)
½ mile E of town centre off A259
Opened in 1903 this cliff railway runs in a cutting 276 ft long at a gradient of 1 in 1.28 on a 5 ft gauge. The 2 cars are operated by water balance.

HASTINGS
Hastings Pier (TQ811091)
W of town centre
Built 1869–1872 to the designs of Eugenius Birch, this pier, 910 ft long, is supported on cast-iron columns and piles. Its appearance now owes most to the 1930s reconstruction of its buildings.

HASTINGS
The Net Shops (TQ827094)
½ mile E of town centre
These tall clinker built net shops are traditionally called 'deezes' and are unique to Hastings They have been a feature in the old town since at least the 16th century and show

HASTINGS: *Net Shops – unique complex of net drying sheds reminiscent of Scandinavia.*

Scandinavian influences in their construction. They vary considerably in height, the tallest being about 30 ft with 3 storeys. Although their number has decreased greatly in the last 100 years there are still some 40 left in constant use for storing net and fishing gear.

HASTINGS
West Hill Lift (TQ822095)
Town centre
This lift runs in a tunnel, formed by a natural cave, some 500 ft long at a gradient of 1 in 3 on a 6 ft gauge. When constructed in 1902 the 2 cars were operated by an endless rope driven by a gas engine. Since 1971 it has been electrified.

HELLINGLY
Hellingly Mill (TQ585124)
2 miles N of Hailsham off A267
The fabric of this 17th-century brick and timber watermill has been extensively restored. It houses 19th-century iron machinery by which 3 pairs of stones are driven, powered by the 10 ft wide, 6 ft diameter iron overshot wheel.

HOVE
Goldstone Pumping Station (TQ286066)
1½ miles N of town centre off A2023
The main structure of this impressive pumping station complex consists of a central boiler house with a tall engine house on either side, overlooking an ornamental cooling pond. The earlier of the 2 compound rotative beam engines, that by Easton, Amos & Sons 1866 has been partly dismantled but the 1875 Easton & Anderson survives intact. There is also a complete 19th-century workshop driven by a horizontal steam engine and the Lancashire boilers were supplied by an internal underground tramway.

LEWES
Ashcombe Toll House (TQ389093)
1½ miles W of Lewes on A27
A small circular brick toll house with a domed roof probably built *c* 1810. It was one of a pair and clearly never lived in. It is significant that traffic between Lewes and Brighton in the early 19th century was such to warrant 2 booths. Re-alignment of the A27 has placed this toll house well back from the main road but its partner has disappeared.

LEWES
Beard's Lamb Brewery (TQ414102)
Town centre
Some of these brewery buildings date from the 19th century and although brewing has ceased they are still used for bottling. There is a primitive single cylinder vertical steam engine of *c* 1860 still *in situ* built by A Shaw of Lewes. Nearby there is a fine stone-built malthouse now used as a store.

LEWES
Cliffe Bridge (TQ419102)
E of town centre
When this elegant humped-back bridge across the Ouse was built in 1727 to the designs of Nicholas Dubois it was only 10 ft wide. Subsequently an overhanging pavement was added in 1808 to the N side and a replica against the S face in 1931–3.

LEWES
Deanery Suspension Bridge (TQ413108)
$\frac{1}{2}$ mile N of town centre
There is some doubt as to the age of this beautiful small iron suspension footbridge over the Ouse between the Deanery and the Pells. Some sources suggest late 19th century, others the early 20th century. The bridge is no longer in use and some of the decking has been removed.

LEWES
Harveys Brewery, Cliffe (TQ419103)
$\frac{1}{4}$ mile E of town centre
This, the largest of the Lewes breweries, is still in use. Much of the external appearance, and the brew tower itself, date from rebuilding in 1868 but much of the interior is considerably earlier. The vat hall itself is substantially unaltered since 1790. Until recently the whole brewery was run by a single cylinder, slide valve, horizontal steam engine of *c* 1880 which is preserved.

LEWES
Offham Chalk Pit Tramway (TQ399118)
$1\frac{1}{2}$ miles NW of Lewes on A275
This tramway served 4 kilns in the enormous Offham Chalk Pit from 1809 to 1890. It ran from the kilns, which still exist in a ruinous state, via a tunnel under the road and descended the very steep scarp to a wharf on a canal cut from the Ouse Navigation. The brick arches of the tunnel portals are the best preserved feature of the tramway.

NEWHAVEN
Piddinghoe Pottery Kiln (TQ432032)
$1\frac{1}{2}$ miles NW of Newhaven on A275
This is the only recorded 19th-century pottery kiln of updraught cupola type in Sussex. It is still complete with floor and firing tunnels under.

NINFIELD
Ashburnham Brickworks (TQ684161)
4 miles W of Battle of A2027
This works, which closed in 1968, was the last wood fired brick kiln to operate in Sussex. They were operated intermittently to provide bricks for the Ashburnham estate. The double kiln, covered firing area and outbuildings still remain while in an adjacent field there are traces of the extraction of sand and loam.

NINFIELD
Ashburnham Iron Furnace (TQ685170)
$4\frac{1}{2}$ miles W of Battle off A2027
This furnace, which ceased operation *c* 1820, was the last smelting works in Sussex. The overgrown masonry wheel pit, dating from the 17th or 18th century, is the most extensive stone relic of the Wealdon iron industry.

NUTLEY
Nutley Windmill (TQ451291)
4 miles N of Maresfield off A22
Situated on the southern edge of Ashdown Forest, this small open trestle post mill probably dates from the late 17th century. It is the only example of this primitive type in Sussex and fortunately the machinery, with gears of both wood and iron, is intact as are the sweeps.

POLEGATE
Polegate Windmill (TQ581041)
$\frac{1}{2}$ mile S of town centre off A22
Built in 1817, the brick tower mill, part tile-hung, is preserved in working order as a milling museum.

PUNNETT'S TOWN
Blackdown or Cherry Clack Windmill
(TQ627208)
3 miles E of Heathfield off B2096
This white weatherboarded smock mill on a brick base once stood at Biddenden, Kent, and was re-erected on its present site in 1856. Its few sails are still occasionally turned and its machinery is in its place.

ROBERTSBRIDGE
Hodson's Mill (TQ736242)
5 miles N of Battle off A21
A large 4-storey 19th-century industrial flour mill. This handsome brick building is now powered by electricity and turbine but the original iron overshot waterwheel 9 ft in diameter and 12 ft in width is intact under the mill.

RYE
Iden Lock (TQ936244)
2½ miles NE of Rye
Situated above Rye at the junction of the Royal Military Canal and the River Rother, this lock was designed to work against a head of water on either side as the river was tidal up to here when the Canal was cut in 1806. This arrangement became redundant with the construction in 1855 of Scots Lock and Sluice downstream. There is a contemporary lock cottage which doubled as a toll house for the collection of canal tolls and possibly also road tolls.

RYE
Town Quay Warehouse (TQ920201)
S of town centre
Rye ceased to be a port in the middle of the 19th century due to the retreat of the sea, and Rye Harbour was constructed *c* 1845 2 miles below the town. The old Town Quay, however, has a number of interesting buildings including an early stone-built warehouse and a cluster of brick and weatherboarded warehouses.

RYE
Water Cistern (TQ922203)
Town centre
Situated in a corner of Rye Churchyard is this very early public cistern. Built 1733–4, it consists of an oval brick tower with a truncated dome. A pump in front of the cistern is dated 1826.

ST LEONARDS
North Lodge Toll House (TQ797093)
¼ mile NW of town centre
Built in 1830, this attractive battlemented building bridges Maze Hill, the original approach to St Leonards. It became redundant 7 years later when the modern London Road was constructed from Silverhill to the sea front.

STANMER
Communal Donkey Wheel (TQ336096)
4 miles NE of Brighton off A27
Housed in a small flint building in the corner of the churchyard this donkey wheel 13 ft 6 in in diameter and 4 ft wide raised water for the village of Stanmer from the middle of the 16th century. The lift was achieved by sprockets on the shaft driving a chain to which buckets were attached at either end.

STANMER
Stanmer House, Horse Wheel (TQ336095)
4 miles NE of Brighton off A27
The present arcaded well house dates from 1927 though the well itself is earlier. The main vertical shaft has 2, 7 ft arms on either side to which 3 horses were harnessed. It raised both water from a well by windlass, and from a rain-water reservoir by pumps.

TICEHURST
Toll Hose (TQ685304)
¼ mile W of village on A266
Originally a 2-roomed weatherboarded cottage, built *c* 1762 for the Flimwell to Hastings turnpike trust, this toll house has been added to on its E side.

WADHURST
Cast-Iron Tombstones (TQ641318)
Village centre on A266
There are very few structural remains of the Wealdon iron industry but these tombstones give witness to one of its abundant products. The collection at Wadhurst Church comprises over 30 items in church floor and churchyard with dates ranging from 1616 to 1799. By this latter date the industry had virtually died out in Sussex.

West Sussex

The industrial history of West Sussex reflects that of its neighbour, East Sussex, in many ways. It shared in the prosperity of the Wealden iron industry but similarly, apart from hammer ponds such as those of the St Leonard Forest, has few above ground remains to attest to the greatness of this industry.

The county has however plentiful remains of its rich agricultural past including many substantial wind and watermills and several limekilns.

Transport has also figured prominently in the county's development, not only are there significant railway structures such as the Ouse Viaduct (*qv*) and Clayton Tunnel (*qv*) on the prestige Brighton line and pleasure piers at Bognor and Worthing but also the remains of a strategic inland navigation route from Portsmouth to London via the Chichester, the Portsmouth & Arundel and the Wey & Arun canals. The Rivers Adur and Arun while providing useful access for shipping far inland also proved something of a barrier to coastal roads. The former was crossed in the 18th century by the old wooden bridge at Shoreham but the latter was only finally bridged at its mouth at Littlehampton in 1908.

Water supply is represented by the unusual turbine driven pumps which raised water to the Arundel estate.

ARUNDEL
Arundel Estate Pumping Station (TQ018077)
E of town centre
Situated at the outlet of Swanbourne Lake below Arundel Castle in the Arun Valley, this pumping installation supplied water to a reservoir on the nearby hill. The building is of a rather ecclesiastical style in common with the nearby ornamented farm buildings. It houses a vertical shaft reaction turbine, drowned in the tail race, driving, through double-reduction spur gearing, 2 3-throw pumps. The head of water is controlled by a butterfly sluice off the adjacent pond. The reservoir itself has a date of 1844 inscribed on it and this may well be the date of the pumping installation.

BALCOMBE
Ouse Viaduct (TQ323278)
3 miles N of Haywards Heath
This viaduct, the major engineering structure of the London to Brighton line, was built in 1839–41 with materials brought up the Ouse Navigation which today is only a small stream 96 ft below the track. Designed by John Urpeth Raistrick the viaduct is 1,475 ft long and has 37 semi-circular headed arches. The 4 Italianate stone pavilions at either end, the ornamental balustrade and the slender pierced-arch pillars combine to make this viaduct one of the most graceful in England.

BOGNOR REGIS
Bognor Pier (SZ934987)
S of town centre
Built 1864–5 by London contractors and engineers at a cost of £5,000, this pier was 1000 ft long and 18 ft wide. In 1910–11 it was enlarged and widened at the shoreward end but in March 1965 the pavillion at the seaward end collapsed into the sea. The pier is now breached and most of the narrow neck section closed.

BOGNOR REGIS
Hotham Park Ice House (SZ936995)
NE of town centre
This rather fine example of an ice house dates from *c* 1792 and was an essential part of the domestic life of Hotham Park estate before the invention of mechanical refrigeration. The ice chamber which is mainly below ground level has a N facing entrance passage with 2 doors and a pebble soakaway for draining the melt water. It is thought that the hooks on the dome itself were for training a prolific growing vine.

CLAYTON
'Jack' and 'Jill' Windmills (TQ304134)
4 miles S of Burgess Hill off A273
Prominently situated on the scarp of the South Downs, these 2 mills date from 1876 and 1821 respectively. The tower mill, locally known as 'Jack', has been disused for many years and has been converted to form part of a dwelling. The post mill, 'Jill', is maintained by the local authority and retains its 4 sweeps and some of its machinery. It was originally set up in Dyke Road, Brighton, and was re-erected at Clayton *c* 1850.

CLAYTON
North Portal, Clayton Tunnel (TQ299141)
3½ miles S of Burgess Hill off A273
Clayton Tunnel, 2,259 yards long, was originally gas-lit when it operated in 1841. It is probably best known, however, for the castellated N portal with a cottage, which is still lived in, surmounting the battlements.

DUNCTON
Limekiln (SU761163)
4 miles S of Petworth off A285

CLAYTON: *Clayton Tunnel portal – a noisy location for an employee's dwelling!*

Built into the steep chalk hillside above the A285 are 3 kilns in one structure. A double brick-and-flint arch is 'stepped' so that the 3 grates at the base are recessed into the hillside. The well behind the central grate is open but fenced off for safety. Some 10 ft across the top it narrows to 7 ft at the base and is almost 25 ft deep.

HENFIELD
Woods Watermill (TQ217137)
1 mile S of Henfield on A2037
The ground floor of this 4-storey cornmill is of stone and brick while the upper portion is timber-framed and weatherboarded. The iron overshot waterwheel, pentrough and machinery are typically mid-19th century. The mill is owned by the Sussex Trust for Nature Conservation.

HIGH SALVINGTON
High Salvington Windmill (TQ122067)
2½ miles NW of Worthing
A well preserved post mill of *c* 1700 with a traditional weatherboarded body, 4 sweeps, and a circular masonry base.

HUNSTON
Poyntz Canal Bridge (SU864022)
2 miles S of Chichester off B2145
Situated some 3 miles S of Chichester, the cast-iron sections of this low level bridge remain *in situ* across the Chichester Canal immediately N of the former junction with the Portsmouth & Arundel Canal. The remains of rails to the E of the bridge suggest that the bridge may have been drawn back over these rails to allow vessels to pass. Alternatively the shape of the beams would allow the structure to pivot vertically or swing horizontally. The Chichester Canal was open from 1822 to 1906 and is still watered although most of the bridges are blocked. A short section above Salterns Lock (SU826012) was re-opened in 1932 for pleasure boat berthing.

HURSTPIERPONT
Cobbs Watermill (TQ274189)
3 miles W of Burgess Hill
This 19th-century brick and timber watermill was in commercial use until 1966. The iron overshot waterwheel drove 4 pairs of stones via an iron layshaft. The layshaft could also be driven by a 1906 Tangye suction gas engine and this engine with its associated gas producer plant is still intact – a rare survival.

LITTLEHAMPTON
Swing-Bridge (TQ023023)
W of town centre
Although this bridge was only constructed as recently as 1908 to replace a ferry, it has already been rendered obsolete by a fixed bridge half a mile upstream. The swing-bridge itself is closed to vehicular traffic. The Arun was the last of the rivers through the South Downs to be bridged below the natural and ancient bridging point at the gap in the Downs – in this case at Arundel.

NORTHCHAPEL
Toll House (SU953296)
5 miles N of Petworth on A283
Situated on the A283 just N of the village green at Northchapel is a dignified single-storey red brick cottage of *c* 1757 in the shape of a shallow 'T' at right angles to the road. The 3 gables are accentuated in moulded brick and carry a central, circular motif also in brick.

OLD SHOREHAM
Adur Bridge (TQ207059)
W of town centre
This bridge originally carried the main coast road from Worthing to Brighton. The site has been by-passed by a dual carriageway to the N and the bridge, which, though frequently rebuilt, preserved the original 1781 design, is now used as a footbridge.

PETWORTH
Ornamental Lamp Standard (SU977217)
Town centre
Situated in the centre of the junction of North and East Street, Petworth, this fanciful piece of road 'furniture' was designed by Sir Charles Barry in 1851.

SHIPLEY
Shipley Windmill (TQ144218)
5 miles SE of Billingshurst
Built in 1879, this is the largest smock mill in Sussex. A 2-storey brick base carries a gallery and weatherboarded smock with revolving cap. The mill ceased operation in 1926 but was restored to full working order in 1958.

STORRINGTON
Toll House (TQ071134)
SW of town centre
A flint and brick single cottage with a slate roof on the Storrington to Auberley road which was turnpiked under an Act of 1812.

TROTTON
Terwick Mills (SU830222)
3 miles W of Hidhurst off A272

An early milling site with 2 adjoining water-mills, the older, timber-framed and tarred, the newer built of local stone with brick trimmings. Between the mills which ceased operation in 1966 are 2 iron waterwheels, a narrow low breast wheel and a conventional sized one.

WASHINGTON
Limekilns (TQ119123)
6 miles N of Worthing off A24
A group of 3 kilns adjoining a cart track which was almost certainly the route from Worthing into the Weald until the turnpike road nearby was made. Two of the kilns are identical with brick arches 10 ft wide by 7 ft high and 10 ft deep tapering sharply to the grate at the rear. The metal grills are still in position though the wells behind are choked with debris. The third arch is smaller with no grate visible. Beneath the undergrowth the kilns are fronted by a stone platform with a loading bay large enough to accommodate a wagon.

WISBOROUGH GREEN
Orfold Aqueduct (TQ058246)
$1\frac{1}{2}$ miles W of Billingshurst off A272
Built *c* 1787 as part of the Arun Navigation, this aqueduct has lost its W retaining wall. The 3 brick arches of the main structure are maintained as part of a weir on the River Arun. The Arun Navigation was part of a chain of canals and navigations providing an inland route between London and Portsmouth.

WORTHING
Worthing Pier (TQ149023)
S of town centre
When originally opened in 1862 this pier was 960 ft long and a neck 15 ft wide with 2 broader sections of 30 ft and a head 60 ft wide. The structure was composed of 24 lattice girder spans supported by 3 rows of cast-iron columns. The pier was widened in 1887–9 and again in 1913–4. The present buildings are very typically twentieth-century, the shore pavilion being built in 1926, the pierhead pavilion in 1935 and the intermediate building in 1959.

YAPTON
Ford Junction Areodrome (SU989029)
2 miles NW of Littlehampton off A259
This abandoned areodrome was originally constructed during the First World War for the Royal Flying Corps but was subsequently used by the US Navy. An engineering works occupies the surviving 3 hangars which are built to a standard pattern with wooden 'Belfast Truss' roofs.

Tyne And Wear

The metropolitan county of Tyne & Wear though physically small has a wealth of industrial monuments alongside the 2 estuaries which comprise the county. The important ports of Newcastle-upon-Tyne, Gateshead, South Shields and Sunderland have numerous transport monuments while their coal mining hinterlands and their connecting rail links provide many more. There are also some notable water supply pumping stations of which Ryhope, with its preserved steam engines, is perhaps the finest.

CLEADON
Pumping Station (NZ388637)
3 miles N of Sunderland on A19
One of the 5 water-pumping stations of the Sunderland & South Shields Water Company (of Ryhope) built in the 1860s and comprising engine house, boiler house, worker's cottage and detached chimney with enclosed staircase to gallery at top. The steam engines were replaced by electrical pumps in 1930.

DUNSTON
Staiths (NZ235627)
2 miles W of Gateshead centre off A6081
Opened by the North Eastern Railway in 1890, these wooden staiths some 1709 ft in length are some of the last on the River Tyne. They could accommodate many ships.

ELEMORE
Colliery Winding Engine (NZ356457)
1 mile S of Hetton-le-Hole
The Isabella Engine is a vertical reciprocating single cylinder double acting non-condensing engine of 1825 of a design peculiar to NE England. The engine house stands in a massive plinth and is surrounded by later 19th-century workshops, stores etc.

FELLING
Old Railway Station (NZ276621)
2 miles E of Gateshead off A184
An early railway station of *c* 1842 on the Brandling Junction Railway of 1839 which linked Sunderland, South Shields and Gateshead.

FULWELL
Windmill (NZ392595)
1 mile N of Sunderland off A184
Built in 1821 of magnesian limestone, this is the most complete windmill in NE England. It is unusual in having a built-up reefing stage. The cap and sails were restored in the 1950s and the machinery is now undergoing restoration.

GATESHEAD
Colliery Pumping Engine House (NZ274632)
1½ miles E of Gateshead centre
Massive ruined ashlar built early 19th-century engine house of a colliery pumping engine at Friars Goose on Gateshead Fell. Preserved by the local authority in a landscaped open space overlooking the Tyne.

GATESHEAD
Engine Works (NZ251633)
¼ mile W of town centre
A massive complex dominating the S bank of the River Tyne. The earliest parts are pre–1856 but the site was continually added to until the 1880s by which time it was the major locomotive works for the NER.

HOUGHTON-LE-SPRING
The Old Brewery (NZ342497)
SW of town centre
Early 19th-century 4-storey building looking more like a maltings than a brewery. It is now being converted into a public house and restaurant.

MARSDEN
Limekilns (NZ404644)
3½ miles SE of South Shields on A183
'An impressive group of kilns dating from the last quarter of the 19th century. The earlier kilns are housed in a massive stone battery but the 2 later circular kilns are brick-built with iron strengthening bands. The magnesian limestone came from quarries immediately to the W, the coal came from Whitburn Colliery to the S.

MONKWEARMOUTH
Station (NZ373561)
A magnificent station built in 1848 as the Sunderland terminus for Newcastle trains. The architect was Thomas Moore (1796–1869) who was responsible for much of Victorian Sunderland and the classical façade of Monkwearmouth Station with its Doric pilasters and huge Ionic portico is his finest work. The station has been converted into a period museum of the late 19th century.

NEWBURN
Lemington Glass Cone (NZ184646)
5 miles W of Newcastle Centre on A6085
The last glass cone in NE England, Lemington cone was built in 1787 and was originally 130 ft high. The uppermost 20 ft have been removed and the cone capped but it is still a most

NEWCASTLE: *High Level Bridge, Stephenson's double decked masterpiece still a vital part of Newcastle's transport system.*

impressive monument to an industry which was of great regional importance.

NEWCASTLE
Chimney Windmill (NZ240656)
1½ miles NW of city centre on B6338
Now occupied by a firm of architects, this gutted smock tower was possibly designed by John Smeaton in 1782 as a 5-sailed mill for grinding corn.

NEWCASTLE
High Level Bridge (NZ251637)
S of city centre
Designed by Robert Stephenson and constructed 1845–9, the High Level Bridge is one of the country's most famous monuments. A double-decked superstructure of cast- and wrought-iron is carried on 5 massive sandstone piers, the tallest of which is 146 ft high. The upper deck carries the 3 railway lines into Newcastle station while the lower deck has a 20 ft roadway and 2 footpaths.

NEWCASTLE
Swing-Bridge (NZ252637)
S of city centre

When it opened in 1876 the Swing-Bridge was the largest ever constructed. It was built by W G Armstrong & Co, the firm which did so much pioneer work in the field of hydraulic power. It replaced a masonry 9-arch bridge of 1781 which had been the limit of navigation for large vessels. The steam-powered hydraulic pumps were replaced by electric pumps in 1959, but otherwise the bridge remains as a monument to hydraulic power engineering at its very best, its 281-ft-long superstructure, weighing 1450 tons, still capable of turning.

NEWCASTLE
Victoria Tunnel (NZ237657)
1½ miles NW of city centre off B6338
Built from 1839–42, the Victoria Tunnel was driven below the city to enable coal from a colliery on the northern outskirts to reach the Tyne near Glasshouse Bridge. It was almost 2 miles long and descended 222 ft. Loaded wagons went down the incline under their own weight and were cable-hauled back by a stationary steam engine. The tunnel went out of use in 1860 but was used as an air raid shelter during the Second World War. Half a mile of the tunnel will be utilized by a sewer but access for visitors to the western end will remain possible.

PENSHAW
Victoria Viaduct (NZ320545)
2 miles S of Washington
Completed in 1838, the Victoria Viaduct is a magnificent stone structure with 4 main spans 120 ft, 120 ft, 144 ft and 160 ft, flanked on either side by 3 small spans of 20 ft each. It carried the first railway between London and the Tyne 128 ft above the River Wear.

ROWLANDS GILL
Whinfield Coke Ovens (NZ152581)
6 miles SW of Gateshead off A692
Of the thousands of coke ovens once in operation in the NE of England, these are the only complete ones to survive. Built in 1861, they were part of a range of 193 beehive coke ovens and they operated until 1958. They have been preserved by the NCB to show various stages in the coke making process and are now in local authority ownership.

RYHOPE
Pumping Station (NZ404524)
3 miles S of Sunderland off A19
Constructed by the Sunderland & South Shields Water Company in 1868 to pump water from the beds of magnesium limestone, Ryhope Pumping Station is a handsome 2-storey ornately gabled building with a pro-

minent ventilator tower. It houses 2 magnificent 100 hp beam engines built by R & W Hawthorn of Newcastle which ran from 1869–1967. The 3 Lancashire boilers were installed in 1908 replacing 6 Cornish boilers. Now operated by a Trust, the engine house is open summer weekends and one engine in steam at bank holidays.

SPRINGWELL
Bowes Railway (NZ285587)
2 miles NW of Washington
The Bowes Railway was the last mineral line in the country to have combined 3 methods of working – locomotives, stationary haulage engines, and gravity incline. The earliest part was designed by George Stephenson in 1826. It was eventually 15 miles long. When the western portion closed in 1974 the county council bought a representative 1¼ miles to restore to working order. The line is now operated by a Trust and besides the rope hauled inclines there are workshops, old colliery buildings, 41 wagons and 2 locomotives.

SOUTH SHIELDS
Coal Chutes (NZ355664)
½ mile SW of town centre
South Shields has been an important coal shipping port for several centuries. Many of the installations such as the wooden staiths have gone while only pillars remain of the 19th-century Stanhope coal drops. Some coal chutes still survive, dating with modifications from 1913.

SUNDERLAND
Docks (NZ412573)
1 mile E of town centre
Developed by the Wear Commissioners from 1717 onwards, the harbour at Sunderland for more than a century depended on the constant improvement of protective piers enclosing the mouth of the river. In 1837 the North Dock was opened, Hudson Dock in 1850 and South Dock in 1857. There are still considerable remains of hydraulic power installations, warehouses, etc.

WALLSEND
Willington Viaduct (NZ316666)
1 mile E of town centre on A695
The Newcastle & North Shields Railway constructed a huge viaduct, 1048 ft long and 82 ft high, across Willington Dene in 1837–39. Built originally with laminated timber arches to the designs of John and Benjamin Green, this timberwork was rebuilt in iron in 1880 to

the original pattern, the abutments and stone piers are original.

WASHINGTON

Colliery Winder (NZ303575)
¹/₂ mile NW of town centre
The Washington F pit was sunk in 1770 and closed in 1968. A headstocks and engine house containing an 1888-twin cylinder horizontal steam winding engine by Grange Iron Co, Durham, has been preserved by the New Town Development Corporation.

WASHINGTON: *Colliery Winder Washington 'F' Pit.*

WYLAM

West Wylam Railway Bridge (NZ112642)
9 miles W of Newcastle off A695
A single span wrought-iron arch railway bridge built in 1876 by the Scotswood, Newburn & Wylam Railway and possibly the first arch rib bridge to support a suspended railway track.

Warwickshire

Warwickshire, shorn in 1974 of much of its industrialized northern area is now an essentially rural county. It has, however, a surprisingly rich stock of industrial monuments in such unlikely places as Stratford on Avon and Warwick. In the former is one of the finest tramway viaducts in the country while the latter has a unique pair of gas holder buildings. The county has also a fine collection of canal monuments including cast-iron aqueducts at Brearley, Leamington, Rugby and Wootten Wawen and basins at Atherstone, Hartshill and Hawkesbury. In the rural heart of the county is the exceptional Chesterton Windmill.

ATHERSTONE
Hartshill Depot (SP328953)
2 miles SE of Atherstone off B4111
An attractive complex of canal company maintenance buildings alongside the Coventry Canal. They date from *c* 1850.

ATHERSTONE
Milestone (SP304971)
$\frac{1}{2}$ mile SW of town centre on B4116
Outside the Red Lion, a fine gabled coaching inn with Gothic windows, stands an old milestone incised '100 Miles London'. The A5 (Watling Street), for long a primary route from the capital, now by-passes this small market town.

ATHERSTONE
Minion's Wharf (SP305975)
$\frac{1}{4}$ mile W of town centre
An early 19th-century complex of semi-derelict buildings grouped round what was once a basin off the Coventry Canal. The basin and its connection with the canal have long since gone but a warehouse with a barge hole and internal wharf survives as does the shell of a steam flour mill.

ATHERSTONE
Viro and Everett's Hat Factory (SP305979)
Group of late 19th-century 2- and 3-storey buildings on Station Street containing a unique range of late 19th-century machinery for manufacturing felt hats. Square chimney stack with datestone 'V & E 1872 repaired 1944'.

BAGINTON
Old Mill (SP339753)
$4\frac{1}{2}$ miles NE of Kenilworth off A429
This rather fine looking mill on the River Sowe is on a Domesday site and although now a restaurant only ceased milling a few years before the Second World War.

BEARLEY
Edstone Aqueduct (SP162609)
5 miles NW of Stratford off A34
This aqueduct, which is similar to that at Wootten Wawen (*qv*) a few miles away, has an iron trough second in length to only Pont Cysyllte Aqueduct. It dates from the later period of construction of the Stratford Canal and, as many of the features are identical, probably shares the same date of construction as Wootten Wawen aqueduct viz 1813. The tow path is carried alongside the trough at a low level and not over the water as in the case of Pont Cysyllte – a much simpler, if less sophisticated design, than the latter.

BEDWORTH
Bedworth Heath Colliery (SP335870)
3 miles S of Nuneaton off A444
The area between Nuneaton and Coventry has long been mined for coal. In the 18th century many of the techniques of deep mining were pioneered in this area to exploit the exceptionally rich coal seams. A Griff colliery (SP356885), now marked by overgrown spoil-heaps, a Newcomen engine was erected in 1714 by Richard & Stonier Parrot – this is the engine displayed at Dartmouth, Newcomen's birthplace. Bedworth Heath Colliery is one of the few pits still to be in production. It was sunk in 1898 by Sir Francis Newdigate – one of a long line of famous coalmasters who were responsible for most of the mining in this area. Bermuda village (SP353899) is a little-altered late 19th-century model colliery village of terraced brick-built cottages.

HARBURY
Chesterton Windmill (SP348594)
5 miles SE of Leamington Spa off Fosse Way
This very unusual windmill was built in 1632 on the estate of Sir Edward Peyto. The design has been attributed, almost certainly wrongly, to Inigo Jones. It is more likely that either Peyto himself or Nicholas Stone, Inigo Jones's master mason, designed it. The low single-storey masonry mill tower is carried on 6-arched base some 20 ft high and the machinery, together with the 4 common sails has recently been restored.

HAWKESBURY
Canal Junction (SP362846)
5 miles NE of Coventry off B4109
A small complex of service buildings has grown up at the junction of the Coventry and Oxford Canals, including a public house, a grocer's shop, a lock keeper's cottage and 2 small terraces of cottages. Across the entrance to the canal basin is a cast-iron bridge with the cast inscription '1837 Britannia Foundry Derby'. There is also the shell of a pumping engine house which formery contained a Newcomen Engine of the mid-1720s erected at Hawkesbury *c* 1821 and moved in 1964 to be a memorial to Newcomen in Dartmouth.

KINGSWOOD
Canal Junction (SP188707)
7 miles NW of Warwick off B4439
At this point the Stratford-on-Avon Canal makes contact with the Grand Union Canal.

HARBURY: *Chesterton Windmill, a magnificent eccentricity high above the Fosse Way.*

From hence the earlier northern section of the Stratford Canal which was completed in 1801 proceeds to its junction with the Worcester & Birmingham Canal at Kings Norton while the Grand Union approaches Birmingham from the SE. The short branch linking the 2 canals was built by the Stratford Canal and includes a lock to equalize the canal levels.

LEAMINGTON SPA
Mill Bridge (SP321656)
¼ mile SE of town centre
A small suspension bridge built 1903 connecting Jephson Gardens to the S bank. Only a footbridge, it has rather unusual cables which radiate from each of the lattice steel pylons to only 2 main points on either side of the walkway which lies on a lattice girder deck frame. Attractively painted railings and finials.

LEAMINGTON
Rock Mill (SP302662)
1½ miles NE of Warwick off A445
A fine large 4-storey mill on a prominent site on the River Avon. The foundation platform and ground floor are stone while the upper 3 floors are red brick. The present mill would appear to be late 18th century and may therefore be the original cotton mill established by Benjamin Smart in 1792. It was converted to flour milling *c* 1830. An attractive red brick 3-storey mill house, 2 ranges of 2-storey outbuildings and a square plan tapering chimney complete the complex.

NAPTON-ON-THE-HILL
Napton Brickworks (SP454615)
4 miles E of Southam off A425
This early brickworks contains a disused single cylinder horizontal engine of *c* 1880 made by J Wilkes, Pelsall Foundry, Walsall. Steam engines remained in use in brickworks long after common usage had ceased because not only could they drive the various machinery and haulage systems, but the waste heat could be used profitably in the drying sheds.

NUNEATON
Anker Mill, Attleborough Road (SP367914)
S of town centre
Originally a typical 4-storey cotton mill built 1861 by Nuneaton Cotton Spinning & Weaving Co, but closed in depression of 1884–5. Bought in 1891 by Lister & Co of Bradford and converted to a worsted spinning mill powered by a pair of beam engines. Conspicuous 159 ft high octagonal chimney.

NUNEATON
Newdigate Canal, Arbury Park (SP335893)
3 miles SW of Nuneaton

This was a private system of canals built *c* 1773 by Sir Richard Newdigate on the Arbury Estate, primarily to carry the estate's coal to the Coventry Canal, but also to facilitate internal communication for goods and pleasure. The system had a total length of 5½ miles and contained 13 locks and a stop lock. Most of these locks have now been weired or dismantled and the canals within the estate itself converted to ornamental waterways. Outside the walled parkland they have largely disappeared though traces can be seen where it crossed the turnpike (B4113) just S of Griff (SP357883). The Newdigate family were responsible for much of the development of the Nuneaton coalfield from the 17th century onwards.

RUGBY
Railway Station and Goods Depot (SP512729)
½ mile NE of town centre
Rugby became an important railway junction as early as 1840 when the Midland Counties Railway obtained a through route to London via the tracks of the London and Birmingham Railway (1838). Midland Station, rebuilt 1886, catered for these and a further 4 lines, hence its size which is disproportionately large for the size of the town. A fine goods depot (SP508759) in red and blue brick with large timber roof on iron columns was built by L & NWR to the W of the station.

RUGBY
Canal Aqueducts and Roving Bridge (e.g. SP503771)
1½ miles N of town centre
The Oxford Canal in the vicinity of Rugby has several interesting structures including a massively built 3-arched red brick aqueduct over the River Avon (SP516765), a brick aqueduct with 3 elliptical arches and metal railings over the River Swift (SP504771), a cast-iron trough aqueduct of *c* 1835 over the Cosford road and a fine cast-iron roving bridge (SP502770) by the Horseley Iron Works over the Rugby branch.

STRATFORD
Canal Wharf and Basin (SP204548)
¼ mile SE of town centre
This wharf is on the section of canal which was restored by the National Trust after it was threatened with abandonment in 1958. The 13½-mile section of the canal owned by the Trust has 36 locks and 26 cantilevered cast-iron bridges in which towlines for barges could be passed through slots in the centre of the bridge. The canal, which finally opened in 1816, was begun in 1793 and because its

sections were constructed at different periods by different engineers there is a variety of building styles displayed by the bridges and lockhouses. The single-storey lockhouses with barrel-shaped roofs on the southern section contrast with the plainer buildings of the earlier northern section.

STRATFORD
Tramway Viaduct (SP205548)
¼ mile SE of town centre
The viaduct is the northern end of a remarkable 16-mile tramway from Stratford to Moreton-in-Marsh built 1826. Engineered by William James and built as an edgeway on a gauge of 4 ft 8½ in it crossed the Avon on a curved viaduct of 9 by 35 ft span brick arches. At the town end is a reconstructed section of track and a wagon.

WARWICK
Canal Aqueducts (e.g. SP301654)
1½ miles E of town centre off A425
Two aqueducts within ¼ mile of each other demonstrate progress made by engineers in the first half of the 19th century. The aqueduct over the River Avon is a massively built 3-arched sandstone structure of 1799 with 2 piers with large cutwaters in the river. The concrete parapet is a 1909 addition. The

WARWICK: *Gasholder Buildings, Saltisford, graceful reminder of concern for safety in early years of gas industry.*

aqueduct over the railway (SP303653) is a light iron trough of *c* 1852 supported by 3 brick piers.

WARWICK
Eagle Warehouse (SP278653)
½ mile NW of town centre on A41
Built in 1796 as a worsted spinning factory for Parkes Brookehouse and Compton, this warehouse on the S side of Wallace Street was the first and for some time the largest factory in Warwick. It is constructed in red brick on a high stone plinth and has stone facings and a parapet while most of the windows in the 4-storey façade retain their iron frames.

WARWICK
Emscote Mills, Wharf Street (SP294656)
1 mile NE of town centre
Large complex of early 19th-century red brick buildings backing onto the canal. Two large ranges of 4-storey mills and several 2-storey buildings, one of which has a columned belfry and clock. An attractive stucco fronted house has 'Emscote Mill' inscribed above door.

WARWICK
Gasholder Buildings, Saltisford (SP278653)
½ mile NW of town centre
The attractive stuccoed street façade of the now demolished early part of the gasworks in Saltisford is an industrial monument of exceptional significance. The octagonal towers at either end with their louvred lanterns are in fact gas-holder houses and date from 1822. Such houses were once common as they were insisted on for spurious safety reasons when gas was first introduced in the early 19th century. These are now the finest surviving examples in the country.

WOOTEN WAWEN
Aqueduct (SP159630)
7 miles NW of Stratford on A34
This iron trough aqueduct on the Stratford-on-Avon Canal was built in 1813 and thus dates from the final period of construction of this canal. The trough, which has a tow-path section built alongside it at its bottom level, is carried over the A34 on a series of brick piers. The canal widens into a small basin at the northern approach to the aqueduct and one of the cast-iron overbridges typical to this canal can be seen to the N of the basin.

West Midlands

West Midlands, the largest of the metropolitan counties in terms of population, is dominated by the city of Birmingham though it also embraces the area known as the Black Country. Though this region has long been the industrial heart of England the continuing prosperity of much of its industry has led to the continuous redevelopment of working sites with the consequent destruction of earlier installations. The West Midlands therefore is not particularly rich in monuments to its heavy engineering industries and most of its monuments derive from its transport systems or craft industries such as jewellery, gun making and glass making. The Birmingham Canal Navigation system is the most intricate network of canals in the country with a wide variety of monuments representing every period of canal construction.

BALSALL
Berkswell Windmill (SP249759)
Off A452 2 miles NW of Kenilworth
Brick-built tower mill of 1826 on the site of a post mill. The post trees of the earlier mill are incorporated into the present mill. The mill, which has its machinery complete is open to the public on summer Sundays.

BIRMINGHAM
The Brasshouse, Broad Street (SP061866)
½ mile W city centre on A456
The fine 2-storey Georgian façade of *c* 1781 in Broad Street now housing the Weights & Measures Department, is the only survival of Birmingham brass merchants' attempts to be independent of their distant suppliers by making their own metal. The smelting works to the rear have gone.

BIRMINGHAM
Curzon Street Station (SP078871)
½ mile E city centre
The original 1838 terminus of the London & Birmingham Railway, designed by Hardwick to provide a northern equivalent to the grandeurs of Euston. Relegated to a goods depot in 1854, the handsome masonry structure with its massive Ionic columns is now the main relic of the country's first main line to the capital.

BIRMINGHAM
Gas Street Canal Basin (SP062866)
½ mile SW of city centre of A456
The terminus of both the Birmingham & Worcester and the Birmingham, Canal Gas Street Basin has recently been landscaped after the demolition of many of its ware-

houses. Originally the Worcester 'bar' kept the 2 canals physically distinct and necessitated transhipment of cargos.

BIRMINGHAM
Guillotine Locks, Kings Norton (SP056795)
6 miles SW of city centre off A441
The northern section of the Stratford & Avon Canal was completed in 1816 to connect with the Worcester & Birmingham at Kings Norton. A guillotine stop lock was necessary to counteract any difference in level that might arise due to water supply difficulties.

BIRMINGHAM
Gun Barrel Proof House, Banbury Street (SP078866)
½ mile E city centre
A graceful 2-storey brick building with a large insignia in a niche above pillared doorway in a cobbled courtyard at the end of Banbury Street. Built in 1813, the proof house was a manifestation of Birmingham's pre-eminent place in the gun trade. The testing shops lie to the rear of the complex.

BIRMINGHAM
Jewellery Quarter, St Paul's Square (SP065874)
½ mile NW of city centre off A41

BIRMINGHAM: *Curzon Street Station – northern counterpart to Euston's Doric Arch.*

Towards the end of the 18th century a distinctive craft quarter developed in the Newhall Street and St Paul's Square area occupying elegant town houses with workshops behind. Though much of the trade moved to Hockley in the mid-19th century some firms survive to the present day, e.g. J Betts & Sons, Charlotte Street.

BIRMINGHAM
Later Jewellery Quarter, Hockley (e.g. SP062882)
¾ mile NW of city centre off A41
Probably the best preserved craft quarter in the country, the Birmingham jewellery trades migrated to this area in the mid-19th century from the earlier quarter around St Paul's Square. Some of the premises are custom built, e.g. Great Hampton Street Works (SP062882), a handsome 3-storey red brick structure of almost Byzantine appearance but others were adapted from large town houses, e.g. Vyse Street (SP061879). A distinctive feature of the trade is the multiple occupation of premises, e.g. Plantagenet Buildings (SP061880), Spencer Street, has 23 firms.

BIRMINGHAM
Model Housing and Factory, Bournville (SP048810)
5 miles SW of city centre off A441
Cadbury Brothers prestige development of the Bourne Brook developed from 1879 onwards. It comprises red brick half-timbered factory buildings of 1899–1902, a baths of 1904 resembling a church, a concert hall, dining room, playing fields and the Green built 1914.

BIRMINGHAM
Sarehole Mill, Hall Green (SP099818)
4 miles SE of city centre off A34
Restored as a museum complex, Sarehole Mill in its present form dates from *c* 1764–7 when it was rebuilt to grind edge tools as well as corn. There are 2 waterwheels, the N wheel, high breast fed, drives the corn mills and the overshot cast-iron S wheel drives the sharpening grindstones. The mid-19th-century steam engine has gone but an early table engine is exhibited in its place.

BRIERLEY HILL
Delph Locks (SO920866)
¼ mile S of town centre
Often photographed flight of 8 closely spaced locks taking the Dudley Canal from the Park Head level to join the Stourbridge Canal. Originally there were 9 locks but these were entirely rebuilt in 1858 in their present form. Near the top there is a Horseley Ironworks cast-iron roving bridge dated 1858.

COVENTRY
Cash's Model Factory, Cash's Lane (SP335806)
¾ mile N of city centre off A444
Terrace of 2-storey houses with 'topshops' above built by John and Joseph Cash in 1857 as part of an ambitious model factory scheme intended to maintain the independence of the individual worker within the factory system. 100 units were planned originally on a site beside the Coventry Canal but only 48 were built. The ribbon trade suffered greatly from competition from French products after the signing of the Cabdeu Treaty in 1860 and the topshops of this terrace were converted to a single factory in 1862.

COVENTRY
Watchmaking Workshops, Chapelfields (SP318788)
1 mile W of city centre
A 19th-century suburb which by the second half of the century had developed as a distinct craft quarter specializing in watchmaking. The workshops with their continuous upper floor windows are typically at the rear of the master watch-makers' houses, e.g. Allesley Old Road.

CRADLEY
Chain making works, e.g. Station Street (SO959867)
1 mile NE town centre off 4100
The Great Western Works of Connop Bros was established 1881 and their 2-storey premises still make all sorts of iron wares including chain for which this area is particularly famous. Other chain works can be found in Corngreave Street (SO946858) belonging to Samuel Woodhouse & Sons. A former chain proving house survives off Newlyn Street (SO948859).

DUDLEY
Cobb's Engine House (SO995884)
2 miles S of town centre off B4171
Dating from *c* 1831, this is one of the most impressive engine houses built to drain several collieries and maintained by the South Staffordshire Mines Drainage Commission. Water from such sources was vital to the operation of the canal system in the Birmingham area.

DUDLEY
Dudley Canal Tunnels (e.g. SO945917)
1½ miles N town centre off A4123
The Earl of Dudley began driving canals into the limestone strata of Dudley Ridge in 1775 and the system of underground tunnels were eventually connected by the Dudley Canal Company to provide a through route in 1792. The main tunnel is of tiny dimensions, being only 8 ft 5 in wide, but it opens up into huge caverns where limestone has been extracted. The Black Country Museum has been established near the northern entrance around a group of limekilns dating from *c* 1840 (SO948917).

DUDLEY
Triangular Crane, Bumble Hole Boatyard (SO953883)
2 miles S of town centre off B4171
A rare example of a 19th-century triangular wooden loading crane on one of the many branches of the Birmingham Canal Navigation. To the N is the Netherton Tunnel, the last major canal tunnel to be built in the country. Completed in 1858, it is 3027 yards long and 27 ft wide with tow paths either side.

HALESOWEN
New Hawne Colliery, Hayseech (SO957846)
¾ mile NW of town centre off A458
Fine complex of red brick colliery buildings

dating from 1865, including engine house, fan house and chimney, offices, workshops and stores. The colliery worked until *c* 1921.

HOCKLEY HEATH
Engine House, Valley Road (SP114743)
$3\frac{1}{2}$ miles SW Solihull B4102
3-storey red brick 19th-century pumping engine house built in conjunction with the Earlswood Lakes water supply to the Stratford & Avon Canal.

LADYWOOD
Stabling and Stores, Sheepcote Street (SP057868)
$\frac{1}{2}$ mile W city centre off A456
A horseshoe-shaped red brick complex of stables and stores, consisting of 2 10-bay single-storey wings flanking a central 15-bay, 2-storey section. Built *c* 1840 for the London and North Western Railway. The different levels are served by cobbled ramps.

LANGLEY
Langley Maltings (SO996883)
Dating from *c* 1860, these red brick maltings with their 5 kilns are a prominent feature alongside the Titford Branch of the BCN. Operated by the Wolverhampton and Dudley Breweries.

SMETHWICK
Chances Glassworks (SP007897)
1 mile NW of town centre off A457
Chances, an illustrious firm which supplied glass for the Crystal Palace and which specializes in heavy glass and optics has since 1834 been based in Smethwick. It occupies a handsome group of buildings, some of which are early 19th-century.

SMETHWICK
Engine Arm Aqueduct (SP015894)
$1\frac{1}{4}$ mile NW of town centre off A457
Built *c* 1828, this fine iron aqueduct carries a branch over Telford's new line of the Birmingham Canal and demonstrates Telford's mastery of the use of cast iron as both a structural and decorative material.

SMETHWICK
Galton Bridge and Canal Cutting (SP015893)
Built in 1829 by Telford across his Smethwick cutting, the Galton Bridge has a single iron span of 150 ft and was considered one of the wonders of the canal age. The cutting itself is a most impressive achievement, being the last of a series of improvements which significantly lowered the summit of the Birmingham Canal from Brindley's original line.

SMETHWICK
Soho Foundry, Foundry Street (SP035888)
$\frac{1}{2}$ mile E of town centre
Site made famous by the firm of Boulton & Watt who opened their new works here in 1796 and here conducted much of their pioneer work on steam engines and foundry technology. Since 1895 the premises have been occupied by W T Avery of weighing machine fame and although most of the early buildings have gone, some offices survive.

SMETHWICK
Toll House, High Street (SP019888)
Early 19th-century 2-storey, stucco, bay-fronted cottages with a panel formerly containing the toll board.

STOURBRIDGE
Glass Cone, Stuart Crystal, Wordsley (SO894865)
$1\frac{1}{2}$ miles NW of town centre off A491
The famous firm of Stuart Crystal have preserved an 87-ft high glass cone dating from *c* 1780 at their works where traditional techniques of glassmaking are still practised.

SUTTON COLDFIELD
Newhall Mill, Wylde Green Road (SP132945)
2 miles SE Sutton Coldfield off B4148
18th-century 2-storey brick-built water mill retaining its waterwheel and much of its machinery.

TIPTON
Horseley Ironworks (SO962927)
$\frac{3}{4}$ mile NE of town centre
Famous ironworks established in 1781 and responsible for casting many fine canal bridges to be found throughout the Midlands and as far away as London.

WALSALL
Albion Corn Mill, Wolverhampton Road (SP005989)
$\frac{1}{2}$ mile W of town centre off A454
Imposing $3\frac{1}{2}$-storey red steam mill built 1898 with 3 assymetrical gables with a huge central archway. Pronounced round-headed windows, semi-circular lunettes and circular window in central gable combine to make this one of the most attractive buildings in Walsall.

WALSALL
Globe Works, Lower Foster Street (SP015990)
$\frac{1}{4}$ mile N of town centre
Walsall is the centre of the British leather industry with an international reputation for saddlery, sports goods, bags, etc. Globe

Works, a typical 3-storey brick factory with polychrome decoration is occupied by Jabez Cliff & Co and was established in 1873. Other leather works are to be found in Whittmere Street (SP016987), Hatherton Street (SP013990), Stafford Street (SP010989), Station Street (SP010985) and Navigation Street (SP009985).

WEDNESBURY
Canal Bridges, Tame Valley Junction (SP977936)
1 mile SW of town centre off A461
The completion of the Wednesbury Canal in 1769 allowed Wednesbury to develop as a major centre for heavy industry. The connecting Tame Valley Canal was opened in 1844. At their junction are 2 cast-iron bridges of *c* 1844 and a tiny bridge dated 1852 over a branch. The canal is a good vantage point to view the extreme industrialization of this area.

WOLVERHAMPTON
Autherley Junction (SJ901021)
1½ miles N of town centre, ½ mile W A449
Junction of Telford's Birmingham and Liverpool Junction Canal completed 1835 and Brindley's Staffs and Worcs Canal opened in 1772 with a fine brick double roving bridge designed by Telford and white painted toll house.

WOLVERHAMPTON
Chubb Works, Wednesfield Road (SO926994)
1 mile NE of town centre on A4124

Wolverhampton is known for all kinds of light engineering, including lockmaking, vehicle components, bicycles etc. The 2-storey Chubb works have been largely modernized but still carry on a famous tradition.

WOLVERHAMPTON
Compton Lock and Wharf (SO883988)
2 miles W of town centre off A454
This was the first lock to be constructed by Brindley shortly after work commenced on the Staffs & Worcs Canal in 1766. Its dimensions were thus to become standard on the Midland narrow canals.

WOLVERHAMPTON
Old Steam Mill, Old Mill Street (SO919988)
⅓ mile E of town centre off A4124
Rebuilt after a fire in 1851 by the noted Wm Fairbairn & Sons of Manchester, this structure has wrought-iron beams as part of its fireproofing – an early example of this technique. Originally a steam engine drove 18 pairs of stones.

WOLVERHAMPTON
Railway Ticket Office, Horseley Field (SO918988)
¼ mile E of town centre
A 2-storey Italianate façade erected in 1849 for Shrewsbury & Birmingham Railway and built of buff coloured brick with stone dressings. Tuscan pilasters lend it some dignity.

Wiltshire

Wiltshire's large size and its situation astride south central England have given it a surprising diversity in its industrial monuments despite its predominantly rural character. It encompasses part of the West of England woollen industry on its western flank and a secondary textile area based on the Salisbury Avon to the south. It has one of the richest stock of transport monuments of any county including Rennie's Kennet & Avon Canal with Caen Hill Locks (*qv*), Dundas and Avoncliffe Aqueducts (*qv*), and Crofton pumping station (*qv*), Brunel's Great Western Railway with the Box Tunnels (*qv*), Chippenham Viaduct (*qv*) and Swindon Railway Town (*qv*) and the Bath road (A4) with its coaching inns and toll houses. Secondary canals such as the Thames & Severn, N Wilts and Wilts & Berks contribute further monuments along with the stone mines and quarries of Box, the maltings of the Warminster area and the breweries at Trowbridge and Devizes.

BOX

Box Railway Tunnel (ST857695–829689)
6 miles SW of Chippenham on A4
The railway tunnel at Box, constructed 1836–41, is one of I K Brunel's most famous achievements. 3,212 yards long at a gradient of 1 in 100 and wide enough to accommodate 2 by 7 ft tracks, the tunnel epitomized Brunel's unorthodox approach to railway engineering and became a focus of attention for his many detractors. Although its construction cost almost 100 lives and some 4000 men and 300 horses were latterly employed by the 2 contractors, the success of the tunnel confounded its critics. The western portal, with its smoothly rusticated quoins and prominent corbelled cornice surmounted by a neat classical balustrade provides one of the finest examples of 'engineer's architecture' and has been immortalized by J G Bourne in *A History and Description of the Great Western Railway*.

BRADFORD-ON-AVON

Abbey Mill (ST826609)
Town centre
Erected in 1875, this handsome stone block was the last major woollen factory to be built in Wiltshire. It is the product of the specialist firm of factory builders – Giles & Gane of London – and has been sympathetically converted into offices for the Avon Rubber Company.

BRADFORD-ON-AVON

Avoncliffe Mill (ST805600)
1 mile W of Bradford-on-Avon
A massive stone weir across the River Avon at this point originally had a watermill at either end. The mill on the N bank has survived and retains its breast shot external waterwheel located below a corrugated-iron cabin on the side of stone-built mill.

CHAPMANSLADE

Weavers' Cottages (ST828479)
4 miles SW of Westbury on A3098
Chapmanslade is a long narrow street village situated at the southern end of the West Country woollen region. However, few traces of the formerly extensive weaving production have survived. On the S side of the street are 2, 3-storey weaving shops where a master weaver would have employed a small team of weavers.

CHIPPENHAM

Railway Viaduct (ST912731)
Town centre
The handsome viaduct, seen from the main road from Bath on entering Chippenham, was built by Brunel as part of his main line of the Great Western Railway.

CHISELDON

Donkey Wheel, Lower Upham Farm (SU208777)
5 miles N of Marlborough off A345
This 14 ft-diameter donkey wheel has survived even though the well it pumped from has been sealed. The rim of the 3 ft 6 in wide wheel is supported by 4 main spokes each with 2 sub spokes while the windlass is 12 in in diameter.

CORSHAM

Stone Mines (ST877685)
4 miles SW of Chippenham off A4
The Monks Park Mine is the sole remaining underground stone mine still being worked in the once very extensive deposits of Bath and Box stone. Production has declined greatly from a peak of *c* 3 million cubic feet per annum in 1900. The freshly mined stone is kept underground until May to avoid frost damage to the 'green' stone.

DEVIZES

Caen Hill Locks (SU976614–995615)
1 mile W of town centre off A361
The Kennet & Avon Canal surmounts a rise of 237 ft between Semington and Devizes by a total of 29 locks. Seventeen of these locks are grouped in an impressive flight at Caen Hill, each with a large side pound to alleviate the effect of their proximity. Although the locks have been derelict for many years they are now being restored by voluntary effort.

DEVIZES

Toll House, Bath Road (SU997617)
$\frac{1}{2}$ mile W of town centre on A361
This attractive, stone-built, battlemented toll house was erected *c* 1840. Its situation, in an acute angle between 2 busy roads, has caused some superficial damage to the stonework and jeopardizes its existence.

DEVIZES

Wadworth's Brewery (SU005615)
$\frac{1}{4}$ mile W of town centre on A361
This tall, brick-built, brewery of 1865 houses a contemporary single cylinder horizontal engine on its first floor. The engine, which is now disused, was made by Geo Adlam & Co of Bristol. The brewery itself is noted for its traditional beer and has recently re-introduced delivery by horse-drawn dray waggons.

DILTON MARSH

Ironstone Workings (ST953507)
2 miles SW of Westbury off A3098
Iron ore, known as the Westbury ironstone, outcrops in a narrow band from the NE of Westbury Station to Dilton Marsh. At Westbury the excavations which date from *c* 1857

are flooded but at the southern end near Dilton Marsh a long narrow gulley some 40 ft deep is witness of later excavation.

DOWNTON

Tannery (SU180215)
5 miles S of Salisbury off A338
One of the many channels of the River Avon at Downton powers a metal waterwheel at Dowton tannery, parts of which date from *c* 1830. The wheel itself is undershot 10 ft diameter by 2 ft 6 in wide and was installed to agitate vats. Across the road a former corn mill powered by the same watercourse was converted in 1931 to a hydro-electric power station which only recently ceased operation.

GREAT BEDWYN

Crofton Pumping Station (SU262623)
7 miles SE of Marlborough off A346
Crofton Pumping Station was built to lift water some 40 ft from Wilton Water to the summit level of the Kennet & Avon Canal. The engine house has 2 Cornish beam engines – the older a Boulton & Watt of 1812

converted to the Cornish cycle of operation in 1845 by Harveys of Hayle who in the following year installed the other engine. These engines are preserved, and occasionally worked by a charitable trust, the steam being supplied by boilers made in the GWR Swindon works.

GREAT CHEVERELL

Corn Mill (ST984548)
7 miles E of Westbury off B3098
This small rural watermill on a tributary of the Semington Brook was rebuilt as recently as 1924 but was disused by 1939. The structure has been converted into a private dwelling but the 14 ft diameter, 4 ft wide overshot waterwheel has been retained.

LACOCK

Key Mill (ST922694)
4 miles S of Chippenham off A350
This 18th-century water-driven mill on the River Avon was originally a corn mill with 5

GREAT BEDWYN: *Crofton Pumping Station on the Kennet & Avon Canal.*

pairs of stones, but now contains 2 turbines by Gilbert Gilkes rated at 76 hp and driving an electric generator.

LIMPLEY STOKE
Dundas Aqueduct (ST786626)
3 miles SE Bath off A36
This, perhaps the most elegant of all masonry aqueducts, was completed to the designs of John Rennie in 1800. The semi-circular 64 ft main span is flanked by 20 ft flood arches of parabolic shape. The aqueduct carries the Kennet & Avon Canal across the River Avon and its curved façade is embellished by Doric pilasters and the entablature has a very deep cornice.

MASTON MEYSEY
Canal Keeper's Cottage (SU132963)
3 miles NE of Cricklade off A419
This characteristic 3-storey Thames & Severn Canal roundhouse was built in 1799 at a wharf and overbridge near Castle Eaton. The main entrance is from the bridge at 1st floor level whence a narrow spiral staircase built partly into the thickness of the wall led to the upper floor. The ground floor was entered from the wharf and was used as a warehouse. The roof was an inverted cone – probably to collect rainwater.

SALISBURY
Canal Cutting (SU200270)
3 miles SE of Salisbury off A36
The abortive Salisbury & Southampton Canal, intended to link the towns of its title, has left few significant remains. At Alderbury, to the SE of Salisbury there is a deep cutting which is the most impressive survival in Wiltshire of this late 18th-century failure.

SWINDON
Railway Housing (SU155850)
W of town centre off A420
The Great Western Railway main line from London to Bristol passed a mile to the N of the market town of Swindon and hence, once this

LIMPLEY STOKE: *Dundas Aqueduct – Rennie's masterpiece on the Kennet & Avon Canal.*

location had been chosen for the company's engineering works, it was necessary to provide housing for the railway workers. During the period 1845–47 an estate comprising some 250 houses was built as well as a Mechanics Institute, market and hostel. The housing has recently been sympathetically restored while the hostel now contains a small railway museum.

SWINDON
Railway Workshops (su140850)
NW of town centre
Daniel Gooch, GWR's noted locomotive builder, persuaded the company to base their engineering works at Swindon – a convenient point on the London–Bristol route to change engines and for passengers to take refreshments. The original engine works were constructed of stone from the excavation of Box Tunnel and were in use by 1843. The works expanded greatly in the succeeding century and only recently have shown some contraction.

TROWBRIDGE
Textile Mills (st855578)
SW of town centre
The area immediately to the SW of the centre of this formerly important textile town contains several mills, some of which are still in operation. In Court Street, for example, the mills display a wide variety of architectural styles ranging from early 19th-century narrow, 3-storey, stone-built mills to multi-storey brick-built, mills of the 1860s.

TROWBRIDGE
Weavers' Cottages, Newton (st853576)
SW of town centre on A361
Trowbridge originally contained numerous terraces of 3-storey weavers' houses built between 1790 and 1830 with the top floor as a workshop. A good example of such a terrace, with characteristically large windows on the uppermost floor has survived in Newtown.

SWINDON: *Great Western Railway's company housing prior to restoration.*

WARMINSTER
Malthouse, Pound Street (ST866447)
½ mile SW of town centre off A362
Warminster and the nearby villages such as Heytesbury were once noted for their malt which was used all over the West of England. In 1818 in Warminster alone there were 25 malthouses in operation but now only the maltings in Pound Street are at work. This impressive masonry range with its large drying kiln was erected in 1879.

WESTBURY
Angel Mill (ST875513)
Town centre
This early steam driven textile mill was built in 1806 and was operated by the prominent Laverton family. The narrow, 4-storey, brick building with its central pediment and segment-headed windows, was in use until recently.

WESTBURY
Prospect Square (ST875511)
¼ mile E of town centre
This spacious square of 39 houses was the result of fierce political rivalry of 2 parliamentary opponents in the elections of 1869. Phipps, the successful Tory candidate, ejected many of his Liberal opponents' work-people for voting for their master. The latter, Abraham Laverton, a prominent cloth manufacturer, laid out this square of vernacular cottages the following year to house those that had been evicted.

WILTON
Wilton Windmill (SU276617)
7 miles SW of Hungerford on A338
This, the most complete windmill in Wiltshire, is owned by the County Council and is currently being restored. Built in 1821, the 3-storey brick tower mill contains most of its original machinery.

WOOTTEN BASSETT
Canal Locks (SU034811)
2 miles SW of Wootten Bassett off A420
The Wilts & Berks Canal ran from a junction with the Kennet & Avon Canal at Semington to the River Thames at Abingdon. Much of its total length of 57 miles has been obliterated but, amongst other remains, are traces of 7 locks to the W of Wootten Bassett.

North Yorkshire

North Yorkshire is a huge new county comprising most of the former N Riding and the northern portion of the West and East Ridings. It encompasses the Dales with their lead mines and smelt mills and water-driven textile mills, the North York Moors with relics of iron mining and early railways, the Vale of York with its important rail links, maltings and breweries and the River Ouse itself with navigation structures and watermills on its many tributaries.

ALLERSTON
Limekilns (SE883832)
4 miles E of Pickering off A170
An impressive masonry bank of 19th-century limekilns built against the scarp bounding the Vale of Pickering. A total view of the whole bank is denied by trees but the kilns are generally in good condition with several unfilled wells and open hearths.

BEAL
Beal Bridge (SE533255)
2 miles NE of Knottingley off A645
This narrow 6-span wooden bridge over the River Aire below Knottingley is typical, in construction, of early 18th-century river navigations. Its structural components will probably have been renewed several times but the larger central span will have remained of

sufficient clearance for any vessel using the river once the parallel Aire & Calder Navigation was constructed.

BOROUGHBRIDGE
Maltings (SE393672)
N of town centre
These maltings, adjacent to a small brewery on the bank of the River Ure, contain a rather unusual kiln built entirely of brick. There is a conventional slated kiln in the same group of maltings and the brick-built kiln may possibly be an early precursor.

BROMPTON-BY-SAWDON
Brick Kiln (SE944817)
6 miles SW of Searborough off A170
This double-sided updraught kiln probably dates from the second quarter of the 19th century. The interior of the kiln is exceptionally tall – 17 ft – and was therefore probably designed to fire mixed goods, e.g. bricks at the bottom, tiles and plant pots at the top. The design of the kiln does not reflect local practice and it would seem likely that this was an experimental kiln designed by Sir George Cayley (1773–1854) the 'Father' of aerodynamics.

CONONLEY
Mine Engine House (SE980462)
4 miles S of Skipton off A629
Lead has been mined at Cononley since the early 17th century but this engine house dates from only 1832 when a shaft was sunk to drain the numerous levels. The engine house was located about 100 yards from the shaft and a set of flat rods connected the engine to the pumps through a balance bob and spears. The tall narrow appearance of the engine house would suggest that it once contained a Cornish-type engine.

DANBY
Esk Mill (NZ707083)
11 miles W of Whitby off A171
This impressive 19th-century mill has only recently ceased grinding cattle food. The waterwheel is located in a small wheel house on the river itself and is in rather poor condition.

DUNNINGTON
Chicory Kiln (SE671526)
4 miles E of York off A166
The growing and processing of chicory was once an important industry in the East Riding. A village like Dunnington, for instance, had several kilns but now production has ceased and most of the kilns have disappeared. This

remaining example is 70 ft by 40 ft and part of the first floor is still laid with the characteristic 11 in square perforated tiles.

EGGBOROUGH
Roall Pumping Station (SE568244)
6 miles SW of Selby off A19
This late 19th-century brick and stone pumping station belonged to the Pontefract, Goole & Selby Water Board. Since 1957 it has used electric pumps and a standby Rushton Hornsby oil engine but one of the pair of 160 hp A-frame beam steam engines has been preserved. It was installed by Easton & Anderson in 1891.

FAIRBURN
Fairburn Canal and Tramway (SE470276)
3 miles N of Knottingley off A1
In the early 19th century the alabaster and limestone quarries at Fairburn were connected to the River Aire by a short canal and tramway. Some of the tramway rails can still be seen at the head of the canal and the associated tramway tunnel also survives.

GLAISDALE
Caper Hill Guidepost (NZ732022)
3 miles SW of Glaisdale unclass road
This rough hewn pillar, high on Glaisdale Moor, is inscribed on all its 4 sides with local distances. It also bears the name of Thomas Harwood, a noted local surveyor, and the date 1735.

GLAISDALE
Powder House (NZ787055)
1 mile E of Glaisdale
This small powder house was built in 1865 to store explosives for the nearby ironstone mines working the Pecten and Avicula seams by the side of the River Esk. The ore was consumed in the adjacent Glaisdale ironworks, a tramway connecting the mines with the top of the blast furnaces. Competition from the Teeside iron industry closed both the furnaces and the mines in 1876 and this small hut is a reminder of a once significant industry.

GOATHLAND
Moorgate Railway Bridge (NZ846944)
7 miles SW of Whitby off A169
A very attractive masonry bridge built in 1835 as part of George Stephenson's original horse-drawn Whitby & Pickering Railway. The bridge itself was subsequently by-passed when the line was converted to locomotive operation a dozen years later and it now merely carries a grassy embankment over a cart track.

GRASSINGTON
Grassington Moor Flue and Chimney
(SE030667)

1½ miles NE of Grassington unclass road
A cupola smelter was established at the Grassington Moor mines in 1792 and as production increased the original flue proved inadequate. Accordingly, in the 1850s an extended flue was built, with 2 Stokoe type condensers in its course, rising 150 ft up the slope of the moor to the foot of a 60 ft high chimney. The total length of the elaborate system of flues was 5,140 ft. At the height of its production the smelter comprised 2 reverberatories, a roasting furnace and a slaghearth.

GRASSINGTON
Linton Cotton Mill (SE002633)
1 mile SW of Grassington
This mill was sited to take advantage of the immense water-power potential of the River Wharfe. Latterly it had 5 turbines at work and a 300 hp uniflow steam engine was installed in 1921 to supplement these in times of low water. In the 1930s cotton spinning ceased and the mill changed its role to that of an electricity generating station supplying the Grassington

area. To this end 4 'Victor' diesel engines were added and the uniflow engine remained on standby. The installation has been disused for several years but the plant is in good condition.

GREENHOW
Panty Oon Stone (SE109645)
3 miles W of Pately Bridge ⅓ of a mile NW of B6265 at Greenhow Hill
This large hollowed out stone with its 3 ft-diameter basin pierced by a 14 in square slot would seem to have connections with medieval dressing of lead ores but its exact function has not yet been ascertained.

GREENHOW
Smelt Mills (SE115649)
3 miles W of Pately Bridge ½ mile N of B6265 at Greenhow
The Greenhow area has been mined for lead since Roman times but while some levels are of very early date, most of the surface remains are of the late 18th or early 19th centuries. 2

GRASSINGTON: *Grassington Moor Flue and chimney.*

smelt mills in the valley below Greenhow Hill village are Cockhill Mill dating from *c* 1785 with considerable ruined remains and slightly older Providence Mill (SE117651) of which little other than the flue and smelting mill gable survives.

GREENHOW
Toft Gate Limekiln (SE131644)
2 miles W of Pateley Bridge beside B6265
A large 19th-century commercial limekiln built in its own quarry. Rather unusually it has a flue over 100 yards long leading to a stumpy chimney further up the hillside. The flue itself is *c* 3 ft broad and 4 ft high and is roofed with single stone slabs. The presence of fixing bolts at the top of the kiln may suggest some form of mechanical assistance to create a good draw.

GROSMONT
Old Railway Tunnel (NZ829051)
5 miles SW of Whitby off A169
This small railway tunnel, with its battlemented portals is a survival from the period of horse operation of the Whitby & Pickering Railway. 119 yards long, built in 1835, it was replaced by a somewhat longer parallel tunnel of larger bore in 1847, since when it has been relegated to use as a footpath.

GROSMONT
Railway Stabling (NZ829053)
5 miles SW of Whitby off A169
A relic of the horse drawn era of the Whitby & Pickering Line, these stables probably date from the opening of the railway in 1836.

HINDERWELL
Port Mulgrave (NZ799178)
1 miles SE of Staithes off A174
This harbour was developed in the 1860s on a stretch of coast notoriously short of safe anchorages. Its primary purpose was to ship ironstone from a mine adjacent to the harbour itself and to serve the extensive mines in the valleys above Staithes. To connect one such mine, Grinkle, a tunnel over a mile long was opened *c* 1875 with waggons rope hauled on narrow-gauge track. The harbour was constructed on concrete and stone piers and demonstrates one of the earliest uses of concrete in the role of a major constructional material. The harbour was badly damaged by storms in 1953 and is semi-derelict, while the entrance to the tunnel, which closed in 1920, has been bricked up.

KILDALE
Warren Moor Chimney (NZ625089)
4½ miles SE of Great Ayton Kildale road

Built-in 1865, this ornamental chimney marks the site of the Leven Vale Iron Company's mine. The nearby shaft drops 220 ft to the main seam.

LEEMING BAR
Canal Lock (SE287892)
6 miles S of Catterick off A1
In a field to the E of, and visible from, the A1 is a small damaged canal lock. This lay on the proposed line of canalized Bedale Beck which was to connect Bedale with the River Swale under a 1767 Act of Parliament. There is no evidence that this lock was ever used.

LOTHERSDALE
Great Wheel, Dale End Mill (SD960459)
6 miles NW of Keighley off A6068
Developed as a silk spinning mill at the end of the 18th century from an old corn mill, the buildings were greatly extended in 1851 and 1861. The huge waterwheel for which the mill is noted was built by Lund's Foundry, Eastburn, in 1862 and developed 30 hp. It is 45 ft in diameter, 5 ft wide with 162 buckets 12 in deep. The shaft, hubs and rim are of cast-iron, the spokes of pine and tensioning rods of steel.

MASHAM
Theakston's Brewery (SE224816)
9 miles NW of Ripon on A6108
A small family brewery with a national reputation for their Old Peculiar strong ale. Founded in 1827, they occupy a stone-built brewing complex with fine maltings with hammer beam roof and a stone with 32 ft-span king post roof.

NABURN
Naburn Lock and Banquetting Hall
(SE594446)
5 miles S of York on B1222
This is the last lock on the River Ouse before the city of York and the Ouse Navigation commissioners developed the site as their headquarters. Besides the usual offices and boat repair facilities there is a monumental banquetting hall. This hall was built in 1823 to accommodate the commissioners formal dinners and must rank as one of the most extravagant gestures to company prestige.

NUNNINGTON
Watermill (SE675794)
3 miles N of Hovingham off B1257
This fine 4-storey mill was erected in 1874 beside the River Rye, and was driven by a leat

GROSMONT: *Old Railway Tunnel – relic of one of the last major horse-drawn railways.*

from the river. It was last worked in 1960 and the wheel and machinery are still in position though the latter is buried in grain as the mill is now used as a grain elevator. The wheel is *c* 15 ft in diameter, metal framed with wooden buckets.

PATELEY BRIDGE
Mill (SE148664)
1 mile NW of Pateley Bridge (Lofthouse road)
A former hemp mill built *c* 1887 with external high breast shot waterwheel 35 ft in diameter by 5 ft wide. Now converted into a country inn.

PICKERING
Pickering Station Goods Yard (SE796838)
Town centre
When the horse-drawn North Yorks Moors railway was converted to locomotive traction *c* 1845 the goods yard was developed in association with York & North Midland Railway. Two find goods sheds were built, one probably designed by G T Andrews in local stone with timber cladding.

REETH
Grinton Smelt Mill (SE050964)
10 miles W of Richmond off B6270
This smelt mill in Swaledale was in operation from *c* 1785 until 1870. From the mill a flue, some 1100 ft long, ran up the hillside to terminate in a short chimney. Alongside the flue stood a thatched building in which would have been stored the peat used as the fuel for smelting.

REETH
Marrick Upper and Lower Smelt Mills (SE089995)
5 miles W of Richmond off Marske-Reeth road
There are 2 smelt mills at this site. The High or Upper Mill was reconstructed *c* 1860 around the chimney of the earlier Low Mill which itself was on the site of a smelt mill of great antiquity. Low Mill must have ceased smelting *c* 1860 but the layout is quite well preserved. Smelting ceased altogether *c* 1890.

RIPON
Ripon Canal Basin (NZ316707)
¼ mile SE of town centre
Surveyed by Smeaton in 1766 and built by his assistant William Jessop, this broad canal was open by 1772. A warehouse designed by Smeaton still stands beside the basin.

ROSEDALE
East Mine, Kilns (SE705989)
10 miles NW of Pickering, Rosedale Abbey road
This battery of calcining kilns was built to serve East Mine in the late 1860s. They are constructed to a different design from the earlier kilns nearby and have suffered greater damage. Only the massive retaining walls and 3 lined box chambers have survived. The linings and the large iron plates across the front of each chamber have almost entirely disappeared.

ROSEDALE
East Mine, Old Kilns (SE706982)
10 miles NW of Pickering, Rosedale Abbey road
These calcining kilns, with their associated chimney, were built in 1865 when a branch line from the North Eastern Railway was opened to this mine. The bank is massively constructed in masonry pointed with huge stone blocks and comprises 16 arches. The kilns were built to reduce the cost of transporting impure ironstone to the Teesside furnaces. The mine eventually closed in 1926.

SANDSEND
'Roman' Cement Mill (NZ861127)
2½ mile NW of Whitby on A174
Owned by the Earl of Mulgrave and operated from 1811 until *c* 1936, the mill produced 'Mulgrave Cement' from nodules in alum shale. The machinery of the water driven grinding mill has been removed but the calcining kiln to the rear is virtually intact.

SCARBOROUGH
Spa Bridge (TA044882)
SE of town centre
This 414 ft long cast-iron bridge was built 1826–7 and widened in 1880. Four segmental braced iron arches of 66½ ft span are carried on tapering stone piers. Originally a toll bridge built to give access to the 'Spa' it was designed by Outhnett and built by Stead Snowden & Buckley.

SELBY
Goods Shed (616322)
¼ mile S of town centre
The building which now serves as a goods shed incorporated some columns and masonry of the 1834 station built for the Leeds & Selby Railway. Other cast-iron columns are dated 1841.

SKELTON
Windmill Tower (SE375695)
4 miles SE of Ripon off B6265

Clearly visible from the nearby A1 road, this windmill tower although converted into a house is the most complete such tower in North Yorkshire.

SKIPTON
Canal Warehouse, Coach Street (SD9851)
S of town centre
A late 18th-century rubble-built 2-storey warehouse with stone flagged roof. Arched openings extend full height of building on both street and canal façades and are now glazed as a feature of the building's new use as the Dales Outdoor Centre.

SKIPTON
High Corn Mill, Chapel Hill (SD989519)
N of town centre
A private museum formed by George Leatt & Co in a restored watermill with numerous interesting milling machines driven by one of the 2 waterwheels. The buildings straddle the Eller Beck.

SLINGSBY
Brick Kiln (SE696762)
6 miles W of Malton off B1257
This small rural updraught kiln is most unusual in that it is clad in stone. Although much overgrown, the stonework and the brick vaulted interior are in good condition. There are several brick-lined stoke holes along each side.

STOKESLEY
Drummer Hill Farm Wheel (NZ570076)
3 miles E of Stokesley
Horse-driven threshing mills were introduced to North Yorkshire *c* 1790. There is evidence of very many sheds in the area but although many buildings survive, physical remains of the horse wheel themselves are now extremely rare. This example is a 4-horse wheel housed in a rectangular shed driving through the wall of the adjacent barn to the thresher.

SWALEDALE
Surrender Smelt Mill (NY988003)
4 miles W of Reeth off B6270
Most of the ruined remains on this site date from an 1840-rebuilding of a late 18th-century mill. They comprise peat store with distinctive tapering stone piers, smelt mill with water-wheel pit, grinding mill and flue with 2 chimneys. The mill went out of use *c* 1880.

TADCASTER
Magnet Brewery (SE484433)
W of town centre
John Smith's brewery built 1883 is notable for the richness of its ornamentation and for its spectacular chimney. The entrance gateway has a fine metal arch proclaiming J Smith The Brewery.

TADCASTER
Viaduct (SE485439)
$\frac{1}{2}$ mile N of Tadcaster
Built over the River Wharfe 1846–49 for a proposed more direct line between York and Leeds, one of the railway mania schemes. As the line never materialized it was disused until 1883 when tracks were laid to serve a mill to the E bank of the river. Eleven arches in rough-faced coursed stone, 2 spannig the river being the widest and framed by paired pilasters on heavier round-faced piers.

YORK
Old Terminus Station (SE598517)
$\frac{1}{4}$ mile W of town centre
The original railway line to York pierced the city walls just to the W of Micklegate Bar and terminated just short of the present railway headquarters. This first station was designed by George Townsend Andrews and opened in 1841. Holroyd & Walker were the main contractors but the fine cast- and wrought-iron platform cover was made by Bingley & Co of Leeds. This cover survives and is now used as a bicycle shed while the adjacent original refreshment rooms are used as offices.

YORK
Queen Street Sidings Water Tank (SE596515)
$\frac{1}{2}$ mile W of town centre
This York & North Midland Railway cast-iron water tank was made in 1839 by W Thomlinson Walker, the firm which made the railings to the British Museum. As such it is certainly one of the earliest railway water tanks in existence.

South Yorkshire

The new metropolitan county of S Yorkshire is dominated by Sheffield but also includes Doncaster Rotherham and Barnsley. Most of its monuments are related to the mining and transport of coal and the manufacture of iron and steel. It has the largest collection of steam winding engines of any of the coalfields and the earliest *in situ* engine in the atmospheric steam pumping engine at Elsecar. Metal manufacture is represented by the early blast furnaces at Rockley and Low Mill, Silkstone, the water-powered hammer forges at Wortley and Abbeydale and 2 early types of steel making at Abbeydale (crucible) and Hoyle Street (cementation) furnaces. The glass and china industries have disappeared but left reminders in the glass cone at Catcliffe and the pottery bottle ovens at Swinton. Early transport links such as the Barnsley and Dearne & Dove Canals and the Silkstone tramway have also left their isolated relics.

BARNSLEY
Junction Lock (SE357068)
¾ of a mile E of town centre off A628
Built in 1804 to connect the Barnsley and the Dearn & Dove Canals, this lock effectively connected the Aire & Calder waterway system with the Don Navigation. The masonry-lined dock is now derelict and forlorn. It is difficult to imagine what it must have been like when thousands of tons of coal passed through it weekly.

CATCLIFFE
Glass Cone (SK425886)
4 miles E of Sheffield A57/B6066
This cone which is some 60 ft high and dates from *c* 1740 is the oldest of the 4 substantially intact glass cones in the country. There were at least 6 such cones in the Sheffield area but only Catcliffe has been preserved. The cone is built of horizontal brick courses tapering sharply from an arcade of arched openings at its base. The piers of the arches are masonry. Prior to restoration the cone was investigated by archaeological excavation.

CONISBOROUGH
Crags Tramway (SK507993)
1¼ miles NW of Conisborough off A6023
This tramway which is formed of shaped stone blocks laid end to end runs down the hillside from a quarry cut into the crags of North Cliff Hill. The lower part of its route to the turnpike has been obliterated but enough survives of the upper part to suggest that it was double tracked in some sections with a gauge of *c* 3 ft 3 in. There is some doubt as to its date; some authorities suggest mid-18th century, but the only parallels elsewhere are from the second decade of the 19th century.

DONCASTER
Sprotborough Water Pump (SE540018)
3 miles W of Doncaster off A630
The original installation on this site was built by George Sorocold, the noted engineer, *c* 1700 for Sir Godfrey Cotley of Sprotborough. This was one of the earliest such installations of its kind and besides supplying the estate and village it was used to fill an open air swimming bath. Water is raised some 150 ft from a well at river level to the village. The present machinery, which is somewhat later, comprises a 15 ft by 3 ft undershot waterwheel driving a 3-throw pump.

DONCASTER
Station and Railway Workshops (SE571032)
¼ mile W of town centre

ELSECAR: *Newcomen Pumping Engine – the only 18th century atmospheric engine* in situ.

The Great Northern Railway at the insistence of E Denison, the local MP, re-aligned their proposals for their main line to pass through Doncaster and this had a great impact on the town. The through route to London opened in 1850 and in 1851 the GNR moved their loco works from Boston to Doncaster and by 1900 4,500 were employed in the loco and wagon works. The station is still an important junction while the works now occupy a huge area of the Carr.

ELSECAR
Coal-mine Footrill (SK387996)
5 miles S of Barnsley off B6097 off A6135
This footrill winds round to the bottom of a shaft of the mid-1790s and is itself probably of that date. It provides pedestrian access to the canal faces in the Barnsley seam.

ELSECAR
Elsecar Village and Ironworks (SE386003)
5 miles S of Barnsley on B6097 off B6135
A planned enlargement of this village was conducted in the mid-19th century by the Earl Fitzwilliam. The original settlement clustered round the ironworks and pumping engine. John Carr the noted architect is credited with some of these later buildings which include terraced housing, a model lodging house, a school, an estate market house, a steam corn mill, a church and a private railway station. Very little survives of the ironworks which had furnaces in blast from 1795 until the 1880s.

ELSECAR
Newcomen Pumping Engine (SK387999)
5 miles S of Barnsley off B6097 off A6135
At Elsecar in an engine house with a 1787-datestone, the National Coal Board have preserved the oldest Newcomen steam engine on its original site in the country. Although the engine underwent several modifications, most notably the wooden beam being replaced by a cast-iron beam, in its pumping life which lasted from 1795 to 1923 it survived in a workable condition late enough to be filmed in operation in the 1950s. The open topped cylinder is 4 ft in diameter with a 5 ft stroke with an indicated horsepower of 13.16.

SHEFFIELD
Abbeydale Industrial Hamlet (SK326820)
3½ miles SW of city centre on A621
A unique industrial monument based round a steel and scythe works dating from the late 18th century. The works comprise a crucible steel furnace with associated pot shop, a tilt forge of 1785, a grinding shop of 1817, a boring shop, numerous hand forges, warehouses, and offices. There are also restored workers' cottages and the manager's house which has been furnished as a lower middle class Victorian home. The complex derived most of its power from a large hammer pond off the River Sheaf, the present dam dating from 1777. A high breast shot wheel 18 ft in diameter by 5½ft wide powers the tilt hammers while the adjacent wheel driving the blowing cylinders is overshot. Further wheels drove the grinding shop and the boring shop. The production of scythes ceased in 1933 but the complex was preserved and eventually re-opened in 1970 as a museum.

SHEFFIELD
Broughton Lane Crucible Shops (SK392893)
2½ miles NE of city centre off A630
These are the largest known surviving melting shops with a capacity of 72 holes – 4 large intermediate stacks ranged parallel to end wall stacks and there are extensive cellar remains below. They were built by Seebolm and Dieckstahl in 1897–8 – a significant date showing how late the process remained in use as the main way of producing tool steels. The works are now owned by Arthur Balfour & Co.

SHEFFIELD
Canal Basin, Exchange Street (SK361877)
¼ mile NE of city centre
The centre of Sheffield was belatedly connected to the rest of S Yorks waterway system in 1819 when the 4 mile Sheffield Canal from Tinsley was opened. Engineered by William Chapman it cost over £100,000 and 12 locks were needed in its short length. The basin in Sheffield has a fine red brick warehouse of 4 and 5 storeys and many later warehouses built out over the basin to give direct loading.

SHEFFIELD
Hoyle Street Cementation Furnace (SK348880)
½ mile NW of city centre
In the premises of the British Iron & Steel Research Association in Hoyle Street is the last complete cementation furnace in the country. At one time, in Sheffield alone, there were over 150. The furnace dates from c 1840 and went out of use in 1951. Externally the furnace resembles a pottery bottle oven in shape but internally it is totally different. The iron bars were roasted in a chest, interspersed with layers of charcoal, to produce blister steel.

SHEFFIELD
Low Matlock Forge and Rolling Mill (SK309894)
4½ miles NW of Sheffield off B6077

This rolling mill in the Loxley Valley replaced an earlier mill destroyed by floods in the mid-19th century. The overshot waterwheel, which until recently drove the mills, is the largest surviving waterwheel in the 5 Sheffield valleys. The 2-high rolling mills are now driven electrically but otherwise are typically 19th-century.

SHEFFIELD
Russell Street Cementation Furnace
(SK352879)
N of city centre
The remains of this furnace have recently been uncovered in Central Sheffield. The furnace is shown in cross section and hence complements to the nearby intact Hoyle Street furnace which hitherto had been thought to be the only surviving cementation furnace of the Sheffield pattern.

SHEFFIELD
Sharrow Snuff Mill (SK338858)
2 miles SW of city centre off A625
One of the 2 surviving water-driven snuff mills

SHEFFIELD: *Tilt hammers, Abbeydale, part of the superb museum illustrating the Sheffield edge tool industry.*

in the country and the only waterwheel operating commercially in Sheffield. Possibly a grinding site, the mill was acquired by the Wilson family in 1794, an overshot wheel powers a ring of pestle and mortar mills for the pulverizing of tobacco into snuff. There is also modern electrically driven equipment.

SHEFFIELD
Shephard Wheel (SK317854)
4 miles SW of city centre
Situated in Whiteley Woods, a public park, is a water-powered grinding shop typical of the 'little mester' system of industrial organization in the early 19th century. Two workshops powered by an 18 ft iron overshot wheel have been restored by a local association and are complete with grinding troughs, bands, saddles and grindstones. It is now part of Sheffield City Museums and open to the public.

SILKSTONE
Silkstone Railway (e.g. SE299075)
2½ miles NW of Barnsley off A635
The Barnsley Canal reached its westernmost point at Barnby Basin *c* 1800 and shortly afterwards a ½ mile tramway was laid to a local colliery. This tramway was incorporated into the line of the 2½ mile-long Silkstone Railway in an Act of 1808 and the railway was open a year later. It was constructed of stone sleeper blocks with iron rails at a gauge of *c* 4 ft 2 in and its course can still be traced by the sleeper blocks. It closed *c* 1870 as by that time most of the local collieries were connected to the standard gauge railway.

SILKSTONE
Low Mill Furnace (SE296067)
2½ miles NW of Barnsley off A635
This small blast furnace was established by Cockshutt & Co *c* 1820 to utilize local coal and ironstone. Although it was connected to the Silkstone Railway (*qv*) by a branch it seems to have operated for only 2 years. The outer masonry cladding of the furnace stack is ruinous and reveals the brick lining standing to a height of *c* 18 ft. The adjacent masonry building with an arched cart opening may be contemporary with the furnace or may be a later purely agricultural building.

SOUTH YORKS COALFIELD
Steam Winders
South Yorks has been the last main bastion of steam-powered winding engines in the English coalfields. In 1976 there were some 10 engines still working mostly grouped around Doncaster but as far W as Gt Houghton and as far S as Dinnington. The majority of these engines were manufactured by Charles Markham & Co of Chesterfield. (I am indebted to G Watkins for the details of the engines in the following list.)

Aldwick Le Street
  Bullcroft Colliery (SE540097) (1976)
  2 × 1910 Markham & Co horizontal twin cylinder   Derelict
Armthorpe
  Markham Main Colliery (SE617046)
  2 × 1920 Markham & Co horizontal twin cylinder   Working
Askern
  Askern Main Colliery (SE558138)
  2 × 1911 Yates & Thom horizontal twin tandem   Working

SHEFFIELD: *Cementation Furnace, Hoyle Street, sole survivor.*

Bentley
  Bentley (SE570075)
  2 × 1908 Fraser & Chalmers horizontal cross compound   Working
Dinnington
  Dinnington Colliery (SK518867)
  2 × 1911 Markham & Co horizontal twin cylinder   Working
Edlington
  Yorkshire Main Colliery (SK544992)
  2 × 1909 Markham & Co horizontal twin cylinder   Working
Hatfield
  Hatfield Colliery (SE653113)
  1921 J Musgrave horizontal twin cylinder Working
Hickleton
  Hickleton Colliery (SE465053)
  1921 Markham & Co horizontal twin cylinder   Working
Little Houghton
  Houghton Main Colliery (SE420060)
  1938 Bradley & Craven horizontal cylinder   Working
Pickburn
  Brodsworth Main Colliery (SE526077)
  1924 Markham & Co horizontal twin cylinder   Working
Thurcroft
  Thurcroft Colliery (SK499897)
  1911 Markham & Co horizontal twin cylinder   Working

SWINTON
Swinton Pottery (SK464992)
1 mile SW of Mexborough off A6023
The Don Pottery at Swinton was established in 1801 on the site of an earlier works and in its heyday employed over 200 staff. It produced more ware than any other pottery in Yorkshire with the exception of Leeds Old Pottery. There are remains of 2 bottle ovens on the site but one has been severely truncated. A lone bottle oven survives at the nearby site of the famous Rockingham works (SK441988).

WORSBOROUGH
Canal Reservoir Dams (and Bridge)
(SE348034)
2½ miles S of Barnsley off A61
The Derne & Dove Canal was opened in 1804 to connect the collieries of Barnsley district to the Don Navigation. It had 2 branches to Elsecar and to Worsborough. At Worsborough there was a basin and a large reservoir ponded back by one of the most ambitious dams to be constructed at that early date. The dam is still in use and an attractive masonry bridge over its outfall leads to Worsborough Mill (*qv*).

WORSBOROUGH
Rockley Furnace and Engine House
(SE338022)
3½ miles S of Barnsley off A61
Built in 1652 the Rockley charcoal blast furnace is one of the most important examples of early blast furnaces although interpretation of its remains is complicated by a much later reworking of the furnace – possibly in Napoleonic times. The free standing furnace retains an inner lining of sandstone blocks. The nearby engine house was probably built *c* 1740 to house a Newcomen engine used by Darwin & Co for draining ironstone mines.

WORSBOROUGH
Worsborough Mill (SE349034)
2½ miles S of Barnsley off A61
A 2-storey stone-built watermill dating in parts from the 17th century has recently been restored as a working museum. A leat diverted alongside the later Worsborough Reservoir worked 3 pairs of stones while in an adjacent 3-storey 19th-century building a steam engine formerly, and now a 1911 oil engine, drove 2 pairs of stones and ancillary machinery.

WORTLEY
Wortley Top Forge (SK294998)
9 miles NW of Sheffield off A629
Parts of this iron working complex may date back to the 17th century but most of the machinery is 19th-century when the works specialized in forging railway axles. There is a massive spring-assisted belly helve hammer worked by a 13½ft breast shot waterwheel. There are also 3 jib cranes of varying date. The works which are currently being restored are open to the public on Sundays.

West Yorkshire

West Yorkshire is the least close knit of the new metropolitan counties and encompasses the classic area of the Yorkshire woollen industry based on Leeds, Bradford, Halifax and Huddersfield. It also takes in the coalmining areas around Wakefield, Pontefract and Castleford. The textile industry has left such illustrious monuments as the Piece Hall, Halifax, the mill and model housing at Saltaire, Marshalls Egyptian Mill, Leeds, the Little Germany warehouses, Bradford, and a host of mills both large and small. The waterways serving the county contribute monuments such as the Bingley Five Rise on the Leeds & Liverpool Canal, Stanley Ferry aqueduct on the Aire & Calder and Sowerby bridge basin on the Calder & Hobble. Of the lesser canals such as the Barnsley, the Bradford, the Halifax and the Huddersfield, only the Huddersfield has significant remains.

ALTOFTS
Mining Settlement, Silkstone Row
(SE387244)
1½ miles N of Normanton
Built in the 1860s by the local colliery company, this is amongst the oldest surviving company settlements in the West Riding coalfield. It consists of a long continuous row of 52, 3-storey through houses with a shorter row at right angles. The rather later Portland Terrace and Portland Street are very early examples of the use of concrete for housing. The settlement also contains 10 deputies' houses, a school (opened 1868), a Wesleyan Chapel and an early co-operative store.

BINGLEY
Five-Rise Locks (SE108399)
6 Miles NE of Bradford off A650
Visually the most impressive flight of locks in the country, Bingley Five-Rise is a staircase of 5 broad locks each of 62 ft by 14 ft 3 in. They surmount a height difference of *c* 60 ft and there are, of course, no intervening pounds – the top gate of one chamber acts as the bottom gate of the next. The flight was opened in 1774

though the Leeds & Liverpool Canal was not finally completed until 1816.

BOSTON SPA
Watermill, Flintmill Grange (SE422472)
3 miles SE of Wetherby off A659
The mill was built in 1722 as a corn mill but it was converted in 1774 to flint grinding using special stones imported from Germany. By 1874 this method of dry grinding had ended due to the deleterious effect of the dust on the health of the workers. The mill is situated on the narrow shelf on the northern bank of the River Wharfe and the undershot waterwheel with most of the driving machinery is located in the basement.

BRADFORD
Illingworth's Mill, Buttershaw (SE137293)
3½ miles SW of city centre on A6036
This woollen mill was established by James Bottomley in 1851. The plain, 5-storey spinning mill carries, at the left hand end, an ornate staircase tower with a lantern top. Between the spinning mill and the long low walls of the preparation shed is the tall engine house which until 1956 contained a beam engine. The mill is surrounded by various ponds and workers' housing and is a very characteristic example of a mid-19th-century woollen mill.

BRADFORD
Conditioning House (SE154339)
½ mile NW of city centre
The moisture content of textile materials can vary greatly and therefore a laboratory examination certifying true weight, length and condition of textiles offered for sale is a valuable protection for all concerned in the sale. Based on continental precedents, Bradford Corporation established a municipal conditioning service in 1887 and constructed this custom-built conditioning house in 1902 – the only such structure in Britain. The 5-storey building is constructed round 3 sides of a narrow rectangular yard and most of the testing equipment is located in the top floor.

BRADFORD
Manningham Mills, Heaton Road (SE146348)
2 miles NW of city centre off B6144
A 2-storey frontage on Heaton Road is backed by 2 massive 6-storey stone-built mill buildings of 1873. They were built by Samuel C Lister (1815–1906), a noted inventor and improver of processes, to exploit his developments in the use of waste silk and their main products were velvet and plush. The architecture is on a grand scale, the main entrance is a massive stone archway with a crest and date (1873) above, while the main mills have a heavy panelled parapet supported by a bracketted cornice. In the centre is the boiler house with a campanile style chimney.

BRADFORD
Little Germany Warehouses (SE168330)
¼ mile E of city centre off A647
The second half of the 19th century witnessed a remarkable expansion of the woollen industry in Bradford and the old Piece Hall built in 1773 was no longer adequate to house the many merchants and their stores. From 1853 onwards an area on either side of Leeds Road was developed by wool merchants in flamboyant architectural styles and became known as Little Germany. Well Street, Vicar Lane and Peckover Street all retain examples of these massive warehouses e.g. the Law Russell warehouse of 1873 and the American & Chinese Export warehouse of 1871 in Vicar Street and Austral House in Well Street.

BRADFORD
Moorside Mills, Moorside Road (SE186357)
2 miles NE of city centre off A658
Bradford's Industrial Museum is housed in a typical late 19th-century/early 20th-century spinning mill complex. Different themes are presented on different floors including transport on the ground floor, worsted textile machinery on the first floor and a variety of textile machinery on the second floor. The mill manager's house has been furnished as a late 19th-century middle-class modest family house.

BRAMHOPE
Railway Tunnel Portal (SE256437)
4 miles SE of Otley off A660
The elaborately detailed and castellated northern portal forms the model of a memorial in Otley churchyard (SE202455) to the men who died in the construction of the tunnel. The tunnel, 2 miles 241 yards long, pierces the watershed between the Aire & Calder rivers and was built in 1845–49 by the Leeds & Thirsk Railway. Of the 20 shafts which were sunk for the construction work, 4, surmounted by substantial towers, remain to provide ventilation.

DEWSBURY
Canal Basin, Mill Street East, Savile Town (SE250204)
1 mile S of town centre
Dewsbury canal basin, off the Aire & Calder Navigation, has interesting warehouses, stables and workshops. A canal museum displaying

200 years of waterway history is housed in the former stables and is open at weekends.

FLOCKTON
Caphouse Colliery (SE253165)
6 miles E of Huddersfield on A642
This small typically 19th-century coal mine still retains its wooden headgear one of the last in the country to do so for coal drawing. Its twin cylinder horizontal steam winding engine of 1876 by Davy Bros is the earliest steam winder still in operation in the South Yorkshire coalfield. It winds from a shaft 440 ft deep.

FLOCKTON
Flockton Engine House (SE254158)
6 miles E of Huddersfield off A637
This engine house dates from the early 19th century and once housed a small pumping engine which drained the nearby collieries. Its present appearance is due to its conversion to living quarters at a later date.

FLOCKTON
Flockton Tunnel (SE254158)
6 miles E of Huddersfield off A637
Flockton tramway was constructed as a wooden waggonway in the mid-1770s and part of the route passed through this 280ft-long tunnel. If this tunnel was indeed on the original alignment of the tramway it would have claims to fame as the oldest such tramway tunnel in Britain. It was last used in 1893 and the entrance is now partially obscured being just inside the fields belonging to New Hall Detention Centre.

GOLCAR
Colne Valley Museum, Cliffe Ash (SE095160)
3 miles W of Huddersfield off A629
Three weavers' cottages, built *c* 1840, have been converted into a museum to display local domestic industries. One of the cottages has been set out as a weaver's cottage with typical workshop and equipment while the other 2 have a variety of exhibits including a clogger's workshop.

GOLCAR
Golcar Mill (SE102153)
3 miles W of Huddersfield off A62
This 18th century textile mill, which has survived relatively unaltered, illustrates the transitional stage in the development of the textile industry between the cottage-based domestic industry and the large steam-driven mills of the 19th century.

HALIFAX
Copley Mill and Housing (SE084225)
2 miles S of Halifax off A6026

In the valley to the S of Halifax lies Edward Ackroyd's small industrial community of Copley which predates the more illustrious Saltaire. The mill itself was built in 1847 and enlarged in 1865, the cottages were begun in 1847 and completed by 1853, the school and library were added in 1849 and 1850 respectively and the church, designed by Crossland was constructed 1863–5.

HALIFAX
Piece Hall, Horton Street (SE095250)
Town centre
This magnificent building was one of the very first industrial buildings to be recognized as an ancient monument. The imposing gateway is surmounted by a pediment and bell tower and bears the date 1779. It leads into a spacious courtyard surrounded by 3 tiers of galleries where the merchants had individual offices. The lower tiers have rusticated square columns while the uppermost tier is a graceful Tuscan colonnade. It now houses the Textile Industrial Museum as well as galleries, antique centre, markets, etc.

HORSFORTH
Pollard Bridge (SE240367)
5 miles NW of Leeds off A65
This cast-iron bridge across the River Aire at Horsforth was erected by John Pollard of Newley House in 1819. It was manufactured at the Shelf ironworks of Ayden & Elwell. It is *c* 92 ft long and 12 ft 6 in wide carrying a 7 ft carriageway of sets between iron kerbs. The ballustrade is 4 ft 6 in high and is composed of 12 sections each 7 ft 8 in long.

HUDDERSFIELD
Canal Wharf (SE149164)
$\frac{1}{4}$ mile S of town centre
Alongside the canal at this point are a number of interesting buildings and fixtures. Amongst these there is a late 18th-century mill, a small counterbalanced hand crane and 19th-century warehouse of unusual wooden construction.

HUDDERSFIELD
Huddersfield Station (SE143168)
Town centre
A magnificent classical station designed by J P Pritchett and built in ashlar by LNWR in 1847. It has a massive portico of fluted Corinthian columns fronting a 2-storey building with colonnaded wings in a most prominent situation in the town centre. It operated as a joint station for the LNWR and L & YR from 1849–1922.

HUDDERSFIELD
Turn Bridge, Quay Street (SE149168)
$\frac{1}{4}$ mile E of town centre

Though only single-track this iron lifting bridge still carries Quay Street across a disused canal. It is dated 1865 and is raised by hand gear.

LEEDS
Armley Mills, Canal Road (SE276341)
1½ miles W of city centre off A647
This mill is now the home of the Leeds Industrial Museum and parts of the building would appear to date from Benjamin Gott's involvement in the use of cast-iron columns in the early 19th century. One of the later buildings has an interesting cast-iron framed roof.

LEEDS
Canal Office (SE296330)
¼ mile S of city centre
This rather modest office/toll house did duty as the headquarters of the Leeds & Liverpool Canal Company in the 1770s.

LEEDS
Obelisk, Holbeck (SE291322)
1 mile SW of city centre off A643
This cast-iron obelisk was erected in 1826 to the memory of Matthew Murray a noted local ironmaster. It was subsequently used as a family memorial.

LEEDS
Temple Works, Marshall Street (SE295326)
1 mile S of city centre
This magnificent Egyptian style flax mill was built for John Marshall in 1840 to designs by Bonomi & David Roberts. Roberts even went to Egypt to study the Temple of Karnak. The massive battered stone walls are 6 ft thick at the base with a line of carved pillars. Lighting is by means of 65 glass domes in the flat roof which was originally covered in grass, drainage is provided by pipes within the stone piers. A uniform temperature all year round was by hypocaust-like air chambers in the basement.

LEEDS
Thwaite Putty Mills, Thwaite Lane (SE328312)
2½ miles SE of city centre
The red brick buildings of this water-driven milling complex date from 1823–5 when an oil seed crushing and corn grinding mill was established on an old milling site. The mills were re-equipped in the 1870s to crush flint and latterly ground chalk for the manufacture of putty. The 2 iron breast shot waterwheels date from the late 19th century being 17 ft diameter by 18 ft wide and 19 ft 6 in by 9 ft respectively. Until recently they drove a variety of machinery including edge runners

and pumps. Besides the main mill building a machine shop, stabling, offices and a drying floor complete a unique industrial monument.

MARSDEN
Standedge Canal Tunnel (SE040120)
7 miles SW of Huddersfield on A62
Located on the highest stretch of navigable water in Britain at 644 ft OD, this tunnel is no longer open. Completed in 1811 it is also the longest canal tunnel in Britain, 3 miles 125 yards. It forms part of the summit level of Benjamin Outram's Huddersfield Canal which provided the shortest trans-Pennine canal route. It was never very successful as its narrow gauge could not compete with the broad gauge of the nearby Rochdale Canal.

NORMANTON
Normanton Station (SE381227)
W of town centre
In 1840 the Midland Railway opened its line through Normanton to meet the York & N Midland and the Manchester & Leeds Railways. Normanton station served as an interchange point for both goods and passengers. By 1875 it was one of the busiest stations in Britain and was the main dining stop on the Midland route to Scotland. Its platform, ¼ mile long, was the fourth longest in the country. By the turn of the century, however, most of this traffic had deserted Normanton and today almost all its spacious appointments are disused.

OTLEY
Railway Memorial, Otley Churchyard (SE202455)
Town centre
See Bramhope Tunnel entry.

SHIPLEY
Saltaire, Mill and Industrial Settlement (SE140381)
4 miles NW of Bradford off A657
Alongside the Leeds & Liverpool Canal is one of the most impressive mills in Yorkshire. Built 1851 onwards, this enormous 5-storey Italianate mill some 60 bays long was the creation of Titus Salt (1803–76), a noted social improver and philanthropist. It was the product of his successful experiments in spinning the wool of the Alpaca goat and was designed to be a model of better working conditions. He also built a village of sturdy terraced houses of vaguely Italianate appearance providing much more generous accommodation than was the norm. By the 1870s a church, hospital, baths and school had been added to form the complete model village which survives to this day virtually unaltered.

SLAITHWAITE
Clough House Mill (SE068144)
4 miles W of Huddersfield on A62
This textile mill built round a courtyard illustrates a variety of mill architecture from the early to the late 19th century. In one corner of the mill is a vertical compound steam engine installed in 1887 by Schofield & Taylor of Huddersfield. The engine, rated at 200 hp, drove one part of the mill by gears and a vertical shaft, by ropes to the upper floors, and by an open shaft across the yard to a third part of the mill.

SOWERBY BRIDGE
Canal Basin (SE067237)
3 miles SW of Halifax on A58
Situated at the junction of the Rochdale Canal and the Calder & Hebble Navigation, this basin was extensively used for the transhipment and storage of goods intended for trans-Pennine carriage. Some of the warehouses survive from the 1790s with some of their associated stabling.

LEEDS: *Temple Works, Marshall Street, exotic elevation to a mill with many innovatory features.*

SHIPLEY: *Saltaire Mill, impressive centrepiece to Salt's model industrial community.*

STANLEY
Stanley Ferry Aqueduct (SE355231)
2 miles SE of Wakefield off A642
The Aire & Calder Canal is carried across the River Calder in a trough hung from a cast-iron arch which has a span of 155 ft. The aqueduct was opened in 1839 and is certainly more allied to railway engineering than to traditional canal engineering. It is protected from damage by collision on the upstream side by a separate fender.

STANLEY
Tramroad Bridge, Canal Lane (SE336246)
An unusually broad bridge built *c* 1840 to carry Canal Lane and 2 tramways – Lake Lock Rail Road and Fenton Railway over a new tramway connecting the Leeds & Wakefield turnpike with the new section of canal at Stanley Ferry. The heavy masonry parapets and causeway span 2 tunnel-like openings constructed of cast-iron beams with brick jack arching between.

STANLEY: *Stanley Ferry Aqueduct, early example of bow string arch construction.*

WAKEFIELD
Aire & Calder Navigation Quays (SE338202)
½ mile S of town centre
Wakefield was the headquarters of the powerful Aire & Calder Navigation Company. Besides several now very dilapidated warehouses there are the company's offices of 1800 with the 1820 classical additions. In the room above the strong room Joseph Priestley, the canal historian, wrote his most important works.

WAKEFIELD
Wakefield Quay (SE336198)
½ mile S of city centre
Wakefield Quay on the River Calder retains a few buildings that are reminders of the town's great trading past. The large stone-built warehouse with the barge hole at one end is late 18th-century while the nearby contemporary maltings are an indication of Wakefield's past as the largest corn market in the north of England.

WAKEFIELD
Heath Hall Water Tower (SE353199)
1½ miles SE of Wakefield off A655
Attributed to Dame Mary Bolles, the mid-17th-century owner of Heath Hall, this tower was erected at the issue of several strong springs. A waterwheel in a chamber below the tower utilized the flow of these springs to pump water to the top of the tower, from whence, reputedly it was conducted in an overhead lead-lined conduit to a cistern at the Hall.

BIBLIOGRAPHY

The following is a selective list of books and pamphets relating to industrial archaeology in England. It is arranged alphabetically by county but is prefaced by a short section of general application to the subject and to the country as a whole.

GENERAL

BAXTER, B., *Stone Blocks and Iron Rails*, David & Charles, Newton Abbot, 1966

BAINES, D., *Transport and Industrial Preservation Handbook 77/78*, Privately published, Crawley, 1977

BODLEY, H., *Discovering Industrial Archaeology and History*, Shire Publications, 1975

BODY, G. and EASTLEIGH, R.L., *Cliff Railways*, David & Charles, 1964

BRACEGIRDLE, B., *The Archaeology of the Industrial Revolution*, Heinemann, 1973

BUCHANAN, R.A., *Industrial Archaeology in Britain*, Pelican, 1972

BUCHANAN, R.A., and WATKINS, G., *The Industrial Archaeology of the Stationary Steam Engine*, Allen Lane, 1976

BURTON, A., *Industrial Archaeological Sites of Britain*, Weidenfeld & Nicholson, 1977

BURTON, A., *Remains of a Revolution*, Andre Deutsch, 1975

CAMPBELL, W.A., *The Chemical Industry*, Longman, 1971

COSSONS, N., *B.P. Book of Industrial Archaeology*, David & Charles, 1975

DE MARE, E., *Bridges of Britain*, Batsford

DERRY, T.K. and WILLIAMS, T.I., *A Short History of Technology*, Oxford University Press, 1960

FORBES, N.N., *Transporter Bridges*, Light Railway Transport League, 1970

GALE, W.K.V., *Iron & Steel*, Longman, 1969

GLOAG, J. and BRIDGWATER, D., *A History of Cast Iron in Architecture*, Architectural Press, 1958

GRIFFIN, A.R., *Coalmining*, Longman, 1971

HADFIELD, C. (ed), *Canals of the British Isles Series*, David & Charles, Newton Abbot, various dates. The whole country is now covered by this excellent series of regional histories, many of which have been written by Charles Hadfield, who is also general editor for the series.

HARRIS, R., *Canals and their Architecture*, 1969

HUDSON, K., *Building Materials*, Longman, 1972

Industrial Archaeology, (Quarterly) produced spasmodically since 1964 by various publishers and editors, latterly Graphmitre, Tavistock, Devon

Industrial Archaeology Review, (3 times a year) Started 1976. Editor S. Linsley, produced by Association for Industrial Archaeology with Oxford University Press

Industrial Past, (quarterly) topical magazine published since 1974 by J. Keavey (editor), Skipton, N. Yorks.

JORDAN, R.F., *Victorian Architecture*, Pelican, 1965

KLINGENDER, F.D., *Art and the Industrial Revolution*, edited and revised by Sir Arthur Elton, Adams and Mackay, 1968 and Paladin paperback, 1972

LLOYD, D. and INSALL, D., *Railway Station Architecture*, David & Charles, 1978

MCKNIGHT, H., *The Shell Book of Inland Waterways*
MAJOR, J.K., *Animal Powered Engines*, Batsford, 1978
MAJOR, J.K., *Fieldwork in Industrial Archaeology*, Batsford, 1975
MORGAN, B., *Railway Relics*, Ian Allen, 1969
MORGAN, B., *Civil Engineering: Railways*, Allen Lane
NEWCOMEN SOCIETY, *Transactions*
RAISTRICK, A., *Industrial Archaeology: An Historical Survey*, Eyre Methuen, 1972
REYNOLDS, J., *Windmills and Watermills*, Hugh Evelyn, 1970
RICHARDS, J.M., *The Functional Tradition in Early Industrial Buildings*, Architectural
    Press, 1958; reprinted 1968
ROLT, L.T.C., *Navigable Waterways*, Longman, 1969
RUSSELL, R., *Lost Canals of England and Wales*, David & Charles, 1971
TARN, J.N., *Working Class Housing in Nineteenth Century Britain*, Lund Humphries
    for the Architectural Association, 1971
Transport History, (quarterly) produced spasmodically since by a succession of pub-
    lishers latterly Graphmitre, Tavistock
WAILES, R., *The English Windmill*, Routledge and Kegan Paul, 1967

AVON

The *Journal* of the Bristol Industrial Archaeological Society produced annually since
    196? contains much useful information on sites
ATHILL, R., *Old Mendip*, David & Charles, 1971
BUCHANAN, R.A. and COSSONS, N., *The Industrial Archaeology of the Bristol Region*,
    David & Charles, 1969
BUCHANAN, R.A. and COSSONS, N., *Industrial History in Pictures: Bristol*, David &
    Charles, 1970
CLEW, K.R., *The Kennet & Avon Canal*, David & Charles, 1968
CLEW, K.R., *The Somerset Coal Canal*, David & Charles, 1970
DAY, J., *Bristol Brass: The History of the Industry*, David & Charles, 1973
GOUGH, J.W., *Mines of Mendip*, Oxford University Press, 1930; reprinted David &
    Charles, 1967

BERKSHIRE

CLEW, K.R., *The Kennet & Avon Canal*, David & Charles, 1968
DALBY, L.J., *The Wilts & Berks Canal*, Oakwood Press, 1971

BEDFORDSHIRE

LAWS, P., *Industrial Archaeology in Bedfordshire*, Bedfordshire County Council, 1967
BOURNE, J.C., *London & Birmingham Railway 1839*, David & Charles reprints, 1970

BUCKINGHAMSHIRE

BOURNE, J.C., *London & Birmingham Railway (1839)*, David & Charles reprints, 1970

CAMBRIDGESHIRE

ALDERTON, D. and BOOKER, J., *The Batsford Guide to the Industrial Archaeology of
    East Anglia*, Batsford, 1979

CHESHIRE

NORRIS, J.H., *The Water-Powered Cornmills of Cheshire*, Manchester, 1969
ASHMORE, O., *The Industrial Archaeology of Lancashire*, David & Charles, 1969

CLEVELAND

ATKINSON, F., *Industrial Archaeology of North East England*, David & Charles, 1974
CHAPMAN, S.K., *Gazetteer of Cleveland Ironstone Mines*, Langbaurgh Museum Service, 1976
HISTORICAL METALLURGY SOCIETY *Early Iron & Steel Making in Cleveland* Conference Papers, 1976

CORNWALL

The *Journal* of the Trevithick Society produced annually since 1972 contains many articles of industrial archaeological interest. In recent years a great many booklets have been published on individual mines and mining areas but reference is given here to works of a more general nature
BARTON, D.B., *The Cornish Beam Engine*, D. B. Barton, Truro, 1965
BARTON, D.B., *A History of Copper Mining in Cornwall and Devon*, D. B. Barton, Truro, 1966
BARTON, D.B., *A History of Tin Mining and Smelting in Cornwall*, D. B. Barton, Truro, 1967
BARTON, R.M., *A History of the Cornish China Clay Industry*, D. B. Barton, Truro, 1966
BOOKER, F., *The Industrial Archaeology of the Tamar Valley*, David & Charles, 1967
CURNOW, W.H., *Industrial Archaeology of Cornwall*, Tor Mark Press, 1970
HARRIS, H. and ELLIS, M., *The Bude Canal*, David & Charles, 1972
NATIONAL TRUST, *Cornish Engines*, National Trust, 1974
TODD, A.C. and LAWS, P., *Industrial Archaeology of Cornwall*, David & Charles, 1972
WILLIAMS, H.V., *Cornwall's Old Mines*, Tor Mark Press, 1970

CUMBRIA

DAVIES-SHIEL, M. and MARSHALL, J.D., *The Industrial Archaeology of the Lake, Counties* David & Charles, 1969
MARSHALL, J.D. and DAVIES-SHIEL, M., *The Lake District at Work, Past and Present*, David & Charles, 1971
SHAW, W.T., *Mining in the Lake Counties*, Dalesman Books, 1972

DERBYSHIRE

The *Bulletin* of the Peak District Mines Historical Society produced twice yearly since 1959 contains many articles of relevance to the county's industrial archaeology
CHAPMAN, S.D., *The Early Factory Masters*, David & Charles, 1967
FORD, T.D. and RIEUWERTS, J.H. (eds), *Lead Mining in the Peak District*, Peak District Mines Historical Society, 1975
HARRIS, H., *The Industrial Archaeology of the Peak District*, David & Charles, 1971
KIRKHAM, N., *Derbyshire Lead Mining Through the Centuries*, D. B. Barton, Truro, 1968
NIXON, F., *The Industrial Archaeology of Derbyshire*, David & Charles, 1969
SMITH, D.M., *The Industrial Archaeology of the East Midlands*, David & Charles, 1965

DEVON

ATKINSON, M., *Dartmoor Mines*, Exeter Industrial Archaeology Group, 1977
BONE, M., *Barnstaple's Industrial Archaeology: a guide*, Exeter Industrial Archaeology Group
BOOKER, F., *The Industrial Archaeology of the Tamar Valley*, David & Charles, 1967
BOOKER, F., *Morwellham*, DART, 1970

BROWN, C.G. (ed), *Industrial Archaeology of Plymouth*, Plymouth WEA Industrial Archaeology Group, 1973

CHITTY, M., *Industrial Archaeology of Exeter: a guide*, Exeter Industrial Archaeology Group, 1971

EDGINTON, C., *Tiverton's Industrial Archaeology: a guide*, Exeter Industrial Archaeology Group, 1976

EWANS, M.C., *Haytor Granite Tramway & Stover Canal*, David & Charles, 1966

HAMILTON JENKIN, A.K., *Mines of Devon*, David & Charles, 1974

HARRIS, H., *The Industrial Archaeology of Dartmoor*, David & Charles, 1968

HARRIS, H., *The Grand Western Canal*, David & Charles, 1973

KANEFSKY, J., *Devon Tollhouses*, Exeter Industrial Archaeology Group, 1976

MINCHINTON, W. (ed), *Industrial Archaeology in Devon*, DART, 1976

MINCHINTON, W., *Windmills of Devon*, Exeter Industrial Archaeology Group, 1976

MINCHINTON, W. and PERKINS, J., *Tidemills of Devon and Cornwall*, Exeter Industrial Archaeology Group, 1971

DORSET

ADDISON, J. and WAILES, R., *Dorset Watermills*, Trans Newcomen Society XXXV, 1962–63

YOUNG, D., 'Brickmaking at Weymouth, Dorset', Journal of Industrial Archaeology, Vol. 9, No. 2 (1972).

DURHAM

ATKINSON, F., *Industrial Archaeology: Top Ten Sites in N.E. England*, Frank Graham, 1971

ATKINSON, F., *Industrial Archaeology of N.E. England*, David and Charles, 1974

MAJOR, J.K., 'Windmills of Northumberland & Durham', Journal of Industrial Archaeology, Vol 4, No. 4, 1967.

ESSEX

BOOKER, J., *Essex and the Industrial Revolution*, Essex County Council, 1974

GLOUCESTERSHIRE

AWDRY, Rev. W., *Industrial Archaeology in Gloucestershire*, Gloucestershire Society for Industrial Archaeology, 1973

HART, C.E., *The Industrial History of Dean*, David & Charles, 1971

HISTORICAL METALLURGY GROUP, *Bulletin* Vol. 2, No. 1, 1968 – *Forest of Dean Conference*

HOUSEHOLD, H., *The Thames & Severn Canal*, David & Charles, 1969

TANN, J., *Gloucestershire Woollen Mills*, David & Charles, 1967

HAMPSHIRE

ELLIS, M. (ed), *Hampshire Industrial Archaeology* – A Guide, Southampton University Industrial Archaeology Group, 1975

ELLIS, C.M., *A Gazetteer of the Water Wind & Tide Mills of Hampshire*, Proc. Hampshire Field Club Vol. XXV, 1968

TIGHE, M.F., *A Gazetteer of Hampshire Breweries*, Proc. Hampshire Field Club Vol. XXVII, 1970

VINER, D.J., *Industrial Archaeology of Hampshire Roads: A Survey*, Proc. Hampshire Field Club Vol. XXVI, 1969

WHITE, W.C.F., *A Gazetteer of Brick and Tile Works in Hampshire*, Proc. Hampshire Field Club Vol. XXVIII, 1971

HEREFORD & WORCESTERSHIRE
BROOK, F., *Industrial Archaeology of the British Isles: Vol. 1 West Midlands*, Batsford, 1977

HERTFORDSHIRE
BRANCH JOHNSON, W., *Industrial Archaeology of Hertfordshire*, David & Charles, 1970

HUMBERSIDE
ALLISON, K.J., *East Riding Watermills*, East Yorkshire Local History Society, 1970
HOLM, S.A., *Brick and Tile Making in South Humberside*, 1976
WHITE, P.R., *An Industrial History of Grimsby and Cleethorpes*, Lincolnshire Industrial Archaeology Group, 1971

ISLE OF WIGHT
MAJOR, J.K., *The Mills of the Isle of Wight*, Charles Skilton Ltd, 1970

KENT
BENNET, C.E., *The Watermills of Kent, East of the Medway*, Industrial Archaeology Review Vol. 1, No. 3, 1977
HASELFOOT, A.J., *The Batsford Guide to the Industrial Archaeology of South East England*, Batsford, 1978
PERCIVAL, A., *The Faversham Gunpowder Industry*, Faversham Society Paper No. 4
VINE, P.A.L., *The Royal Military Canal*, David & Charles, 1972
WEST, J., *The Windmills of Kent*, Charles Skilton, 1974

LANCASHIRE
ASHMORE, O., *The Industrial Archaeology of Lancashire*, David & Charles, 1969
GEORGE, A.D., *The Industrial Archaeology of Preston*, privately published, 1974

LINCOLNSHIRE
LEWIS, M.J.T. & WRIGHT, N.R. (ed.), *Boston as a Port*, I A Group Lincolnshire Local History Society, 1974

LONDON
ASHDOWN, J., BUSSELL, M. & CARTER, P., *Industrial Monuments of Greater London*, Thames Basin Archaeological Observers Group, 1969
DENVEY, M., *London's Waterways*, Batsford, 1978
ENFIELD ARCHAEOLOGICAL SOCIETY, *London's Industrial Archaeology*, GLIAS Journal Vol. 1, 1979
LONDON TRANSPORT (Pamphlet) *London's Industrial Archaeology*
THOMAS, R.H.G., *London's First Railway*, Batsford, 1972
WILSON, A., *London's Industrial Heritage*, David & Charles, 1967

GREATER MANCHESTER
ASHMORE, O, *The Industrial Archaeology of Lancashire*, David & Charles, 1969
ASHMORE, O., *Industrial Archaeology of Stockport*, University of Manchester, 1975
GEORGE, A.D., *An Introduction to the Industrial Archaeology of Manchester and South Lancashire*, Manchester Polytechnic, 1977
SHARP, D. (ed), *Manchester*, Studio Vista, 1969

MERSEYSIDE

ASHMORE, O., *The Industrial Archaeology of Lancashire*, David & Charles, 1969

HUGHES, Q., Seaport – *Architecture and Townscape in Liverpool*, Lund Humphries, 1964

NORFOLK

ALDERTON, D. & BOOKER, J., *Batsford Guide to the Industrial Archaeology of East Anglia*, Batsford, 1980

NORTHAMPTON

STARMER, G.H. (Ed), *Industrial Archaeology: Northamptonshire Northampton Museums and Art Galleries*, 1970

NORTHUMBERLAND

ATKINSON, F., *Industrial Archaeology of N.E. England*, David & Charles, 1974

MAJOR, J.K., 'Windmills of Northumberland & Durham', *Journal of Industrial Archaeology Vol 4 No 4*, 1967

NOTTINGHAMSHIRE

NOTTINGHAMSHIRE COUNTY COUNCIL, *Canals in Nottinghamshire: A Survey in Industrial Archaeology*, 1976

NOTTINGHAMSHIRE COUNTY COUNCIL, *Maltings in Nottinghamshire: A Survey in Industrial Archaeology*, 1977

SMITH, D.M., *The Industrial Archaeology of the East Midlands*, David & Charles, 1965

SHROPSHIRE

BROOK, F., *Industrial Archaeology of the West Midlands*, Batsford, 1977

BROOK, F. & ALLBUTT, M., *The Shropshire Lead Mines*, Moorland, 1973

SOMERSET

The *Journals* of both the Somerset Industrial Archaeological Society and the Bristol Industrial Archaeological Society contain a variety of general and specialized articles on industrial sites in Somerset

ATHILL, R., *Old Mendip*, David & Charles, 1971

BUCHANAN, R.A. & COSSONS, N., *The Industrial Archaeology of the Bristol Region*, David & Charles, 1969

CLEW, K.R., *The Dorset & Somerset Canal*, David & Charles, 1971

GOUGH, J.W., *Mines of Mendip*, (1930), David & Charles (Reprint), 1967

HUDSON, K., *The Industrial Archaeology of Southern England*, David & Charles, 1965

PONTING, K.E., *Wool and Water*, Moonraker, 1975

ROGERS, K.H., *Wiltshire and Somerset Woollen Mills*, Pasold Research, 1976

SELLICK, R., *The West Somerset Mineral Railway*, David & Charles, 1970

STAFFORDSHIRE

BOOTH, G., *The Midlands: Industrial Archaeology*, Wayland, 1973

BROOK, F., *The Industrial Archaeology of the British Isles: Vol 1 The West Midlands*, Batsford, 1977

COPELAND, R., *A Short History of Pottery Raw Materials and the Cheddleton Flint Mill*, Cheddleton Flint Mill Industrial Heritage Trust, 1972

ROBEY, J.A. & PORTER, L., *The Copper and Lead Mines of Ecton Hill, Staffordshire* Moorland, 1972

SHERLOCK, R., *Industrial Archaeology of Staffordshire*, David & Charles, 1976
THOMPSON, W.J., *The Industrial Archaeology of North Staffordshire*, Moorland, 1976

SUFFOLK
ALDERTON, D. & BOOKER, J., *The Batsford Guide to the Industrial Archaeology of East Anglia*, Batsford, 1979

SURREY
HASELFOOT, A.J., *The Batsford Guide to the Industrial Archaeology of South-East England*, Batsford, 1978
PAYNE, G.A., *Surrey Industrial Archaeology*, Phillimore, 1977
VINE, P.A.L., *London's Lost Route to Basingstoke*, David & Charles, 1968

SUSSEX E & W
Sussex Industrial History the journal of the Sussex Industrial Archaeology Society published by Phillimore contains a wealth of material on industrial monuments in the two counties
HASELFOOT, A.J., *Batsford Guide to the Industrial Archaeology of South-East England*, Batsford, 1978
HENNING, P., *Windmills in Sussex*, Daniel, 1936
STRAKER, E., *Wealden Iron (1931)*, republished Library Association, 1967
VINE, P.A.L., *London's Lost Route to the Sea*, David & Charles, 1965
VINE, P.A.L., *The Royal Military Canal*, David & Charles, 1972
WEALDEN IRON RESEARCH GROUP *Wealden Iron*, 1969

TYNE & WEAR
ATKINSON, F., *Industrial Archaeology of North East England Vols 1 & 2*, David & Charles, 1974
ATKINSON, F., *Industrial Archaeology: Top Ten Sites in North East England*, Frank Graham, 1971

WARWICKSHIRE
BROOK, F., *The Industrial Archaeology of the British Isles: The West Midlands*, Batsford, 1977

WEST MIDLANDS
BOOTH, G., *The Midlands: Industrial Archaeology*, Wayland, 1973
BROOK, F., (See Warwicks)
SHERLOCK, R., *The Industrial Archaeology of Staffordshire*, David & Charles, 1976

WILTSHIRE
CLEW, K.R., *The Kennet & Avon Canal*, David & Charles, 1973
CORFIELD, M.C. (ed), *A Guide to the Industrial Archaeology of Wiltshire*, Wilts. Arch. & Nat. History Soc. and Wilts. County Council, 1978
DALBY, L.J., *The Wilts & Berks Canal*, Oakwood Press, 1971
HUDSON, K., *The Industrial Archaeology of Southern England*, David & Charles, 1965
PONTING, K.G., *Wool & Water*, Moonraker, 1975
ROGERS, K., *Wiltshire and Somerset Woollen Mills*, Pasold, 1976

YORKSHIRE N S & W
BARRACLOUGH, K.C., *Sheffield Steel*, Moorland, 1976
BINNIE, M. et al, *Satanic Mills*, SAVE Britain's Heritage, 1978

CLOUGH, R.T., *The Lead Smelting Mills of the Yorkshire Dales*, privately published 1st Ed 1962, 2nd Ed enlarged 1979

GOODCHILD, J. (ed), *Cusworth Hall Museum Monographs*

HADFIELD, C., *The Canals of Yorkshire and North East England Vols 1 & 2*, David & Charles, 1973

RAISTRICK, A. and JENNINGS, B., *A History of Lead in the Pennines*, Longman, 1966

RAISTRICK, A., *Lead Mining in the Mid-Pennines*, D. B. Barton, 1973

RAISTRICK, A., *The Lead Industry of Wensleydale and Swaledale Vols 1 & 2*, Moorland, 1975

Index of Sites by Industry

This index is arranged by subjects to show the places where material relative to a particular subject may be seen.